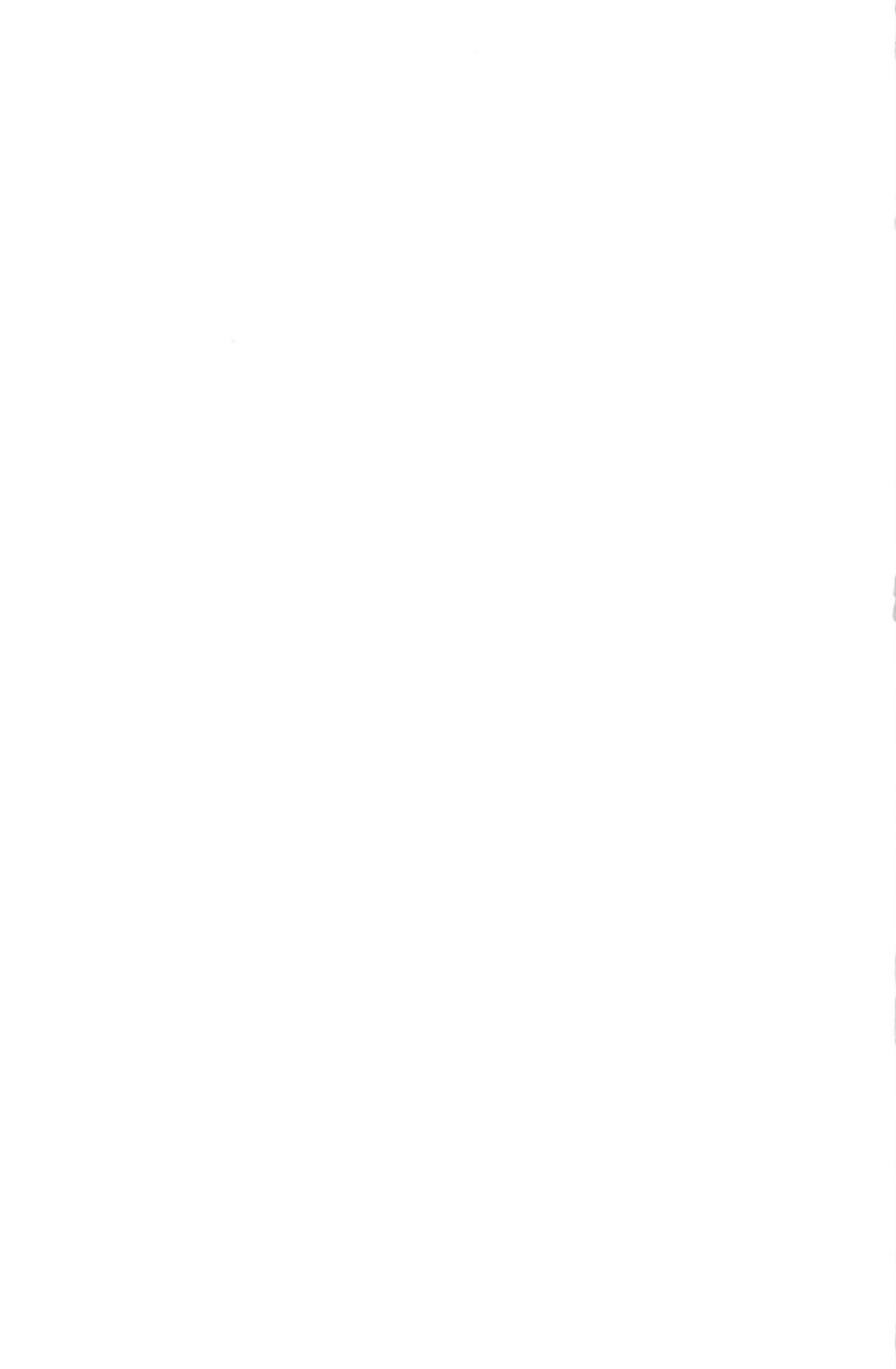

THE ASHES OF BABI YAR

George L. Mosse Series in the History of European Culture, Sexuality, and Ideas

THE ASHES OF BABI YAR

The Massacre of Jews in Kyiv

Antonella Salomoni

Translated by Antony Shugaar

THE UNIVERSITY OF WISCONSIN PRESS

Publication of this book has been made possible, in part, through support
from the George L. Mosse Program in History at the University of Wisconsin–Madison
and the Hebrew University of Jerusalem.

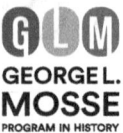

This book has been translated thanks to a contribution from the Italian Ministry of
Foreign Affairs and International Cooperation / Questo libro e' stato tradotto grazie a un
contributo del Ministero degli Affari Esteri e della Cooperazione Internazionale Italiano.

The University of Wisconsin Press
728 State Street, Suite 443
Madison, Wisconsin 53706
uwpress.wisc.edu

Library of Congress Cataloging-in-Publication Data

Names: Salomoni, Antonella, author | Shugaar, Antony, translator
Title: The ashes of Babi Yar : the massacre of Jews in Kyiv /
Antonella Salomoni ; translated by Antony Shugaar.
Other titles: Ceneri di Babij Jar. English | George L. Mosse series in the history of
European culture, sexuality, and ideas
Description: Madison, Wisconsin : University of Wisconsin Press, 2025. | Series: George L.
Mosse series in the history of European culture, sexuality, and ideas | Originally
published as Le ceneri di Babij Jar: L'eccidio degli ebrei di Kiev, copyright ©2019 by
Società editrice il Mulino, Bologna. | Includes bibliographical references and index.
Identifiers: LCCN 2025001975 | ISBN 9780299351205 hardcover
Subjects: LCSH: Babi Yar Massacre, Ukraine, 1941 | Holocaust, Jewish (1939–1945)—
Ukraine—Kyïv | Jews—Persecutions—Ukraine—Kyïv—History—20th century |
Kyïv (Ukraine)—Ethnic relations
Classification: LCC DS135.U42 K546813 2025 | DDC 940.53/18445—dc23/eng/20250401
LC record available at https://lccn.loc.gov/2025001975

Contents

Preface

Babij Yar was a large ravine near Kyiv between the suburbs of Lukyanivka, Kurenivka, and Syrets. On 29 and 30 September 1941, German troops exterminated 33,771 Jews there by shooting them.[1]

Lightning, purple black and silent, flared
Out across the horror-frosted land.
The suburb sank beneath its evil glare,
Tarnishing the Kyiv households. And

The people, from their mournful cellars, saw
How, past the graveyard poplars with their graves,
And past the domes of Cyril with their wreathes,
Their very flesh and blood went up in flames.

The ash from deathfires, corpses charred.
And Kyiv, angry Kyiv, witnessed this
As flames rose toward the sky from Babi Yar.
There is no penance for this kind of fire.

(Mykola P. Bazhan, "Jar" [Ravine], 1943)

In Kyiv, in Babi Yar, a little girl cried out:
"But why are you throwing sand in my eyes!"
The earth stirred.
The earth implored.
No one with a heart will ever be able to forget that cry.

No one with a heart will ever be able to forget mass graves and ravines.
Those ghosts will be with us all our lives.

> (Ilya Ehrenburg, "Oni otomstjat za vsë"
> [They will avenge everything], 1944)

Why does the breeze from the riverbank so dear to me
Scatter furious dust on the passerby?
And the dust grains, impregnated with smoke and blood,
Choke me and blind me.

The wind has crossed the charred walls,
Sweeping ashes from the old places of fire.
It swirls the sacred ashes on Khreshchatyk,
Suffocating dust that descends from Babi Yar.

If under the foliage of the blooming chestnuts
In this city you have forgotten the past pain,
You will remember it suddenly
As you are struck by a desolating cloud of dust and ashes.

> (Yakov Chelemsky, "Nikogda v etom gorode ne bylo pyli"
> [Never in this city was there dust], 1946)

Note on Transliteration

Transcriptions from Russian, Ukrainian, and Belarusian follow the standards adopted by Italian Slavists. Transcriptions from Yiddish use the Yivo system. Hebrew words are mostly transcribed in Ashkenazi pronunciation. Place-names are generally indicated in Ukrainian, but when they come from texts written in Russian or Yiddish, the form in which they appeared in the writer's original language has been retained. The established Italian names for Kyiv and Babi Yar have been preserved.

THE ASHES OF BABI YAR

Introduction

Kyiv was taken by the Germans on 19 September 1941 after seventy-three days of siege. It was one of the greatest defeats suffered by the Soviets, who lost about one million men, half killed in battle, half taken prisoner. The Ukrainian capital was a multiethnic, multireligious, and multilingual metropolis. According to the 1939 census, 224,236 Jews lived there, accounting for 26.48 percent of the population.[1] One-third of them were evacuated.

Assaults upon shops and warehouses, followed by devastating waves of looting, began immediately after the withdrawal of the Red Army and continued "until midday on 19 September both in the city center and on the outskirts."[2] Properties of Jews were targeted in particular, especially in the Podil district. What followed were the first arrests of Jews, carried out by German soldiers in collaboration with citizens of Kyiv. Soon it was dangerous for Jews to appear both in the city streets and in the very courtyards of their buildings. Even voluntary segregation was insufficient to ward off the dangers of break-ins and looting, which were often accompanied by beatings or murders.[3]

"A Vulgar Provocation"

Babi Yar was immediately identified as the place to carry out the first summary executions.[4] Ivan S. Yanovych lived about a kilometer away. Shortly after the liberation, he testified that as early as 20 September, groups of prisoners of war were being marched there. He had not witnessed the executions because guards had been set to prevent access, but he had heard the distinct sounds of screams and gunshots. From that date on, which is to say, from the first day after they arrived in the city, "the Germans conducted daily firing-squad executions of hundreds of people."[5] The survivor Mikhl Tanklevski also reported that a great many Jews, including his seventy-two-year-old father, as well as non-Jews with a Semitic appearance, had been confined in a camp set up in

Darnytsia.[6] They were executed by gunfire after being ordered to dig their own graves.[7]

In the territories of Operation Barbarossa, the "criminal orders" were already being implemented.[8] Normally, the slaughter of the Jewish population was preceded by operations of registration, concentration, marking, and segregation. In Kyiv, however, the Jews who remained in the city were *immediately* liquidated. What prompted this decision to accelerate the process? Before they abandoned the city, Soviet security services, working in conjunction with special units of the Red Army, had mined a number of strategic locations in the city, as well as undertaking various acts of sabotage.[9] On 20 September an old arsenal blew up near the Pechersk Lavra (Monastery of the Caves), where German troops had been quartered. On 24 September on Khreshchatyk, the main street of Kyiv, a series of buildings were blown up, some of which had been chosen as military command headquarters. That explosion triggered a catastrophic fire that lasted several days and destroyed hundreds of residential and administrative buildings. Those explosions not only demolished a considerable part of the historic city center but also resulted in significant losses to the occupying forces who were engaged in fighting fires.[10] That offered a pretext for reprisals, which were mainly leveled against political commissars, partisans, and Jewish officials. According to some eyewitnesses, the Germans even made use of human shields, marching hundreds of prisoners through the streets of the city on the assumption that the streets had been mined.[11]

The "motivations" for the killings are listed quite concisely in an official German report that was compiled a few weeks later. That document, in addition to providing an account of the repressive measures adopted till that point ("fifty-one thousand executions"), also listed the array of ideological categories of individuals subject to punitive actions: officials of the Soviet state bureaucracy; activists and specialists in Communist propaganda; partisans and Red Army instructors; agents and informers of the political police; and agents of agitation and rebellion, sabotage, and armed insurrection. That list was followed by the categories of those who had taken part in the deportation of the local ethnic German population; then came socially undesirable individuals, spreaders of pestilence, looters, Russian bandits, and young criminals. There were also mentions of Jews who had obtained release from prison camps on the basis on false declarations of identity, as well as those who, out of pure "sadism," harbored a thirst for vengeance. But what mattered most was the final clause: "Jews in general." And indeed, as the document specified, "most of the people [involved] were Jews."[12]

The fires and explosions left thousands of inhabitants without a roof over their heads and without the basics for daily life. The occupying forces had no difficulty exploiting the situation for propaganda purposes. The young librarian Irina Khoroshunova noted in her diary on 28 September that "many myths" about the attackers were circulating in Kyiv and that those myths had been fabricated to shape the populace's mood: "Among all the rumors that have circulated in recent days, those about the responsibility of the Jews for the fires devastating the city have been repeated so persistently that for many they have become reality. It is quite clear to us that this was a vulgar provocation. Something was being plotted, but no one could exactly foretell the result."[13] In her novelistic account about the occupation of Kyiv, Ukrainian writer Dokia K. Humenna even staged a sort of "spectacle" set in an "atmosphere of expectation" among the citizens and centered around the figure of the Jewish arsonist. A disheveled and terrified woman is dragged out of her house by two Germans; she stammers something, trying to offer an explanation, but is beaten by the soldiers for a very long time before being killed: "People gather. Why are they torturing her? Not everyone can hear what is happening in the middle of the crowd. She is a Jew. Someone very simply saw her pouring kerosene into her stove and lighting it. 'The Jews that have remained are responsible for the fires, they set fire to every third building. One of them came from Boryspil', set fire to his own house, and fled.'" Shortly thereafter, another woman, pushed out into the street almost naked, suffers the same fate: "It unfolds like [a] pantomime, a medieval scene, against the backdrop of fire and explosions, before the eyes of the crowd." The main character, Mariana, feels "complicit just for having watched." Someone beside her offers explanations for what is happening: "They caught a guy in Bessarabka, too, pouring kerosene in the covered market"; "Look, now the pharmacy is on fire, and the fire started at the top of the building"; "I saw a huge number of kerosene bottles on the top floor of the department store, but I couldn't understand the reason then. But now I understand!"[14]

The mass slaughter of Kyiv's Jews was preceded by a series of individual or group killings, primarily for demonstrative purposes and as reprisals. They were carried out at various locations in the city and surrounding areas, on the streets, and at the exits of social centers and places of worship.[15] The first systematic executions at Babi Yar almost certainly began on 27 September at the hands of the Southern Police Regiment.[16] They are presumed to have involved sixteen hundred people, arrested regardless of age or sex, calculated on the basis of the capacity of thirty-five to forty trucks.[17] The daughter of the custodian of the Orthodox cemetery of Lukyanivka, Maria S. Lutsenko, on a date in September that was not specified, witnessed the arrival of about ten open-bed trucks loaded with Jews. The occupants were immediately killed.[18] The Russian Nadezhda T. Gorbacheva, who lived very close to the ravine, placed the executions she witnessed on the date of 22 September, but it is more plausible that the events she recounted actually occurred a few days later.[19] The fact remains that they predate the massacre of 29–30 September. Gorbacheva declared that she saw about forty trucks arrive loaded with entire families—men, women, and children, including infants in their mother's arms. She had moved closer with other residents of her neighborhood and was thus able to witness the victims being forced to disrobe and then run along the edge of the ravine, after which they were finally shot: "I saw with my own eyes that the Germans threw infants into the ravine, along the bottom of which lay not only dead people but also injured and even still-living children. Despite that, the Germans filled the pit with dirt so that you could see that thin layer of soil moving due to the movements of the people beneath it. Many, sensing their imminent deaths, lost their senses, tore their clothing and hair, and threw themselves at the feet of the German soldiers. In return, they received only clubbings."[20]

Another neighbor, Natalia F. Petrenko, confirmed that testimony, right down to the date, but specified that the Jews had walked in a kind of chain, being passed from German to German, until their final execution near the edge of the ravine.[21]

Official report no. 97, dated 28 September 1941, regarding the activity of Einsatzgruppe C, and reporting on ongoing operations—particularly concerning the demolition of defensive military installations, handling explosions, detonating mines, and putting out fires—stated that there was "evidence that the Jews had played a prominent part" in hostilities against German military forces. In Kyiv there were "presumably 150,000" Jews, although it had been "impossible" to verify the accuracy of the information. During the "first action," measures had been "taken to neutralize the Jewish population as a whole." Furthermore, a specific plan had been "laid out to liquidate at least fifty thousand Jews." Those measures had been "welcomed" by the Wehrmacht, which urged "drastic methods."[22]

"Large-Scale Actions"

On 26 September a meeting concerning the evacuation of the local Jews was held between the military governor of Kyiv, Kurt Eberhardt, and the leadership of the Waffen-SS: Friedrich Jeckeln, *Obergruppenführer, Höherer-SS*, and *Polizeiführer* for the territories of southern Russia; Emil Otto Rasch, *Brigadeführer* and commander of Einsatzgruppe C; and Paul Blobel, *Standartenführer* and commander of Sonderkommando 4a.[23] It was decided that in retaliation for attacks against German installations, all Jews in Kyiv would be liquidated. The operation was entrusted to Sonderkommando 4a, a subunit of Einsatzgruppe C that was led by Blobel and composed of men from the Sicherheitsdienst and the Sicherheitspolizei, the third company of the Waffen-SS Special Services Battalion, and a team from Police Battalion No. 9. Arriving in Kyiv with the army, Sonderkommando 4a was reinforced by Police Battalions No. 45, under the command of Martin Besser, and No. 303, under the command of Heinrich Hannibal, as well as auxiliary Ukrainian units. It could also count on the full cooperation of Wehrmacht general Friedrich-Georg Eberhardt.[24]

On 28 September approximately two thousand copies of a communiqué prepared by Propaganda Company No. 637 in Russian, Ukrainian, and German were distributed. The communiqué instructed all Jews residing in Kyiv and its surroundings to assemble at eight o'clock the following morning at the intersection of Melnyk and Dehtyarivs'ka Streets—"in the cemetery area," it was vaguely added. The street names were not entirely correct as published, revealing a vague (at best) knowledge of the capital's topography, but the instructions were nevertheless comprehensible to the populace at large. Those summoned were required to bring with them identity papers, money, and other securities and valuables, as well as warm clothing and undergarments. Anyone who failed to obey the instructions of the communiqué would be shot summarily. The same fate awaited citizens of Kyiv who took possession of housing or other property left behind by the Jews.[25]

The action had been prepared expeditiously. Official report no. 106 on the activity of Einsatzgruppe C in Soviet territory, drafted on 7 October 1941, provides details on the "liquidation" of Jews and "further measures." The order to assemble, issued "in coordination with the military authorities of the city," had been widely distributed with the assistance of members of the newly established Ukrainian militia. Rumors had also been put into circulation concerning the "impending transfer of all Jews from Kyiv to another location."[26] A "sufficient number of collaborators" were assigned the task of "studying local conditions." In particular, instructions were issued, with the issuance of specific orders, to facilitate the expulsion of Jews from their homes on 29 September by retrieving house keys and forcing even the sick, elderly, and mothers with infants out onto the streets.[27]

To all building administrators in the city of Kyiv: you are hereby ordered, prior to 2400 hours, to declare to the nearest district police stations and to the Ukrainian police command in Kyiv, at Korolenko Street 15, 2nd floor, the presence of all Jews, security service workers, and members of the Communist Party living in your buildings.

Hiding these individuals will result in a sentence of death.

Building administrators and caretakers have the right to deliver the Jews
themselves to the internment camp [reserved for them], located near the prisoner camp on Kerosynna Street. (Commander of the Ukrainian Police in Kyiv,
Orlyk)[28]

As a result, building administrators and caretakers gained power over the lives
and deaths of Jewish tenants as well as members of the secret services and the
Communist Party.[29] With the concentration order directed at the entire Jewish population, caretakers' agreement and collaboration with the occupiers
became even closer—as explained in a report written shortly after the city's
liberation: "The Germans and the 'police chiefs' of the buildings dragged
elderly people, no longer able to walk, out of their homes and left them on the
sidewalk or in the street, where they could die of hunger and cold to the indifference of passersby."[30]According to official reports sent to Berlin at the end of
October and the beginning of November, even German military commands
were surprised by the huge influx of people at the appointed hour:

Some retaliatory measures were implemented within the framework of large-
scale actions [Grossaktionen]. The largest of these actions took place immediately
after the occupation of Kyiv. It involved only Jews with all their families. The
difficulties associated with carrying out such a significant operation—primarily,
the logistics of assembling them—were overcome in Kyiv through posters
announcing to the Jewish population that they had to leave the city. Although
the initial expectation was for a turnout of about five to six thousand Jews, over
thirty thousand showed up, fully convinced that they were only being moved
out of the city until the actual moment of their deaths—thanks to extraordi-
narily skillful organization.[31]

Why did the Jewish population comply so passively with these summonses?
Soviet authorities, faced with the imminent occupation of Kyiv, had not prepared special rescue plans for Jews. The categories that took advantage of the
evacuation opportunities offered by state institutions largely corresponded to
the categories of the remaining population that were not expected to be mobi-
lized: workers in the war industry or other critical sectors, party members,
administrative personnel with their families, members of politically integrated
scientific and cultural elites. There were Jews who managed to leave the city
entirely under their own steam because they had money, means of transportation, and/or family or social connections in areas far from the front lines. But
there were also those who had chosen to stay at the side of sick or elderly relatives who were too frail to undertake a journey under such difficult and

precarious conditions. Finally, there were those who harbored feelings of hostility toward the Communist system and believed that the Nazi regime was unlikely to worsen their situation.[32]

The elderly often looked back fondly upon the occupation that had occurred during the First World War, when the Germans themselves put an end to the pogroms and restored order. Elena Gorodetskaya's grandfather dismissed the idea of the family leaving the capital precisely because, based on his own past experiences, he considered Germany to be a "civilized nation."[33] A similar account comes from the poet Nahum Korzhavin, who explained why an uncle vehemently refused to participate in the evacuation and therefore met his death at Babi Yar: "Since he did not believe a single word of Soviet propaganda, he would not even believe what was said about the Nazis, especially since he had personally observed the Germans in 1918 and therefore considered them to be what the Bolsheviks were not: 'people of culture.'"[34] Neli Ya. Melman, then fifteen years old, was transferred with her closest relatives to Turkmenistan. Her paternal grandparents, however, categorically refused to follow them, partly due to age and poor health, but partly due to the trust they felt in German expertise and knowledge. A maid of theirs later reported watching the elderly couple as they walked down Saksahanskoho Street toward Babi Yar: "Grandma Ita was pushing a wheelbarrow with some 'household items' ahead of her, while Grandpa Duvid could barely keep up with her. That is all we know about the last days of their lives."[35]

There is, however, another and far more important explanation for the passivity with which the Jewish population complied with the 29 September summonses. Soviet Jews, as a result of the pact of alliance signed by Molotov and Ribbentrop, had failed to receive any significant information from the public media (newspapers and radio) about the anti-Semitic policies of German National Socialism following Kristallnacht, nor were they informed about the forcing of Polish Jews into ghettos and the massacres that followed the territorial invasion of Poland.[36] Most Jews, taken in by the regulation language (*Sprachregelung*) used, remained ignorant and unsuspecting until the very last instant of the actual meaning of the order they had received. Many believed they were being resettled: some spoke of "labor mobilization," others reported a "transfer" to some provincial city, while still others recounted a deal struck between the German high command and a Soviet commission, according to which "one Jewish family would be exchanged for every German prisoner of war." For this last reason, for example, Tamara Mikhaseva, the young Russian wife of a Jewish commander in the Red Army, went to Babi Yar with the intention of passing herself off as Jewish. She hoped to reunite with her husband in Soviet territory. She went through all the stages of the "procedure":

she passed through the barrier, stood in line to hand over her belongings, and presented herself for registration. However, she was recognized by a Russian naturalized German who had accompanied his own Jewish relatives (his wife, son, and mother-in-law) and who managed to have her sent away just as they began to hear "the barking of numerous guard dogs, gunshots from automatic rifles, and the screams of the victims."[37]

The grandparents of sixteen-year-old Konstantin Miroshnik began preparing for the journey immediately. They decided, however, to entrust the boy to an acquaintance who lived in a village located twenty-two kilometers away from Kyiv. "Sonja," the grandfather told this friend, "the Germans have ordered us all to report to a certain assembly point, I believe because the situation in the city is tense; there might be pogroms against the Jews, and they want to take us to a safe place. Where? No one knows. . . . As for us, as soon as they have taken us to the place in question, we will try to get settled. I will write to you, and then [Konstantin] can join us."[38] In the family of twelve-year-old Sergey Tauzhnyansky, whose mother was Jewish, the adults discussed the orders at length: "Some thought that those who showed up would be sent to the train station, and from there to Israel. Others thought they would be sent somewhere to work." Finally, Sergey's mother decided to join the rest of the Jewish population: "After filling two large backpacks with a couple of changes of clothes and some biscuits that we had in the house, we ventured out into the courtyard. I remember that even the neighbors who hadn't yet had time to evacuate came out with us and escorted us out the gate. A woman gave my mother a small cross on a chain, and she hung it around my neck." That cross would be the talisman that saved the boy from the massacre.[39]

That doesn't mean that some didn't view the objectives of the summons differently. But the prevailing decision was almost always not to evade it. Genya Batasheva, seventeen years old, recalled that the ordinance sparked many discussions in her family and neighborhood: "Some hypothesized that people would be sent to work, others said they would be transported somewhere along the railway, but no one knew anything specific." A neighbor advised Genya's mother not to obey the orders until more reliable information could be gathered. But after a few hours, the woman, frightened by the possible consequences, decided to join her children in the "immense torrent" of people: "Women with babies and children, middle-aged people and teenagers, decrepit old men and women."[40] On the other hand, Shelya Polishchuk's mother chose not to obey because she did not believe in the hypothesis of mass relocation.[41] Elena Efimovna Borodyanskaya-Knysh, on the other hand, set off with her four-year-old daughter, bringing no luggage because she "was aware that they would kill us."[42] Izabella N. Mirkina-Egorycheva, a Jew married to a Russian, sensed the anxiety that filled not only Jews "but anyone who retained even a little humanity." Some, seized by "ominous presentiments," plunged "into the darkest despair." Others clung "to the last faint thread of hope" because—as Izabella testified after the liberation—"the thought of an imminent violent death, the disappearance of relatives and friends, and especially of the youngest children, was so terrifying that everyone tried to suppress it."[43] Everyone? In truth, the numerous suicides demonstrate that many had a full understanding of events.[44] And in the Podil neighborhood, some gathered with their rabbi for the entire night: "He calmed them down and prepared them for death. The next morning they set off, bidding farewell to their Russian friends."[45]

"Families Had Baked Bread for the Journey"

At the first light of dawn on 29 September, a large crowd gathered at the designated location. The future writer Anatoly Vasilyevich Kuznetsov, then twelve years old, had decided to witness "such an incredible spectacle as the expulsion of the Jews from Kyiv" and observed that many had started to move when "it was still dark" because they wanted "to be in good time to get seats in the train."[46] After the liberation, the poet and literary critic Lev A. Ozerov gathered accounts from some witnesses, providing a powerful recollection of the exodus:

> Families had baked bread for the journey, sewn shoulder bags, hired carts and carriages. The elderly, men and women, walked supporting each other. Mothers held babies in their arms or pushed prams. People dragged sacks, bundles, suitcases, and crates. Children walked alongside their parents. The boys had almost nothing, while the adults had tried to bring as much as possible with them. The elderly, pale and breathless, were supported by their grandchildren. The sick and infirm, wrapped in blankets and sheets, were carried on stretchers by relatives. The crowd moved like an uninterrupted current along Lvovskaya Street, while German patrols stood on the sidewalks. From early morning until late at night, such a large number of people advanced on the road that crossing Lvovskaya became problematic. This procession of death lasted three days and three nights. The city fell silent. From Pavlovskaya Street, Dmitrievskaya Street, Volodarsky Street, and Nekrasovsky Street, the crowd poured into Lvovskaya like tributaries into a river.[47]

Izabella Mirkina-Egorycheva used the same imagery. Humans of all ages and social conditions "streamed from all parts of the city to pour, like individual streams, into one endless torrent."[48] The survivor Dina M. Pronicheva recalled streets so packed with people that it was difficult to move forward even a few steps:

> People with bundles, with prams, various carts, wagons, even a few trucks—all stood still, then moved forward a bit, stopped again. There was a loud noise of voices, the roar of the crowd, and it seemed like a demonstration, but there were no flags, no bands, no festive atmosphere. Strange, those trucks: where had they come from? It happened that the inhabitants of an entire building had collected money and rented a means of transportation for their luggage, and so now they all stood at the sides of the cart or truck. In the midst of bundles and suitcases lay the sick, and clusters of children sat. Infants were also carried two or three in one pram. . . . All this procession moved very slowly, and Artem Street is very long.[49]

In her diary, the teacher L. Nartova noted the image of "an incessant parade of people" invading streets and sidewalks: "Women, men, young girls, children, the elderly, whole families proceed. Many carry their belongings on carts, but most carry their possessions on their shoulders. They advance in silence, without noise. Terrifying. It all lasted a long time, an entire day, and only towards evening did the crowd begin to diminish. But the next day they resumed marching and continued like this for many days in a row."[50]

Several accounts focus on the composition of the crowd. With the exception of the males of conscription age who had already been the subject of a specific arrest order on 22 September, at the time of this concentration the Jews remaining in Kyiv were mainly elderly people, women, and children, with an especially high percentage of those underage (perhaps 30 percent were children under the age of eight). Fedir P. Pihido (pen name Pravoberezhny), later a prominent figure in the Ukrainian diaspora, was struck precisely by this detail: "Many thousands of people, mostly elderly (but there were also middle-aged people), were moving toward Babi Yar. And the children, the children. . . . Lord, how many children there were! Everything was moving, laden with bundles, luggage, and children. Occasionally, the elderly and the sick who did not have the strength to move on their own were transported on carts, probably by their sons or daughters. Some cried, others remained calm. Most of them advanced in a composed manner, in silence. They looked like condemned people. It was a terrible sight."[51]

Anatoly Kuznetsov was struck by the fact that it was mostly the poorest and most grievously suffering people who poured into the streets: "You see, in normal times, the crippled, the sick, the old stay at home, you don't see them. But here, everyone had to come out—and they did too." Many had only the bare essentials with them: "There were bundles roughly tied together with string, worn-out cases made from plywood, woven baskets, boxes of carpenters' tools. . . . Some elderly women were wearing strings of onions hung around their necks like gigantic necklaces—food supplies for the journey."[52] Even Nartova observed that the crowd was mostly made up of the elderly and infirm: "They advance so slowly and with such painful faces that it's painful to watch them. It's evident that they're all sick. Behind them, three women are being carried on carts. Their legs dangle and bump against the sidewalk." As the procession moved forward, doubts about the fate of the refugees thinned out. Even a seven-year-old girl, with a tone of total indifference, could ask: "Are they Jews? Where are they being sent? Will they be killed?"[53]

After several kilometers of marching past the Jewish cemetery, the human stream arrived at the area that overlooked the ravine of Babi Yar:

> As the crowd approached Babi Yar, the murmuring grew louder, mingling with moans and sobs. An outdoor office had been set up, complete with desks. However, the crowd, halted at the checkpoint organized by the Germans at the end of the road, could not see them. Thirty to forty people at a time were escorted out of the crowd and brought under surveillance to be "registered." Documents and valuables were confiscated. The documents were immediately thrown to the ground; witnesses recounted that the area was covered with a thick layer of discarded papers, identity documents, and torn work permits. Then the Germans forced everyone, without exception—including girls, women, the elderly, and children—to strip completely. The clothes were collected and neatly folded. Rings were torn from the fingers of the naked men and women.[54]

The precious items were seized on the spot by German officers and gendarmes; warm clothing and other usable materials were collected to be distributed among the Volksdeutsche. Fritz Höfer, the driver of Sonderkommando 4a, tasked with loading and transporting the piles of items elsewhere, described during a postwar trial the meticulousness of the operations preceding the execution:

> The Jews arriving—men, women, and children—were taken in charge by Ukrainians and led to different places, where one by one they had to deposit, in order, their luggage, coats, shoes, clothes, and even underwear. Similarly, they had to place their valuables in a designated area. For each type of garment, a separate pile was formed. Everything proceeded very quickly, and if someone hesitated, they were prodded with kicks and beatings. I believe no one took

more than a minute from the moment they removed their coat until they were completely naked. There was no distinction made between men, women, or children here.[55]

Dina Pronicheva fetched up near the entrance to the Jewish cemetery, close to a barrier of *chevaux de frise* (barbed-wire obstacles) where Germans and Ukrainian policemen regulated the foot traffic. She was with other members of her family. She wanted to find out where people were being taken and for what purpose. She left her family and made an attempt to go find out what was happening beyond the barbed wire. She expected to see a specially outfitted train for mass transportation but suddenly found herself facing a scene of people stripping:

> I went back to my folks. But I told them nothing to keep from upsetting them, and we continued together. They took my parents' possessions first. We went straight ahead, then to the right. And that was where I lost them. The crowd took them away from me, and they continued forward. It felt as if I walked for a long time. . . . Then I saw an open space where Germans were lined up on both sides. . . . They all had rubber truncheons or large and heavy sticks. We were forced to walk the entire length of that corridor.[56]

It was impossible, Dina went on, to avoid the beatings: "Cruel blows that immediately drew blood rained down on heads, backs, and shoulders from left and right. The soldiers shouted: 'Schnell! Schnell!' [Quickly! Quickly!] and laughed cheerfully, as if they were having fun at an amusement park, and they made an effort to strike particularly hard blows in the most vulnerable spots."[57] Confirmation of this method comes from Genya Batasheva. After being forced to abandon her luggage, the young woman was pushed toward a point where she could hear gunfire. On either side of the path, she saw German soldiers armed with automatic rifles and sticks. Many of them had dogs. To reach the pit, she had to walk through "a kind of human corridor" that led everyone, indiscriminately, to a wide, flat area. Anyone who tried to escape out the sides was brutally beaten and chased by dogs: "They beat people, and they did it for no reason. We were forced to constantly dodge the blows. Many years have passed, and I cannot help but recall with horror the nightmare of what happened in that clearing. It was hell in the truest sense of the word."[58]

Fritz Höfer described the subsequent phase of the operation: how the Jews were herded into the bed of the ravine and piled high. there. According to his testimony, the prisoners were taken under the command of members of the

Schutzpolizei and neatly arranged by a "packer" "in regular layers" atop the corpses of those who had already been killed: "There were only two shooters who carried out the executions. One acted at one end of the ravine, the second at the other end." They worked "standing" atop the "piled-up" bodies, killing the Jews "one after the other" and proceeding "like on a conveyor belt."[59] The executioners alternated in teams and were abundantly supplied with alcoholic beverages to muddle their sensibilities. Kurt Werner, the member of Sonderkommando 4a, participated in the massacre for the entire day of 29 September:

The whole commando, except for one sentinel, set off that day around 6:00 in the morning, heading to the place of these executions. I was on a truck. We were ordered to take with us everything that was available. We drove for about twenty minutes north and stopped on a paved road until it ended in open country. There, a very large number of Jews had been gathered, and a place had also been arranged where the Jews were obliged to deposit their clothes and luggage. After a kilometer, I saw a large natural ravine. The ground was sandy. The ravine was about ten meters deep, about four hundred meters long, about eighty meters wide at the top, and ten meters wide at the bottom.

Immediately after my arrival at the execution grounds, I was ordered to descend with my other comrades into this ravine. It wasn't long before the first Jews were brought down the walls of the ravine and made to lie face down. In the ravine there were three groups of shooters, a total of twelve. The Jews were brought down in a rush, all together, from the heights above down to these shooters. The Jews who followed had to lie down on the corpses of those previously shot. The shooters stood behind the Jews and killed them with gunshots to the back of the neck. I still remember today the state of terror in which the Jews fell when, from up above, at the rim of the ravine, they were first able to glimpse the bodies down at the bottom: many shouted loudly in fear.

One cannot even imagine what grim determination it took to carry out that dirty business down there. It was a gruesome thing. . . . I had to stay down in the ravine all morning. There, I had to continue shooting for a while, then I was busy loading ammunition into the magazines. During that time, other comrades were employed as shooters. Around noon, we were brought out of the ravine, and in the afternoon, I, along with others, had to lead more Jews back to the ravine. During this time, other comrades were shooting down into the ravine. We led the Jews to the edge of the ravine, and from there they ran down the slope on their own. All the shootings that day may have lasted until around . . . 5:00 or 6:00 in the evening. Later, we were taken back to our quarters. That evening, there was a further distribution of liquor.[60]

"The Action Was Carried Out Smoothly, and There Were No incidents"

Some of the people in the pits took a long time to die. Two women from the area, Natalia Petrenko and Nadezhda Gorbacheva, testified that "the layer of earth [thrown on the corpses] was astir with the movements of people still alive."[61] During the phase when the shootings were still being carried out by lining up a row of people at the rim of the ravine, some people managed to claw their way out. Nesya Elgort, who had lost touch with all her family in the crush, arrived at the ravine clutching her son to her naked body. The bullets missed her, but she fell into the empty space practically unconscious: "It's hard for me today to understand how I managed to get out of that ravine of death. All I know is that I did. Evidently what drove me was the survival instinct. That evening, I found myself back at Podol, with my son, Ilyusha, beside me. I really can't understand by what miracle he managed to survive. It was as if he had melded with me and we hadn't separated for a moment."[62]

Dina Pronicheva had managed to pass herself off as Ukrainian and had waited all day, along with other people recognized by the soldiers as non-Jewish, to be able to return home. She witnessed harrowing scenes: "People were going mad, turning white [with terror], atrocious screams and moans echoed through the air, continuous gunshots issued from rifles. I saw the Germans snatch babies from their mothers and hurl them down the slope into the bottom of the ravine." Finally, at the order of an officer unwilling to leave any witnesses alive, Dina too was taken to the edge:

> I was in a group of about twenty-five to thirty people. I saw those around me drop off the cliff as they were shot. Even before I could be shot myself, I threw myself into the void. I landed on the bodies of people who had just been shot, and I pretended to be dead. I could hear the Germans come down and shoot the wounded. I was afraid to move; a policeman approached me and saw that I wasn't bleeding. He called a German and told him I seemed still to be alive. I held my breath; one of them pushed me over with his foot so that I lay face up. The German stepped up so that he had one foot on my chest and the other on the back of my hand. After making sure I had no reaction, they left. . . . After a while, they started covering us with dirt. The layer of soil was thin, and I managed to work my way out of it. By now it was dark, and I silently crawled to the rock wall and with enormous effort began to climb it. I managed to make my way up the lip of the ravine, not far from where they had made us undress before the shooting. During my climb, I was called by a boy who had also survived. For two days, he and I both tried to escape from Babi Yar together. On the first day, I hid in the branches of a tree, and the boy hid among the bushes; on the second

day, I hid in a garbage pit. On the morning of the third day, the boy was killed while trying to reach the Kurenivka district. I heard two gunshots, but I couldn't see who had shot him. That same third day, still in the morning, I reached a hut, where the owner found me. I kept the whole story of my escape from Babi Yar secret from her and told her that I came from the trenches. I asked her to direct me to the city. She seemed willing to do so and gestured to her seventeen-year-old son. He vanished somewhere but returned a few minutes later with a German officer and, pointing at me, told him, "Here, sir, is a Jewess."[63]

Elena Borodyanskaya-Knysh arrived at Babi Yar with her column of people when it was already dark, together with her four-year-old daughter, Lyudmila. When the time came to disrobe, she was allowed to keep her undergarments only because they were so tattered and worn:

> Around midnight, the Germans ordered us to line up. Without waiting for the next order, I immediately pushed my daughter into the pit and threw myself in after her. A second later, dead bodies started falling on top of me. Then there was silence. Fifteen minutes passed, and the next group was brought in. Gunshots rang out again, and once more bleeding, dead, or dying people began to fall into the pit. It seemed like my daughter wasn't moving anymore. I pressed myself against her, shielding her with my body, clenched my fists, and put them under her chin so she wouldn't suffocate. The child began to show signs of life. I tried to lift myself a little to avoid crushing her. There was plenty of blood everywhere. The shootings had been going on since nine in the morning. I had corpses above and below me. I heard someone walking on the bodies and cursing in German. A soldier was using a bayonet to make sure there were no survivors. It just happened that he came to a halt on top of me, and that's why I avoided the bayonet thrust. As soon as he left, I raised my head. There were noises in the distance. It was the Germans arguing over the division of our belongings. I freed myself, got up, and took my unconscious daughter in my arms. I crossed the ravine. When I had walked about a kilometer, I realized that the child was barely breathing. There was no water anywhere, so I moistened her mouth with my saliva. After another kilometer, I started collecting dew from the grass and wetting her lips. Gradually, the little one came to. I caught my breath and then went on. Crawling from ravine to ravine, I reached the village of Babi Yar. I reached the courtyard of the kiln and took refuge in the basement. I stayed there for four days and four nights, without food and without clothing.[64]

Some residents of Kyiv were witnesses to what happened. Their accounts, in some cases offered by different individuals from the same family, were collected during the investigations undertaken after the liberation by the Soviet government. The caretaker of the Lukyanivka Orthodox cemetery, Sergei I. Lutsenko, who lived a few hundred meters from the ravine, reported what he had seen to the Extraordinary State Commission for Investigation of Nazi War Crimes:

> [The condemned] were ordered to pile all their personal belongings on the ground. The Germans then led the people . . . to Babi Yar in close-ranked lines of a hundred at a time. From the cemetery guardhouse, it was clearly visible how the first column stopped near the edge of the cliff, how people were ordered to disrobe, how their clothing was carefully piled up, how people at the ravine's edge were shot with rifles and automatic weapons, how women were seized, and how children were hoisted by the ankles and tossed into the ravine.[65]

The caretaker's daughter, Maria Lutsenko, stated in 1943 in the presence of the Soviet security service inquiry that she distinctly heard the gunfire and "the heartbreaking screams of children and women."[66] In a much later deposition to the KGB, the same witness specified that in the final stages "the Germans were in a hurry" to finish and therefore "hurried people to their execution without making them undress."[67]

Likewise, Ivan Yanovich, who lived nearby, clearly saw columns of Jews passing by. From the window of his house he had observed in particular the moment when the Jews, before being led to the ravine, were stripped of whatever belongings they had brought with them. He hadn't seen "how they were shot," but he had heard "the gunfire of automatic weapons and people screaming."[68]

Anatoly M. Yevgenyev, a seventeen-year-old Ukrainian who had observed the "endless stream" from a hilltop for twenty to thirty minutes along with his cousin Vasily Tkachenko, continued to hear rifle and machine gun bursts from his home for many days. Just over a week later, he went to the massacre site. It was strewn with corpses, which, in many places, were covered with fresh earth. Often, however, the limbs of "new victims" could be seen.[69] Lyudmila I. Zavorotnaya, Anatoly's sister, lived "in the immediate vicinity of the ravine." She hadn't witnessed the massacre herself, but she had distinctly heard the noise of "incessant shootings, the wailing and screams of a multitude of people." When, after a few days, it seemed that the executions were over, she noticed that "streams of blood flowed from the ravine," that "blood spurted from the sand with which the corpses had been covered."[70]

Official report no. 101 on the activity of Einsatzgruppe C, drafted on 2 October 1941, laconically announces: "Sonderkommando 4a in collaboration with

Einsatzgruppe HQ and two Kommandos of police regiment South executed 33,771 Jews in Kyiv on 29 and 30 September 1941."[71] The same figure is indicated in the aforementioned and much more detailed official report no. 106 of 7 October, which noted how essential it was for the success of the operation to have the support of the citizens of Kyiv:

> The population has an extremely hostile attitude toward the Jews, partly because of their privileged economic status under Soviet rule and their activities as informants or agents of the security services, partly as a result of the explosions in the city and the fires that resulted from them. It has indeed been possible to demonstrate that the Jews were involved in arson. The population expects appropriate reprisals from the Germans. . . . In collaboration with the command of Einsatzgruppe C and two detachments of the Southern Police Regiment, Sonderkommando 4a liquidated 33,771 Jews on 29 and 30 September. Money and valuables, clothing and linen were secured; a part was entrusted to the NSV [Nationalsozialistische Volkswohlfahrt (National Socialist People's Welfare)] for the use of the Volksdeutsche, and a part was assigned to the administrative authorities of the city to be distributed to the needy population. The action was carried out smoothly, and there were no incidents. The population approved the plan to transfer the Jews to another location. It is unlikely that it was known that the Jews, in fact, were liquidated. In any case, based on the experience gained so far, this would not provoke any reaction. The Wehrmacht also supported the measures taken. The Jews who have not yet been caught or those who return to the city after fleeing will be subjected to the same treatment.[72]

Irina Khoroshunova recounted in her diary how it had actually been quite easy for the citizens of the capital to learn of these events within a few days. On 30 September she still didn't know "what they did to the Jews":

> Terrible rumors are coming from the Lukyanivka cemetery. But so far they have been impossible to verify. It is said that Jews are being shot. People who accompanied them to the designated assembly point saw them all being ushered past a line of German soldiers and ordered to surrender all their possessions, and then other Germans pushed them farther on.
>
> Yesterday, the old Skrinskaya woman died. Her people hurried to find a coffin and ask for authorization to bury her. They were unable to locate a coffin until today, and that with great difficulty, because yesterday and today there were large numbers of suicides among the Jews, and it seems that there is an order from the city commander to bury those Jews before anyone else. Yesterday, her family went to Lukyanivka cemetery (the Germans had prohibited burials in

Baikove cemetery). Impossible to reach the cemetery by the usual route. The entire route is filled with Jews surrounded by German soldiers. To reach the cemetery, you have to pass by way of the prison. There a hole has been cut in the fencing, and the deceased are brought in on that side. On the far side of the Russian cemetery, there is silence. When they were there, they heard continuous gunfire from the Jewish cemetery.

It is said that the Jews are shot, that they are being liquidated one by one. Others say that sixteen trains have been formed up for them and that they will be sent away. To where? No one can say. Only one thing is certain: they confiscate all their identity papers, belongings, and foodstuffs. Then they push them along in the direction of Babi Yar, and there—I have no idea what's there. All I know is that something terrifying, something terrible, something unthinkable is happening, something that can be neither understood, recognized, nor explained.[73]

By 2 October Irina knew, because "by now, everyone says they're killing the Jews":

No, it's not that they're *killing* them, they have *already* killed them. All of them, indiscriminately, old people, women, children. Even those who returned home on Monday have been executed by firing squad. That's just what people are saying, but there can really be no doubt as to its truth. No train has left Lukyanivka. People have seen winter shawls and other such things being carried off from the cemetery. German "attention to detail." They've already split up the trophies!

A young Russian woman accompanied a friend to the cemetery and went through to the other side of the fence. She saw people being led naked to Babi Yar and heard bursts of machine-gun fire. These news items / rumors continue to proliferate. They are so monstrous that we cannot accept them into our minds. But we really have no choice but to believe them, because the execution by firing squad, the shooting of the Jews, is clearly a fact. A fact that is starting to cause us all to lose our minds. It is impossible to live with the awareness of all this.

Women all around us weep. And what about us? We too wept on 29 September when we thought they were taking them away to a concentration camp. And now? Can we really cry?

I write, and my hair stands on end. I write, but these words express nothing. I write because it is important that everyone become aware of this monstrous crime and avenge it. I write, and at Babi Yar, the mass murder of children, women, and elderly, innocent people continues, many of whom, it is said, are buried half-alive because the Germans are frugal and don't like to waste unnecessary bullets.

The cursed blue paper [a likely reference to the assembly order] weighs on the brain like a red-hot iron slab. And we are absolutely powerless! . . . But at Babi Yar the executions continue, the wholesale slaughter of innocent people. Has anything like this ever taken place in the whole history of humankind? No one could ever have devised anything remotely similar. I cannot bring myself to write anything more. No one can write this, no one can understand this, because full awareness of what is taking place would simply drive us mad. And there is no advantage to this for anyone, for anyone—They incessantly drive prisoners through the city. They parade Jews naked. They kill them if they beg for water or for bread.

That is all. And still we live. And still we cannot understand why we suddenly find ourselves with a greater right to live for the simple fact that we are not Jews.

Cursed century, cursed horrible era![74]

"Muffled Sounds Still Came"

In the month of September, approximately 130,000 Jews were exterminated in Ukraine—at least 40,000 in the Kyiv region alone.[75]

"After the savage reprisal" at Babi Yar, "the ground continued to move for a long time; from under the berm, muffled sounds still came."[76]

Sonderkommando 4a member Anton Heidborn returned there with his comrades three days later. He came face-to-face with some survivors, who were immediately executed by men from the Sicherheitsdienst, who assigned civilian teams to bury those new bodies by detonating explosives to bring down part of the wall of the ravine.[77] That detail actually reached Germany. The philologist Victor Klemperer noted it in his diary on 19 April 1942: "At the tram stop Eva was greeted by Lange, the carpenter (in the uniform of a corporal). She went to a pub with him, and he had a beer and talked. He had been in Russia for several months during the winter (until Christmas) as a driver for the military police. Ghastly mass murders of Jews in Kyiv. The heads of small children smashed against walls, thousands of men, women, adolescents shot down in a great heap, a hillock blown up, and the mass of bodies buried under the exploding earth."[78]

The executions continued at an intensive pace until at least mid-October, causing the death of thousands more Jews.[79] But they continued with some regularity even in the weeks and months that followed.[80] For the overall period of roughly two years, various armed units, varying in composition and nature, took turns one after another, and the executions took place at various points in the greater area, though most frequently within the relatively small perimeter of the area generally referred to as Babi Yar.[81] The extermination process might occasionally vary in its pattern. Thousands of victims were killed in their homes or shot down on the streets, drowned in the waters of the Dnieper River, or shot on the edge of other ravines, which are common in the area around the capital. Alongside Jews, Russian and Ukrainian civilians were also slaughtered, as were ordinary citizens and intellectuals taken prisoner as acts of military intimidation, prisoners of war, sailors from the Dnieper flotilla, partisans, members of the Communist Party, activists belonging to Ukrainian nationalist groups, mentally ill individuals, and residents of nomad camps. According to a population census conducted by the city administration, as of 1 April 1942 Kyiv had a population of 352,139, including 281,611 Ukrainians, 50,263 Russians, 7,874 Poles, 40 Gypsies, 131 Karaites, and 20 Jews (seven men and thirteen women).[82]

While most of the victims "voluntarily" showed up for the assembly summons on 29 September 1941, the Jews killed later were taken during roundups or on the basis of informants' denunciations. Indeed, there were quite a few who contributed, out of antisemitism or greed, to the expulsion of Jews from their homes and later to reporting their presence if and when they were found. In some cases, these informants even went on to take part in violence and street killings. Joseph Goebbels noted in his *Tagebuch* on 19 October 1941 that it was necessary to further encourage anti-Jewish propaganda in the occupied territories: "Bolshevism has gradually reduced the antisemitic instinct in the peoples of the Soviet Union. In a sense, we have to start again from scratch."[83] The population of Kyiv was therefore subjected to a "reeducation process" based on a linkage between Judaism and Bolshevism. The history of the Soviet Union was presented, in accordance with a model that had become accepted in Germany since the 1920s, as a history of the Jewish conquest of power through the tools of communication (movies, theater, radio, newspapers) and cultural hegemony. According to an official report, it was necessary to "give Ukrainians the opportunity to discover that practically only Jews enjoyed the advantages associated with membership in the Communist Party."[84]

Starting on 26 September 1941, the newspaper *Ukraïns'ke slovo* (Ukrainian word) was published in Kyiv.[85] Printed without any identification of ownership or composition of editorial staff, the paper initially manifested a rather moderate temperament in the language used: "There was an absence of insults and blasphemies." But as noted by Irina Khoroshunova, its "exaltation of the 'blond and noble Teutonic knights'" who had come to generously "liberate" the Ukrainians and its willingness to spread "the watchword of the destruction of Bolshevism and Jews" immediately caused concern in some sectors of the population.[86] *Ukraïns'ke slovo* then regularly published and publicized the edicts of the occupation forces.[87] A few days after the Babi Yar massacre, on

9 October, it called on the population to hunt down Jews or provide information about the presence of Jews who had assumed a false national identity (Greek, Armenian, Ukrainian, Russian) by paying high prices for the identity documents required. Ukraine had "a large number of true patriots" who were eager "to cleanse their lives, their villages, dense forests, and wonderful cities of partisans, Jewish arsonists, and Red commissars." The newspaper even announced the address where informants could anonymously report Jews trying to avoid liquidation: "These patriots come on a daily basis to a small house at Boulevard Shevchenko 48 and denounce enemies who, as a rule, hide under false names."[88] Calls for denunciation by informants must surely have been heeded, given the fact that the commander of security services in Kyiv, Hans Schumacher, testified after the war that informants were so common and active in the city that his own men could not keep up with the reports.[89]

Collaborationists were quite common and could be found among all nationalities and across all social classes. In the German Reichskommissariat Ukraine (which included Volhynia, central Ukraine, and parts of eastern Ukraine), the number of those serving in various auxiliary police forces had risen by August 1942 to no fewer than 150,000 individuals; by January 1943, that number had reached 170,000, amounting to roughly 1 percent of the entire population.[90] Collaborators not only were present in administrative agencies and bodies but also participated in patrol, escort, and defense operations and took part in investigative activities, political surveillance, and the issuance and monitoring of identity cards. But what matters most, as was the case in the Baltic countries, is that the Ukrainian police conducted antipartisan and anti-Communist operations alongside the Germans, they conducted guard duty in concentration camps, and they took part enthusiastically in the arrest, interrogations, and shooting of Jews.[91] There were multiple reasons why the Ukrainians collaborated with the Germans. There was certainly a significant number of "political activists" of nationalist persuasion who had experienced the Holodomor and the 1930s repressions (collectivization and dekulakization). Consequently, they saw Soviet power as an enemy force and held it responsible for requisitions, confiscations, and famines. However, according to some historians, the most important component of that activity should be sought in the "enterprising conformists" and "willing executioners" who, for the most part, were simply eager to avoid the threat of forced labor in Germany.[92]

There were many cases when Jews managed to obtain help by paying for it. For example, Maria I. Konstantinovskaya, after escaping the massacre along with her daughter, Shelya Polishchuk, decided to return home, claiming to her neighbors that she was of Ukrainian nationality and that only her husband was Jewish. With the assistance of an acquaintance, she managed to pay the building administrator to register her under a false identity and thereby obtain a forged passport. That, however, was not enough to prevent her from being reported. Mother and daughter were summoned by the police for investigation and questioning. Allowed to return home pending further verification, the women discovered that their apartment had been looted in their absence. Their photo album would be exhibited the following day during a new interrogation as proof of the two women's Jewishness.[93] They managed, nevertheless, to survive thanks to the assistance of people who, often independently, offered them hospitality, lied to the police, and illegally procured employment for them.[94]

"I Stayed Hidden with Her"

Many of those who managed to survive owed it most frequently to the spontaneous assistance of ordinary acquaintances, if not in some cases to the outright courage of strangers—indications of a solidarity that composed a mosaic, too large to be mapped, of small acts of kindness. There were, first of all, genuine gestures of understanding and support, as noted by Dina Pronicheva as she walked through the streets of Kyiv on her way toward Babi Yar: "There were many escorts: neighbors, friends, relatives, Ukrainians and Russians, who helped carry luggage and supported the sick, sometimes even carrying them on their shoulders."[95] Even the mother of the writer Viktor P. Nekrasov, who had unsuccessfully tried to persuade many Jewish friends not to obey the concentration order, escorted some of them. When she reached the Jewish cemetery, she was turned back, along with others who had accompanied Jews, by soldiers and policemen: "In the distance, gunfire could be heard, but my mother at the time understood nothing."[96] There was no shortage of individual attempts at rescue that put the lives of the would-be rescuers at risk, too. Even though the Germans circulated leaflets immediately after the massacre declaring that anyone who provided fugitives with shelter or accommodation would be immediately executed along with their families, attempts at rescue still persisted.

After great hesitation, the mother of Elena Gorodetskaya started walking toward Babi Yar with her three daughters the morning after the first concentration of the Jewish population. After a short journey, she was stopped by a friend and neighbor, Marusya Bantysh, who ran after her to warn her about the continual shootings. Her husband, who had just happened to return to Kyiv, decided in disbelief to check that report out in person:

He returned five or six hours later with a vacant gaze and trembling hands: "It's true, I crossed past the barricades and saw how the policemen were searching for valuables, stripping and piling up stacks of still-warm clothing." From that day forward, he began to go slowly mad; he was seized by a silent madness out of the fear he felt for us. I remember my parents in bed with ropes tied around their necks: "If they knock at our door at night, if they come looking for us, we'll strangle ourselves." Mama: "What about the children?"—"They have red hair, they'll survive; the Germans are looking for people with curly black hair and hooked noses—that's their stereotype of a Jew."[97]

The family took shelter in a hole excavated next to the stove in their apartment and covered with iron plates. Elena's father committed suicide just a few months later, and her mother tried to take her own life more than once. Her survival was ensured by her neighbors, who provided food in exchange for valuables.[98]

Among the few who managed to escape the Babi Yar ravine was Nesya Elgort. After reaching Podil with her child, she was assisted by a Russian woman, Maria Grigorievna, whose surname Nesya could no longer remember. That woman offered her overnight hospitality and then helped her to get home the following morning.[99] Elena Efimovna Borodyanskaya-Knysh, who—as we have already seen—escaped the massacre with her four-year-old daughter, remained hidden for several days in a chance hidey-hole from which she could hear bursts of machine-gun fire in the distance. Finally, she decided to venture out and managed to make her way into the attic of a nearby house:

> I found a worn-out knit skirt and two old jackets. I dressed the child in one of those jackets. Then I went to see an acquaintance named Letoshenko. When she saw me, she felt her blood freeze. She gave me a skirt and a dress and hid me along with my daughter. I stayed hidden with her for more than a week. Then she gave me some money, and I went to another acquaintance, Fenya Plyuyko. She also helped me a lot. Her husband had been killed at the front. I spent a month in her apartment. None of the neighbors knew me. Whenever they asked who I was, Fenya replied, "She's my husband's sister, come from the countryside." I then moved to stay with Shkuropadskaya. I stayed with her for two weeks. Since everyone in Podil knew me, I couldn't leave the house during the day.[100]

Given shelter for one month by a colleague from work, Elena finally left Kyiv and took refuge in a village in the region. There she found shelter with a peasant family, the Grigorenkos, who saved her and her daughter from roundups and raids. Returning to Kyiv after liberation, she continued working for the city transport company alongside her rescuer, Valentina Ya. Litvinenko.[101]

Revekka Shvarcman was accompanied to Babi Yar by an acquaintance, Praskovya Taraday, who even brought her own two daughters, aged eleven and sixteen. A German soldier, seeing Revekka with her very blond fifteen-month-old son in her arms, asked if she was Jewish. Upon being told that in fact she was, he unexpectedly suggested that she escape. The young woman barely managed to break free of the crowd along with her sister and their respective children. They abandoned their other kin (their parents and their aunt, their father's sister, as well as the aunt's husband and three children). After finding hospitality for roughly two months with acquaintances in a village in the provinces, Revekka was forced to flee once again and returned to Kyiv, where she turned to a pair of family friends, Ganna I. Radchenko and Savely Klimentevich, hoping they might take in her son before she was forced to surrender to the Germans. Instead, they offered her hospitality and assistance. Thanks to the support of an entire support network (the Radchenko, Nechai, and Taraday families), she managed to survive. They even provided her with a passport under the false Ukrainian identity of Raisa A. Kiseleva (the surname actually belonged to her husband), and they procured a forged birth certificate for her son and had him baptized. Her sister, on the other hand, was instead denounced after several months in hiding and killed along with her two children.[102]

Genya Batasheva and another teenager living in her same apartment building, Manya Z. Palti, managed to escape the massacre by convincing German soldiers that they weren't Jewish and that they had wandered into Babi Yar merely out of curiosity. Once back in the city, they were helped by a neighbor, who procured false identity papers for them, along with a map of Ukraine, suggesting a route to cross the front line.[103] Uncommon but every bit as significant were attempts at rescue by members of the Ukrainian police. V. Alperin, a five-year-old boy, was saved from death along with his mother and grandmother by a policeman still remembered as "Gordon." He managed to spirit them out of the group of people slated for execution; the next day, he provided them with "Aryan" identity documents and new accommodations.[104]

One of the most notable cases of rescue occurred in the Podil district. The Orthodox priest Aleksey Aleksandrovich Glagolev, son of a prominent biblical scholar at the Kyiv Theological Academy, hid several Jews who had survived the shootings and requested his help at the Pokrovskaya church, along with the active support of his family.[105] Izabella Mirkina-Egorycheva turned to the Glagolevs after her closest relatives disappeared at Babi Yar. Glagolev's wife, Tatyana Pavlovna, gave Izabella her identity card and baptism certificate; with those documents, the woman lived for eight months in the house of some acquaintances in the countryside. Faced with suspicion from the village authorities, however, she was forced to return to Kyiv. From that moment on, she spent two years, along with her ten-year-old daughter, Ira, in the Glagolevs' home or in the church's bell tower. Polina D. Sheveleva, a Jewess married to a Ukrainian, and her mother, Evgeniya A. Sheveleva, were offered accommodations in a small building adjacent to the parish church. When in August 1942 Polina's husband, Dmytro L. Pasichny, managed to rescue them, the two women had a baptism certificate that, although legally worthless as proof of personal identity, could still be somewhat useful.[106] Other people hidden by Father Aleksey were issued documents accrediting them with the qualifications of chorister, sacristan, and custodian without the Germans realizing that a church only occasionally open to the public and in any case rather poor as the Pokrovskaya could hardly hope to have such a large staff in its employ.[107]

"According to a Reliable Source"

In the first week of October 1941, a group of foreign journalists was taken to Kyiv to observe the effects of the explosions that followed German occupation. The journalists asked Reichskommissar Erich Koch, who had accompanied them, about Babi Yar. They put no stock in his denials.[108] The first information reported by the international press was limited yet nonetheless timely and accurate. On 21 October 1941 the Jewish Telegraphic Agency (JTA) reported that the capital was now "completely *judenrein* [cleansed or free of Jews]." The source was a report from the Ukrainian newspaper *Krakivs'ki visti* (Krakow news), at that time published in Krakow. The collaborationist newspaper had reported that all Jews—men, women, and children of all ages—had been expelled. Pried out of their homes and concentrated in the suburbs, they had been "led on foot to a secret destination." Their fate remained "unknown."[109]

Meanwhile, unequivocal news reports reached Germany through the Germans who had taken part in the operations. "Ludwig B.," probably a private stationed in Kyiv or nearby, drew a link explaining the summary executions as a response to the urgent need for reprisals in a letter he wrote at the end of September 1941: "In Kyiv there has been one explosion after another. The city continued to burn for eight days: it has all been the work of the Jews. Consequently, Jewish men between fourteen and sixty years old, as well as women, were shot; otherwise, there would never have been an end to it."[110] Historian Willy Cohn heard about a "great bloodbath" in Kyiv during the last days he spent in Breslau. He noted it in his diary on 11 October 1941, shortly before being deported with his family to Lithuania.[111]

On 16 November the JTA stated that according to a "reliable source," fifty-two thousand Jews—men, women, and children—had been systematically and methodically killed in Kyiv. The victims had been killed not in a pogrom but in a process of "ruthless and consistent execution, carried out in accordance with a premeditated Nazi extermination policy."[112] On 19 November both *Pravda* and *Izvestia* reported that according to "reliable sources," the Germans had killed "fifty-two thousand Jews in Kyiv: men, women, and children."[113] On 21 November Lev Z. Mekhlis, head of the Red Army's Political Directorate (GlavPUR), was presented with the accounts of several officers who had escaped captivity and had had a chance to see the concentration order. The Jews, "unsuspecting," had obeyed the order and had gathered near the Jewish cemetery awaiting relocation: "They were all killed."[114] A few days later, on 28 November, the Russian armed forces newspaper *Krasnaya zvezda* (Red star) published an account from Major Pyotr Stepanenko. The officer, a special envoy to the southwestern front, having collected information "from Soviet citizens who had escaped," provided an important account of the *pogromy* (a recurring term in the text). The violence and looting, rapes, and murders, which had affected "almost every family," had taken on "a mass character" two days after the German occupation. The massacre of "fifty-two thousand men, women, and children," which went on for quite a while, had targeted "not only Jews" but also "Russians and Ukrainians" of all ages and walks of life. The correspondent also referred to the "furious antisemitic agitation" promoted by the Germans and their collaborators (*ouenovcy*), who had heaped blame on the Jews for sabotage, and in particular actions targeting administrative offices and army high commands. The reprisal was unleashed not only on adults, who were forced to dig their own graves, but also on children, who were buried alive. Despite highlighting that the victims were "peaceful citizens," "defenseless and guiltless individuals," Stepanenko devoted ample space to the specificity of the concentration order, which masqueraded as an evacuation plan. Addressed to "all the Jews residing in the city," it had ordered them to present themselves with baggage and provisions for a journey, even though "the intention was not evacuation but murder."[115]

On 4 December 1941 Serhiy R. Savchenko, commissioner for internal affairs of the Ukrainian Soviet Socialist Republic, while mentioning in passing the festive welcome that several hundred people had given the first German detachments, submitted to Nikita S. Khrushchev, then first secretary of the Ukrainian party organization, a report on the creation of new government agencies and the first administrative measures issued by the occupying forces; the recruitment of collaborators and intense anti-Soviet propaganda; the registration of male laborers and the presence of forced-labor battalions; and food supplies, transportation, and the provision of electricity and water. The importance of that document lies mainly in its status as evidence of full and detailed knowledge of the massacre of the Jews at Babi Yar, so complete that it even included a description of the work of the packer as reported by the Sonderkommando 4a driver, Fritz Höfer, mentioned above:

> Even as the fires were still blazing, the Germans began to spread rumors, officially declaring in the press that it was Jews who had been responsible for the explosions and fires. On 28 September notices were distributed in the city concerning the concentration of the entire Jewish population at Lukyanivka cemetery on 29 September at 8:00 p.m. The Jews were to bring documents, valuables, and warm clothing. Failure to comply with the order would result in execution. The entire Jewish population, mostly elderly, women, and children, showed up at the designated gathering place, where they were all shot. According to the testimony of prisoners of war, the Germans stripped the Jews who showed up, took away their valuables, then piled them on top of each other and, with a single shot, killed several people. Thus, in Kyiv as many as thirty thousand Jews were shot.[116]

The figure of fifty-two thousand victims reported on 16 November by the JTA, on 19 November by *Pravda* and *Izvestia*, and on 28 November by Pyotr Stepanenko was found in a note that Foreign Minister Vyacheslav M. Molotov sent on 6 January 1942 to the governments with which the Soviet Union had diplomatic relations. This was the first official document that not only reported the looting and reprisals carried out by the occupying troops, the violations of international law in the treatment of prisoners of war and civilians, and the mass executions but also extensively described the massacres of Jews in the occupied territories, especially at Babi Yar:

> A horrible massacre and pogrom were perpetrated by the German invaders in the Ukrainian capital, Kyiv. Within a few days the German bandits killed and tortured to death fifty-two thousand men, women, old folk, and children, dealing mercilessly with all Ukrainians, Russians, and Jews who in any way displayed their fidelity to the Soviet government. Soviet citizens who escaped from Kyiv gave an agonizing account of one of these mass executions. A large number of Jews, including women and children of all ages, was gathered in the Jewish cemetery of Kyiv. Before they were shot, all were stripped naked and beaten. The first persons selected for shooting were forced to lie face down at the bottom of a ditch and were shot with automatic rifles. Then the Germans threw a little earth over them. The next group of people awaiting execution was forced to lie on top of them and shot, and so on.[117]

Despite considering the fate of different nationalities within the broader context of an attack on their "loyalty to Soviet power," the statement contained a clear reference to the annihilation of a single group of the citizenry: "These bloody executions were especially directed against unarmed and defenseless Jewish working people."[118]

A long communiqué from *Pravda* on 19 December 1942 followed the declaration signed two days earlier by the governments of the twelve anti-Nazi coalition countries.[119] The Soviet government acknowledged that a campaign of extermination (*istreblenie*) of the Jewish population of Europe was under way: "In proportion to their modest numbers, the Jewish minority of the Soviet population" had suffered "particularly harshly" because it was targeted by a "plan for total annihilation."[120] Some ecclesiastical leaders soon weighed in as well. Metropolitan Andrey Sheptytsky, head of the Ukrainian Greek Catholic Church in Galicia, who saved the lives of 150 Jewish children and 15 rabbis, publicly spoke out against all forms of murder and protested to Nazi authorities about the involvement of the local population in their *pogromy*.[121] At the end of August 1942, he informed the Vatican: "Not a day goes by without the most horrendous crimes being committed. . . . The Jews are the first victims. The number of those killed in our country has certainly exceeded 200,000. As the army advanced eastward, the number of victims increased. In Kyiv in a few days there were executions of about 130,000 [actually, 30,000] men, women, and children. All the small towns of Ukraine witnessed similar massacres, and this situation has lasted for a year."[122]

"All Traces Were Destroyed"

The Germans weren't especially interested in disposing of their victims' bodies, which were often hastily covered with a bit of calcium hypochlorite and a thin layer of soil.[123] Once winter ended, however, the water running everywhere as a result of the spring thaw caused those bodies to bob to the surface and float. The stench of rotting bodies spread to the settlements closest to the sites of the massacre, eliciting protests from the local population as well as from German army units deployed in the area.[124]

In the spring of 1942, driven by fears that the National Socialist leadership, in the event of Germany's defeat, might be held accountable for war crimes, Heinrich Himmler ordered the establishment of a special unit within the Schutzstaffeln (SS): Sonderkommando 1005, under the command of SS Standartenführer Paul Blobel, commander of Sonderkommando 4a, was thereby assigned to erase all traces of the executions. After several experimental efforts, the operation was carried out in a methodical manner. Covering extensive

geographic territory, the operation entailed training unit leaders. That training was done at the Janowska camp in Lviv. The task was to exhume bodies,
burn them, and scatter the ashes. The instructions were kept strictly secret,
and it was decided that the matter would only ever be discussed verbally. From
the summer of 1943 until the end of the occupation, hundreds of mass graves
were exhumed by Jewish prisoners and prisoners of war across the entire Eastern Front. It was only the advance of Soviet troops that prevented the operation's completion.[125]

At Babi Yar in the summer of 1943, the work was entrusted to unit 1005a,
under the command of SS Sturmbannführer E. Topheide, who had been one
of the perpetrators of the massacre in the first place. The work was placed
under the overall command of SS Hauptsturmführer Julius Baumann. On
18 August 327 men were taken from Syrets concentration camp, one hundred
of them Jews.[126] They were assigned to carry out tasks that immediately
appeared anything but "ordinary." The prisoners were sent to Babi Yar in the
greatest secrecy, following pathways surrounded by barbed wire and under the
escort of SS officers and noncommissioned officers. They were housed in a
special shelter carved into one of the ravine walls. The following day, the exhu-
mations began. The graves were opened with the help of excavators, and the
inmates, armed with shovels, were ordered to unearth the corpses. A heap of
tens of thousands of corpses came to light. At the sight of the heaps of bodies,
some of the prisoners went mad: "The bodies, having been underground for a
long time, had fused together to such a degree that it was necessary to use
grappling hooks to separate them." That first day, work lasted from 4:00 a.m.
until late at night.[127]

The Germans ordered granite gravestones and iron fences to be transported
from the nearby cemetery. Immediately following liberation, some survivors
from the group of prisoners reported the use of these materials:

> We made platforms with the gravestones, and we laid rails atop them. On the
> rails, we placed iron fences to serve as grills. We placed a layer of firewood atop
> them and atop the wood a layer of bodies. Atop the bodies, we placed another
> layer of firewood and then poured gasoline over it. In that sequence, several rows
> of bodies were stacked, and then we lit the fire. Each pyre included up to 2,500–
> 3,000 bodies. The Germans detached special teams of men who removed ear-
> rings and rings from the bodies and extracted gold teeth from the gums. After all
> the bodies were burned, new pyres were prepared, and so on. The bones were
> smashed into small pieces with hammers. The ashes had to be scattered through-
> out the ravine so that no trace remained. We worked like this for twelve to
> fifteen hours a day.[128]

The hard work of the Syrets prisoners continued until 28 September and led to the cremation of about seventy thousand bodies. The destruction of the mass graves was pursued so thoroughly that the subsequent Soviet commission assigned to investigate German war crimes proved incapable of accurately establishing the number of victims and had to settle for approximate figures.[129] Blobel himself participated in the action at least once. He described his inspection in a deposition given during legal proceedings on 18 June 1947: "I had the opportunity to witness the cremation of the bodies from a mass grave near Kyiv during my visit in August [1943]. The grave was fifty-five meters long, three meters wide, and two and a half meters deep. After the surface layer was removed, the bodies were doused with fuel and set on fire. It took almost two days for the fire to burn completely. I personally made sure that everything was done as it should be. After that, the grave was covered back over, and all traces were destroyed."[130]

At the end of the "cleanup job," the prisoners—well aware that they were going to be killed—made an escape attempt at dawn on 29 September 1943. They caught the SS guards by surprise before they could immediately open fire. Most of the prisoners were killed by the ensuing hail of bullets, but about twenty managed to get over the fences alive, and they managed to make it to safety on the outskirts of Kyiv.[131]

What happened in the months of August and September 1943 was unfailingly perceptible to the *senses* of the city's inhabitants: "In that ravine, day and night, a fire burned, emitting black smoke and an unbearable smell. Word spread among the inhabitants that the Germans were digging up all the bodies with a machine that resembled an excavator, dousing them with gasoline, and setting them on fire."[132] It was only thanks to the escape of the prisoners, however, that the incineration of the bodies buried at Babi Yar became known with certainty to the population. The writer Vasily S. Grossman reported on this in a letter written in the city's immediate vicinity in October 1943, shortly before the Soviet troops arrived: "People arriving from Kyiv report that the Germans have thrown a cordon of soldiers around an enormous pit at Babi Yar, where the bodies of fifty thousand Jews, killed in Kyiv at the end of September 1941, were thrown. The Germans are feverishly unearthing the corpses and burning them. Could they be so foolish as to believe they can cover their terrible tracks? Tracks imprinted forever with the tears and blood of Ukraine, tracks that stand out even in the darkest night."[133]

"It Is Not in Our Interest"

Kyiv was liberated on 6 November 1943. Among the first to enter the city with the Soviet troops was Boris N. Polevoy, war correspondent for *Pravda*:

The city was still burning. But all of us correspondents were eager to go to Babi Yar. We had heard about it many times. But it was important to see everything in person. Now I can no longer remember the name of the woman who took it upon herself to take us there. I recall only vaguely that she was a schoolteacher and had lived through the occupation. We arrived at Babi Yar and felt the blood freeze in our veins. Enormous, deep ditches. The day before, the city had been bombed, and one of the bombs had fallen along the ravine's escarpment. The explosion caused a piece of the ravine wall to break away. And we saw something inconceivable: a kind of geological deposit of death—a monolith of human remains compressed between layers of earth. Not even in the most horrible dream will anything of this sort ever appear. . . . [I]t was impossible to believe that any of this was real. Terrible . . . fear washes over you at the memory alone. . . . I haven't seen anything more frightful in the entire war. After it came Auschwitz, Dachau, Buchenwald, dozens of other places of mass extermination. But the most terrifying, the most inconceivable to the human mind, was there at Babi Yar.[134]

There are any number of accounts from soldiers and correspondents who, upon entering Kyiv, discovered the bodies scattered in the sands of Babi Yar, but none of them managed to express their emotions in words at the level achieved by Mykola P. Bazhan in the poem titled "Jar" (1943).[135] The reader is confronted with "a rotted-out ravine, full of waste" and "putrid winds from far-off rustlands":

Don't flinch; don't pale; don't turn away.
Stand tall, as though before a judge, a soldier.
We cannot find the curses to condemn.
The oaths—we cannot find the oaths to swear.

Straightforward pit!
Disordered pit, untidy,
The branches of two white aspens tremble.
No. Here among the dead it isn't silent:

A hundred thousand dying hearts are sobbing,
And human cinderbones burn silver.
A person's forehead, broken into bits.
The crumbling slopes have slid into the void. . . .

And buried underground beneath the mud

Are a hundred thousand moldering bodies.
It's slippery—this greasy clay, this flesh
Of mangled, headless human carcasses.

Here the angry tongues of fire hissed,
Here folks fueled the raging flames with gas,
But not before (the shame!) they'd searched each corpse,
Treasure hunting in the murdered mass.

There rose above the terrible ravine
A heavy, suffocating smoke,
Inhaling death, exhaling nightmares, choking
Its way into the homes—a deaf-mute fiend.

Lightning, purple black and silent, flared
Out across the horror-frosted land.
The suburb sank beneath its evil glare,
Tarnishing the Kyiv households. And

The people, from their mournful cellars, saw
How, past the graveyard poplars with their graves,
And past the domes of Cyril with their wreathes,
Their very flesh and blood went up in flames.

The ash from deathfires, corpses charred.
And Kyiv, angry Kyiv, witnessed this
As flames rose toward the sky from Babi Yar.
There is no penance for this kind of fire.

There is no vengeance for this kind of murder.
Damn the ones who say it's in the past.
Damn the ones who say, "Forgive, it's over."[136]

The Soviet government staged a visit for the international press. The welcoming committee was chaired by Bazhan himself, a member of the Ukrainian Commission of Inquiry into German War Crimes, which summoned three former Jewish inmates from Syrets concentration camp, Fima A. Vilkis, Leonid K. Ostrovsky, and Vladimir Yu. Davidov, as witnesses. The Moscow correspondent for CBS and *Newsweek*, Bill Downs, upon returning from his visit to Babi Yar, wrote: "As substantiating evidence, while walking over the mass graves, I saw bits of hair, bones, and a crushed skull with bits of flesh and hair still attached. Walking down the ravine, I constantly came across shoes, spectacle cases, and in one place found gold bridgework." If the Germans— unlike what had happened in the early days of the war—had set out to erase the traces of the massacres, this meant on their part "a policy which presupposes the possibility of defeat" and an effort to escape the punishment announced in the Allied declarations.[137]

The *New York Times* correspondent William Lawrence, however, expressed a certain incredulity ("On the basis of what we saw, it is impossible for this correspondent to judge the truth or falsity of the story told to us"), placing in diametric opposition what he saw in the ravine's ruins and the story told by the three crematorium attendants: "It is the contention of the authorities in Kiev that the Germans, with characteristic thoroughness, not only burned the bodies and clothing, but also crumbled the bones, and shot and burned the bodies of all prisoners of war participating in the burning, except for a handful that escaped, so that the evidence of their atrocity could not be available for the outside world. If this was the Germans' intent, they succeeded well, for there is little evidence in the ravine to prove or disprove the story."[138]

The Extraordinary State Commission into war crimes committed by the Germans in all occupied territories worked—from late 1943 to early 1944—to document the methods, establish the extent, and assign criminal responsibilities for those crimes.[139] Work began in Kyiv as soon as a delegate arrived from Moscow.[140] A first report on the mass graves found at Syrets and Babi Yar was produced on 27 November 1943. The official version was published by the press starting on 29 February 1944.[141] The document denounced "the policy of Germanization of the Ukrainian people" and the "mass extermination of peaceful citizens and Soviet prisoners of war."[142] The accusations were grouped into three sections: economic exploitation, destruction of culture, and mass executions. In conclusion, the report listed the names of those deemed responsible for the atrocities. In just over two years of occupation in the Kyiv region, over 195,000 people were tortured to death, shot, or asphyxiated in gas trucks: over 100,000 men, women, children, and the elderly at Babi Yar; over 68,000 prisoners of war and civilians in the Darnytsia district; over 25,000 civilians and prisoners of war near or within the Syrets internment camp; 800 mentally ill in the territory of the Kyrylivska psychiatric hospital; about 500 civilians in the vicinity of the Pechersk Lavra; and 400 civilians in the Lukyanivka cemetery.[143] These were incomplete data based on provisional calculations, but they were not too far astray from those that became available a few months later (October 1944), which estimated the number of people killed in Kyiv and the surrounding region at 127,273 civilians and 69,021 prisoners of war.

The document, however, provided no information about the types of victims. The reduction of nationality (Jewish) to citizenship (Soviet) obeyed the order of the larger constitutional discourse and reformulated in institutional language the watchword of that military context (the Great Patriotic War): Nazi aggression had been unleashed against the Soviet Union, not against any of its individual components. The report of 27 November 1943 on the massacre of Babi Yar was subject to review at the highest levels of the political hierarchy. The vice president of the Council of People's Commissars and minister of foreign affairs, Vyacheslav M. Molotov; the president of the Soviet Information Bureau, Aleksandr S. Shcherbakov; the Ukrainian leader, Nikita S. Khrushchev; and the deputy minister of foreign affairs, Andrey Yanuaryevich Vyshinsky, agreed to accept the proposal of the head of the propaganda department of the Central Committee of the Communist Party, Georgy Fedorovich Aleksandrov, to replace the word "Jews" with the expression "peaceful Soviet citizens." We can get some sense of the radical nature of that interference from a letter dated in February 1944 and addressed to Molotov by Nikolai Mikhailovich Shvernik, president of the Extraordinary State Commission, which allows us to see the corrections made by the recipient. In the text revised by Molotov, every reference to Jewish victims had been removed, replacing "Jews" with "peaceful Soviet citizens." In the report, we find this phrasing: "The Hitlerite bands carried out a brutal mass extermination of the Jewish population. They issued an ordinance that ordered all Jews to appear on 29 September 1941 at the intersection of Mel'nikova and Dorohozhytska Streets, bringing personal documents, money, and valuables. The executioners pushed the Jews who had gathered there toward Babi Yar, robbed them of all their valuables, and then shot them."[144]

It is difficult to assess relations between Moscow and Kyiv based on the instructions provided by the Extraordinary State Commission of inquiry into German war crimes to the investigating bodies of the individual republics. One scholar who examined the model of the capital city's intervention in the outlying areas highlighted the weakness of the state structure and the lack of any operational plan, but he also emphasized the rushed conduct of the work and the rough approximation of calculations sent by a bureaucracy incapable of selecting and distinguishing between reports of atrocities. In April 1944 the perception of a situation of stalemate and the clear concern that the necessary conclusions were not being drawn from the immense documentation now available prompted the Ukrainian minister of foreign affairs, Oleksandr Yevdokymovych Korniychuk, to write a memorandum to Khrushchev, proposing (unsuccessfully) that they undertake the publication of a sort of "red book" on Nazi crimes.[145]

With the opening of the Nuremberg trials on 20 November 1945, about which the daily press sought to provide the most complete coverage possible, further investigations were conducted; following the establishment of conventions between the Allied powers, a number of local trials were held. One such trial of German officers was prepared in Moscow during the preliminary investigative phase and then held in Kyiv from 17 to 28 January 1946, resulting in twelve death sentences. Reversing the model of identification proposed by Georgy Aleksandrov to the state leadership, the officers placed on trial by the Ukrainian judiciary were charged with having caused the deaths at Babi Yar of seventy thousand Soviet citizens of Jewish nationality.[146]

This verdict was important because it was dangerous. In Ukraine, the process of rebuilding popular consensus for the socialist state was undertaken decisively in the wake of the collaborationist deviation and the prevalence of separatist political positions. The Kyiv government had no intention of discussing the suffering endured by Jews as Jews, only the suffering endured by the Ukrainian citizenry, of which Jews formed a part. In a report sent to Stalin from Kyiv on 8 November 1943, immediately after liberation, Khrushchev, in addition to reporting on the aftermath of destruction and the initial measures being taken to ensure order and the restoration of essential services, went on to report on the testimony and accounts he had collected from various residents, who tearfully told of "the horrors of the German occupation." But he didn't go much further than that: "The Germans have managed to empty the city of the vast majority of its population. Kyiv gives the impression of a dead city."[147] The desire to establish reconciliation and pacification with the more extreme sectors of Ukrainian nationalism is evident in the report that Khrushchev himself—already appointed head of the Kyiv government (1944–47) and previously in charge of the Sovietization campaign for the annexed area (1939–41)—delivered on 1 March 1944 to the Supreme Soviet of the Soviet Socialist Republic of Ukraine, which was meeting for the first time since liberation. After dwelling on the torments and destruction caused by the occupation regime, he paid tribute to the hundreds of thousands of victims of Nazism. But he made no mention whatsoever of the extermination of 1.5 million Jews. On the contrary, he guaranteed amnesty ("complete forgiveness [*proshchenie*] of their mistakes") to those who had "found themselves by mishap in the ranks of the nationalist gangs, whether they had been deceived or forcibly recruited," even though those individuals had fought against the Red Army and had, in a number of cases, personally participated in the genocide.[148] Furthermore, Khrushchev was more than explicit on other occasions as well. In a private conversation shortly after the liberation of Kyiv, while expressing the hope that no surviving Jews would be repatriated to Ukraine, he reportedly declared: "The Jews have committed many sins against the Ukrainian people in the past. Which is why the people hate them. We don't need Jews in our Ukraine. . . . It is not in our interest for the Ukrainian people to interpret the return of Soviet power as tantamount to the return of the Jews."[149]

All that remained was to contrast the "heroism" of the Ukrainian population ("our people," as Khrushchev added) with the "cowardice" of the Jewish population.[150] One particular factor helped to facilitate the construction of that myth. According to the Soviet view, every survivor was suspected of some crime tantamount to disloyalty to the homeland, and that held true to a far greater extent than in other countries that had been subjected to German invasion occupation and therefore the temptations of collaborationism. Why had they obeyed the enemy's orders instead of resisting? Had they been contaminated not only in their ideas and feelings but also, most importantly, in the sphere of ethics by their prolonged exposure to the regime of military occupation, which demanded collaboration? Had they supported the enemy in any way, even through mere passivity? All these questions were more than understandable, since the level of the populace's voluntary and involuntary participation in the Reichskommissariat Ukraine was not limited only to a few fringe pro-Nazi or simply anti-Soviet elements. In fact, it included a wide-ranging array of adherents who had little to do with ideology. Hence, "Jews who'd merely tried to survive the occupation," having hidden to escape raids instead of resisting and fighting, were suspected of having "collaborated with the Germans."[151]

In a report on the incipient formation of a partisan movement that was sent to Stalin in early July 1941, the secretary of the Central Committee of the Communist Party in Belarus, Panteleimon K. Ponomarenko, mentioned the efforts of Nazi propaganda, "written and oral," which waved "the flag of the fight against Jews [zhydy] and Communists: two terms used as synonyms." While the peasant population had rejected every offer, reacting with "extraordinary courage, tenacity, and intransigence," a portion of the urban population, adept at servility, had concerned themselves with nothing "other than saving their own skin." That was explained chiefly by the high number of Jews in the cities, who, gripped by an "animal terror in the face of Hitler," fled "instead of fighting" in partisan formations.[152] With that contemptuous judgment on the instinctive fear that sees retreat as the only option, Ponomarenko contributed to the reinforcement of the myth of "Jewish passivity," constructed in ancient times by those who unleashed violence, and revived the prejudice regarding the Jews' inclination to evade military service.

Form and Truth

"Poetry" wrote Paul Celan, "is the place where that which can be perceived and reached through language gathers around that center from which it derives form (*Gestalt*) and truth; around that individual existence (*Dasein*) that poses questions at the present hour, both its own and that of the world, to the beat of the heart and of the century."[1]

On the "truth" of Babi Yar, politics and its institutions remained silent.[2] Jews and non-Jews, men and women, soldiers and veterans, survivors and witnesses, war correspondents, investigators, researchers, or ordinary citizens instead wrote.[3]

Verse gave shape to suffering.

"From the Trench Rises Boundless Pain"

Ilya Selvinsky's poem "Ja eto videl!" (I saw it!), written in January 1942, begins with these lines:

One may choose to dismiss people's tales
Or disbelieve printed columns of news.
But I saw it! With my own eyes.
Do you understand? I saw it. Myself.

Here—the road. Over there—a higher plain.
Between them,
Just so—
A trench.

From the trench rises boundless pain
And sorrow—without end.[4]

The trench, or antitank ditch, from which the pain rises was located near Kerch, in Crimea. It was filled with Jews, thousands of them, whom the Germans, together with their collaborators, had shot there over the course of a few days in early December 1941. Selvinsky saw it and seems to have abandoned any belief in the representative power of words: "What words? The words have turned to rot."[5] These lines were reprinted several times in 1942 in army newspapers, national periodicals, and even books. It was the first work of poetry by a Jew about the extermination of Jews to receive such widespread public attention. The future poet Evdokia Olshanskaya, then fifteen years old, recalls that it was her older sister who first introduced her to the poem in the spring of 1944. The poem spoke of another massacre, but in Kyiv it was received "as a description of the tragedy of Babi Yar" and therefore "passed from hand to hand, copied, memorized."[6]

A twenty-year-old Ukrainian named Liudmila Titova had accompanied a female neighbor to Babi Yar. Upon reaching the place, she realized that the Jews had not been summoned there for a population transfer, as she had first thought. Indeed, she barely managed to escape execution by showing her passport of nationality. Between 1941 and 1942 she composed short and acerbic verses in Russian:

No one believed in the tales of misfortune.
All night the city was in the grip of nightmares,
And like a nightmare the new, difficult day was born
In a suffocating grip of soot and burning coals.
Silence hung over the city,
The gray soldiers closed ranks,
And on that cursed day many fates
Were irrevocably decided.

They went away like the children of Hamelin town,
Disappeared underground, vanished into thin air,
Gone forever into the farthest recesses
With the late, dark year of forty-one.
The eyes are those of the condemned,
The miserable haversacks on their backs . . .
And the procession advances silently
Amid the furious barking of the soldiers.[7]

There is a poem from 1943 in four movements, fifty-one lines, entitled "Kyrylivskyi Yari."[8] Olga Nikolaevna Anstei recalled in the first three movements the times of childhood when the wild gorges of Babi Yar were "the freest of free places," the times of a reckless adolescence when one could run "in the evening along the damp path in the ravine," and the times of a more prudent and conscious youth in the "most fragrant of fragrant places." The fourth movement, constructed with the imagery and rhythm of Christian suffering, is that of a desolate space covered with the objects and symbols of those who were summoned "to the crossroads of ancient tombs, far from [their] sweet and silent home," to be buried "in a nameless tomb":

> The last chalice. Those same places
> Where nature exulted quietly,
> Became Golgotha, the base of the cross,
> For a people hunted and persecuted.
> Listen! They lined them up in order,
> Their belongings piled up on the gravestones.
> Half suffocated, half dead,
> They covered them halfway over with earth . . .
> Don't you see those old women with shawls,
> The elders, majestic like Abraham,
> And the curly-haired defiant children, like those of Bethlehem,
> In their mothers' arms?
> I find no words for this:
> Don't you see—here on the road—the crockery,
> The worn tallit, the fragments of Talmud,
> The rain-washed shreds of passport?
> A black, scorched cross ahead!
> The most terrible of terrible places![9]

Despite the fact that, throughout the years of the war, all literature was expected to celebrate and commemorate the suffering of the Soviet people, without distinction of nationality, in 1942 Pavlo Tychyna, a Ukrainian poet who knew both Yiddish and Hebrew, expressed compassion for the persecution and faith in the "immortal spirit" of the Jewish people.[10] Also in 1943, Maksym Tadeyovych Rylsky wrote poetry not only to show solidarity "with our brothers in both joy and sorrow" but also to express confidence in "a shared path through the darkness of adversity."[11]

Rachels, Hayims, and Leahs Wander

In January 1941 Ilya Ehrenburg composed poems that gave shape to the war against the Jewish "race" in Europe. They seem like a foreshadowing:

They wander, the Rachels, the Hayims, the Leahs,
Like lepers, half-alive.
A weight oppresses them; blind and deaf
They wander, barefoot before death, the old women.
The children wander, awakened in the night.
Sleep carries them, the earth rejects them.
An old wound, alas, has reopened.
My mother was called Chana [Hannah].[12]

Jewish by birth and Russian by language and culture, Ehrenburg was born in Kyiv, a city with which he maintained strong emotional and intellectual ties over the years.[13] He was a renowned war correspondent, and when the capital of Ukraine was taken by the Germans, the press was ordered not to publish details. For several days, official statements remained studiedly vague, and on 22 September 1941 the Sovinformburo (Soviet Information Bureau) announced in the simplest terms that "after fierce and prolonged fighting [Soviet troops had] left Kyiv." All journalists respected the orders, and the city went radio silent. Ehrenburg, however, wrote two short articles to celebrate the "cradle of Russian culture," inasmuch as it had been "the progenitor of the ideas of law and justice," as well as to incite the people to draw strength for redemption through suffering: "We shall liberate Kyiv. The enemy's blood will wash away the stains it left there. Kyiv, like the ancient phoenix, will rise from its ashes, young and beautiful. Grief feeds hatred. Hatred strengthens hope."[14]

For some time, hewing faithfully to the Soviet model of narrative, Ehrenburg addressed the persecution of the Jews only indirectly.[15] In his earliest articles that mentioned the Babi Yar massacre, he made no reference to the victims' national identity. In December 1941, in his commentary on an order from the Wehrmacht high command that prohibited "photographing the work of special units [*Einsatzgruppen*]," he alluded to the probable existence of "snapshots of the atrocities in Kyiv" but spoke of "women shot to death in the cemetery of Kyiv" without specifying that they were Jewish women who had been shot to death in a Jewish cemetery.[16] It was not a full-fledged omission. In much of Ehrenburg's reporting, we find a rhetorical device that refers to the eloquence of places: "We shall take particular satisfaction in killing them [the Germans]—for all the gallows, for the mass grave of Kerch, for Kyiv's Lukyanivka cemetery."[17] "A year ago, in the cemetery at Babi Yar, fifty-five thousands citizens of Kyiv were shot to death."[18] The writer put forth unreservedly the idea that the Nazis' war was a war of extermination of the Soviet peoples. But he became increasingly aware, as months went by, that the Nazi destruction of the Jews had specific motivations, and he did his best to convey this idea without in any way undermining the patriotic narrative. Those who read his work as a correspondent hardly needed to know that the "cemetery" in Kyiv he spoke of was the Jewish cemetery: just reading "Lukyanivka" was sufficient to direct his readers to the network of Jewish memory of the *khurbn* (destruction) that Ehrenburg, together with other writers, was beginning to construct.

In one famous article from May 1942, Ehrenburg added a new literary figure who appeared alongside the mute eloquence of the massacre sites. The writer collected documents found on the bodies of dead enemy soldiers, especially through letters sent to him from the front. As he gazed upon a family photograph of a soldier who "had killed a Russian child" but who "certainly loved his own children," he wrote: "For the Germans, murder is no manifestation of some mental disorder but instead a methodical activity." Drawing inspiration from another artifact, he added: "After killing thousands of children in Kyiv, one German wrote: 'We slaughter the diminutive representatives of an accursed race.'"[19] That phrase is of great importance to our understanding of Ehrenburg's thinking. Many Ukrainian and Russian citizens were killed in Kyiv because they were partisans or Communists, but only Jewish *children* were taken and dumped into the mass graves of Babi Yar. The "accursed race" in question, therefore, is the race to which the writer himself belongs. The extermination of Jewish children is understood by Nazism as a biological guarantee because it halts the reproduction of that race. Ehrenburg returned to the same issue about two months later. He once again made use of documents that highlight the mindset, ideology, and motivations of the occupying soldiers: "One German writes to his brother: 'It's not true that we kill children. You know how we love children in Germany. . . . If in Russia we kill the diminutive representatives of an accursed race, it's only because that is a state necessity.'" Ehrenburg thus displayed a complete understanding of the mechanism by which Nazism had freed the soldier of any moral qualms. It was the state that undertook infanticide and assumed full responsibility for having done so: "[The German soldier] feels at peace with his conscience. . . . He's not killing children, he's only killing 'the diminutive representatives of an accursed race.'"[20]

In fairly short order, Ehrenburg's attitude underwent a further evolution, thrusting into the narrative of the war avenging Jews bringing justice for Jewish children: "Hitler wanted to turn the Jews into a target. Russian Jews taught him that targets can shoot back. . . . Once Jews dreamed of the promised land. Now Jews have a promised land: the front line of defense. Here [they] can take revenge on Germans for the women, old men, and children."[21] Here we catch a glimpse of the writer's abandonment of the official position that he had adopted in the earliest stages of the war, his growing awareness of the difference between the extermination of Jews and the extermination of other Soviet nationalities. In an article addressed to the Jewish community, using words redolent of the patriotic rhetoric of citizenship, he celebrated the warlike heroism of Jews fighting in the war against the Germans. At the same time, a declaration of national belonging emerged:

> The regions in Soviet Russia that were occupied by the Germans have been completely devastated. There are no longer any Jews alive out of those who failed either to evacuate or to leave along with the partisans: all those have been shot. They were executed in Kyiv, Minsk, Gomel, Kharkov, in Crimea, and in the Baltic republics. For two years, the German army has waged war on defenseless women, old people, and children. Now the Nazis will boast of having exterminated all the Jews, right down to the very last one.
>
> But the Jewish people are still alive. The bloodthirsty executioner Hitler failed to realize that you cannot simply murder a whole people.
>
> Yes, there may be fewer Jews than before, but now every Jew amounts more than before. The Jews have not responded to bloody massacre by sobbing at the Wailing Wall. Brandishing weapons, every Jew swore to themself, to their conscience, to the ghosts of the dead: we may die, but we will destroy our hated tormentors. Jews are hardly a people eager to plunge recklessly into every brawl that presents itself; they do not practice the habit of flexing their muscles. In the midst of this explosion of dark diabolical forces, Jews have not stopped believing in the victory of human reason. They have perfected their skills of argument, they have sharpened their biting irony, they have used their own thoughts to tear through the darkness. They are the People of the Book. But when times of danger have arrived, these men of thought and work who for centuries had suffered torments in the ghettos have become firm, unyielding soldiers. Jews don't cry, Jews do not rush recklessly into harm's way, but Jews fight.
>
> . . . Whenever I speak to German prisoners, I like to tell them: "I am a Jew." And when I do, I like to see that look of animal terror on the dull face of these "supermen."
>
> Stalingrad, Kastornoye, the Don—they are only the beginning. The war will go back to where it began. We Jews remember our right: to stand among the judges, to prosecute the persecutors of old people and children. On the stones of Berlin's Victory Avenue (Siegesallee), we shall carve the names of Kyiv, Vitebsk, Kerch, the names of cities where Germans buried alive thousands and thousands of children: let these names call down vengeance. Let the executioners and their children no longer know as much as a moment's rest, let them never know repose, let them nevermore find a place just for them here on Earth.
>
> Jews everywhere, rise up! Waste no time! Let us fight for our honor, for our right to breathe the air around us. We will wage battle on behalf of the majority:

for those who can no longer speak, to demand respect for our dead, for Jews slaughtered in France and in Poland, in the Soviet Union, and around the world.

Come, we are the judges of the righteous. We may well give up our place to others on festive occasions. But there is one place we shall never surrender: our place among the accusers. We shall make sure that no one takes away our right to say: On your feet, child killers! On your feet, and hear the verdict that you face! Our conscience dictates that verdict; our soldiers' bullets write it clearly.[22]

"Where Are the Languages of the Prophets?"

Ehrenburg anxiously awaited the liberation of Kyiv, an event that he saw as crucial to the outcome of the war and therefore to the very future of the country: "The Germans want Kyiv to be their stronghold. But Kyiv must become their tomb."[23] In a letter that he wrote at the end of October 1943, shortly after arriving in the zone of operations around Kyiv, he expressed in a few words his "expectations of the aftermath." The Germans were now in disarray and in full flight, but they were also leaving behind them "horrifying ruins" and "a morally corrupted people."[24] In an article published a few days later, on 29 October, he offered a more exacting account of the devastation and massacres, the sheer scale of the catastrophe: "In Ukrainian cities there are no longer elderly Jews, eccentric dreamers, no tailors, no cobblers. Hundreds of thousands of children have been killed by the Germans." As he accompanied fighters across the devastation of Ukraine who, "nearing Kyiv, thought in anguish and anger about the villages burned to the ground, the fresh graves, all the things they had seen," he declared that he shared their feelings: "Who will answer for Babi Yar in Kyiv?"[25] The image of a region from which an entire Jewish population had disappeared—at least all those who had not been evacuated to the rear—was accompanied by the image of a land desecrated and scattered far and wide with mass graves:

Once ashes were something you sprinkled over your head in grief. People would rend their garments. Now ashes are something that covers the earth. . . . *Where are the languages of the prophets?* What words do we have to recount such a great disaster, such a great misfortune? What we need are not words but blood! Since ancient times, Jews have lived in Ukraine and Belarus. They are not guests here. They have long lived in these lands as native residents born here. The remains of their ancestors sleep in the cemeteries here. Generations of Jews have grown up here. They have built, they have suffered, and they have paved their way to a bright future. Philosophers and poets, tailors and cobblers, coachmen and employees have all lived here.

On mild autumn evenings, old gray-bearded Jews held deep conversations. Jewish women carrying baskets wandered through the markets, their gazes intense and melancholic. Graceful young maidens experienced the first sorrows of their lives among the cherry trees. Restless youths sought paths to knowledge. In those streets Jewish children played, boys and girls, black as coal, fair, red as fire, or delicate as flowers of Canaan.

. . . This land was not some place of transit for Jews. It was their homeland. Who can imagine the cities and villages of Ukraine and Belarus without Jews? I saw this desert, these frightening ruins sprawling over a sea of blood. I have terrible words to say. Let everyone read them. May no one have the courage to turn their back. May no one forget these words until they draw their last breath: IN UKRAINE THERE IS NOT A SINGLE JEW LEFT. The Germans have completed their work. It's pointless to number the dead. I repeat: not a single Jew is left alive. I have heard so many stories about how this all happened. I couldn't stand to listen to them, yet I listened.[26]

In relating some of these stories, Ehrenburg harked back to the image of graves still twitching and groaning in the heart of the one remembering them: "In Pyryatyn, the soil undulated. The earth screamed. The earth pleaded also in Kozelets, in Lubny, in Poltava, in Chernihiv. Is there a single soul on this earth who can sleep peacefully? Is there a single soul on this earth who fails to hear the pleading of the earth? . . . You who have rifles, kill! Do it for this elderly man. For this ancient Jewish mother. For these children. For Babi Yar. For the death pits in Vitebsk and Minsk. For all our pain."[27]

Also, during the Kharkiv trial of war criminals between 15 and 18 December 1943, Ehrenburg summoned a place to judgment: Drobytsky Yar. If all the witnesses had testified, the trial would have lasted for years: "Cities, trees, dead children, stones, the ashes, and the earth" would all have spoken; all those who had been "mutilated, insulted, trampled underfoot." Thereupon, "those shot, suffocated, and burned would have risen from the pits and ravines." Finally, "the Jews buried alive would arrive."[28] The victims could no longer regain the age-old usage of the word *yar* (ravine), a word that contained "grass, a stream, sand, the oversized chamomile flowers that girls plucked to find love," because that word had now become terrifying. "There is a ravine in Kyiv." But it is not the only ravine. "There is a ravine in every Ukrainian city, and everywhere it is all the same: scraps of undergarments, corpses long since stiffened, toys for children smeared with blood."[29] The time of vengeance and reprisal, however, was drawing to a close, as was the war. The hour of legal reckoning had arrived. Ehrenburg invoked the death penalty for the defendants as an act of compensation, saying that it should be applied in every judicial proceeding that recognized perpetrators of genocide. Had "the murderers of Krasnodar and Babi Yar survived," it would have been simply "too shameful and desolate to live on this earth." The perpetrators of the crimes absolutely had to be punished, "lest children laugh at the sound of the word 'justice.'"[30]

On 6 February 1944 Ehrenburg described the need to hunt down and prosecute criminals as a deed devoutly owed to the defenseless ones. And this is where the image of the girl shouting from the pit probably appeared for the first time: "Why are you throwing sand in my eyes?"[31]

Marshal Günther Zessner writes to his brother: "Sure, it's a shame I had to leave Kyiv, I lived well there for a year and a half. Sometimes it became necessary to resort to strict measures, but, frankly speaking, I'm anything but sentimental, and my nerves are strong. So I enjoyed myself for a year and a half: good food, vodka, wine, women, walks. I had everything that I had coming to me from life."

As I read this letter, I remembered what had happened in Kyiv, at Babi Yar, to a little girl. For three days and three nights in a row, the Germans killed old people, women, children. To save bullets, they threw live children into the pit. Then came the cry of the little girl: "Why are you throwing sand in my eyes?" The girl didn't realize they were burying her alive; she didn't understand that Günther Zessner was having his fun. At night I hear this childish cry and I think: Günther Zessner left Kyiv. He is still alive. He still drinks vodka and wine. He still takes walks. He still remembers the days when, in Kyiv, he buried children alive. Perhaps even now, Günther Zessner is burying a girl in Minsk or Lviv and saying with a smirk: "Severe measures are necessary." Can it be that Günther Zessner still escapes punishment? Can it be that one day he will be tending to one of his granddaughters in Schweinfurt and that he tells them: "Damn! I used to enjoy myself in Kyiv"?

Can it be that thousands and thousands of child murderers will escape punishment? Can it be that German arsonists and executioners who drenched Belarus in blood will have their lives saved? Can it be that Germans, having reduced young girls to slavery, should spend a peaceful old age in Dresden or Karlsruhe? Can it be that Germans, having thrown newborns down wells, should return home and play skittles? Can it be that Germans, after tying old women to the tails of horses, should smell the scent of flowers and start up music on a gramophone? They'll disguise themselves. If necessary, Günther will become Kurt or Karl. They have so many identities, so many shelters, such arrogance. They'll play the guitar, water a flower bed, pass themselves off as peaceful citizens. They'll cry, pray, and bleat like sheep. They'll set out to prove that they are not guilty. Ten witnesses will state that Günther Zessner was never in Kyiv, that he spent the whole war in Schweinfurt planting roses. They'll have witnesses and lawyers. They still hope to go unpunished. They hope to say, "We came to Russia, but then we left, and now all that lies in the past."

If you've ever seen the ashes of villages, you won't forget. If you've ever seen a mother's tears, you won't forgive. You won't delegate your rights to anyone: You yourself are the judge. You must track down Günther Zessner. You must track down all the perpetrators: woe betide you if you postpone it to some future day. Track down the accursed Günther, and Kurt, and Karl. All of them! You owe them a reckoning. Remember that little girl who cried: "Why are you throwing sand in my eyes?" Don't let her tormentors escape. Hurry! They are trying to escape, vanish, hide.

They came to us, and they won't get away from us.[32]

In the belief that it was the determination to destroy Jews that "led to Majdanek, to Babi Yar, to Treblinka, to ditches filled with children's corpses," in his preface to a selection of documents published in March 1944, Ehrenburg conjured up an image in an attempt to defy the doubts and reservations expressed by the international press (British and American) about the nature of German war crimes: "When at Babi Yar . . . they were burying Jewish children alive, the desperate cry of a little girl rang out: 'Why are you throwing sand in my eyes?'"[33] In the accompanying material, he provided the reasons for the war of extermination conducted by the *narodoubiycy* (people killers" against the defenseless:

I will not list again the crimes of the Hitlerian army. I will not tell once again of the cities and villages of Russia set ablaze, the executions of entire villages, gallows, brutal raids against the helpless population. I will now focus on just one thing: the extermination of the Jews. I choose this charge because it so clearly explains the nature of Hitler's army. Having conquered Ukraine and Belarus, where so many Jews lived, the Germans encountered almost exclusively elderly and sick people there, women and children, since the young male Jews had moved eastward. The German army thus, carefully and thoroughly—in accordance with a plan and on a vast scale—destroyed women, the elderly, and small children. Can there still be hypocrites who call this "overblown propaganda"? We can remind them that the Führer himself has stated repeatedly that, once the war is over, there will be not be a single living Jew in Europe. As far as he was able, he achieved this part of his plan: in the occupied regions of Russia, Hitler literally annihilated all Jews.[34]

A variant of this text states: "I have heard many stories about mass executions. I have read hundreds of letters written in blood, and I can say . . . : the groaning of the earth, beneath which the elderly were buried alive, keeps me from sleeping. In Kyiv, a little girl whom the Germans had tossed into the pit cried out: 'Why are you throwing sand in my eyes?' I hear this child's cry at night. All our people hear it. Our conscience is outraged, our conscience refuses to give us peace. It demands: Death to the murderers of peoples." Here Ehrenburg entered the realm of discourse established by Raphael Lemkin during the war: "The execution of infants is part of the genocidal program [*narodoubiystvo*]" of Nazism; the murder of Jewish children is the prelude to universal extermination.[35]

In a speech delivered on 2 April 1944 on the occasion of the third anti-Fascist assembly of representatives of the Jewish people of the USSR, the writer revisited the images that most disturbed him ("at night we're enveloped by the specters of the dead"). It was the wailing of Jews buried alive that gave him no peace: "In Kyiv, in Babi Yar, a little girl cried out: 'But why are you throwing sand in my eyes!' The earth stirred. The earth implored. No one with a heart will ever be able to forget that cry. No one with a heart will ever be able to forget mass graves and ravines. Those ghosts [*videniya*] will be with us all our lives."[36] In verse he wrote in 1943, the "ghosts" seem like so many fragments of pain derived from letters received from the front:

Remember this grave. You have learned everything:
The grinning leer of the burned city,
The black lips of the murdered child,
The towel red with blood.
Be silent—words are not how you alleviate misfortune.[37]

Anyone who looks at a pit filled with human bodies has not received the candle of the *Yahrzeit* (the anniversary of a person's death) or the stone for the *matzeyve* (headstone) in order to fix the memory to the earth. You must refrain from seeking words. You must not be enchanted by nature. If you have looked upon the mass graves of the dead, you can only heed a twofold imperative:

You want to drink, but you may not seek water.
You have been given neither wax nor marble. Remember—
You are the most homeless stray of all this world's wanderers.
Do not allow yourself to be seduced by a flower: it too lies in blood.
You have seen all. Remember and live.[38]

For Ehrenburg to resort to poetry was hardly crossing a red line considering that (as one astute Western observer wrote) "Russia is probably also the

only country where poetry is read by millions of people" and that, even during the war, poets "were read by everybody." People read "between the lines"
in search of hidden truths and had learned to "decipher the adjectives."[39]
Even in 1943 the writer questioned the "meaning of words" for a man who
was burdened with the "memory of others" and had "a rock on his heart."
This poem, the first of a cycle of six short poems, later came to be known
by the title "Babi Yar."[40] It is read today as a "prayer for the dead," a
secular kaddish created by someone who hardly seemed familiar with that
liturgy.[41]

What meaning do words and the pen possess
When there is a rock weighing on my heart,
And I carry with me the memory of others
Just as a forced laborer drags his own weight behind him?
I once lived in large cities,
And I loved the companionship of the living.
Now I am forced to dig graves
In fields empty and deserted.
Now every ravine is known to me,
And every ravine is my home.
The beloved hands of that woman,
I once kissed them.
Even so, when I was among the living,
I did not know that woman at all.
My darling child! My red cheeks!
My great big family!
I hear you calling to me
From the bottom of every grave.
I speak for the dead. We shall rise,
We shall make the bones rattle: There,
Where the cities that still live
Are odorous of bread and essences.
Dim the light. Run down the flags.
We have come to you, not we—but the ravines.[42]

Ehrenburg visited Kyiv at the end of 1944. Alongside his awareness that
there had been a war against the Jews within the larger war against the Soviet
peoples, he also discovered during that visit the sheer vigor of antisemitism.[43]
To Hersh Smolar, a Jewish partisan leader Ehrenburg met in Moscow in
December of that same year, he admitted: "This was my hometown, and I will

never go back there."[44] All that remained with him of that city was the image of destruction in the sands of Babi Yar:

> There were none of my relatives among the dead, but I doubt I have ever felt such anguish anywhere, I have never felt so completely orphaned, as I felt upon the sands of Babi Yar. More or less everywhere was the sootiness of ashes, charred bones (shortly before retreating, the Germans had ordered prisoners of war to exhume the bodies of the victims and burn them). It struck me, who can say why, that here my relatives, friends, and contemporaries had found their death, people I had seen forty years ago, busy in their childish games on the melancholy streets of Podol or Demievka.[45]

It is with the image of those "ghosts" before his eyes that the writer walked the path to liberation:

> In moments of repose the heart beats harder, in the throes of bottomless rage. It is not only divisions and armies that march toward Berlin. Also toward Berlin march horrified mothers, inconsolable widows, children already old. Toward Berlin march all the cliffs, ravines, and gullies. All the lands razed to desolation. To Berlin march the cabbage soups of Majdanek and the trees of Vitebsk where the Germans hanged their wretched victims. To Berlin march the boots, shoes, and clogs of all those who were asphyxiated, as well as the slippers of a two-year-old child. The dead knock at the doors of houses on Joachimsthaler Strasse, Königsallee, and Unter den Linden, all the accursed streets of an accursed city. The children the Germans buried alive have risen from their mass graves, from their antitank ditches, and they're already at the border, clamoring to enter the houses of Berlin, where the wives of senior sergeants and privy councilors say, as they finish the last bottle of Champagne and having already severely whipped Gapa or Oksana or Masha: "There's an east wind, a terrible wind out of the east. Put on the fur coat your husband brought you from Kyiv, don't catch cold now . . ." It's not a wind. It's the children her husband murdered at Babi Yar, and they've arrived. These children won't go away. They are our conscience. They are leading our tanks and our infantry. We shall reach Berlin! We say this not boastfully or gleefully. We say it with clenched teeth, with pain and determination—as one soldier wrote: "With tears of blood."[46]

"New, Unprecedented Challenges, More Complex Than Ever"

In the fall of 1943 Pavel G. Antokolsky traveled through various provinces of Ukraine as a war correspondent. He returned to Moscow a few days before the liberation of Kyiv. He mentioned the catastrophe in a long and famous poem composed in memory of his son, who fell at the front at age nineteen:

> For the glowing ashes of all the burned Bibles,
> Of all the Polish ghettos and concentration camps,
> For everyone, for all those who are dead,
> He awakened, half Russian and half Jewish,
> From his childish slumber
> For the war and felt only one thing:
> He had to do all that others were doing!
> And so it was all decided . . .[47]

In a diary entry dated 25 October 1943, Antokolsky confessed that he found himself in a state of "utter failure" in terms of his creative capacity. Not only did he feel "incapable of writing poems," but he also no longer felt the desire: "Any language strikes me as crude, inadequate, alienating. Rhyme and meter irritate me as [if they were] merely conventional. There is nothing I can say in verse that hasn't already been said a thousand times before."[48] It was not until he arrived with the army in Poland in the fall of the next year that the poet found the words: "Lager' unichtozheniya" (Extermination camp). The poem was conceived in late 1944 or early 1945. It opens with the figure of elderly Rachel, who had come from afar through burning *shtetlach* (small towns), waving her hand in the direction of a collapsed grave, wondering how she could find the bodies of her children:

> Perhaps in the Polish plains,
> Perhaps among the broken skulls I will find
> My Joseph and my Benjamin . . .
> But under our feet there is no gravel,
> Only dense and blackened dust,
> Only the ash of charred bodies.[49]

In the poem "Ne vechnaya pamyat'" (In noneternal memory), published in 1946, Antokolsky expressed a new awareness ("Forgive these three centuries of delay / And these three millennia of silence") of his bond with the fate of the Jewish people: "I have built bridges in eternity / For the meeting day to come. / The whole universe listens: 'Shema Yisrael.'" The poem frequently touched on the theme of the impossibility of recognition ("What life? What passage beyond without home, without sleep") for those who walked and trampled underfoot the places of extermination ("the steep slope of death"):

We lose track in centuries of wandering
Through the burned cities,
In the sands around Babi Yar, in nasty rumors,
In black markets, in junk—and there

The searchlights prowl across the horizon,
Traverse ditches, crawl over bridges
And somewhere something is burning, breaking, grinding, and glowing
white hot,
Rotting behind rusty barbed wire—and there

The hypocrite shows compassion, and the miser clutches his purse,
And the false witness speaks as commanded,
And the journalist already transcribes—there

We find no tracks—in the cities of Europe,
On no imaginable planet,
In the black entrails of the earth,
Neither in heaven, nor in hell—there are no more tracks.[50]

Leonid Pervomayskiy (pseudonym of Illya Shlyomovych Hurevych), in a short composition in Ukrainian titled "V Babynim Jaru" (At Babi Yar), depicts a father focused on protecting his son in the last moment of life:

Stay, my son, stay close.
I will shade your eyes with the palm of my hand
Lest you see death in the face.

See only the blood on my fingers in the sun,
That blood, which has become your blood,
And must now spill on the ground.[51]

The poet returns later to the theme of death in the ravine in a poem he wrote in 1964, left long unpublished, where the proximity of a cemetery and a slope seems to refer to the Babi Yar massacre:

I was among the crowd in the cemetery,
Naked among tombstones and mounded earth,
And I remembered elevated aspirations,
A world without pain and without blood.

And as I fell dead down the slope
Into the dreadful clay of bleeding bodies,
I firmly believed and without fear
That you would come to bring me back to life.[52]

Lev Ozerov mourned the slaughtered Jews in a poem he wrote in 1944 or
1945. Published in the spring of 1946, this work is one of the most expressive
parts of the Babi Yar cycle, understood as a collective creation of the poets of
Kyiv (included in the epilogue).[53] The author himself recalled their gestation:

Kyiv immediately after the war, Kyiv in ruins. I reconnect with surviving relatives and friends. I am carrying with me Ehrenburg's request to take down anything and everything that can be known about Babi Yar. I have no experience,
no instructions. I learn as I go. Mishaps teach valuable lessons. The heart cannot
withstand the violent impact of discovering the details of how this all happened.
I count . . . I cannot count the family members, relatives, and friends dead at
Babi Yar. I take refuge in poetry. The short poem "Babi Yar" practically wrote
itself:

I have come to you, Babi Yar.
If pain has an age,
Then I am terribly old,
You cannot even count it in centuries.

Everything connected to Babi Yar takes greater and greater hold of me. I went
there alone. I went there with the poet Tychyna and the painter Shovkunenko. I
walked the path that Kyevans followed in the procession that led them to their
deaths.[54]

The task that Ozerov assigned to poetry is clearly set forth in an essay published in early 1944 that attracted harsh criticism from the Communist Party's
leading committees:

Let's return to Ukraine. Poetry here encounters a people who have endured Hitlerian slavery, a populace whose absence has long been felt and lamented, with
new ways of life, new characters, new relationships. This newness poses new,
unprecedented challenges, more complex than ever for Ukrainian poetry. During the years of Hitlerian domination, the populace endured so much sorrow
and grief in Ukraine that a news-gathering approach to reality could only explain
very little. If the young Ukrainian woman Maria has begun to call herself Marta,

and a filthy street urchin, asked his age, replies, "Four," then behind these facts "of life" there is some spiritual upheaval, enormous suffering, a tragedy that [only] a great artist can show us. If an artist shows to that Ukrainian girl exactly what has happened in the world and in the human soul over these last years, . . . then she, the Ukrainian Maria, will begin to ponder her own fate. She will want to be worthy of the image of the motherland that has been created by Ukrainian poetry.[55]

As a war correspondent, Ozerov collected extensive information concerning the genocide. Part of the documentation served him in writing an article to reconstruct that history ("Kiev, Babiy Jar") based on eyewitness accounts from inhabitants, along with other material, for the Extraordinary State Commission for Investigation of Nazi War Crimes.[56] That text was selected as the opening text of *The Black Book*, which is about the extermination of Jews in Soviet territory.[57] Like Ehrenburg, Ozerov also allowed the places and objects to speak for themselves: "Not all the bodies were burned; not all the bones were ground to dust—there were too many of them. Even now, anyone who comes to Baby Yar will see bits of skulls and bones mixed with charcoal. He will find a boot with a decayed human foot in it, as well as slippers, galoshes, scarves, and children's toys. He will see the cast-iron gratings torn from the cemetery wall. These cast-iron gratings served as the oven racks on which the exhumed bodies of those murdered during the terrible days of September 1941 were burned."[58]

Ozerov's essay failed to circulate at all, because publication of the book in which it was supposed to appear was blocked. Censorship heavily affected all of the literary activities of the Soviet Jewish Anti-Fascist Committee, created in 1942 to support the war effort and increasingly committed, as the war came to an end, to the work of reconstructing the methods and extent of the massacres. The committee asked Andreĭ Aleksandrovich Zhdanov on 28 November 1946 to speed up publication of *The Black Book*.[59] Georgy Aleksandrov, head of the propaganda department of the Central Committee of the Communist Party, wrote, in a note sent to Zhdanov himself on 3 February 1947, that reading the typescript, especially the "section on Ukraine" to which Ozerov himself had contributed, produced "a mistaken idea of the true nature of Fascism." It suggested, in fact, that the Germans had persecuted and exterminated only Jews or had even fought against the Soviet Union for that purpose while treating "with leniency" Russians, Ukrainians, Belarusians, Lithuanians, Latvians, and other nationalities. Moreover, many accounts reported that in order "to save themselves" from death, "it was enough to obtain a 'Russian passport,' not look like a Jew, and so on." That was why, for example, it was necessary to firmly reject the previously mentioned testimony of Izabella N. Mirkina-Egorycheva, who attributed her survival to the availability of a false identity document with Russian nationality. The publication, Aleksandrov concluded, was "not advisable."[60] *The Black Book*, in fact, never made it out of the print shop, where it had already reached the stage of proofs.[61]

The Soviet government acted decisively to obstruct any editorial initiative that informed the public of sources concerning the extermination of Jews because they were Jews, and it simultaneously censored poetic, narrative, artistic, and musical productions concerning every Jewish "point of view." The removal of documents from the archive of the Great Patriotic War went hand in hand—as we shall see—with the project to make Babi Yar disappear from the cityscape of Kyiv by leveling and reforesting the site, which was to be surrounded and crisscrossed by an extensive road network; by designing an urban plan that envisaged development of the entire adjacent area; and by destroying the remains of cemeteries once present in the area.

Return, Reconstruction, Recognition

When Jews returned to Kyiv following liberation, they were faced not only with fellow city dwellers who had taken possession of their property, set up housekeeping in their homes, or taken over their jobs but also with institutions unwilling to support them in disputes over the restitution of property and rehiring in their old jobs.[1]

The writer Arkady I. Vaksberg found a letter in his family files dated 22 February 1946, sent to his mother, who was a lawyer, by Sofia Kuperman, requesting legal assistance. Kuperman had unsuccessfully tried to enforce a court ruling recognizing her right to reclaim the apartment she had been allocated before the war. She had appealed for justice to the provincial committee of the Communist Party and, bringing to bear "emotional as well as legal arguments," pointed out that she had lost eleven family members during the occupation. The first secretary, however, accused her of harboring hostile preconceptions regarding the established authorities and being uninformed about the "sufferings of the Jews." He therefore urged her to "make greater efforts to find" the relatives whose deaths she bemoaned. Perhaps they were still alive, hiding "somewhere in Tashkent," in Uzbekistan, where they had surely been evacuated and had "changed their names to live like wealthy gentlefolk." There was no shortage of menace in the official's response: "And just where did *you* hide? Certainly not in the partisans' lairs and hideouts. After fattening yourself up behind the front lines, now you're even demanding a house! I shall forward your request to the security services, and they can take care of matters."[2] A few months later, the poet Nahum Korzhavin became convinced that the situation had become so stark that it amounted to "a granite-hard and oppressive anti-Semitism," a sentiment of hostility that, as he later wrote in his memoirs, he "would never encounter again, anywhere, at such a high level of concentration and strength."[3]

"Beat the Jews"

An internal report sent on 13 September 1944 to Nikita Khrushchev by Serhiy Savchenko, at that time in charge of the republic's security services, reported cases of mistreatment and violence at numerous locations. In the city of Kyiv, incidents often took the form of interethnic pogroms. Among the holdover legacies of German propaganda subsequently adopted by Ukrainians during the occupation was the widespread perception of the Jewish population as an element foreign to *their* nation.

The report noted that many heads of economic or administrative institutions, implementing a "distorted" interpretation of hiring regulations, refused to accept Jews for open jobs. Savchenko, however, adduced a factor in their defense: significant blame was placed upon the "provocative" nature of activity organized by elements of the Jewish community for the spread of antisemitic sentiment. In particular, adopting one of the most established Judophobic communication techniques, Savchenko reported "rumors" of the impending assignment of prestigious positions in government offices to Jews, with a resulting purge or punishment of Ukrainian citizens accused of antisemitism. At the same time, Savchenko denounced a legend, also allegedly fabricated by elements within the Jewish community, about the intention of the Ukrainian republic's government—namely, in the person of its top representative, Khrushchev—to promote policies of reformulation and restructuring of the ruling class at the expense of the Jewish component. These allegations, he concluded, found their way into the most retrograde portion of the population, fomenting animosity among the populace. The same report highlighted new standard clichés of prejudice highlighting the foreignness, if not outright hostility, of Jews toward the homeland: their low percentages in the ranks of the Red Army; their tendency to dodge military service and labor duties in basic sectors of production; their involvement in cases of commercial speculation and profiteering. Great attention was focused, in a mélange of real and imaginary elements, upon instances of Jewish "nationalism": their admiring mentions of better living conditions in the United States and their incitement to emigrate from the Soviet Union; their expressions of sympathy toward Zionism; their unconditional defense of all those who had faced discrimination for being Jewish and demands for the Soviet leadership to undertake a decisive fight against anti-Judaism, to start with Ukraine; their belief in rumors that the authorities were preparing to relocate the entire Jewish population currently residing in territories previously subjected to enemy occupation to new areas of settlement; their creation and spread of false reports concerning the imminent ousting of First

Secretary Khrushchev (and his supposed replacement by Andrei Zhdanov) as punishment for his twisted view of the national question and his indulgent attitudes toward antisemitism.[4]

A few weeks later, a special commission of inquiry delivered the results of its investigation to the second secretary of the Communist Party of Ukraine's Central Committee, Demjan Korotchenko. This investigation aimed to ascertain the validity of the three main issues raised in Savchenko's report: the "alleged increase in anti-Jewish actions"; the "nationalistic manifestations by individual members of the Jewish population"; and the "spread of provocative rumors about the government's alleged antisemitic policy . . . and imaginary changes in its composition."[5] While acknowledging that remnants of Nazi propaganda from the period of the war persisted in Ukrainian society, the investigation significantly downplayed the extent of antisemitism. The "verified" incidents were by and large attributed to hooliganism (*chuliganstvo*) or material hardships, particularly the housing shortage. In short, there was nothing to suggest that these isolated incidents reflected the "authentic political and moral attitudes of the populace," nor was there any evidence of any spread of anti-Judaism among the citizenry.[6] On the contrary, in line with the reversal already indicated in Savchenko's report, the commission instead placed the blame on Jewish nationalism for distorting reality for purposes of agitation by claiming that antisemitism was a "political current" in the Ukrainian republic, if not an outright "government policy." The security services were accused of negligence on two fronts: they had failed to act adequately in order to counter the infiltration of the German espionage network into Ukrainian nationalist organizations, and they had likewise failed to promptly identify enemy agents still at large and operating in the region. Because of their "weak" perception of the danger, they were also unaware of the "attempt by Zionist circles to organize a mass demonstration of the Jewish population in the city of Kyiv on the anniversary of the massacre perpetrated by the Germans at Babi Yar."[7]

A year later, the pogrom took place. The event triggering the outbreak of violence was the killing on 4 September 1945 of two Red Army soldiers, Ivan Z. Hrabar and Mykola A. Melnykov, by a security services officer of Jewish nationality, Iosif D. Rozenstein, who had reacted with an armed response to a racist attack. The officer in question was immediately arrested, but during the victims' funerals on 7 September riots broke out: the procession, passing through densely populated streets, swelled to several hundred people and headed toward the bazaar in Halytska Square. There, the ensuing riots resulted in the deaths of five Jews and the injury of around a hundred, thirty-six of whom had to be hospitalized as a result of the beatings they suffered.[8]

An appeal signed that same month by a group of former Jewish combatants and conveyed to the Central Committee of the Communist Party through Stalin, Lavrentiy P. Beria, and the chief editor of *Pravda*, Pyotr N. Pospelov, establishes the moral context for the events.[9] The combat veterans, upon returning to their city—like all those who had been included, for strategic reasons, in the evacuation to eastern territories—found themselves face-to-face with a deeply altered social landscape. They had already sensed it while at the front but had chosen not to believe it until then. Now, however, the city appeared politically "unrecognizable" to them. There was indeed a perceived continuity between the occupation regime and the liberation regime:

> There is a strong perception of German influence. No struggle is conducted against the consequences of their political sabotage. Nationalists of all kinds, sometimes with party membership cards in their pockets, have begun to act without restraint. . . . Unprecedented ANTISEMITISM rages in our Soviet reality. The word "Jew" and the imperative "beat the Jews" [*bej zhidov*] . . . resonate loudly in the streets of the Ukrainian capital on trams and trolleybuses and in shops, markets, and even some Soviet institutions. In a somewhat different, more veiled form, we find the same atmosphere within the party apparatus, up to the Central Committee of the Communist Party of Ukraine. All this ultimately led to the pogrom against Jews that recently took place in Kyiv.[10]

The authors of the document therefore appealed to the highest authorities of the party to restore the dictates of the constitution (article 123), which formally recognized equal rights for Soviet citizens regardless of nationality or ethnicity and punished any violation of the law, particularly instances of racial hatred. How had it come to pass that, precisely in Kyiv, "the first pogrom against Jews under Soviet rule" had occurred?[11]

After recounting the events of 4–7 September and warning the city authorities of the danger—city authorities who had limited themselves to countering antisemitic demonstrations by merely bolstering the defense of Jewish synagogues, theaters, and markets while failing to undertake any basic political and educational intervention in order to redefine norms of civil coexistence—the former combatants warned of the active preparation for a new and even more devastating uprising. In their view, the Communist institutions in Ukraine were responsible for "fomenting discord among nationalities" and "pursuing a shameful antisemitic policy alien to the party and Soviet power" and for "establishing a special regime against Jews" and "orchestrating their exclusion from Soviet and party apparatuses." A simple historical analysis could have easily explained the reasons for the dense

Jewish presence throughout the republic and especially in Kyiv, where entire neighborhoods (Podil, Stalinka [Demiivka], and others) had become homes to the Jews. It would have combatted the stereotypes of Jewish otherness with respect to their shared Ukrainian homeland, stereotypes that had generated widespread intolerance: "Here, Jewish war invalids and children who lost their parents under German occupation are now returning to their native land. But they are not welcomed, nor are they given work; residence permits are denied them, and they are mistreated." Many veterans and survivors had already lost many family members and had also been deprived of their homes and other possessions. Now they faced the hostile attitudes of fellow citizens and even authorities. To their most urgent needs and pressing employment demands, they were met with responses focused "especially on the principle of nationality," that is, on numerical relations between nationalities, effectively adopting "a new political attitude toward Jews, one completely alien to our party" and "very similar" indeed "to that held by Goebbels's office."[12]

The document meticulously examined the individual discriminatory measures adopted immediately after the war: the exclusion of Jews from party leadership positions, both centrally and locally (with isolated exceptions for technical cadres); the limited reintegration of Jews into ministerial and administrative apparatuses; the introduction of special admission rules for institutions of higher education and universities (numerus clausus, following the czarist model); the failure to reintegrate Jews into employment and the refusal to return misappropriated housing, alongside attempts to hinder Jews' return entirely ("many Jews, native to Kyiv, are not allowed to return to their hometown, where they had lived all their lives and where they lost their families, solely because they are Jews"); the adoption of a "depersonalization" system in the distribution of aid from abroad, resulting in financial or material support from international Jewish organizations rarely reaching the intended recipients; the boycott of the Jewish theater in Kyiv, still lacking a venue for its activities; the absence of any information in the press and publications regarding the condition of Jews and their needs ("as if this people did not exist, as if it had disappeared from the horizon, as if it had been excluded from cooperation among nations in the Soviet Union"). All this set the stage for the Kyiv pogrom and an increasingly menacing policy of ostracism throughout the republic that was fueled by apparatus cadres who had actively collaborated with German occupation forces, "individuals with a prominent Ukrainian surname but with a politically dubious past," completely unqualified professionally "but greatly experienced in matters of Ukrainian nationalism and antisemitism."[13]

The deterioration of the material situation also had moral repercussions for the Jewish population in Ukraine. The appeal described a state of panic that had led many people to take their own lives. At the same time, challenging the narrative put forth in reports from the secret services and the investigation commission established by the Communist Party, the appeal highlighted how the assertion of a national identity often manifested as a straightforward reaction to the intent to exclude Jews from the nationalities constituting Soviet citizenship:

> There are cases where individual Jews here in Kyiv, having personally experienced all the disadvantages of the new political situation, have ended their own lives through suicide. There are Communist Jews who have appeared before provincial party committees and torn up or thrown away their membership cards, considering it shameful to be part of an organization advancing racial policies akin to those of the Fascist Party. There are Jews fleeing Ukraine, fleeing Kyiv like madmen, trying to escape as quickly as possible from the whirlwind of antisemitism to save their lives from these imitators of Hitlerian actions: some flee to other Soviet republics; others try to cross the border, heading to Poland or America. . . . There are Jews in Kyiv who once considered themselves internationalists before the war and did not feel Jewish at all; sometimes, in fact, they had even forgotten they were Jewish because there was nothing to provoke such a state of mind. Only now, in relation to the new course undertaken by the Central Committee of the Communist Party of Ukraine and the Council of People's Commissars of the Ukrainian Soviet Socialist Republic, they have realized they are Jews and have felt their national sentiment.[14]

Even family relationships had been affected and compromised. There were mixed couples who could not reunite, couples in whom racial hatred crept between spouses, causing previously unknown friction and hostility. Things were especially sensitive for minors, as they experienced these circumstances with particular pain: antisemitism had already penetrated pioneer organizations, schools, and vocational institutes, and Jewish children, until then "blithely unaware of it all," felt the weight of hostility from their peers who had nationalist Ukrainian parents, leading to a rapid decline in "the spirit of internationalism" among the youth. Therefore, faced with the lack of protection from local authorities and obstacles encountered in the battle to restore violated rights, several Jews had "taken up arms," defending, like Iosif Rozenstein, "the honor and pride of their people against all camouflaged antisemites and nationalists." Only these considerations could explain the incident in Kyiv that led to a pogrom whose resonance extended far beyond Soviet borders.[15]

The grim atmosphere of hostility and intimidation toward Jews is captured in the verses Boris A. Slutsky devoted to antisemitic legends:

Jews don't sow grain,
Jews do business in shops,
Jews go bald early,
Jews steal more than any others.

Jews are evil people,
They are terrible soldiers:
Ivan fights in the trenches,
Abram profiteers in the market.

I have heard it since childhood,
And soon I'll be old,
But one can never escape
That cry: "The Jews, the Jews!"

I haven't profiteered once,
I haven't stolen once,
But I carry within me like an infection
This cursed race.

The bullet missed me,
Confirming what they say:
"The Jews were not killed!
They all came back alive!"[16]

"She Could Have Been My Sister"

In such a morally depraved situation, no attempt to commemorate the annihilation of the Jews at Babi Yar, however provisional and rudimentary, could help but clash with the narrative protocols of the Great Patriotic War, which, on the one hand, pursued national reconciliation based on the principle that divisions within the people were merely the malign legacies of Nazi propaganda and the degradation caused by the war while, on the other hand, aiming to build a cult of active heroism that diverted attention from the fate of helpless victims.[17] The leadership of the republic therefore rejected proposals such as the one put forward in December 1943, less than a month after liberation, by the party committee's secretary for ideology in Kyiv, Maria M. Pidtychenko, to set up an exhibition of photographs of mass graves, internment sites, and deportations. Instead, what prevailed was the directive to avoid overly empha-sizing the Soviet victory in Ukraine and to maintain strict control over any memorial or museum projects, as well as work aimed at investigating the methods and outcomes of the occupation.[18]

The annihilation of the Jews, however, was a well-known fact to the popu-lation. Writer Vasily Grossman portrayed a sense of physical emptiness in a letter to his wife in January 1944: "Yesterday I was in Kyiv. You cannot imagine what I felt and how much I suffered visiting the addresses where my relatives and acquaintances lived. Everywhere there was nothing but death and desola-tion."[19] In one of the news accounts from the Nuremberg trials, another writer, the Ukrainian Yuri I. Yanovsky, could not help but recall that the dust from the bodies unearthed and burned by the Germans at Babi Yar in 1943 had hung over Ukraine for months and months: "The ashes of the victims stirred in the wind. There was so much human ash that the wind was powerless to disperse it. The ash was buried in the ground. But the earth groaned, the ash refused to scatter, stubbornly awaiting fitting punishment."[20] In 1946 poet Yakov A. Chelemsky, formerly a war correspondent, published verses in *Ogo-niok* that give us an image of destruction glimpsed right through the most elementary form of matter, now part of the daily life of the people of Kyiv:

Never in this city was there dust,
Only the pollen of flowers caressed the face.
With the water of the Dnieper they washed the streets;
Even now the neighborhoods shine with cleanliness.

Why does the breeze along the riverbank, so dear to me,
Sprinkle the passerby with furious dust?
And why do the grains, soaked in smoke and blood,
Choke and blind me?

The wind has passed through charred walls,
Sweeping ashes into old burn sites.
It swirls sacred ashes on Khreshchatyk,
Choking dust descending from Babi Yar.

If under the foliage of blooming chestnuts
In this city you have forgotten past pain,
You will suddenly remember it
Struck by a desolate cloud of dust and ashes.[21]

Anatoly Kuznetsov, son of a Ukrainian mother and a Russian father, was born and raised in the suburb of Kurenivka, not far from Babi Yar. After the Germans arrived, access to the ravine was prohibited, but the teenager figured out something from hearing, day after day, the sound of gunfire coming from there. At the end of the second year of occupation, he had also observed for several weeks the thick, heavy smoke rising on the horizon. He returned to Babi Yar immediately after the end of the conflict:

> When it was all over, despite the fear of mines, my friend and I went to see what was left. It was an enormous ravine, one could even say magnificent—deep and wide like a mountain gorge. If you shouted standing on the edge of a wall, on the opposite slope they could barely hear it. It stretched between three districts of Kyiv, Lukyanivka, Kurenivka, and Syrets, and was surrounded by cemeteries, groves, and gardens. A clear and pleasant stream always flowed at its bottom. The walls were steep, in some places even vertical, and landslides were frequent at Babi Yar. Moreover, it's not uncommon in those parts: the right bank of the Dnieper is all marked by such ravines, Kyiv's main street, Khreshchatyk, formed from the Khreshchaty Yar, and there are also the Repyachov Yar, Syretsky Yar, and many others. . . . We knew that stream like the backs of our hands; as children, we dammed it with small dams made of branches and twigs, which we called *gatkas*, and we bathed in it. There was always nice coarse sand at the bottom, but now, who knows why, it was all sprinkled with small white pebbles. I bent down and picked one up to examine it closely. It was a small piece of burnt bone the size of a fingernail, white on one side and black on the other. The stream had carried them away who knows where and dragged them along. We deduced that they had shot Jews, Russians, Ukrainians, and people of other nationalities farther upstream. And so we followed those little bones for a long time until we reached the very beginning of the ravine, and the stream disappeared: that's where it originated from many springs dripping from the sandy slopes below, and it was precisely from there that it had carried away the bones. Now the ravine narrowed, branching into different arms, and at one point the sand had turned gray. Suddenly we realized that we were walking on human ashes.[22]

Academician Isaac M. Trachtenberg, then a medical student, recalled in an account written much later how the perception of the "name" of the place suddenly changed for him and his classmates. Until recently, Babi Yar had meant "green gullies" opening on the slopes of the ravine, "reflected sunshine" that strangely glinted off the foliage of ancient trees, "welcoming clearings" imbued with a pungent scent of wormwood. Then, suddenly, "like a

poignant and tearing cry of pain," those same words "burst into consciousness," bringing with them a "completely different" content. Now they indicated "blood and lifeless bodies in the moving earth"; they denoted "the darkness swallowing the gullies," which—closing over—had become "a huge
tomb of innocent victims." After that "terrible discovery," Trachtenberg left,
along with his companions, overcome by a "bewilderment" alternating
between "pain and anger."[23]

The Jews arriving from the front or returning from civilian evacuation zones
were among the first, from the very day the city was liberated, to head toward
Babi Yar.[24] On 6 November 1943, at six o'clock in the morning, Simon Sherbin-
ski found himself in the destroyed Khreshchatyk Street; by eleven, he was at
Babi Yar: "It was a cloudy day, with a steady, fine rain. [At Babi Yar] there were
few people. Some soldiers were wandering around the site where the bodies had
been burned. And there was a terrible silence. It had been a great bonfire. In the
ashes lay torn iron railings from the tomb fences [used for cremating the bod-
ies], bones of adults and children, skulls, rotting children's shoes. I then wandered among the destroyed gravestones of the [Lukyanivka] cemetery, covered
in weeds and fallen leaves. I left when it started to get dark."[25]

There were those who gathered in silence in front of the ditches, trying to
collect the scattered remains of the victims for proper burial.[26] A certain Gutin,
who arrived on 15 April 1944 with a field military hospital where he served as
a doctor, went directly there from the station: "I descended into the chasm. A
young woman was digging in the ground, lamenting, crying, pulling at her
hair: 'Thirteen,' she cried, 'thirteen of my kin and my beloved are here. I'm all
alone now.'" Some distance away, someone recited the prayer for the dead:
"Each time he read *El Malei Rachamim*, he pronounced a different name.
Clearly, many of his relatives were buried there." Gutin even encountered a
Ukrainian who, improvising as a guide for visitors, recounted what he had
seen for a fee, easily gathering a small crowd of people seeking news about
their loved ones.[27] Sarah Tartakovskaya, returning from the rear, arrived on the
third anniversary of the massacre at the place where she had lost her father,
mother, sister, and other relatives: "From the slope, I pulled out by the hair
(which hadn't had a chance to burn) the head of a young girl with the remnants of a handkerchief attached, two braids, two clips, and a hole in her
temple. I stood there crying: she could have been my sister." From that day on,
Sarah began collecting bone fragments charred from the fire. Throughout
1944, before the site was turned into a city landfill and the local government
proceeded to destroy the Jewish cemetery, she returned almost daily. She thus
participated, along with many others who came on pilgrimage, in the heartbreaking discovery of remains and their burial not far from the ravine.[28]

In the spring of 1944, at the age of eight, Aleksandr Burakovsky went to
Babi Yar with his war-disabled father shortly after returning from the territories where the family had been evacuated: "The steep gullies were covered
with thorny bushes. I ran down the winding paths easily and swiftly, clinging
to the bushes. My father walked slowly, still unable to move his right arm. He
walked and cried. . . . I never saw him cry again. In those ravines lay my elder
brother, his wife and five daughters, my elder sister and her family, and other
relatives. At the bottom of the ravine, dug and eroded by rain, it was very
cold. And, a frightening thing, it felt like being in a damp underground cel-
lar." Burakovsky continued to visit Babi Yar and almost always found small
bunches of flowers, some fresh, others wilted, almost "falling by chance" in
various spots, as there was no recognizable or acknowledged place to lay
"flowers to memory" of a deceased loved one.[29] The writer Yuri Shcheglov
(Yuri M. Varshaver) recalled that, at least until Stalin's death, Babi Yar was
"one of the most desolate outskirts of Kyiv." He frequented the place, starting
in the spring of 1944, but he viewed things differently: "I never saw flowers
there, people with distressed looks, or heard prayers for the dead. . . . The
rare passersby stopped briefly and without entering into conversation." What
prevailed was the image of people forced to undertake furtive expeditions
("they arrived, lingered, were silent, nothing more"), unable to hold commemorative gatherings or even propose, "not even in a whisper," a monument for the victims: "The epithet 'Zionist' was no joke at that time! Visiting
Babi Yar was considered an act of Zionism." The threat of imprisonment as a
direct consequence of such an accusation "weighed heavily, intimidated, and
compelled caution."[30] Some families adopted a strategy of silence almost to
shield the younger ones from trauma, as suggested by Boris M. Shifman's
testimony: "I became aware of Babi Yar immediately after returning from
evacuation. At home, it was a forbidden topic, spoken of with obvious pain
and tears, only in Yiddish. Despite living nearby, I was categorically forbidden to go there." In January 1946 the boy witnessed, along with some peers,
the public execution of German soldiers tried in Kyiv, and the curtain began
to lift on his family's tragedy: "Not all our relatives could be evacuated; many
had stayed and died at Babi Yar. My mother saw that I was absent from home
for long periods and that I asked many questions about the fate of our relatives. That's when she began to take me with her."[31]

At the end of September 1945, an assembly was held in Kyiv to celebrate the
twenty-fifth anniversary of the establishment of the State Jewish Theater. A
Moscow delegation led by actor Solomon M. Mikhoels participated, and he
took to the speaker's platform holding a crystal vase: "I have brought you some
soil from Babi Yar. Throw some of your flowers into it so they can symbolically

grow for our people" were his words. He had gone to the massacre site earlier with other members of the delegation and filled the vase "with soil that had absorbed the screams of mothers and fathers, of children who did not live long enough to grow up." If one looked closely into the vase, one could possibly find "the shoelaces of children's shoes" and "the tears of an elderly Jewish woman"; with even greater focus, one might encounter "parents in the act of crying out 'Shema Yisrael,' with pleading eyes turned toward the sky and the hope that an angel would come to save them."[32]

Back in Moscow, the actor spoke on behalf of the Jewish Anti-Fascist Committee, of which he was president, about the urgent need to promote "a movement for the creation of monuments to the victims of Fascism," especially at Babi Yar, "a neglected and abandoned place completely without enclosure fences."[33] Mikhoels's conservation effort took form in many other initiatives. Shortly thereafter, for example, he suggested including in his repertoire the theatrical work of writer and playwright Leonid M. Leonov, *Zolotaja kareta* (The golden coach, 1946), set in a small provincial town reduced to rubble overnight by German bombings. He wanted to play the minor role of the old Jew Rachum, who, when asked about the fate of his loved ones, points to Babi Yar as the place where they all disappeared—a fact considered relevant not so much to any "individual biography" but rather to "collective history." The performance of the drama, slated for Moscow's Maly Theatre (Small Theater), was, however, prohibited due to the "tragic" and "pessimistic" nature of the text, which did not align with the party's recent guidelines on art and literature.[34]

In 1947 the same fate befell the project of Aleksandr Borshchagovskiy, author of the theatrical drama *Do konca vmeste* (Together until the end), prohibited by Glavrepertkom, the Central Committee for Repertoire Control (a commission for approval of performers' repertoires) at the Ministry of Education. The author addressed a theme that he would be able to explore—in an even more intense form—only many years later: the fate of a Jewish actress, Rachael, unable to flee Kyiv before the arrival of the Germans because of serious illness, intertwined with that of Oksana, her Ukrainian sister-in-law, who voluntarily impersonates Rachael to save her from arrest after a tip to the authorities. The plot was intricate and constructed, basically, around feelings of human brotherhood and altruism, the contrast between nobility and honor, on the one hand, and racism and cowardice, on the other. This drama also caught Mikhoels's attention, and he pledged to stage it despite the ban, immediately commissioning its translation into Yiddish. The only request he made to Borshchagovskiy was to modify the character of Rachael to move her away from a role strictly as a victim and instead make her a protagonist aware of her choices: "'This is how one can construct a drama. And even a tragedy,' he told me after a pause. 'How do temples rise? A broad base on the ground, large volumes, plenty of air, and only gradually everything narrows, rises upward, toward God.'"[35]

"State of Abandonment"

The war left physical and psychic ruins behind it across Europe. But in Eastern Europe, everywhere one looked there were expanses of mass graves, the wreckage of torched synagogues, and the debris of ravaged cemeteries.[36] Soldiers and civilians were forced to confront the trauma of places scattered with human remains in every direction. The awareness that the desecration of bodies was virtually endless emerges from correspondence and recollections: thousands of corpses lay in pits and ditches without fencing or in fields crisscrossed by roads; the sites of massacres, although well known, were left unmarked and in complete neglect; there was a widespread attitude of contempt for the victims that demoralized former residents returning to their homes and veterans visiting their homelands.[37] In a letter to Solomon Mikhoels sent in December 1945 from the region of Bryansk, Colonel David A. Dragunsky, one of the Red Army's best-known commanders and a protagonist in the capture of Berlin, lamented the fact that the authorities in his village did not have a list of the people massacred or a map of the execution locations: "In my land, the Germans brutally exterminated my whole family—a total of seventy-four people. But what troubled me most was that no graves were prepared to receive their remains. The bones of my sisters and their children are scattered in fields, trampled underfoot by cattle." To avoid "the denial of every human dignity," it was necessary to mark out the massacre sites with fences, erect funeral stelae and pillars, and inscribe them with epitaphs calculating the number of the fallen and ascertaining the dates of the massacres. Commemorating the "victims heaped with insults" and preventing the oblivion of the "unprecedented abuses" they had suffered would also have constituted a powerful counter to the antisemitism that infiltrated the country during German occupation.[38] Three years later, in the fall of 1948, the poet Boris L. Brainin (Sepp Österreicher) evoked similar arguments in a message to Ilya Ehrenburg about the "scandalous state of abandonment and neglect" in which Babi Yar was kept. Cows grazed in the place of the massacre, human bones scattered beneath their hooves. Through the local press, the proposal to establish a park "on the picturesque slopes" of the ravine was advanced, while the proposal to erect a monument to the victims advocated by Brainin seemed to make no progress.[39]

Initiatives commemorating the victims of the genocide became increasingly widespread over the passing years. The need to gather in commemorative assemblies, to safeguard the sites of massacres, to promote the installation of simple gravestones or other burial markers, to exhume violated bodies and provide for their reburial, and to restore vandalized cemeteries is expressed both by individual citizens and by communities in the process of rebuilding.[40] Where survivors succeeded in their intentions, this happened mainly because they avoided direct confrontation with the authorities, raising the resources needed for the work on their own initiative and usually limiting the construction of memorials within the confines of old Jewish cemeteries.[41] But in 1947, coinciding with the start of the campaign against "nationalistic deviations" in several provinces, there came the first refusals by major institutions to acquiesce to particularistic initiatives, with the justification that it was the exclusive prerogative of central bodies of power to perpetuate, in whatever form it deemed necessary, the memory of events.

Cases where the construction of named memorials for Jewish victims were officially sanctioned are few and far between. In Ternopil, on the initiative of Rabbi Ch. A. Klainer, who arrived in the city in October 1946, funds were raised to provide proper burial for those who had been shot, and a monument with inscriptions in Russian and Yiddish was inaugurated in the presence of authorities. The president of the municipal council and the secretary of the city committee of the party even delivered official speeches on the occasion. (The issue was soon brought to the attention of regional leaders, and the monument was probably demolished.)[42] In July 1948 representatives of the Jewish community in Kamianets-Podilskyi, on the other hand, protested against the high-handed decisions of local administrators who denied them the right to observe a day of mourning. "For over three years," the complaint reads, "we have walked the streets of the city treading upon stones used to pave sidewalks during the German occupation. When we have asked for them to be removed and replaced with other stones, our requests were refused." A similar rejection met the request to "respectfully arrange mass graves." Urgent action was needed, since if "another year" passed, the "place" would no longer be recognizable: weeds were growing up over the graves that would "erase every trace and memory of life."[43]

Those Jewish cemeteries that had not been destroyed and looted because they lacked gates and fences and now had open, sadly violated gravesites, with remains exhumed and scattered, had become vast, empty nonplaces. It is fair to say that at the time of liberation, neglect afflicted burial sites of all faiths and communities. In the face of a general absence of oversight, widespread neglect, and the indifference of government bodies, local populations looted anything that could provide "some form of income or usefulness": crosses and fences served as firewood, stone walls and tombstones became construction material, chapels and mortuaries came in handy as stables, grassy areas were thrown open to grazing animals, and plots of land were plowed up as gardens or turned into dumps.[44] In the case of Jewish necropolises, institutional indifference was compounded by a more general hostility, to the point that venturing into these places, where looting and vandalism had become so frequent, was an increasingly dangerous prospect. Sarah Kolchinskaya wrote about the risk of going to Babi Yar due to the presence of antisemitic thugs: the adjacent Jewish cemetery was soon devastated, the graves robbed of anything of value.[45] Writer and poet Abram Ya. Kagan was aware that in the summer of 1942, occupying authorities had decided to "scatter and distribute" among the population "everything they had not destroyed, lest even the slightest trace remain." The ordinance allowing anyone who wished to "freely take slabs of funerary monuments and iron gates" had not, however, met with wide acceptance. The work of "profanation and destruction," therefore, had to be managed in some other fashion, employing the labor of prisoners of war and interned civilians repeatedly for over a year. They were forced to "shatter the graves and tombstones, which were then used to pave roads." Kagan now had an opportunity to confirm as an eyewitness the results of that "intolerable outrage" to the eternal rest of the deceased, a travesty that had disfigured Kyiv's famous Jewish cemetery, rendering it unrecognizable:

The cemetery occupies a very large area. Once, there were a great number of rich marble monuments of every color: black, white, dark green. Most of them have been uprooted, then smashed into small pieces and scattered on the streets like gravel. The path leading to the cemetery is cluttered with tombstones. At the bottom of the ravine, for example, I saw a fragment of marble with an inscription in gold letters still intact: a mother had wanted to immortalize the memory of her untimely deceased child. A little farther away, a remnant of the funerary monument of Isaak Kruglyak, a well-known doctor from Kyiv. It is impossible to recognize the cemetery of Kyiv. Near the entrance there are entire piles of vaults [made of reinforced concrete conglomerate] that were too difficult to completely extract from the ground. Therefore, they were broken. Above the piles of stones, bent and twisted fences have been stacked. We approach the tomb of Rabbi Moishe Mordheim. His burial site is filthy, the walls have collapsed, the ancient inscriptions in Hebrew are covered with black soot. Now we stand before the crypt of the Brodsky family, wealthy merchants well known in Kyiv. It's the same sight: photographs and plaques have been stolen, marble slabs smashed into a thousand pieces. . . . For a year, the Germans forced Hungarian Jewish soldiers to work here and smash the tombs, which were then used to pave the streets. Russian soldiers from the nearby concentration camp were also assigned to this type of work. This went on for months. The Germans had many

iron grates transported to Babi Yar. All the bars and other fences were used for
the pyres on which the German criminals, before fleeing, burned the bodies. At
Babi Yar, we also saw a large number of marble relics from the cemetery. There
are areas entirely covered with the ashes of consumed bodies.[46]

"Vu zaynen mir? Ot do iz es shoyn?"

In November 1943 the Yiddish poet Dovid Hofshteyn (David Hofstein) composed verses to celebrate liberation and avenge "the shame of two terrible
years."[47] Transported to Ufa, the capital of Bashkortostan, Russia, before the
occupation, he managed to return to Kyiv in early 1944, despite severe restrictions on passes and residence permits.[48] For months, he had tried to prepare
himself psychologically for the trauma: at Babi Yar, he had lost his mother and
younger brother. Approaching the anniversary of the massacre, he attempted
to organize a gathering as an act of public acknowledgment and restitution to
the victims for whom they were murdered. Local authorities denied authorization, claiming the initiative could lead to serious antisemitic demonstrations.
Furthermore, anticipating an attitude that would subsequently characterize
every official position, they declared it would be an expression of Jewish
"chauvinism" or "nationalism."[49] Soon, Ukrainian security services identified
Hofshteyn as the main focal point of the "Jewish nationalistic intelligentsia in
the city of Kyiv."[50]

Despite the obstacles, on 29 September 1944 a crowd of "soldiers, workers,
clerks, women with children, youth, and elders" gathered at Babi Yar "from
early morning until late evening."[51] The writer Itzik Kipnis depicted the event
in a eulogy that evokes the "suspension" of the *Yahrzeit*.[52] It was impossible "to
light a candle and recite the Kaddish for each deceased individual because
there was no space capable of containing so many flames." Immediately after
recalling the religious tradition, the speaker is seized by a secular thought "foreign" to worship—vengeance—and focuses intensely upon that sentiment.
He sees "enemy cities burning like torches" and their inhabitants, instead of
being "killed on the spot," "suffering at length before dying."[53]

Kipnis calls for a symbolic repetition of the massacre. With a "supplication
from the bottom of the heart," he urges the crowd to repeat the journey on
foot without using public transportation: "Let's walk there. Let's follow the
same path. Let's tread those identical streets, then unbelievably crowded by the
living bodies of our brothers." Pushed out "treacherously" from their homes,
Jews had come from all districts of Kyiv: "From Podil and Demyivka, from
Kurenivka and Shuliavka, . . . entire families and solitary individuals, young

and old, children and elderly, mingled together on Lvovska Street in a river of destruction and death"—a mass of individuals "drawn by deceit, plundered, piled up" in a march that had generated "dismay among onlookers."[54]

Kipnis's oratorical strategy revolves around the pathos of reminiscences of ordinary people. Sisters Emma and Yeva, "two elderly women," look at each other, "lost and terrified." They were only able to carry with them "two small bundles in which, along with a photo album, they remembered to place the ritual goblets inherited from their parents: the ancient goblets, now yellowed, for the kiddush." Their mother's candlesticks, on the other hand, were too heavy, and they abandoned them. "Perhaps it wasn't right," say the two sisters, "to leave them on the windowsill behind the curtain. Wouldn't it have been better to entrust them to the Christian neighbor or hide them well in the back of the closet?" The evocation continues with images of a doctor walking with his wife, a rabbi, an elderly woman with many children but left alone in the crowd, "a ten-year-old girl, the best child in her building, where she lives on the fifth floor," with her mother, who is "shy and quiet" by nature and who cannot understand being "in the midst of such a large crowd" and doesn't know what to do, because her daughter "clings to her legs" and blocks the flow of people. Finally, alongside the bitterness of the survivor ("it would have been better if I were the victim instead"), again an appeal to those present: "That is why, three years later, we should go there on foot. It wouldn't be the same if we go by tram. The atmosphere would be, if I may say so, prosaic and suffocating. A stranger's glance, if placed indelicately, could touch my wound, and from that contact would come immense pain, because the wound has not yet healed."[55]

Those who find themselves on that "day of mourning" and in that "sorrowful march" come "from every corner of the liberated homeland," Kipnis continues. They cling to the native city, which, "like a mother," should have "welcomed, comforted, and brought them back to life." During the journey, the writer tries to interpret the feeling that all those travelers hold "quietly enclosed in their own hearts, without display and clamor," because "everyone has their own burden of sorrows and grievances, which must be gradually let go of; everyone has their own sadness, mourning for relatives, and even family discord that need not be revealed."[56]

Gradually, as they move away from the city, other groups of people join the procession, "coming from the most diverse and distant streets," and they "learn about each other." But it is mainly silence that unites them: "Those who do not know the route ask no questions, because they understand that everyone is going 'there.'" The composition of the crowd becomes more evident along the way: "Many women and few men. And it's no wonder. The war, though nearing its end, has not yet concluded. And for us, it is a matter of no small consolation and pride to know that our young people and our men in the Red Army uniform are fighting the enemy and relentlessly hunting them down."[57]

As they approach the destination, Kipnis observes that everyone maintains an attitude of restrained composure, even though their faces betray distress, and he begins to understand that "everyone, as soon as the knot of anguish is loosened, will pour out their pain." Soon the first lamentations are heard. Faces grow tense; many of them cannot help but start to cry softly. Finally, two simple questions reveal the difficulties of using words to guide the heart and controlling emotions in the face of the open space where the massacre took place: "Sandy cliffs crumble under our feet and drag us down. . . . Large ravines covered, deep ditches, thickets. 'Where are we?' 'Is this the place?' [Vu zaynen mir? Ot do iz es shoyn?] Other people have already arrived at the site. There are no words of greeting. Hearts beat in unison, and gazes are fixed on an area that resembles a square ritual chalice":

> In the bottom of the goblet, there is no wine left over. Only blood that has lost its color in the rain and snow. Over there, you can see a piece of crumpled, dirty, white fabric. It used to be a shirt. . . . And there is hair, what remains of it, that once adorned [a face]. And there is something more terrifying than death in all this. Also, torn beards with skin attached, an old cap. Practically at the center, a soft shoe that a foot lost in that moment, that last moment we could not experience with you. There will never be words to write about a shoe that a stumbling foot lost in the very instant the body, in the whirlwind of death and screams, parted from life. No one touches the shoe, no one approaches it where it lies. Just as no one approaches a fragment of skull on the other side of the ditch. A piece of bone, one side bare; the other covered in skin and tousled hair. It's a fragment of a blessed human body, the messenger of Babi Yar, of an entire tortured community, of a world of hundreds of thousands of victims, accusing and demanding an answer from heaven. It accepts no compromise and seeks no mercy. Indeed, it can devour your heart with its terrifying grin. Yes, even yours, even if you are family, even if you are flesh of their flesh and blood of their blood.[58]

The testimonies left surviving by the fire tell something the human mind cannot grasp and the voice cannot express. The onlookers seem to await someone to say even just a few words to understand. It is at this point that Kipnis decides to address them with an oration:

Brothers and friends! We throw ourselves to the ground, we roll in the ashes, we beat our heads, we plunge into tears. Could it be otherwise? Who would dare to say that, as great as the catastrophe may be, it is too much to shake ourselves in despair, to let our faces be torn by thorny bushes growing on the sides of the ravine until we bleed, until we reach spasms, until we scream in pain?

And yet, to each of you, to you who are of my own blood, I want to say this:

Jews, dear brothers, let us rise from the ground, shake off the ashes, and let all the light that our people bear shine forth. A man who has lost a leg, or an arm, even just a finger feels diminished by how he has become. But a people . . . a people from whom, without ever uttering a complaint, as happened to us, half, if not three-quarters, of the body has been torn away, that people will nonetheless be able to reconstitute itself like a drop of water or a mercury ball. Take away half of it, and what remains will assume the rounded shape and restore itself as a whole.

Let us rise from the ground, stand tall, and raise our flag high! Peoples, even now, benefit from the light they have brought. And you will see how they will treat us with respect even for our physical strength.[59]

On the way home, when parting from a young Jew, Kipnis dwells on the feeling of revenge: "Three years ago the enemy was convinced that Babi Yar was the word with which the history of a people would end. Now, on the other side of Babi Yar, you can see a concentration camp where German prisoners, covered with sores, drag themselves in their rags and devour the lice from their bodies. We look at them with disgust, like rotting carcasses, while envy sparkles in their eyes: they see human beings in front of them."[60]

"A Zionist Symbol"

At the end of the war, Kipnis wrote a short story titled "On khokhmes, on kheshboynes" (Without pretense, without calculations). It tells the story of a Ukrainian peasant woman who, risking her life, offers aid and shelter to two small Jewish children in her family. The author expresses admiration for the woman's courage and nobility of spirit but cannot help thinking that Soviet Jewry, from which—as he had previously written in his eulogy at Babi Yar—"half, if not three-quarters, of the body has been torn away," had also lost those two children.[61] That is why he is increasingly "anxious to preserve intact what has survived" the catastrophe, symbolically represented by the mother tongue: "When I see a student, a beautiful girl, a brave and handsome soldier, an academic, or even just an ordinary Jew, I ardently desire them to address me in Yiddish." His aspiration is that "all the Jews who now march confidently and triumphantly through the streets of Berlin should wear on their chests, along with decorations and medals, a small Mogen David." That gesture of pride possesses the power to transform a mark of death into an emblem of courage and life: "[Hitler] wanted everyone to see the Jew tortured, insulted, and despised. I now therefore want everyone to see that I am a Jew and that my dignity as a Jewish man is no less than that of all other freedom-loving citizens."[62]

"On khokhmes, on kheshboynes" was published in the newspaper *Eynikayt* on 26 July 1945, but all passages deemed to be nationalistic were excised. Kipnis's decision to publish an unabridged version abroad in 1947, bypassing official channels, had grim consequences for Kipnis.[63] On 3 July of that year the writer was virulently attacked by the Jewish Anti-Fascist Committee, an attack that was understood as a reaffirmation of just how unacceptable any deviation from the principle of Soviet citizenship remained. The author's "sentimental" aesthetic, the note stated, like the same motif found in the work of other Jewish writers, seemed to draw inspiration only from the *shteyger* (way of life) of Yiddishland.[64] As a result, it conflicted with the ideology that was meant to guide the intelligentsia as a body in its efforts to overcome the trauma of the war and to rebuild a normal life.[65] The polemic kindled against Kipnis should be read as an integral part of the project of "purification" and "moralization" of intellectual life traditionally attributed to Andrei A. Zhdanov. In a famous speech given in the summer of 1946, the secretary of the Central Committee of the Communist Party criticized all and any "servility" toward foreign culture and denounced the deviationist positions of two Leningrad newspapers, *Zvezda* and *Leningrad*, which were deemed responsible for spreading "ideologies alien to the party spirit" because they had published works by the poet Anna Akhmatova and the writer Mikhail M. Zoshchenko.[66] The battle against "bourgeois nationalism" and "Western decadence" was summarized in a resolution approved by the Central Committee's organizational office on 14 August 1946.[67] Inspired and personally managed by Stalin, the resolution resulted in a program of standards for literature and art that condemned, among other things, any expression of "nostalgia, pessimism, and disappointment."[68] The prescriptive effects were immediate even in Jewish circles, as demonstrated by the criticisms directed at poets Margarita Aliger and Olga Bergholz, deemed guilty of spreading defeatist ideas and writing verses of gloomy lamentation.[69] In September *Eynikayt* began publishing increasingly harsh reprimands against the "nationalism" of writers who claimed cultural autonomy, put forward the idea of a people's unity relatively independent from all geographic or class divisions, or overemphasized the themes of Judeocide.[70]

In Ukraine, during a plenary meeting of the Communist Party's Central Committee of the republic held on 15–17 August 1946, First Secretary Nikita

Khrushchev, along with Ideology Secretary Kostyantyn Z. Lytvyn and Propaganda Secretary Ivan D. Nazarenko, asked intellectuals to reconsider and correct public discourse in immediate response to new central directives for literature and art. From that moment on, there ensued a series of official meetings in which alleged errors were denounced and criticism of nationalism in literature was combined with calls to uphold the Soviet present at the expense of the "separatism" of national cultures.[71] The ideological campaign was entrusted to Lazar M. Kaganovich, who in February 1947 was tasked with replacing Khrushchev as first secretary in Ukraine.[72] In a secret report on "anti-Soviet manifestations in the leading circles of the intelligentsia" transmitted to him during the summer, great emphasis was placed upon the role played by "individual Jewish researchers and writers" who, taking advantage of this particular point in history, had insinuated the presence of "national-bourgeois conceptions regarding the history of Ukrainian literature." Moreover, they had assigned themselves the task of "criticizing and exposing those conceptions." In so doing, those researchers and writers spread "provocative rumors" solely to demonstrate that the Central Committee of the Communist Party of Ukraine acted "under their influence." It had also been ascertained that there was a close connection "between the Jewish nationalist writers Hofshteyn, Kipnis, and Kagan" and representatives of the Kyiv religious community.[73] On 25 July 1947 the Jewish section of the Union of Writers convened a meeting that had only one item on the agenda, namely, Kipnis's "harmful story." Gershl (Hershel) Polyanker, an important war writer, pointed out that the accused had already been reprimanded for "ideological falsehood" and "petty-bourgeois nationalist narrow-mindedness." Attempts had been made to guide him on the path he should follow in his literary profession in order to be considered, in all respects, a "Soviet artist," but to no avail. Even in his latest work, he had dealt with "the noble theme of friendship between peoples" from "nationalistic positions." In his response, Kipnis tried to draw attention to the reason that led him to imagine a Magen David, alongside other war decorations, on the chests of Jewish soldiers parading through the streets of Berlin: to transform the "symbol of shame" into a "symbol of pride." He also noted that just two years earlier the story would have been interpreted in a "creative" sense, whereas now it was seen as "nationalistic in genre." The meeting concluded with the proposal to expel Kipnis, forwarded to the presidium of the Union of Writers of Ukraine.[74]

On 15 September, during a session discussing the Central Committee's resolutions on the newspapers *Zvezda* and *Leningrad*, writer Oleksandr Korniychuk criticized "On khokhmes, on kheshboynes" for "bourgeois nationalist deviationism." Kipnis was accused of proposing "a Zionist symbol" and thereby "defaming the Soviet man."[75] This was followed by further attacks in the press, often coming from Jews within the Communist apparatus. On the one hand, the writer was invited to recognize that "the Soviet five-pointed star [had] long replaced both the six-pointed Star of David and the trident of Petlyura, as well as any eagle and other nationalistic emblem."[76] On the other hand, it was argued that one of the most disturbing aspects in the story of the "outrageous tale" was the determination with which the author had sought to publish the chauvinistic paragraphs already removed from the first edition of the text.[77]

On 25 June 1949 Kipnis was arrested under article 54–10/2 of the criminal code of the Ukrainian Soviet Socialist Republic. Among the documents seized from him was a manuscript used during the criminal proceedings to denounce his "idealization of the shtetl, rituals, and religious customs of ancient times."[78] On 25 January 1950 the writer was sentenced to ten years of forced labor for engaging in "anti-Soviet nationalist activities" and inciting hatred against the Ukrainian people. He was released on 30 December 1955, but he could not be rehabilitated and was forced to live in Boyarka, a town on the outskirts of the capital. The sentence was later repealed on 21 June 1957.[79]

"Rootless Cosmopolitanism"

On 20 November 1948 the Politburo of the Central Committee decided to liquidate the Jewish Anti-Fascist Committee. The execution of the order was entrusted to the Ministry of State Security on the grounds that the committee was "a center of anti-Soviet propaganda" that was responsible for "regularly providing information to foreign intelligence services." For that reason, it was specified that "the press organs of the committee must be closed, and its activities must be blocked," although "for the moment, no one need be arrested."[80] Actually, several writers had already been detained, and Dovid Hofshteyn was imprisoned in Kyiv on 16 September 1948.[81] The operation was part of the dismantling of major Jewish cultural institutions. In particular, between the summer of 1948 and that of 1949, the systematic suppression of all Jewish theater collectives operating in the country was carried out: in Moscow, Odessa, Minsk, Chernovtsy, and Birobidzhan.[82]

On 28 January 1949 *Pravda*, in a lengthy unsigned article, gave a strongly antisemitic twist to the ongoing ideological campaign, directing it against "rootless cosmopolitanism" (*bezrodny kosmopolityzm*).[83] The expression, which quickly came into use, left "no doubts as to whom it was directed against."[84] The epithets "cosmopolitan," "rootless," and "antipatriotic" were indeed "masks" behind which "the harsh word Zhyd [Jew] was lurking." If no one dared "to tear them off and loudly proclaim the original and sweet[-sounding] word," it was only because the Soviet criminal code severely punished the crime of antisemitism.[85] Literature was called upon to reflect on the "miserable and dangerous consequences" that arose from every writer "detaching themselves from the life and struggle of the Soviet people." Cosmopolitanism not only had an "antinational" character but also was "barren" and produced damages similar to those caused by "parasites in the plant world, attacking the shoots." In particular, theater critics, many of whom were Jewish, were accused of being the most reactionary cultural sector, within which "bourgeois aestheticism under the guise of an unpatriotic, cosmopolitan attitude was corrupting Soviet art."[86] This marked a linguistically new turn, although the entries in the Soviet dictionary were largely drawn from the lexicon of political antisemitism: the press as a whole quickly aligned with it, and literature engaged in experimenting with its narrative approach.[87]

On 3 February 1949, during a meeting of the secretariat of the Central Committee of the Communist Party chaired by Georgy M. Malenkov, an order was handed down for the dissolution of the associations of Jewish writers in Moscow, Kyiv, and Minsk, along with the suppression of the Yiddish art and literature periodicals *Heymland* in Moscow and *Der shtern* in Kyiv. The resolution, inspired by the secretary of the Union of Soviet Writers, Alexander A. Fadeyev, was ratified during a Politburo meeting on 8 February.[88] A few days later, the poet Nikolai M. Gribachev published a violent attack "against cosmopolitanism and formalism in poetry" in *Pravda*, thus expanding the horizon of party criticism. Among his targets was Pavel Antokolsky, considered "the leader of poets who spread and protected decadence." He was accused in particular of corrupting young writers, some of whom had already shown their talents, dragging them "into the swamp of formalism and subjectivism." Essentially, Antokolsky was accused of having taken advantage of the lack of control over his role as an educator at the Literary Institute of the Union of Writers to inspire in the students themes alien to the "traditions of Russian poetry" and indifferent to the "heroic actions of the Soviet people."[89] The poet was expelled from the institute and was effectively forced to cease all composition of poetry for the next several years. Gribachev's indictment also affected literary criticism. Particularly significant was the condemnation of Daniil S. Danin (Plotke) for publishing essays against the "embellishment of reality" in poetry and for advocating a "dramatic principle" as a necessary aesthetic condition to support the truthfulness and moral significance of poetic metric compositions.[90]

In Ukraine the campaign against cosmopolitanism was even more extensive. In January 1949 the Office of Jewish Culture at the Academy of Sciences was dismantled, and its director, Elia Spivak, was imprisoned.[91] The same fate befell, among others, two scientific collaborators of the institute, Chaim Loytsker and Moisei E. Mizhiritsky; the editor in chief of *Der shtern*, the same Polyanker who had expelled Kipnis from the Jewish section of the Union of Writers; and the writers and poets David Bergelson, Peretz Markish, Leib Kvitko, Motl Talalayevsky, Abram Kagan, and Itzik Kipnis.[92] This wave of arrests caused great concern in intellectual circles.[93] Meanwhile, Glavlit, the Soviet body responsible for censoring printed works and protecting state secrets, prepared lists of hundreds of books that were to be withdrawn from public libraries and removed from the market.[94] Scientists, artists, and writers who had shown interest in the massacre of the Jews in Kyiv were accused of "nationalism," "cosmopolitanism," "Zionism," and inciting hatred toward the Russian people. In March 1949 the Jewish Ukrainian poet and playwright Sava O. Holovanivsky, a war correspondent during the conflict, was accused by the secretary of the Ukrainian Writers' Union, Lyubomyr D. Dmyterko, of composing a work that was "nationalistic and manifestly hostile to the Soviet people." The poem *Avraam* (1943), which had sought to critically address the theme of the relationships between Jews and other local communities during the occupation, contained, according to Dmyterko, "a frightening and unheard-of calumny." The author had "blatantly lied" in describing an elderly Jew led by the Germans through the streets of Kyiv to the place of execution under the indifferent eyes of Russians and Ukrainians. It was "a terrible defamation" of a people who had defended "the freedom and independence of Soviet citizens of all nationalities in a harsh and bloody struggle at the cost of enormous efforts and sacrifices."[95]

Ostracism affected every form of artistic expression. Even in the visual arts there was a reversal that, to borrow Kipnis's judgment, made what had recently appeared "creative" now appear "nationalistic." The painter Vasyl F. Ovchinnikov, director of a Kyiv museum, had served on the Stalingrad front. Upon his return, as his daughter recalled, he discovered that many of his Jewish neighbors had been slaughtered: "The tragedy was not an abstraction for him. It had the concrete faces of people who had lived beside him." The next day, he walked toward Babi Yar, wandered around, and drew pictures in a small album of clay gullies, leafless skeletons of trees, and old funeral stelae.[96] Later, he began to conceive the idea of transforming those sketches into an ordered succession of pictorial elements commemorating the massacre, a project initially supported by the Union of Writers and the Ministry of Culture in order to create a sort of frescoed pantheon. In May 1949, during a plenary session of the Union of Soviet Artists of Ukraine, he was accused of having formalistic positions alien to Soviet art due to the Babi Yar cycle and other works in which deformed images of the Soviet population were depicted.[97] His unpatriotic tendencies were sanctioned along with those of Zinovy S. Tolkachev, who was accused of "deeply reprehensible" inspiration and a "Zionist-religious orientation," especially in relation to the graphic works *Okkupanty* (Occupiers), *Majdanek, Christos v Majdaneke* (Christ at Majdanek), and *Cvety Osvencima* (The flowers of Auschwitz), created between 1944 and 1945. These works had been widely and favorably received at the time of the liberation of Poland. Now they were found to be imbued with "bourgeois nationalism and rootless cosmopolitanism" and were judged as "an insult to the dignity of the Soviet people" because the works showed them "as helpless victims in the face of the enemy."[98] Already for some time now, "due to well-defined prejudices," having relations with Tolkachev was considered a "criminal" attitude.[99] Great concern was aroused especially by the painting *Taleskoten* (1944, from the *Majdanek* series), which depicted a worn *tallit katan* hanging on barbed wire like a proud flag against the backdrop of a desolate and completely lifeless landscape.[100]

Dmytro L. Klebanov, originally from Kharkiv, resolved to write a symphony in memory of the victims of Babi Yar in 1945 as soon as he returned to his city from the evacuation zone in Uzbekistan.[101] Jewish by birth but Russian by culture, he had not received an education tied to nationality. To realize his project, he turned to an expert. Maestro Zynoviy D. Zagranychny provided him with the necessary sources: folk songs and synagogue liturgical chants that he used to infuse the classical Ukrainian symphonic repertoire with Jewish-inspired materials. Klebanov's composition was entirely constructed in the ways of a traditional melody using a Freygish scale. The music, with its characteristic Jewish intonations, was significant even without words up to the final soprano lamentation, which evoked a Kaddish. The work was first performed in Kharkiv in 1947 and then reprised in Kyiv in 1948 under the direction of Natan H. Rakhlin. It soon underwent an ideological examination. During the First Congress of Soviet Composers, held in April 1948, Andriy Ya. Shtokharenko, a member of the governing council of the Union of Ukrainian Composers, spoke out against "formalism" and "bourgeois modernism," drawing inspiration from Klebanov's symphony. According to him, one of the major flaws lay in the way it represented, "completely falsely," the tragedy of Babi Yar as if it were "a passive acceptance of death." There was also a "sense of despair," so that the "music perverted the historical value of the Soviet man, who fell fighting for freedom and the independence of peoples."[102]

On 12 March 1949, during a meeting of composers, musicologists, and other workers from specialized cultural institutes in the city of Kyiv— convened to indicate "the tasks of musical criticism in light of the decisions of the Twenty-Sixth Congress of the Ukrainian Communist Party and the interventions of the newspapers *Pravda* and *Kultura i zhizn* [Culture and life] on an antipatriotic group of theater critics"—Klebanov was again targeted. The speaker Valerian D. Dovzhenko accused him of writing a work "permeated by the spirit of bourgeois nationalism and cosmopolitanism based on ancient Jewish religious chants." Essentially, the "sources" used—namely, "the rituals of ancient Palestine, the book of Lamentations, and Hebrew cantillations"—had inspired the author to create an "antipatriotic" work. With his "symphony full of biblical motifs and imbued with the feeling of a tragic destiny," the author had "defamed Russians and Ukrainians," since he had forgotten "the friendship and brotherhood of peoples" and had instead supported "the idea of the total solitude of Soviet citizens tortured by the Germans in Babi Yar."[103] Composer Levko M. Revutsky, a professor at the Kyiv Conservatory, in a speech denouncing the pernicious influence (or "ideological deviation") of "cosmopolitan" artists on musical education in Ukraine, accused Klebanov's "nationalistic symphony" of propagating "Zionist melodies." Despite the defense attempt by conductor Natan Rakhlin, the "cosmopolitans" were already considered responsible for spreading a "dangerous theory" to stifle Ukrainian musical tradition and talent. The poet Andriy S. Malyshko, speaking on behalf of the Union of Writers of Ukraine, offered further insight into this alleged scheme. In his view, the "rootless cosmopolitans" had moved "cohesively against Soviet culture in all its expressions." Just as literary critics had found accomplices among composers, "Klebanov's Zionism, manifested in the symphony in memory of the Babi Yar victims, coincided with the Zionism of Pervomaisky and Holovanivsky."[104] The consequences of these attacks were almost immediate: Klebanov was dismissed from his positions as director of the composition department at the Kharkiv Conservatory and president of the local section of the Union of Ukrainian Composers. Any performances of his composition were suspended, and it was only on 29 September 1990 that the symphony was reprised in Kyiv under the baton of conductor Igor I. Blazhkov.[105]

One must not underestimate the consequences of repressive measures and censorship that prohibit or inhibit any possibility of discussing the extermination of the Jews in poetic, literary, musical, or pictorial form. Within a few years, conditions for an even more radical purge in the cultural world would be created. In March 1953 the leadership of the Union of Writers, represented by Aleksandr A. Fadeyev, Aleksei A. Surkov, and Konstantin M. Simonov, sent a report on the results of the cleansing campaign conducted within the Moscow section. The goal was to get rid of "inactive" members, meaning those writers who had not produced "works of original artistic value" for five to ten years and who therefore were considered "a dead weight hindering the organization's work," not to mention that, in some cases, they brought "discredit to the high reputation of the Soviet writer." Expulsion was possible, according to the report, in response to the "cessation of artistic-literary and critical-literary activity for a certain number of years."[106] The report made no secret of the identity of the targets of the ongoing purge:

> A significant part of this ballast consisted of people of Jewish nationality, including members of the former Jewish Literary Association (Moscow section of Jewish writers), which was liquidated in 1949. Of the 1,102 members of the Moscow organization of the Union of Writers, 662 are Russian (60 percent), 329 are Jewish (29.8 percent), 23 are Ukrainian, 21 are Armenian, and 67 belong to other nationalities.
>
> When the Union of Soviet Writers was created in 1934, 351 people were admitted to the Moscow organization, of whom 124 were Jewish writers (35.3 percent). From 1935 to 1940, 244 people were accepted, of whom 85 were Jewish (34.8 percent); from 1941 to 1946, 265 people were admitted, of whom 75 were Jewish (28.4 percent); from 1947 to 1952, 241 people were admitted, of whom 49 were Jewish (20.3 percent).[107]

According to the report, these were individuals who, in most cases, should not even have been admitted to the union due to a flagrant lack of "literary merits." But they had been able to take advantage of the lax control of formal requirements, friendships, and, in some cases, "masked forms of nationalist sentiments."[108]

3

Transforming Space

On 13 March 1945 the Council of People's Commissars and the Central Committee of the Communist Party of Ukraine adopted a resolution, signed by Nikita Khrushchev and Demyan Korotchenko, "on the construction of a monument in the territory of Babi Yar" in honor of the "140,000 citizens of Kyiv, savagely tortured there by the Nazi barbarians."[1] The project entailed an estimated cost of about three million rubles and called for an initial allocation for 1946, the year work was to begin, of almost half that amount. The execution of the work, which was supposed to be completed in 1947, was entrusted to architect Oleksandr V. Vlasov and sculptor G. T. Kruglov. The plan included the construction of a black granite triangular pyramid with a base of fifteen meters, a bas-relief in the center, and a composition of steps that echoed the contour of the ravine.[2] However, the "monument to the victims of Fascist terror at Babi Yar," as it was still described in the reconstruction and development plan of urban facilities and services for 1948–50, was never carried out.[3]

Where to Lay a Wreath?

The reconstruction of Kyiv saw all resources committed to restoring the industrial base, rebuilding the road network, and rebuilding for public and residential use. The mastermind of this massive urban redevelopment plan was Oleksandr Vlasov, the city's chief architect from 1944 to 1950.[4] For several years, the Babi Yar site was not touched by the planned works and remained almost unaltered. It was often possible to find bones and burnt objects there, and there were those who continued to scour the bottom of the ravine in search of valuables missed by German inspections (money, diamonds, rings, or gold teeth).[5] The authorities were well aware of the excavation activities and tried to limit them. A directive from the city council's executive committee, issued on 14 August 1946, emphasized the need to restore order in the area, where "unknown malefactors" were digging up the pits: first, the holes that had been dug needed to be refilled; second, it was necessary to prohibit anyone from freely accessing the sand quarries.[6] Despite the bans, the residents of the area continued to use large portions of the land "simply as a dump."[7] The dismay this caused is evident in the bitter lines of verse written in 1949 by Roman Levin, a teenager who had survived the Brest ghetto, after he had visited the ravine, now reduced to a garbage dump. The victory had been an act of justice for the victims, but what was the point of avenging the outrage done to them if there was no respect even for the corpses? Levin had come across graves of all kinds filled with the corpses of women and children:

But I have never seen and never would have thought
That human Reason could sink so low
And that the living could so matter-of-factly
Trample on the bodies of the dead.[8]

Students at the Military Medical School, located nearby, used the large space for shooting practice, unaware that their empty bullets were landing next to other bullets the Germans had used to commit murder. One of those recruits recalled, sixty years after the end of his training session, "If only we had known, my comrades and I, . . . that we were marching, running, advancing, crawling over the bodies of our grandfathers and grandmothers, mothers and sisters."[9] At the same time, many survivors visited "every year"—as David Budnik, a survivor of Operation Sonderkommando 1005, reported—the place where tens of thousands of people were "killed simply because they were Jews." There was no designated stopping and gathering point: "We would arrive and, in silence, stand before the abandoned ravine."[10] Mourning was expressed in the simplest and most spontaneous way: "We went there to cry and scatter flowers around us. No wreaths. Besides, where to lay it, where to place it? Neither a monument nor an obelisk. Only wild brush and weeds around."[11]

In the mid-1950s commemorative works were erected in various locations that had been the scene of war crimes. It was a need that had been widely felt. Some verses by Boris Slutsky seem to testify to this fact:

And the sculptor marked the measurements on the stone.
The grimace of the face, deformed by the cry,
Smoothed, leveled with the sharp chisel.
I died small, but when I arose, I came up big.
And I had turned to granite, but I was alive.[12]

Nothing similar, however, happened at Babi Yar. The issue was discussed in 1957 by the Central Committee of the Communist Party of Ukraine, about to come under the leadership of Nikolai V. Podgorny, who decided to erase the site by building a stadium or other sports facilities and setting up a public park.[13] Lev Ozerov composed verses in 1958 that remained unpublished for a long time, in which the dead appealed silently to the living not to forget and not to forgive the sins that the institutions wanted to pardon:

> Meandering moat. Grayish burdock.
> The abundance of quietness made me deaf,
> The abundance of light dazzled me.
> I find no peace in the silence.
> Poisoned water and bitter bread,
> And I can't understand: What is this?
> The dead appeal silently to the living.
> Friends, have we truly forgiven
> And forgotten the simple truths,
> Which are no longer needed by them now?
> Bring the children here.
> Let them cross again
> The slippery edge of the covered ditch. . . .
> Forgive? No, we do not forgive!
> We do not have the right to forgive.[14]

Yuri G. Kaplan wrote a lengthy poem in 1959 that likewise remained unpublished for many years, in which he dared to assert that the remission of crimes could be neither achieved nor carried out. Kaplan had escaped the massacre because he and his mother had managed to board one of the last freight trains to the rear. At nineteen, a student at the Kyiv Polytechnic, he had been struck by the thought that his salvation had meant the condemnation of another:

> Ravine—with twisted banks, a huge gaping wound,
> You are deserted and wild, only the winds blow over you.
> You turn black as an abyss,
>   when darkness descends,
> The city lights encircle you like beasts.
> A hundred thousand sleep in you. Their names are not engraved in granite,
> They sleep unknown in your depths, brown as iodine.
> Their names are forgotten forever. But thousands upon thousands

Will never forget your name of blood . . .
I grew up in distant areas behind the lines—I barely remember the sky of war,
I have not encountered the enemies and have not seen death in the face.
Teach me fury, Ravine, teach me anger.
I come to you as they come to their father's grave.
I come to you as they come, probably, to God,
Entrusted with the most hidden to simple prayers.
Give me strength, Ravine. Stir up tumult in my heart
So that I do not forget, so that I do not forgive.
Let no one forgive, let the multitude of the nameless rise.
Help them rise, help them wake up to fight.
No fences, no garlands—let it be an open wound
So that it hurts, so that the pain helps to attain victory.[15]

The image of a wound that time cannot heal is also found in the opening declaration of some verses from "Konec veka" (End of the century), written by Nahum Korzhavin around the mid-1950s. The poem opens by posing to the reader the problem of an intimate collective experience of pain that "is not yet history." And in fact, the institutions, with their linguistic games that nullify all specific qualities ("peaceful Soviet citizens"), do their best to marginalize the reality of the extermination of the Jews ("At Babi Yar thick and lush grass sprouts"), fighting against those who know what lies underground, in the extermination camps, and want to preserve the traces so that this chapter can one day be written:

It is not yet history.
It is a recent wound
That is still alive in people.
In the camps, the ruins of the crematoria are still intact.
At Babi Yar
thick and lush grass sprouts.[16]

Shike Driz emerged during the 1950s as one of the most original poets in Yiddish. At the end of the war, a reference to Babi Yar that surfaced in a children's ballad is almost indecipherable. But there it is:

A Jew bought a balloon.
It was the green color of grass.
It seemed to him like a valley
Floating in the air, hanging on a string.

He takes it, the valley,
And brings it to Babi Yar
To give to his grandson
And buys a new ball.

So the grandfather brings
Gifts to the grandson:
Once a forest, once a field,
The sun with the moon.[17]

In 1954 Driz composed the song of a mother who could no longer put her
children to sleep:

I would like to hang the cradle on the beam
And rock and rock my baby, my Yankl.
But the house vanished in the flames of the night.
How could I rock you, my dear child?

With thorns and nettles,
The paths are covered
With thorns and nettles. The white doves of peace
Have turned to ashes.

I would like to hang the cradle from a tree
And rock and rock my child, my Shleyml.
But not even a thread of a cloth remains to me.
Not even a shoelace remains to me.

Not even a branch, not even a leaf
Of the barren oak.
Only a small pile
Of burning embers remains.

I would like to cut my long braids
And hang the cradle, the cradle from the braids.
But I do not know where the bones might be,
The beloved bones of my two children.

Help me, mothers, help me
To let my song flow.

Help me, mothers, help me
To lull Babi Yar to sleep.[18]

These verses managed to reach a wide audience in the form of a folksong.
Nechama Lifshitz, one of the most popular performers of melodies in Yiddish
and Hebrew, sang the lullaby in Kyiv in December 1959 in the packed hall of
the operetta theater. The music was by Rivka Boyarskaya.[19] Lifshitz concluded
her performance by singing the "lament" with the entire audience standing in
absolute silence. No one applauded. There was only "a curtain of tears."[20]

A series of drawings by Boris I. Prorokov, *This Must Not Happen Again!*, was
exhibited at the Manezh in Moscow in 1961. One was titled *At Babi Yar* and
depicts three women with their heads covered by black shawls. One hides her
face with her hand so as not to look at the ravine full of bodies. In the com-
ments that accompanied the exhibition, there was never any reference to the
Jewish identity of the victims.[21] But those who saw knew. The painter and
graphic artist Aleksandr D. Tikhomirov was known as the author of portraits
of the Communist Party leaders. For example, he created the largest depiction
of Lenin ever made (42 × 22 meters). In 2013, long after his death, his daughter
found a series titled *Babi Yar* in his personal archive, created between the 1950s
and 1960s. These drawings, which were not even known to the people closest
to the artist, were recently exhibited.[22]

"Underline the Space"

In October 1959 Viktor P. Nekrasov appealed to public opinion to denounce
the fact that, eighteen years later, there was nothing to remember the place
where "one of the most heinous crimes in all of human history" had been
committed.[23] From that moment on, the commitment to marking Babi Yar
would become, as critic Anna Berzer noted, "an integral part of his personal,
social, civil, and literary life."[24] In 1946 the magazine *Znamya* published the
novel *V okopakh Stalingrada* (Front-Line Stalingrad), which, printed in a single volume in several million copies, was translated into over forty languages,
making its author a prominent figure in modern war literature.[25] Why did a
famous realist writer become a custodian of the memory of Babi Yar?

Nekrasov had studied architecture with a strong inclination toward constructivism and the style of Le Corbusier.[26] In the final stages of the conflict,
he showed great concern for the reconstruction plans of liberated cities and
the ways in which victory was to be celebrated. On 8 June 1944 he reported to
his family that he had sent a letter to *Pravda*, along with a fellow architect and
comrade, Gyorgy A. Obradovich, in which he expressed doubts about the
proposal advanced by academician Aleksey V. Shchusev to set up "a park of

culture and leisure on Mamaev Kurgan," the hill on the right bank of the
Volga that was the scene of fierce fighting between German assault troops and
Soviet defenders and where Nekrasov himself had spent five crucial months in
the Battle of Stalingrad.[27] Supported by academician Karo S. Alabyan, Nekrasov believed that the reconstruction should indeed be conceived "as a majestic
monument of heroic deeds in the war, symbolizing the power and vitality of
the great Russian people," but, with respect for the "tragic epic of the fighters,"
it was also necessary to demonstrate "artistic sensitivity and thoughtfulness."[28]
The hypothesis, shared by Alabyan, was "to include in the architectural composition authentic fragments of trenches, machine gun nests, underground
shelters, and passageways and to combine them with the monumental works"
to be erected.[29]

Nekrasov advocated reconstruction and celebratory theories very different
from those held in high esteem by Soviet institutions. He outlined them in
May 1945 in a short essay in which he foreshadowed the demythologized reading of the conflict that would characterize all his subsequent activities. An
exhibition had provided him the opportunity to reflect on the function of
those who created drafts and sketches of the wartime experience while it was
"still alive in memory," transforming them into a finished painting or writing.
The artist had to be aware that he would produce, in the most varied represen-
tational and compositional forms, "historical documents" destined to influence
the way the war would be judged for a long time to come. Therefore, at the
center of the representation, whatever its colors and shapes, there should
always be "the truth." Writing or painting with "the language of artistic truth"
was not the same thing as depicting "the feeling of indignation" of the combatant or attributing to him "a wonderful and young face with the expression
of an angry knight." It meant having the courage to portray "a soldier with a
tattered coat and without a helmet" without worrying about "diminishing his
image as a defender of the homeland." Alongside the most celebrated heroes
(Nikolay F. Gastello, Aleksandr M. Matrosov, Zoya A. Kosmodemyanskaya),
there were indeed "hundreds and thousands of fighters and commanders
whose courage and dedication lay not only in being on the front lines for
entire weeks" but also "in retreating and then advancing again." To Nekrasov,
"the dust-covered soldier, tired, in his worn overcoat, rolling a cigarette after
the attack" seemed far more real and noble than "the sweet, artificial, and
oleographic soldiers of the Red Army with their gleaming helmets." The war
was not "only made of bold attacks and the entry of troops, with flags waving,
into liberated cities." It was also "the nerve-wracking tension to the limit,
clenched teeth, the bitterness of retreat, the death of comrades with whom you
slept under the same overcoat"; it was also "the nighttime crossings in

knee-deep mud, the backpack stuffed with ammunition, the mortar on the shoulders, the muddy puddles into which soldiers plunged their thirsty mouths."[30]

To those who wanted to commemorate Stalingrad with "granite, marble, bronze, sculptures, monuments," it was necessary to remind them of the reality of the slain combatant: "He lay on his back with his arms outstretched and a cigarette butt still clenched in his lips. A small butt that was still smoking. And this was more frightening . . . than the destroyed cities, the disemboweled bellies, the severed lips and legs. The outstretched arms and a cigarette butt between the lips. A moment ago there was still life, thoughts, desires. Now there is death."[31] Those who wanted to commemorate Stalingrad with "a magnificent park of culture and leisure" should remember that soldiers and officers would not have been able to share the choice of turning into a recreation and entertainment ground a hill of which they knew "every hollow, every trench, every machine gun site." Who would want to laugh "where, after removing one's cap, one must stand in silence"? And then "why not preserve all these trenches? Why not transform them into a sort of museum of the defense of Stalingrad? At the top of the kurgan there is an abandoned tank for which a three-month battle was fought. Isn't it, destroyed and riddled with bullets as it is, the most vivid monument of those days?"[32] Nekrasov thus intended to remind the architects that it was not easy at all to "immortalize historic sites." Ukraine was full of places that should have been "preserved in the form they had." The function of architecture was to "highlight, underline the space." It was not to "overload, suffocate, replace the noble simplicity and gravity of the territories where battles had raged just a short time before." It was still too early to predict how the events would "materialize," what configuration ("pantheon, triumphal arch, obelisk, column?") the "monuments to the [martyred] cities, the memorials on the mass graves, the works dedicated to the victories" would take. The exhibition of the projects for the reconstruction of Khreshchatyk in Kyiv, as well as Oleksandr Vlasov's proposal to commemorate the victims of Babi Yar and other results of a competition aimed at celebrating the war heroes, provided a wide range of hypotheses and discussions. But whatever the final choice, it was necessary to keep in mind the words of those fighters and adhere accordingly to principles of "simplicity, nobility, and restraint."[33]

"An Empty Space"

The theme of preserving historical sites reappears in the essay that Nekrasov devoted to Babi Yar in 1959, "Pochemu eto ne sdelano?" (Why wasn't it done?). Lev Ozerov reconstructed the rather unusual circumstances of the genesis of that brief article. Returning from one of his frequent trips to Kyiv, having composed a narrative that seemed to have some "provisional coherence," he tried to share with relatives and friends "the tremendous impressions" he felt every time he visited the site of the massacre. He also felt, however, that the words he used never fully conveyed his feelings until he realized that there was no need for "pathetic elements," even if reduced to a minimum: "The drier and more succinct the description, the stronger the impression it produced." Among those who had listened to him, there were those who advised him to consider publication. The contacts with *Literaturnaya gazeta*, the weekly organ of the Union of Soviet Writers, were positive, and the poet committed himself to preparing the text for printing. But just a few hours after making arrangements, he was invited to reflect on whether it would not be more appropriate to pass on the material he had to "a Ukrainian writer," who would then be entrusted with the task of literary elaboration. From the editor in chief's "intonation" in his reconsideration, there was only "the barbaric custom—which is not adopted anywhere else in the world—that a man of a certain nationality should not write about people of his own nationality, lest he be accused, God forbid, of nationalism." Instead of accepting the proposals to involve Mykola P. Bazhan, Pavlo H. Tychyna, or Maksym T. Rylsky, three of Ukraine's leading poets, Ozerov named the writer Viktor Nekrasov, "a Kyivite, Russian, soldier, well known to the general public, a lover of freedom, with a good reputation and excellent style." The suggestion was welcomed by the editorial staff. Nekrasov accepted and delivered the article in about two weeks.[34]

The critic Lazar Lazarev, editor of *Literaturnaya gazeta*, recalled some stages of the text's drafting. Nekrasov had sought him out at the end of September and asked him to come to Kyiv as soon as possible:

First he took me to the old Jewish cemetery—I didn't know that Babi Yar was in its immediate vicinity. A cemetery is always a sad place, especially an old abandoned cemetery. But that one provided, in a heartbreaking way, a gloomy impression because it did not have the peace and respect due to the deceased: recently knocked-down stelae, shattered tombstones, antisemitic graffiti, a Fascist swastika. "To make it clear that I haven't only written about the past," said Nekrasov. From there we went to Babi Yar. What had once been a ravine was now quite a large artificial lake. It was sunset, it was getting dark, besides us and two elderly people visible in the distance, there was no one. "In the morning and during the day, there were many people," observed Nekrasov, and he explained to me that in those days [of September] the first shootings had taken place. We remained there in silence, I took some photographs, I still have them. I am a terrible photographer, and my shots do not convey the feeling of anguish and grief that image of unnatural and intentional oblivion produced.[35]

The writer had already finished the essay. Lazarev read it shortly after and found "the feeling that, just an hour and a half earlier, that place had inspired in me." He suggested modest corrections and discussed the title at length. Regarding the publication date, the author insisted with particular stubbornness: the article had to come out almost at the same time as Yom Kippur.[36]

At that time, Nekrasov adhered to the dictates of ideology, and for him, too, the victims were "peaceful citizens, innocent of any crime."[37] He therefore avoided naming the Jews massacred as Jews. The only element that could denote their identity was in the beginning: "On the outskirts of Kyiv, in Lukyanovka, behind the old Jewish cemetery, there is a large ravine whose name is now known worldwide: Babi Yar." Eighteen years had passed since the day of one of the most heinous crimes in the history of humanity:

> And here I am in the same place where, in September 1941, thousands of Soviet citizens were savagely murdered, here I am at Babi Yar. Silence. An empty space. On one side of the ravine, houses are being built. At the bottom of the chasm, there is water. Where does it come from? An elderly couple climbs up the slope of the ravine, making their way through the bushes. What are they doing here? They have a son who died in this place. They have come to visit him. . . . I also have a friend who died here. There is no person in Kyiv who does not have a father or a son, a relative, a friend, an acquaintance, . . . who does not rest (no, another term is needed) at Babi Yar.
>
> I am at Babi Yar and, without meaning to, I think of other places where, like here, innocents were killed at the hands of Fascists. Lidice, Oradour-sur-Glane, Oświęcim, Majdanek, Dachau, Sachsenhausen, Ravensbrück, Buchenwald . . . I was at Buchenwald last year. On a high hill overlooking the valley where Weimar lies comfortably, there is a monument. Granite pillars with the names of the countries whose children were tortured in that camp, and on the pillars, a tower. And continuously, on this tower, a bell rings so that what happened here is never forgotten.[38]

Walking through the deserted space now invaded by water, Nekrasov remembered the first commemorative project, the "monument-museum" conceived by Oleksandr Vlasov ("severe, simple, pyramid shaped") and the "sketches for a fresco" that Vasyl Ovchynnikov had worked on in preparation for the "interior design of the place." Where had those drawings gone, and why were they abandoned? He knew that the city's administrators wanted to "fill" the chasm. They wanted, in other words, to "cover" Babi Yar, "level" the ground, build a stadium there, and set up a public park. "Is it possible? Who could have thought of filling a thirty-meter-deep ravine and then having fun and playing soccer on the site of an immense tragedy? No, it cannot be allowed! When a man dies, he is buried, and a stela is placed on his grave. Is it possible that 195,000 Kyevans, brutally killed at Babi Yar, Syrets, Darnytsia, the Kirill-ovka hospital, the Lavra, the Lukyanovka cemetery, do not deserve such a respectful act?"[39]

Why So Much "Ambiguity, Reticence, and Secrecy"?

Nekrasov's intervention had a strong resonance and emotional impact.[40] It provoked favorable reactions not only in civil society but also in some institutions.[41] A few months later, the response from the city administration attributed the inaction to the lack of a general "district restructuring plan." However, the administration promised that within the year, "reforestation work on the slopes" would begin, and "in the very near future" a large green space would be set up. In the center of the park, in accordance with the decision of the republic's government, "a pedestal-obelisk bearing a commemorative plaque in memory of the Soviet citizens tortured to death by the Nazis in 1941" would be installed.[42] However, a London periodical monitoring the living conditions of Jewish communities in Eastern European countries noted that "throughout the discussion, there was no mention of the Jewish victims, nor was there any promise to remember them at the site where their bodies lay buried," even though it had become an important "destination for pilgrimages."[43]

Indeed, there are numerous testimonies from Western visitors who, through their travel reports, helped keep the international public's attention alive during those years, despite the obstacles that Soviet authorities devised to hinder access to Babi Yar. Most often, these visitors were delegations from Jewish Diaspora communities (especially American), who, at the end of their missions in the USSR, raised thorny issues such as the absence of Jewish schools, the limitation of literary and theatrical heritage, the closure of synagogues, the scarce prospects for emigration, and finally, the obstacles placed on attempts to pay homage to the dead. Some individuals also took explicit positions, urging the authorities to erect a monument.[44]

Edward Crankshaw, author of a famous biography of Nikita Khrushchev, was authorized to visit Kyiv for the first time in 1955. He immediately asked the local director of Intourist (Inostrannyj Turist [Foreign Tourist]), the state agency responsible for foreign travelers in the USSR, to take him to Babi Yar. "At first, [the director] pretended he had never heard of Babi Yar. But when I insisted, he said, 'Why do you want to go and look at a lot of dead Jews? If you're interested in Jews you'll see more than enough live ones on the streets!'"[45] Similarly, in August 1959 writer Joseph B. Schechtman tried to break through the "ambiguity, reticence, and secrecy" that seemed to surround the chasm. Faced with the guide's refusal, he then asked to be taken to the Lukyanivka cemetery, but in vain. Arriving at the site on his own by using public transport, he found that, unlike the Orthodox cemetery, the Jewish cemetery was in a state of complete neglect: "There was no office at the entrance, which appeared dilapidated. The burial records were gone. Paths and trails were overrun with weeds and brushwood. Hundreds of gravestones were displaced, overturned, shattered, as were the railings. There was not a living soul around, not a single visitor, and, of course, no one to provide information."[46] Schechtman finally found an escort willing, despite initial reluctance, to listen to his requests:

> After a short drive, the escort stopped and said in a low voice: "Here is your Babi Yar." I realized he was right, there was nothing to see. It was just a steep embankment without recognizable landmarks. A vast, empty, devastated, and desolate plot of land stretched out, uncultivated, neglected, covered with bushes and weeds, left to waste, terrible in its solitude. There was nothing alive around. The ruins of the Warsaw Ghetto, as I had seen them in August 1947, came to mind. I don't know how long I stayed there. "So this is Babi Yar? Is this all?" My guide mumbled: "What did I tell you? Haven't you had enough? Let's go! It's unhealthy to stay too long in a place like this. Let's go!"[47]

In the same year, the journalist Patricia Blake provided an account, the result of a two-month stay in the USSR, on the intensification of the antisemitic campaign.[48] In a climate increasingly tense due to the evident hostility of the authorities—as evidenced by the closure of synagogues; impediments to the production and sale of matzos, kosher foods, books, and prayer shawls; the denunciation through the press of the misdeeds of the Jews ("thieves" and "enemies of socialism"); and discriminatory measures in access to education, professions, or services provided to citizens—acts of hooliganism and violence multiplied. In particular, "no Jewish life of any kind is permitted in Kiev, except that which is contained in the hearts of the people."[49] Blake managed to find a willing taxi driver and reached Babi Yar despite everyone denying its existence:

> At Babi Yar, I found a garbage dump and a few scruffy trees on the edge of a ravine. I walked for a while among tin cans and pop bottles until I met an elderly

man who was dumping refuse from a truck. Did he know where the massacre had taken place? He stopped working and led me to an open space. "Here," he said gesturing vaguely, "the Germans and the Ukrainian collaborators set up desks. When they had taken the Jews' papers and clothes, they lined them up on the edge of the ravine and shot them. They killed 96,000 in three days."[50]

Since there was no monument, "except in the form of garbage," and since the victims' bodies had been "left here to rot," the elderly man suggested that Blake visit the nearby Jewish cemetery. The road leading to it was "a stream of mud," and the journalist barely managed to walk it. She knew that Jews take great care of their graveyards. But here the place was "wild and untended," with fallen tombstones, broken fences, and weeds everywhere. Blake questioned some young people she met there about the reasons for the neglect but couldn't overcome their reluctance and mistrust. Only later did she learn that the previous year, "a mob of Ukrainians" had desecrated the cemetery on the anniversary of the massacre, vandalizing the graves and leaving inscriptions such as "We are starting with the dead and will continue with the living."[51]

"That Moving, Viscous Mire"

But how to explain the "stream of mud" that Patricia Blake encountered?

Great investments were made in the reconstruction of Kyiv. According to the guidelines of the ten-year plan for 1951–60, the reconstruction was not only about repairing the damage caused by the conflict, ensuring development that met the needs of modern life, and giving the city a face suitable to the ideological and cultural aspirations of socialist construction but also about meeting the housing needs of a population constantly growing due to both rising birth rates and the predictable increase in internal migration. It was necessary to provide for the construction of entire neighborhoods, the preparation of infrastructure (from paved roads to the water supply system and gas pipelines), and the expansion of equipped green areas (parks and gardens). But above all, it was considered urgent to carry out a radical modernization of the entire urban road network to improve connections between the different areas of the city, an indispensable prerequisite for any further expansion. Consequently, the tram, trolleybus, and bus lines that would have to transport thousands of workers had to be strengthened.[52]

In this context, the authorities decided to level Babi Yar. No one, except Viktor Nekrasov, seemed publicly concerned about the ethical aspects that such a decision entailed. The project was presented in 1950. The leveling began the following year and continued in various sections of the territory until 1961. The manufacturing waste of building material extracted from the area's clay pits, which were intensely exploited, was mixed with water, and the semiliquid debris was poured into the ravine. To prevent the now muddy ground from shifting, a dam was built, with wells and diversion channels for water drainage. The expectation was that the sludge would be deposited and then settle while the water flowed through the embankment's channels. The embankment continued to grow until in a few years it had reached the height of a six-story building: "I went there," recalled Anatoly Kuznetsov later, "and stared in amazement at the lake of mud that swallowed the ashes, bones, piles of tombstones. The water was putrid, green, still, and the pipes that poured that murky [flow of water and mud in suspension] rumbled day and night."[53] By the beginning of 1961, with the planned filling level attained, the completion of the works and the transfer of businesses were scheduled. But since the preparation of the new reservoir had not been completed, the relocation did not take place, and dredging continued despite some clear signs of danger. On 13 March 1961 the catastrophe occurred: the waters from the spring thaw suddenly filled the entire Babi Yar basin, the channels failed to filter them, and the sludge overflowed the embankment, which gave way.[54] The engineers' calculations, which had been ambitiously experimental in nature, proved wrong at that point: the sludge that had been pumped for years had not compacted, and the clay slopes of the ravine had preserved the sludge in its fluid form. A torrent of mud four meters high and twenty meters wide then rushed at high speed over the Kurenivka district below, dragging along people and houses, a tram depot, the hospital, the stadium, and a machinery workshop. "In an instant," wrote Kuznetsov, capturing the calamity in literary terms, "crowds of people were swallowed by the wave. The people in the trams and cars died, probably without having time to understand what had happened. Emerging from that moving, viscous mire, or somehow breaking free from it, was impossible."[55] That same day, the first secretary of the Central Committee of the Communist Party of Ukraine, Petro Shelest, noted in his diary: "I visited the site of the disaster. Horrible situation. Everything was flooded with 2.5–3 meters of water, mud, sand. People took refuge on the roofs of houses, in trees."[56] Physicist Sergei Tiktin, who visited the site about a month later, described the disaster scene as follows: "The traces of the sand are still clearly visible on the slopes of the ravine, indicating the level of the flow. The small private houses at the top remained as if nothing had happened. Of those at the bottom, there was no trace. The flood had cut through those along the path in half, by a quarter, by three-quarters."[57]

The relief efforts were entrusted to a special commission led by the second secretary of the Central Committee of the party, Ivan P. Kazanets, who provided constant updates on the progress of operations to internal bodies. In the last report on record (25 March), the victims numbered 137, but many people were still missing.[58] Another expert commission, led by the president of the Ukrainian Academy of Construction and Architecture, Pavel F. Bakuma, was assigned the task of determining the causes of the incident. Initial findings revealed that it was an "inevitable" disaster due to the negligence and lack of skill with which the work had been carried out. It was true that, without a strong "influx of water from above," the overflow might not have occurred "precisely on 13 March 1961," but it could have happened "later," given that "the stability of the dam had not been adequately ensured." Essentially, events had been "simply accelerated" and would have "happened sooner or later."[59] During its work, conducted between 14 and 19 March, the inquiry commission monitored the operations to clear the debris after the embankment's collapse and checked the methods of removing the soil; the commission also examined design materials and technical documentation and heard the responsible individuals and other personnel from construction companies, as well as witnesses of the flood. The final report established that the disaster was attributable to both "planning errors" that had gone unnoticed "because the project verification and approval procedure had not been followed" and "execution defects in the installation work."[60]

In the immediate aftermath of the dam collapse, the authorities issued no statements. The area was isolated by the militia and closed to traffic, mainly to prevent news about the number of victims from leaking out. Security services, for their part, tightened population controls to prevent anyone from "using the event in an anti-Soviet and provocative manner." One of the first reports (14 March) stated that such episodes had not yet occurred, but it nevertheless reported citizens' discontent and dissatisfaction. Those citizens continued, "in conversations and letters," to discuss the causes and consequences of the incident. In particular, citizens accused the political-administrative apparatus of not having addressed residents' reports and not providing any explanation for what had happened. The same political police report—immediately resorting to its ancient skills of inventing reality by creating another possible scenario to shift responsibility for the event—reported the circulation of disturbing rumors. The vice president of the Jewish community was said to have attributed the upheaval "to the corpses of the Jews shot by the Germans." Other residents of Jewish nationality were said to have shared the idea that "the dead could not endure" the insult and that instead of filling Babi Yar, it was necessary to erect a monument there. In particular, a man in the crowd was said to have publicly stated: "One should not have profaned the memory of those killed here, and that is why the disaster happened."[61] Surveillance of the mail had already, by that date, identified fifteen letters, extensively cited in the report, that provided the most diverse and sometimes implausible details about the disaster.[62]

The agencies responsible for maintaining public order continued for weeks to collect data on citizens' reactions. They gathered expressions of public sentiment about the reasons for the water's overflow from the reservoir; accusations of insufficient supervision directed at the authorities; and complaints in which the resignation of the president of the city council's executive committee, Oleksiy Y. Davydov, was even requested.[63] The absence of official statements contributed to giving rise to the most uncontrolled rumors, fueling the belief that the authorities were hiding the severity of the disaster and the reality of thousands of victims.[64]

The extent of the "exaggerations" was such that the security services found themselves having to advise various party or corporate organizations, public bodies, and educational institutions to "carry out work to clarify matters among the population."[65] In particular, the rumor continued to circulate that, through the flooding, Babi Yar had "taken revenge" for the blood of the Jews. On the one hand, there were those who judged the incident "as a divine punishment inflicted on the Kyiv authorities for deciding to fill the ravine of memory and build a park with bars and dance halls on the bones of the Jews"; on the other hand, there were those who, while agreeing with the idea of punishment, attributed the disaster instead to "the greed manifested by the decision to save on drainage, despite the recommendations of hydraulic engineers."[66] There were also many rumors about the consequences of greed ("everyone says it happened because they were digging for gold teeth and rings") and the contempt with which the burial issue was treated ("we covered the bones of the Jews with mud and dirt").[67] But from the moment the incident was linked to the crimes perpetrated at Babi Yar in 1941, a feeling of compassion seemed to make its way among the local population: "It was reported that peasants went to church to light candles and pray for the killed Jews and that in many parish churches Orthodox priests held memorial services and spoke of the victims of the massacre."[68]

At the end of March, an official statement was published to summarize the results of the government investigation and report on the measures taken to secure the area. It mentioned errors made in the design phase and in the execution of the work that were in clear violation of technical standards, and it provided information on the considerable material damages, the organization of the rescue efforts, and, for the first time, the number of victims: "In the district of the incident, 145 people died. Of the 143 injured admitted to city hospitals, as of 30 March, 84 have been discharged. The remaining are still receiving medical treatment."[69] However, as the security services immediately found, rumors about the death toll being grossly underestimated continued to circulate.[70] The same statement announced that those responsible for the disaster would be subjected to criminal prosecution.[71] The trial took place between 2 and 24 August 1961 at the regional court of Kyiv. The charges referred to the violation of article 165/2, abuse of power or official misconduct causing serious consequences.[72]

"Any Ordinary Place"

The almost complete erasure of Babi Yar did not put an end to the pilgrimages. Writer and journalist Ben Zion Goldberg, who had immigrated to the United States as a boy in 1908 and who became the son-in-law of Sholem Aleichem, arrived in Kyiv in 1962, having already visited in 1937 and 1946. He had been to Babi Yar on his second visit, and now, after sixteen years, he was interested in understanding what initiatives had been taken to commemorate the victims. When he learned from the guide that the ravine had been filled in and leveled and that city officials had simply placed "two tablets with inscriptions," he had an instinctive reaction of anger and refused to "go to the dead."[73] Michael Kaufman, who fled Kyiv when he was a young adult, on the other hand, faced all sorts of difficulties when he tried to reach the site, overcoming more or less clumsy attempts by his companions to prevent access. During his visit to the site he read Tehillim (the book of Psalms) and recited El Male Rachamim, the prayer for the eternal rest of the deceased.[74]

Elie Wiesel left us a brief account of his secular pilgrimage to the place that was not supposed to be part of the Soviet tourist programs in the mid-sixties.[75] In his opinion, in whatever location, the Jewish visitor in Kyiv could not free himself from the feeling that something substantial was being hidden, namely, "the dead souls that populate that seemingly serene landscape, the innocent blood that flows in the veins of that splendid and bloody city." The official guides refused to talk about it: "If you insist, they reply: 'It's not worth the trip, there's nothing to see.' And they are right. It's not worth bothering. You won't discover anything. No monuments, no commemorative plaques. At Babi Yar, the essential is covered up."[76] Wiesel did not miss the wild specificity of the massacre:

Fifty thousand victims? One hundred thousand? Add them up, and you'll get closer to the truth. But in the numbers, one gets confused. Defective accounting. Not like at Auschwitz. At Auschwitz the accounting experts did their work with impeccable precision. There, no. They shot in the crowd. Without counting. . . . Even today, one walks on corpses. From time to time, a mass grave is discovered that is never the last. And so it seems impossible to determine definitively the exact number of victims: it seems that the dead themselves intervene to confuse the calculations and force historians to constantly revise everything.[77]

The writer felt the profound and guilty silence surrounding the most trau-matic event that the Ukrainian capital had ever known. Especially since, with the population as a whole having "seen and heard" but "no one raised a voice in protest, not a single tear was shed," the massacre of the Jews had taken on a public nature: "Stores remained open; sellers and customers chatted about this and that. At the communal school, children learned to read, to count, to play. Life went on. And so did the shooting. Many of those impassive witnesses are still alive. Who knows, maybe some occupy important positions in the high spheres of government and the party. It is better not to cast a shadow: one ends up in a minefield. To avoid offending the guilty, it is wise and prudent not to mention the victims."[78]

Wiesel ended his stay without finding anyone willing to accompany him to Babi Yar:

> Finally, I decided to go there alone. By taxi. I put twenty rubles in the driver's hand. He pocketed the money and, smiling, started the engine. We crossed the city, emerged in the old Jewish quarter of Podil, and circled around a cemetery. The slaughterhouse was two kilometers farther. With a circular gesture of his hand, the driver, still smiling, announced: here it is.
>
> I got out of the car. To look. To search. To murmur the Kaddish, the prayer of the dead. But there was nothing to see. Nothing remained of the massacre. The dead had taken away their shadows, their traces. Beautiful autumn day. Blue sky. Some white clouds slowly moving toward the mountains. Calm and serenity. To the right, a square of buildings. Children were playing, and I won-dered what at. To the left, a road under construction. In the distance, the city with uncertain contours. One hundred fifty thousand corpses don't even make an image. For an hour, nailed to the spot, I scanned the place. A sign, just one. A trace, just one. A drop of blood, just one. A tear. Nothing.[79]

A week later, while in Moscow, the writer learned from some diplomats that other travelers had been prevented from officially visiting Babi Yar and had to resort to private means. But, even more disturbingly, there was no certainty that the drivers had not deceived them by showing them "any ordinary place"; indeed, it seemed that this deception was "common practice" in Kyiv: "Then I recalled my driver's smile: had he deceived me too? The disappointment was short-lived. The driver didn't know, but I saw Babi Yar. The real Babi Yar is different from a name, different from a place. Babi Yar, a poem of mourning, denies and surpasses all geography. Babi Yar is not only at Babi Yar. And despite himself, the driver showed it to me."[80]

Acts of Justice in Poetry, Music, Prose

On 26 July 1966 twenty-two American Reform rabbis, who had arrived in Kyiv as the final stop of a trip to the Soviet Union for purposes of study, gathered in prayer at Babi Yar. The president of the Central Conference of American Rabbis, Jacob J. Weinstein, said these words: "We stand here on hallowed ground where many thousands of our brethren lie buried in a musty pit. We cannot separate their comingled bones. But we can perform an act of poetic justice. We can insist on a special memorial for those who were so singularly selected for this bitter martyrdom." During the service, the poem "Babi Yar" by Yevgeny A. Yevtushenko was recited in English.[1]

"Shame as a Coauthor"

"No monument stands over Babi Yar," begins the first verse of the poem that, in the autumn of 1961, the twenty-nine-year-old Yevgeny A. Yevtushenko wrote in dedication to the massacre of Kyiv's Jews. It was a time, the author writes in his "precocious autobiography," when, once the veil had been ripped open that had so long distorted the truth, people seemed to return to "seeing with their own eyes."[2] The poet had to take a stand because "a poet in Russia is more than a poet":

> Here, in order to be born a poet,
> You must have a proud civil spirit,
> You must be someone who cannot find refuge, cannot find peace.[3]

Yevtushenko had long wished to write verses about antisemitism, but only after visiting Kyiv and seeing "that terrible place" did the intention find a "poetic solution."[4] He had been invited to attend an evening of readings and

had also invited Anatoliy Kuznetsov, who had told him about Babi Yar, to
accompany him to the site:

> When we arrived, I was shocked by what I saw. I knew there was no monument,
> but I expected to find some commemorative sign or some well-kept place. What
> I saw instead was an ordinary dump of foul-smelling compressed garbage. And
> this in the place where tens of thousands of innocent people lay buried: children,
> old people, women.
>
> Before our eyes, trucks continuously dumped heaps of waste on the spot where
> the victims lay. I asked Anatoliy why there was a conspiracy of silence around that
> place. During the war, Ilya Ehrenburg had written verses about it, and Lev Ozerov
> had also written very beautiful ones. So why now a conspiracy of silence? Anatoliy
> Kuznetsov said there were many reasons. But about seventy percent of those who
> participated in the atrocities were Ukrainian policemen who had collaborated
> with the Nazis; the Germans had left them the dirtiest work in the massacres. It
> was thought, therefore, that this somehow undermined the prestige of the Ukrai-
> nian nation. I replied that we [in Russia] also had traitors and that talking about
> it did not weaken the nation but rather absolved it of the crimes committed [by
> individuals]. He replied: "Try explaining that to them. After all, how can a nation
> be considered heroic if it is again suspected of all sorts of guilty acts?"[5]

Moved by the "feeling of shame," Yevtushenko composed "Babi Yar" in a
few hours.[6] He then presented the poem to a number of listeners (among others, poets Ivan F. Drach and Vitaly O. Korotych and literary critic Ivan M.
Dziuba) and read it over the phone to one of his mentors, Alexander P. Mezhi-
rov, who was in Moscow. The next day, he realized he had attracted the attention of the authorities, who seemed ready to cancel the planned public decla-
mation at the October Palace (now the International Center of Culture and
Arts). He was obliged to go to the headquarters of the Central Committee of
the Communist Party of Ukraine and threaten them, saying that if the even
ing's events were canceled, he would denounce that decision as "a lack of
respect for poetry, literature, and the Russian language." And so it was that he
recited "Babi Yar" for the first time before an audience in public: "[At the end]
there was a moment of silence, and it seemed to me that it was an intermina-
ble silence. A small elderly woman crossed the hall, limping, leaning on a cane,
and slowly climbed onto the stage toward me. She said she had been at Babi
Yar, one of the few who managed to crawl out [of the pit] through the corpses.
She bowed before me in a gesture of heartfelt gratitude and kissed my hand.
No one in my life had ever kissed my hand."[7]

It is possible, as some critics have claimed, that Yevtushenko's memories of the evening are imprecise, that he did not read the poem in its entirety—and even that he had not yet finished writing it. But in those verses of that public reading, his audience perceived his will to *tell* the truth.[8] On 16 September 1961 Yevtushenko appeared for a reading in a famous venue of the lyrical tradition, the auditorium of Moscow's Polytechnic Museum. It was his habit to recite his verse from memory, but this time he found himself "so deeply emotional" that he was forced to keep the poem within sight: "When I finished reading the last lines, a deadly silence fell in the hall, and I stood on the podium, clutching the sheet nervously, afraid to look up. . . . At last, I raised my eyes and saw the entire audience on its feet. Then the applause thundered, continuing for roughly ten minutes. There were some who rushed onto the stage to embrace me, to kiss me. I had tears in my eyes."[9]

The hall, wrote Ilya M. Levitas, had lacked the capacity to accommodate all those who wanted to attend the event. Every passageway was packed, and so was the stage, where a space of no larger than one square meter had been left for the poet, who arrived quite late because he'd been unable to make his way through the crowd:

> Yevtushenko read his well-known verses and new ones written after his recent trip to Cuba. However, it was felt that the audience was expecting something unusual. And so, at the end of the second part, Yevtushenko announced: "Now I will read you a poem written after my visit to Kyiv. I have just returned, and you will understand what I am talking about." He pulled out some sheets with the text from his pocket, but I don't think he even looked at them once.
>
> And in the silent hall, the words resounded slowly, clearly: "No monument stands over Babi Yar . . ." In the dead silence, the poet's words echoed like hammer blows: they struck the brain, the heart, the soul. A chill ran up the spine, tears flowed freely from the eyes. In the tomb-like silence of the hall, sobs could be heard.
>
> Halfway through the poem, people began to stand up as if by enchantment, and they listened standing until the end. When the poet concluded with the words "by all the antisemites, as if I were a Jew, and for this reason, I am a true Russian," the hall remained silent for a few moments more. Then it exploded. Literally, exploded. I couldn't find another word to describe what happened. People were jumping, shouting, everyone was in a state of ecstasy, of wild enthusiasm. Shouts resounded: "Zhenya, thank you! Zhenya, thank you!" People who were perfect strangers wept and hugged and kissed one another. And it wasn't just the Jews: the majority of those present, of course, were Russians. But at that moment in the hall, there were neither Jews nor Russians.

There were people who had had enough of lies and enmity, who wanted to free themselves from Stalinism. It was 1961, the famous "thaw" had begun, when the people—after many years of silence—had a chance to speak the truth. The jubilation lasted for quite a while. A passageway formed through which dozens of people offered the poet bouquets of flowers, then they began to hand them up from person to person. The flowers were placed directly on the proscenium at his feet.

"Zhenya, more! Zhenya, more," the crowd shouted as he stood there stunned and confused. Finally, Yevtushenko raised his hand, and the hall fell silent. No one took their seat: everyone stood as they listened to the verses.

And, after the second reading, "Babi Yar" resonated as a memory of the murdered Jews, a condemnation of antisemitism, an execration of the past. For the first time, it was said aloud that those who were shot at Babi Yar were not simply "peaceful Soviet citizens" but Jews. And that they were shot *only* because they were Jews.[10]

The verses were published three days later, almost coinciding with the twentieth anniversary of the massacre.[11] Received as the "cry" of "an angry young Russian," they stirred up one of the most violent storms in the history of Soviet literature.[12] In a private conversation, writer Vasily Grossman commented on the event: "Finally, a Russian man has written that antisemitism exists in our country." He considered the poem to be, as a poem, "barely passable," but what mattered was "the act itself, admirable, even courageous."[13] Yevtushenko denounced the persistence of Judophobia in the country:

The arrogant drunks in the tavern
Reeking of vodka and onion
While I, powerless, am kicked to the ground by a boot
As I beg in vain for mercy from the pogromists.
They shout: "Kill the Jew! Save Russia!"
A shopkeeper beats my mother.[14]

He also identified alternately as an ancient Israelite, as Dreyfus, as a child from Białystok, as Anne Frank.

No monument stands over Babi Yar.
A drop sheer as a crude gravestone.
I am afraid.
     Today I am as old in years
As all the Jewish people.

Now I seem to be a Jew.
. . . .
The wild grasses rustle over Babi Yar.
The trees look ominous, like judges.
Here all things scream silently,
And, baring my head,
Slowly I feel myself turning gray.
And I myself am one massive,
Soundless scream above
The thousand thousand buried here.
I am each old man here shot dead.
I am every child here shot dead.
Nothing in me shall ever forget!
. . . .
In my blood there is
No Jewish blood.
In their callous rage,
All antisemites must hate me
Now as a Jew.
For that reason
I am a true Russian![15]

The poem resounded as a challenge at a time when antisemitism, despite Levitas's conviction that "the people" had finally had the "opportunity to tell the truth" about Babi Yar and that there were "neither Jews nor Russians" in the hall of the Polytechnic Museum, was gaining strength in political and cultural circles that tolerated increasingly frequent acts of vandalism and desecration. In 1958 Patricia Blake had denounced, on the eve of Yom Kippur, the plundering of the Jewish sector of the Baikove Cemetery in Kyiv. Numerous graves were destroyed, and threatening inscriptions were left on many others. The authorities downplayed the incident. The president of the city's executive committee, Oleksiy Davydov, during a visit to the site the following day, promised the municipality's commitment to urgently rebuild the demolished graves and claimed that the devastation was nothing more than the result of Nazi propaganda influence during the occupation.[16] The delegate for religious cults, P. Ya. Vilkhovy, presented a report to the Central Committee of the Communist Party and the Council of Ministers of the Soviet Socialist Republic of Ukraine in which the destruction of thirty-nine tombstones (in eight other cases, photographs of the deceased were shattered) appeared simply as an act of hooliganism akin to a petty theft ("two window curtains and two tablecloths") in the synagogue on Shchekavytska Street during the holidays. Although some in the Jewish community were "inclined to see these acts as manifestations of antisemitism," he assured committee members that even the leaders of the community shared the hypothesis of pure *chuliganstvo* (hooliganism).[17]

In the autumn of 1959, in Malakhovka, a suburb about thirty kilometers from Moscow where around three thousand Jews lived among a population of thirty thousand, there were attacks.[18] At dawn on 4 October, the second day of Rosh Hashanah, a mysterious organization started a wave of violence that ended with the burning down of the synagogue as well as the destruction of the building adjacent to the cemetery where bodies were prepared for burial, resulting in one victim.[19] The authorities tried to deny the facts. Then, especially due to pressure from the Israeli embassy, they were forced to admit that the synagogue had been set on fire.[20] At the same time, they announced that a judicial investigation had been undertaken, resulting in the identification of the culprits: two young members of the Komsomol, who were quickly sentenced to six years in prison. According to Ilya Ehrenburg, the possibility of a public trial was briefly considered. But in the end, it was decided otherwise: "The committee for religious cults informed some foreigners of the sentence, while Soviet citizens, even those living in Malakhovka, knew nothing of the trial."[21] The episode was, in any case, considered "a case of hooliganism carried out by an isolated group of individuals and not an organized action."[22] In reality, it was one of numerous antisemitic attacks: the cemetery had already been repeatedly violated, the synagogue had suffered damage several times, and there had even been an attempt, foiled by some of the faithful, to set fire to the Torah scrolls. The night before the most recent devastations, hundreds of flyers signed BZhSR—an abbreviation for "Bej zhidov, spasaj Rossiyu" (Beat the Jews, save Russia), one of the most common slogans during the pogroms of the czarist period—were posted on the doors of buildings and public offices.[23]

In Yevtushenko's verses on Babi Yar, as we have seen, there was a reference to "the pogromists." It also appears that, during a public reading held before the publication of the poem, the poet had included a stanza about antisemitic feelings that arise among Russians "in the fumes of alcohol."[24] But even earlier, in the composition "Ochotnorjadec" (The pogromist, 1957), still unpublished at that time, he had unequivocally evoked the antisemitic mob:

He drank and drank alone, the merchant.
He poured more liquor into his glass
And with a fork, grim and menacing,
Picked up an onion ring.

He laughed loudly, groped the cook,
Slipped his hand under her knit skirt,
And his lacquered boots shone,
While upstairs, in an elegant tailcoat,
His daughter performed a polonaise.
He laughed loudly, he was no layabout. . . .
He was happy to distract himself this way,
To be able to slip his hand under the skirt.
He had already devoured Russia
But wanted to finish devouring it.
He got up drunk and strong,
Drank kvass and was ready for anything,
And to save Russia,
He went out to beat up students and Jews.[25]

"The Spit of a Pygmy"

When Yevtushenko went to the editorial office of *Literaturnaya gazeta* to propose the publication of "Babi Yar," it elicited great emotion among the newspaper staff but also doubts about the possibility of publishing it in the organ of the Union of Soviet Writers. After a couple of hours of waiting, the author was summoned by the editorial director, Valery A. Kosolapov:

"Nice verses," said the editor in chief, enunciating each word and staring at me inquisitively, as if to test me. I knew from experience that when they start saying that, they usually don't publish the verses. "And correct verses," continued the editor in chief, again pausing at each word. And at that moment, I was certain they wouldn't go through. "We'll publish them," said the editor in chief. And the usual mischievous look disappeared from his eyes: now his gaze was full of seriousness. "I am a Communist," he said to me. "Do you understand? How could I not publish them? Of course, anything can happen, keep that in mind."[26]

In fact, the official bodies in charge of selecting and administering everything related to the cultural sphere immediately sent a very negative report on the content of the freshly printed poem to the leadership of the Communist Party, a sort of distillation of the criticisms that, from that moment on, would accompany the official statements of position:

In his recollection of the mass murders of Jews at Babi Yar, Yevtushenko sees only a manifestation of the age-old persecution and oppression of the Jewish people, completely omitting the fact that it was precisely Fascism, a product and instrument of the reactionary bourgeoisie, that was responsible not only for the bloody crimes at Babi Yar but also for the extermination of millions of people of other nationalities.

There isn't a word about the Fascists in the verses. On the contrary, it speaks of the Russian people on behalf of whom antisemites conducted pogroms against Jews. Instead of arousing hatred against Fascism and the Fascist ideology that was reawakened in West Germany, Yevtushenko follows a line of artificial, historically false parallels and makes ambiguous allusions. And although he specifies that "the Russian people are essentially internationalist," the verses remain equivocal from start to finish. . . .

Yevtushenko, a Russian poet, proclaims that he wants to defend the martyred Jewish people, to fight contemporary antisemitism, to be ready to suffer for the Jews. In conclusion, he affirms that "The Internationale" will resound victorious only when "the last antisemite on earth is forever buried." . . .

Aimed at fomenting nationalist prejudices that are offensive to the memory of Soviet citizens who died in the fight against Fascism, Yevtushenko's verses objectively possess a provocative character. Their publication must be considered a serious political error on the part of *Literaturnaya gazeta*.[27]

A few days after the publication, the poet Alexei Ya. Markov improvised denigrating verses ("But what kind of true Russian are you!") accusing Yevtushenko of having "forgotten [his] people" and introduced a statement denying the specificity of the event represented in "Babi Yar": "It seems to me . . . to be a Jew"; "I am every old man, every child shot here." He evoked the series to which it needed to be assimilated: "The world shuddered at Babi Yar, / But that was only the first ravine." It would have been necessary to inscribe on stone, "one by one," the names of the millions of young Russians who fell in the war so that they would not be "swept away by the wind" or "defiled by the spit of a pygmy" writing verses. The demand was peremptory: "To excavate the graves" would cause not only suffering but also indignation in those who remained faithful to the spirit of the nation:

As long as even one cosmopolitan
Treads the cemeteries
I will say: "I am Russian, people!"
And the ashes pulse in my heart.[28]

In a long review, literary critic Dmitry V. Starikov—although he did not deny the atrocities suffered by Jews at the hands of the Nazis—recalled the vast number of places that had been scenes of massacres similar to Babi Yar and the boundless number of mass graves where "the earth moved" from the struggles of the dying, barely covered by a thin layer of sand. The Nazis had insulted *all* nationalities, not just the Jewish one. For this reason, evoking antisemitism was nothing more than a "provocation" to be answered with the weapons of doctrine:

> Why, right now, in 1961, did Yevgeny Yevtushenko take up this theme? Did he perhaps recall Babi Yar to warn the world against Fascism? Had he perhaps understood that he could not remain silent after hearing the hysterical complaints of West Germany's revanchist bastards? Did he want to remind some of his peers of the exploits, heroic acts, and great sacrifices of their fathers? . . . Nothing of the sort. In the face of the steep ravine of Babi Yar, all the Soviet writer found here was a theme for verses about antisemitism! And reflecting today on the victims—the old man shot, the child shot—he thought only that they were Jews. This was the essential for him, this was the most important and burning issue![29]

Starikov tried to rely on a Jewish authority. He indeed drew from war correspondences and from the poem that Ilya Ehrenburg had dedicated to the Kyiv massacre, words that served to show that class internationalism—in the face of the very "nature of Fascism," indifferent to the national identities of those it wanted to annihilate—ruled out the possibility of affording privilege to the sufferings of one people over those of another people. Therefore, Yevtushenko was responsible, with his "comparisons and 'recollections,'" for fomenting "reverse racism," discrediting the "solid and monolithic friendship" of the Soviet peoples, "insulting the triumph of the Leninist policy of nationality." In his "Babi Yar" there was a clear deviation from Communist ideology; therefore, *Literaturnaya gazeta*, as an organ of Soviet writers, was called upon to protect the honor of the homeland.[30] But the chauvinism of the detractors was not well received. Markov's verses and Starikov's article indeed generated a "wave of public indignation."[31]

At that time, Ehrenburg was in Italy but was immediately informed of the reckless abuse of his name. It was the poet Boris Slutsky who communicated to him on 30 September that Starikov's "unworthy article" had had "widespread resonance," and Slutsky suggested that Ehrenburg react "immediately and in an authoritative forum."[32] On 3 October the writer sent a letter to *Literaturnaya gazeta* to clarify that Starikov had expressed thoughts completely contrary to Ehrenburg's own, but the culture section of the Central Committee of the Communist Party refused to authorize the publication of the letter.

On 9 October, through the mediation of one of Khrushchev's closest collaborators, Vladimir S. Lebedev, Ehrenburg proceeded to send a message to the first secretary to officially dissociate himself and explain how the wide international echo of Markov's verses and Starikov's article placed Ehrenburg in a difficult situation, associating him with antisemitic positions that were clearly aimed at reviving the climate of the "fight against 'cosmopolitanism.'" He therefore requested support in attempting to "dampen the latest anti-Soviet campaign in the West," showing publicly that he was being allowed to refute the opinions falsely attributed to him.[33] He thus succeeded in having a brief but nevertheless explicit note published a few days later declaring that he had learned only belatedly of Starikov's article, since he had been abroad, and that he felt obliged to clarify that it quoted "arbitrarily" from his articles and poems, "twisting them to fit *his* thinking and contradict *my own*."[34] A few years later, Ehrenburg spoke even more clearly of his intentions, writing that he knew perfectly well that at Babi Yar, during the long period of occupation, people of different nationalities were killed. But "in the popular memory," the days of September 1941 remained when the victims ("all the Jews who hadn't managed to leave Kyiv—elderly, sick, women, children") were selected for slaughter on a racial basis. It was true that the Germans had killed "Russians or Ukrainians suspected of being part of the underground resistance, of being in contact with partisans, of sheltering Jews or Communists, of violating ordinances." But the Jews were killed "just because they were Jews, all without distinction, even the old and newborns." Yevtushenko's verses had thus rendered a "great service" because they had finally affirmed "the right of Kyiv's Jews to a stone slab."[35]

There were several texts composed in support of Yevtushenko that, following a custom of the time, circulated mostly in handwritten and anonymous form. Notable among them are the satirical verses of Samuil Ya. Marshak, who juxtaposed the name of the Communist Alexei Markov with that of Nikolai E. Markov, member of the Black Hundreds, founder of the Union of the Russian People, and instigator of pogroms under Czar Nicholas II. The Communist Markov could not restrain himself from saying, here is "a non-Jewish poet," a poet who had said he was proud to be a true Russian, who "felt sorry for the dead Jews." This man, "seething with rage," as Marshak writes, had thus unleashed "the iron fist of the thug, endowing it with the form of a verse."[36]

In the immediate aftermath, however, there were relatively few individuals willing to stand up in support of Yevtushenko. Director Mikhail I. Romm, in a famous speech delivered in November 1962 during a meeting of cinema and theater workers, defined the publication of Starikov's article and Markov's poem in the pages of *Literatura i zhizn'* as "our shame." He had been in Italy and the

United States shortly before that, and he was bewildered by the press's requests to comment on the "new wave of antisemitism in the USSR." He thus realized that what had most forcibly struck Western public opinion was not so much Yevtushenko's poem as the unrestrained reactions against it.[37] General David A. Dragunsky, who prioritized his Soviet citizenship over his Jewish nationality, even found himself forced to address the issue in a press conference during an official visit to France. After criticizing Yevtushenko for "diminishing the role played by the Russian people in saving Jewish lives," Dragunsky stated that "violent language" had been used against Yevtushenko.[38]

The poem "Babi Yar" was welcomed, regardless of its literary value, as a manifestation of a new style that not only rejected the "primitive and reactionary" way in which "Russian nationalism" expressed itself but also violated the "conspiracy of silence" observed by the Soviet regime on the specific issue of the extermination of the Jews.[39] Despite the hostile climate and the feelings of aversion that some attempted to arouse in the population (Yevtushenko found the word "Jew" carved into his car), the verses had great civil resonance, especially among young people (a Komsomol chapter offered the poet bodyguards for personal protection), and inspired a broad solidarity movement.[40] In the institutions of the Jewish community, these verses were received with such favor that some Western newspapers reported that they were recited "in synagogues as a prayer."[41] Public readings were attended by passionately devout readers, and listeners recited the composition aloud in time with the poet. Journalist Patricia Blake, present at an evening held at the Polytechnic Museum in Moscow in the summer of 1962, got the impression that Yevtushenko's popularity had formed largely "outside the domain of the literary." As talented as he was, it was the "occasional audacity of the subjects," particularly "the protest against anti-Semitism," that contributed to the formation of his "national and international reputation."[42]

"'Represent[ing]' in Music the Problem of Conscience"

It is fair to say that Yevtushenko's verses would not have achieved such wide resonance if they had not been included in Dmitri Shostakovich's Symphony No. 13 in B-flat minor (op. 113, subtitled *Babi Yar*) for bass soloist, male choir, and orchestra.

It was Isaak D. Glikman who shared the newly published text with Shostakovich on 20–21 September 1961, and the composer was so disturbed by it that he decided to immediately transform it into a vocal symphonic poem.[43] He was convinced that the combination of "music and words" facilitated the understanding of what the composer, usually communicating through the art of sound alone, intended to convey, thus preventing any "misunderstanding" of the message.[44] There were considerations of civil engagement behind this choice: Poems such as "Babi Yar" and "Nasledniki Stalina" (The heirs of Stalin), printed in hundreds of thousands of copies and read by millions of people, brought unexpressed truths to individual consciousness and made an important contribution to the moral progress of society. Anyone who wanted to read Yevtushenko could now do so "quietly, legally, without having to look around, without fear": They had only to go to a bookstore, a newsstand, or a library.[45]

The Jewish theme, driven by motivations that were not purely musical, played an important role in Shostakovich's work.[46] It harked back to the understanding that Jews, in a sort of "latter-day return to the Middle Ages," had become "the most persecuted and defenseless group in Europe." For this reason, the composer had turned them into a kind of "symbol" of all "human weakness and helplessness." After the war, he tried to pour this sentiment into his music: "Many had heard of Babi Yar, but it took Yevtushenko's poem to truly make them understand what had happened there. A memory that the Germans first and the Ukrainian government later tried to erase. But following the publication of Yevtushenko's work, it became clear that this episode would never be forgotten again. That's the power of art. People knew about Babi Yar even before the poet wrote about it, but [everyone] remained silent. And when they read the poem, the silence was broken. Art dissolves silence."[47] Assigning to art the task of bringing forth what has been repressed would have found critics ready to invoke "other and nobler goals" of creativity: "beauty, grace, the sublime." But Shostakovich had no intention of giving up the idea of music that embodied "tragedies, victims, the dead."[48] The so-called war symphonies were a reaction to the Nazi attack. However, it was necessary to broaden the "theme of invasion" and strike at other "enemies of humanity":

> I feel endless pain for those killed by Hitler. But the pain I feel for those killed on Stalin's orders is no less. I suffer for all those who were tortured, executed, or starved to death. And in our country, before the war with Hitler began, there were millions of them. The war brought great new waves of suffering and destruction, but I for one have certainly never forgotten the terrible years that preceded the war. That is what all my symphonies are about, starting from the Fourth and including the Seventh and the Eighth.
>
> I have nothing against calling the Seventh the Leningrad Symphony. But it is *not* a symphony about Leningrad under siege. It's about the Leningrad that Stalin starved and Hitler destroyed. Most of my symphonies are tombstones. Far too many people have died and been buried in places unknown to anyone.

Unknown even to their families. That happened to too many of my friends. Where should we place a memorial plaque for Meyerhold or Tukhachevsky? Only music can do that. I wish I could write a symphony for each victim, but that would be impossible. It's why I dedicate all my music to them.

I never stop thinking about the victims. And in almost all my major works, I attempt to summon up their memory. The conditions of the war years were actually favorable, as the authorities at the time were less restrictive about music and really didn't care if that music had dark tones. But later, all and any suffering was attributed to the war, as if it were only during the war that people were tortured and killed.[49]

Initially, Shostakovich conceived the work as a cantata. In contrast with his usual practice, he started writing a piano score and then on 21 April 1962 completed the orchestral score, asking the poet for permission to set "Babi Yar" to music. Upon receiving Yevtushenko's authorization, Shostakovich admitted that he had already done so and invited the poet to his home to hear it:

What a pity that [Shostakovich's] performance was not recorded. It was truly extraordinary. He sang in his hoarse voice. When he reached the line "It seems to me that I am Anne Frank," he burst into tears. The music here transitioned from an epic requiem to a lyricism typical of springtime. I was overwhelmed. I have no musical expertise. Some of my poems had previously been set to music, but the music almost never matched the melody I heard with my inner ear while writing the poem. I hope this doesn't sound immodest, but if I knew how to write music, I would have written it exactly as Shostakovich did. It seemed that he had pulled the melody out of my innermost being, as if by magical telepathy, and then fixed it in the form of musical notes. That was how I felt. He astonished me with his deep interpretation of the poem. His music made the poem greater, more significant, more powerful. In a word, it became a much better poem.[50]

Toward the end of May, Shostakovich decided to add other compositions to the cantata. He wrote Isaak Glikman: "A small volume of Yevtushenko's verses [*Vzmach ruki* (A gesture of the hand)] inspired me to write a symphony in which Babi Yar would be the first or second movement."[51] The symphony was completed on July 20.[52] It included the poems "Jumor" (Humor, 1960), "V magazine" (In the store, 1956), and "Kar'era" (Career, 1957), which became the second, third, and fifth movements, respectively.[53] The musician, attracted by the poet's "thought and humanity," also proposed that he write verses about Stalinist terror.[54] Among those Shostakovich received, he chose for the fourth movement (as more in line with his expectations despite "the length and a bit of verbosity") "Strachi" (Fears, 1962), which he revised in collaboration with the author.[55] The poem denounced the effect of the 1930s Stalinist repression upon human character and described the process of liberating individual citizens from the traumatizing experiences they had lived through: "Fears are dying in Russia."[56]

The war brought great sorrows and made life very difficult. Much pain, many tears. But before the war, life had been even more difficult because at that time everyone had been alone with their pain.

Before the conflict, there was probably not a single family in Leningrad that hadn't lost *someone*, a father, a brother, or if not a relative, at least a dear friend. There was no one who didn't have *someone* to mourn, but it had to be done in silence, under the covers, lest anyone notice. Everyone feared each other, and the pain and grief oppressed and suffocated us.

I too was suffocated by it. I had to write about it, I felt it was my responsibility, my duty. I had to write a requiem for all those who had died, who had suffered. I had to describe the horrific killing machine and raise my voice against it in protest. But how could I do it? At the time, I was constantly under suspicion, and the critics kept track of how many of my symphonies were in major keys and how many in minor keys. All of this filled me with distress and stripped me of the desire to compose.

Then the war broke out, and sorrow and grief spared no one. We could talk about it, we could cry openly, weep for our lost loved ones. People were no longer afraid of tears.[57]

The fourth movement of the symphony developed on these verses:

Fears are dying in Russia
. . . .
I remember them in power and strength
At the court of triumphant lies:
Fears slipped everywhere like shadows,
Penetrated every floor.
. . . .
The secret fear of someone's denunciation,
The secret fear when they knock at the door.

And the fear of talking to the foreigner?
A foreigner, you say? What about just talking with your wife?[58]

In a letter sent to Yevtushenko, Shostakovich explained that he had chosen "Strachi" to "restore civil rights" to conscience:

> After reading "Babi Yar," a kind of rebirth occurred in me. When I started read-
> ing your book *A Gesture of the Hand* and decided to continue working, I simply
> couldn't tear myself away from the sheet of paper. It had been a long time since
> anything of the sort had happened to me. . . . But today your verses arrived, and
> I am once again at the mercy of a debt, a debt that I absolutely must pay, a debt
> to my conscience. In short, I am grateful to you for this. . . .
>
>   It seems appropriate to dedicate a few words to conscience. We have forgot-
> ten about it, but it is essential to remember it. We must rehabilitate conscience,
> restore its civil rights, offer it a decent living space in the human soul. When I
> finish the Thirteenth Symphony, I will bow at your feet because you have helped
> me "represent" in music the problem of conscience.[59]

Generally, Shostakovich preferred not to talk about his music and, above all, preferred not to offer indications for interpreting it. Shortly after finishing his Thirteenth Symphony, however, he confided to writer Marietta Shaginjan that what had always caught his attention was "the behavior of the individual as a citizen." It was precisely the issue of "civil ethics" that led him to Yevtush-enko's poetry and to use it in his latest work. Among the five compositions he had chosen, none dealt with the theme of courage. However, Shaginjan com-mented, if one tried to grasp the effect it had on the listener, the entire sym-phony revealed itself to be "a lofty song about human courage, a powerful appeal to civic nobility."[60]

Yevtushenko's reaction when he heard Symphony No. 13, performed on the piano by the composer just for him, was one of great surprise. He was particu-larly struck by the choice of texts that had seemed to him "completely dispa-rate." In the volume, they were stand-alone units. He could never have imag-ined fusing together the requiem form of "Babi Yar," with its rhetorical conclusion, and the graphic structure of the melancholic stanzas of "V maga-zine," about Russian women standing in line, dropping with fatigue, or the painful evocation of the feeling of fear and the playful, antibureaucratic tones of "Jumor" or "Kar'era." Especially unexpected was the effect of "Strachi," as Shostakovich had interpreted "the poem in his own way, giving it a depth and penetration it previously lacked." The musician, "by linking all those verses," managed to reveal to the poet "a greater school of composition," making him feel that "in art there are no elements that cannot be assembled," that "one must have courage and attempt to bring together things that might seem incompatible."[61] From listening to the work, Yevtushenko thus got the impression that if he—"a total ignoramus from a musical point of view"—had "suddenly acquired hearing," he would have written "absolutely the same music." The reading was "so precise in tone and sense" that the composer seemed to have "invisibly entered" the poet and "composed the music at the very moment the verses were born."[62] At the same time, he had "never seen a man so similar to his own overwrought fate" and who expressed it with a body that "shook and twisted." He appeared both "vulnerable" and "powerful" in that way, and "without pretending to be so, he accepted the burden of protecting all those who were more defenseless than him."[63]

"Sometimes Even Silence Is Equivalent to Lies"

In the fall of 1962 Shostakovich proposed to a select group of colleagues and friends, including conductor Kirill P. Kondrashin and composers Aram I. Khachaturian, Moisey Vainberg (Mieczysław Weinberg), Revol S. Bunin, and Yuri A. Levitin, that they attend a performance. They were all forewarned that it was an "unusual work for a symphonic cycle in five parts." According to Shostakovich himself, it was the five poems that made it a "symphony" marked by a "unified thought."[64]

There were quite a number of difficulties, and especially numerous defections, that plagued the preparation of the first public performance. Conductor Yevgeny A. Mravinsky, who was one of Shostakovich's closest interpreters and who had worked closely with him on several difficult occasions, declined the assignment.[65] He was replaced by Kondrashin, who had a Russian father and a Jewish mother.[66] Ukrainian bass Borys R. Hmyria, an artist the composer especially admired and considered particularly suitable for singing the new opus, refused to be involved in any way.[67] In proposing that Yevtushenko collaborate with him, keenly aware of how uncertain it was that the theme might be widely accepted, especially in Ukraine, Shostakovich tried to defend the poet from the accusations of his own critics: "It is true that there are people who consider 'Babi Yar' to have been a failure on Yevtushenko's part. I cannot agree with them in any way. His great patriotism, his burning love for the Russian people, his genuine internationalism have entirely won me over, and I 'translated' or, as they say now, 'attempted to translate' all these feelings into a musical composition. For that reason, I would very much like 'Babi Yar' to be heard in the best possible interpretation."[68] On 16 August Hmyria communicated his decision to Shostakovich. He had had a "consultation" with the Ukrainian authorities and had been informed that the Communist Party did not approve of the musical composition based on Yevtushenko's poetry. Therefore, Hmyria would be unable to take part in the performance.[69]

Even Bolshoi Theater soloist Aleksandr F. Vedernikov, recommended to Shostakovich by soprano Galina P. Vishnevskaya, declined the invitation.[70] Bass singer Viktor T. Nechipailo, who had agreed to perform as a soloist, failed to show up for the dress rehearsal because he had suddenly been "conscripted" for the staging of an opera at the Bolshoi Theater, where he was a member of the staff.[71] He was replaced at the last minute by the young Vitaly A. Gromadsky. Finally, on the eve of the symphony's premiere, Kondrashin himself received strong pressure from the Russian Republic's minister of culture, Alexey I. Popov, to eliminate the first movement from the performance. The conductor avoided mentioning it to Shostakovich but refused to allow himself to be intimidated, replying that the work had been "conceived as an indissoluble whole." If a part were canceled, the performance would be irreparably compromised. The consequences would be even more severe if the first movement, which everyone was "already aware of," were suppressed; it would only cause "great turmoil" and "utterly needless curiosity."[72] On such a fraught eve of performance, it is hardly surprising that the composer should have confided to his friend Isaak Glikman: "If after the symphony the public jeers and spits at me, don't defend me, I will endure everything."[73]

Symphony No. 13 was performed by the Moscow State Philharmonic Orchestra on 18 December 1962, the day after Nikita Khrushchev's famous meeting with four hundred representatives of literature and the arts, including Yevtushenko and Shostakovich. It was an occasion to bring the greatest resonance to the campaign against formalism and abstract art and to manifest a firm intent to curb the growing influence of artists inclined to creative thinking and the autonomy of aesthetic research.[74]

The Central Committee secretary, Leonid F. Ilyichev, argued in the introductory report against the propriety of performing the symphony. He questioned whether it was legitimate to present antisemitism as a theme of "extreme seriousness and topicality," given that the law categorically prohibited any manifestation of it: "There are no dissenting opinions in the party. Antisemitism is a revolting phenomenon; the party has fought, fights, and will continue to fight against all its proponents." The verses Shostakovich had chosen for the first movement were, in Ilyichev's view, formally correct. But by adding the resonance of musical accompaniment, wasn't there a risk, in a country that had lost twenty million people during the war "representing all the peoples of the Union," of provoking a "reverse reaction" to the one desired? "No problem exists," warned Ilyichev, "but evoking it will create a problem."[75]

Khrushchev intervened to reiterate that at Babi Yar not only Jews, as Yevtushenko's verses implied, but also Gypsies and, above all, Slavs were killed. The premise was inconclusive because it lumped together different kinds of events, but it did not allow for rebuttals ("this is certain"), as the rhetorical form of the clause assumed a repetitive response of the axiom. "If we were now to perform the arithmetic of which peoples were exterminated to a greater extent, Jews or Slavs, those who claim the existence of antisemitism would see that more Slavs have been killed than Jews. This is certain. So why make distinctions, why sow discord? What purpose do those who raise the issue pursue?" The first secretary then informed the audience about the episode that gave rise in September 1945 to the Kyiv pogrom, even though he placed it at an earlier date and reduced its scope, attributing credit to the city authorities for having prevented violence. Concerning the determination of Jewish quotas in the party's leading bodies, he energetically affirmed that it should not be thought of as a discriminatory measure bearing the distinguishing features of antisemitism but rather as a legitimate and necessary criterion in order to curb the excessive role played by the Jewish component. Moreover, he hoped that Poland and Hungary, too, would initiate a rebalancing process in the party's structure to prevent any automatic identification of Judaism with Bolshevism. Evoking antisemitism, as Yevtushenko had done with poetry and Shostakovich was now doing with music, was a dangerous step heralding unpredictable popular reactions. The proposed model was now consolidated: "One can write something against antisemitism, only thereby to nurture antisemitism."[76] In the attempt to "restore justice," one ended up favoring "chauvinistic" impulses and hindering the affirmation of a society truly free of barriers between peoples.[77]

During the debate, Yevtushenko reiterated his conception of the poetic testimonial: "What was Stalin's main mistake? Believing that truth could be achieved through lies. But lies are not only made of concrete words or actions. Sometimes even silence is equivalent to lies."[78] That is why, according to an unofficial account of the meeting that circulated widely on an international circuit, the poet attempted to read aloud a few lines of "Babi Yar." The intention had been to integrate antisemitism into Stalinism, thereby broadening the spectrum of errors committed by socialism in its development. In response to Khrushchev's censorious reaction ("these verses are out of place here") and his firm refusal to begin a discussion of the topic ("this is not a problem"), Yevtushenko seemed to respond with equal determination:

It *is* a problem, it cannot be denied and cannot be evaded. We often have to deal with it. Anti-Semitism exists. I myself have witnessed it. Moreover, it exists because of people who hold official positions and, in this way, it has assumed an official character. We cannot move towards communism with such a heavy burden as Judeophobia. There can be neither silence nor denial on this; the problem must be solved, and we hope it will be solved. The entire progressive world is watching us, and the resolution of this issue will further enhance our country's authority. By resolution of the issue, I mean the end of anti-Semitism, that is, by initiating judicial procedures against anti-Semites.[79]

"Applause, Like Bright, White Seagulls"

The performance of Symphony No. 13 elicited triumphant ovations at the Moscow Conservatory. The work resounded as a call for the necessity of overcoming the fear that had prevailed during the Stalin era, resulting in the suppression of speech during the Stalin era. It was, the poet recalled, the only symphony in the world that had provoked such contrasting reactions in the audience as tears and laughter, euphoria and reflection.[80] Kondrashin perceived "a jubilation almost akin to a political demonstration." Already at the end of the first movement, the audience had begun "to applaud and cheer uncontrollably." The atmosphere was so tense that the conductor was forced to signal the spectators to calm down, and he immediately started the second movement to avoid putting Shostakovich in an "embarrassing position" and, at the same time, to "avoid altering the form" of the composition.[81] The reminiscences of sculptor Ernst I. Neizvestny focused on the final moments of the concert: "It was magnificent! There was a feeling that something incredible was happening. . . . When the symphony ended, there was no applause, just a strangely long pause. So long a pause that I even thought there might be some sort of conspiracy. Then the audience burst into a frenzied applause." Neizvestny closely observed the reactions of the members of the *nomenklatura*, the ruling elite of the party, present in the hall: "There were many of them, those black beetles, along with their permed ladies. I was sitting right behind this company. The wives, being more emotional and respectful of success—the whole hall had stood up and was applauding standing—stood up as well. And suddenly I saw it: arms reaching up—black sleeves, white cuffs—and every official, placing his arm on his better half's hip, decisively seating her back in her place. They did it as if on signal. What a Kafkaesque scene!"[82]

Young Yevgeny Yu. Sidorov, later a major scholar of Yevtushenko's work, was struck by how the words made the music more fully capable of deeply touching the listener's soul. It was the intonation, more than the rhythm or melody, that achieved the fusion, "as if the poet's verses had been regenerated for another life, now inseparable from the music."[83] To Yevtushenko, who had not fully understood the meaning of the finale ("too neutral, too far outside the boundaries of the text"), the effect seemed overwhelming.[84]

The applause, like bright, white seagulls, took flight from all the arms, and the great genius was onstage beneath that noise, bowing awkwardly. . . . Suddenly he approached the edge of the stage, and he too began to applaud someone, only at that moment I couldn't understand who. The people in the front rows also turned to applaud. I also turned, searching with my eyes for the person to whom the applause was directed. But someone lightly touched my shoulder—it was the director of the conservatory, Mark Borisovich Veksler, beaming and at the same time irritated: "Well then, aren't you going onstage? They're calling you. . . ." You may believe it or not, but, listening to the symphony, I had almost forgotten that the words were mine, so captivated was I by the power of the orchestra and the choir. Truly, the main thing in that symphony is the music. And when I was onstage next to the genius, and Shostakovich took my hand in his—dry, burning hot—I still couldn't believe it was real.[85]

The performance was not broadcast on the radio. There was no official commentary, and the press limited itself to a few brief mentions.[86] The silence of the critics seemed more than eloquent, given the party leadership's position, but there were no immediate consequences. On 20 December a new perfor-mance, again under Kondrashin's baton, was also hailed enthusiastically by the audience, though ignored in silence by the music critics.[87] The only political reaction was an editorial in the Ministry of Culture's newspaper, which, how-ever, did not explicitly mention the symphony:

Under the banners of the fight against the cult of personality, some artists have started rummaging through the garbage in the backyards of our houses and do not want to see what is happening on the front line in the development of our life. . . . This is all the more outrageous when it involves works that are great in form and conception, created by masters of enormous talent, whose voices are particularly authoritative in their professional fields and whose works have long been beloved by a wide audience. . . . What might seem to be a single peculiarity in minor works acquires traits of categorical generalization in important and very complex musical works. If, for example, a composer has written a sym-phony about our shared reality and has placed at its foundation images of dark-ness, the embodiment of evil, sarcastic parody, or mournful pessimism, then, whether the author likes it or not, the result will be to denigrate our life, depict-ing it in a false and distorted way.[88]

There were, of course, expressions of unconditional support for the ruling executive's cultural policies. For example, at the end of December, the assembly of the Union of Composers of Ukraine adopted a resolution titled "Our

Principles Are Loyalty to the Party and the People," which echoed Khrushchev's statements and reiterated the aversion to any form of innovation.[89] But the Symphony No. 13 established itself as a cultural event of enormous significance. It was a work, Kondrashin said, that solicited "civic spirit" and would cause "eternal unrest."[90] Soprano Galina Vishnevskaya described it as "a great victory of art over politics and the party's ideology."[91] Pianist Maria V. Yudina, after attending the second performance, wrote to Shostakovich expressing, alongside her own thanks, the gratitude "of those who already lie dead, because they could not survive a life marked by an endless sequence of torments." She spoke for all the victims of oppression: "I think I can say thank you on behalf of the deceased Pasternak, Zabolotsky, and *countless* other friends; on behalf of the Meyerholds, Michoelses, Karsavins, and Mandelstams, all tortured to death; on behalf of the hundreds of thousands of anonymous 'Ivan Denisoviches'—*impossible to count them all*—of whom Pasternak said: '*We live in torment.*'"[92] In a letter she sent to acquaintances residing in France a few days later, Yudina still hailed the performance as a "great event" and exalted the "archaic language" that the composer had adopted—"perhaps intentionally." Yevtushenko's verses had found themselves "elevated to an enormous height," although they were already "magnificent for their synthesis and precision."[93]

Punitive measures, however, were not long in coming. Shostakovich was ordered to make changes to the score, and in the face of his refusal, repressive measures proliferated: further performances were deferred and canceled, and the entire run of the recording intended for the Soviet market, performed in the recording studios of the Melodiya label, was inexplicably lost, while the rest of the records were sent abroad.[94] Yevtushenko accepted a revision of the text. During a meeting of the party's ideological commission, held at the end of December, he explained that after the meeting with Khrushchev, he had reconsidered the "profoundly friendly" remarks made to him. He had therefore carefully reread his verses and, although finding them "subjectively correct," concluded that in some cases they needed "some clarification and addition." He recalled an incident that had come to his attention during the early months of the Ukrainian occupation when, as a teenager, he wandered through the region: the interrogation, conducted by Einsatzgruppen men, of a Russian peasant woman who had hidden a Jewish girl. Consequently, he had wanted, with "sincerity" and "deep conviction," to include the theme of rescue in the poem. He was convinced that the whole had thus become "more powerful not only politically but also poetically."[95] He made the corrections in January 1963 in spite of the opposition of Shostakovich, who found himself in a very delicate moral situation.[96] On 15 February, a few days after a repeat of the symphony, he wrote to Marietta Shaginjan: "I don't like the new verses. But the situation was this: either the new verses or nothing. It's clear I lacked courage. Yevtushenko, for his part, sent them to me and then went abroad for two months."[97]

The modifications did not substantially alter the musical form of the first movement but seemed to address some of the main objections raised against Yevtushenko. The first correction was intended to dispel the accusation of being a partisan of Jewish nationalism. By introducing the principle of brotherhood among peoples and placing Jews on the same level as other victims, it returned to the starting point. The original lines read:

> It seems to me today that I am a Jew.
> And wandering through ancient Egypt
> And dying crucified: I still have the stigmata.

They were replaced with these lines:

> I stand here,
> As if near a spring,
> From which I draw faith in our brotherhood.
> Because here lie Russians and Ukrainians,
> Lying with Jews at their side.

A second correction introduced a reversal. The defenseless victims disappeared, and the heroes were once again exalted. The original lines read:

> I myself am a silent scream
> Over the many thousands buried.
> I am every old man,
> Every child shot here.

The new version read:

> I think of Russia's deeds,
> That barred the way to Fascism.
> To the last drop of dew
> I feel close to her in all her essence
> And her destiny.[98]

With the text thus revised, the symphony was repeated on 10 and 11 February 1963 at the Moscow Conservatory, once again under Kondrashin's direction. Yevtushenko was in Paris. Interviewed by a French newspaper, he denied yielding to party pressure and, reiterating the motivations offered during the meeting of the Central Committee's ideological commission, clarified that he had made only a modest addition that did not in any way distort the poem's meaning.[99]

In reality, the addition could not at all be described as modest, and the poem had in fact been altered. Shostakovich was fully aware of this, so much so that in the Minsk performance, held in his presence on 19 March 1963, he imposed the original version. The artistic director of the Belarusian State Symphony Orchestra, Vitaly V. Katayev, faced great difficulties casting certain performers (the choir basses), but above all, he encountered a number of obstacles to keeping the score in his hands. He was even obliged to advise each musician to take the sheet music home after the dress rehearsal and to make a copy of it to prevent last-minute issues. The concert was held without a hitch and met with a triumphant reception: "As the symphony ended, there was a silence full of tension in the hall. The audience, gripped by the authenticity of the dramatic scenes and the acute social ideas set forth in the symphony, remained mute. Then the hall exploded with applause. People clapped without moving, acclaiming the composer, who had taken the stage."[100]

The Belarusian journalist Mikalaj Ya. Matukowski sent a detailed report to Leonid Ilyichev on 24 March 1963 to inform him of the audience's reactions:

> Already the first sounds of the symphony divided the hall quite palpably between Jews and non-Jews. The Jews did not hesitate to show their feelings, behaving quite oddly. Some of them cried, while others occasionally scrutinized their neighbors. These glances revealed evident hostility. . . . The other half, of which I was a part, felt a bit uncomfortable, as if we were guilty of something in the eyes of the Jews. Then the feeling of heavy embarrassment turned into a sentiment of protest and indignation. . . . The worst thing, in my opinion, is that people (and I do not distinguish myself from them) who were neither antisemites nor chauvinists before could no longer speak calmly either about Shostakovich's symphony or about Jews. . . . We do not have a "Jewish question," but people like Y. Yevtushenko, I. Ehrenburg, Shostakovich may yet create it. The Thirteenth Symphony is a compelling confirmation of this idea. It breeds the germs not only of a highly dangerous Jewish nationalism but also of a no less dangerous chauvinism: antisemitism.[101]

A review published a few days later in the main Belarusian newspaper— while attributing to the composer the best intentions of a "patriot-artist" and admitting that, at first impact, the music "gripped, moved, shook"—emphasized the "substantial flaws" of the symphony, which had not "fulfilled its social responsibility." In particular, musicologist Ariadna B. Ladygina questioned whether the work's beginning was evidence of "civil courage or a loss of civil discretion." The first movement "artificially" tried to revive the Jewish question, raising issues created by the old class society and now erased in the Soviet civilization of equality. Shostakovich had lost one of his main qualities: the "perception of time" understood as "a sense of high responsibility" toward the present. On the contrary, he had the symphony performed, "as if intentionally," at the same time that the country was discussing lines of cultural intervention. He thus demonstrated a total "misunderstanding of the party's demands regarding art." The problem was clear in these words of the reviewer: "When the poet, and behind him a composer loved by all, a composer we consider a great thinker, elevates an insignificant case of life almost to the rank of a national tragedy, the idea of falsity inevitably arises, and an inexorable feeling of internal protest matures in the soul." Shostakovich did not understand the needs of Soviet society, he did not understand what could "objectively" serve the citizens, inspiring them in the struggle for Communism, and what, on the contrary, was "an obstacle" and generated "useless passions." The composer, although deserving "unanimous recognition for the purely musical (and even formal) merits" of the symphony, was to be deprecated for "the insufficient ideological significance of the work." After all, Ladygina asked, was it permissible for something to be "aesthetically excellent without having any connection to the doctrinal aspect"?[102]

Simultaneously with the conception and execution of the Symphony No. 13, another important Soviet composer, Moisei Vainberg (Mieczysław Weinberg), commemorated the victims of genocide with his Symphony No. 6 in A minor, op. 79, for children's choir and orchestra, employing verses by poets Leib Kvitko, Shmuel Halkin, and Mikhail K. Lukonin. The work was performed for the first time in the Great Hall of the Moscow Conservatory on 12 November 1963 under the direction of Kirill Kondrashin. The choir evoking a small violinist and the children shot at Babi Yar left a particularly powerful impression.[103]

"Judaism without Embellishment"

Every critical intervention and every impulse toward censorship of the Symphony No. 13 met with the applause and support of Nikita Khrushchev. In a speech on the cultural orientations of the Communist Party delivered on 8 March 1963 during a meeting with six hundred representatives of art and literature held at the Senate Palace in Moscow, the first secretary once again condemned writers, painters, composers, sculptors, filmmakers, and theater workers who exhibited "dangerous tendencies" in the ideological field, displayed "negligent attitudes" in the duty of participating in social construction, and revealed "serious shortcomings" in the work to be done.[104] Among those being admonished in particular were those who—driven by "preconceived, deviant, and subjective ideas" and influenced by "artificial and sterile schemes"—depicted reality "in a deliberately altered form" and resorted to "dark tones," putting readers or viewers "in a state of dismay, anguish, and despair."[105] A particular concern was that some authors preferred "events of criminality, arbitrary behavior, and the abuse of power."[106] While it is true that the years of the cult of personality had left a heavy legacy in the nation, it was unacceptable to retrace the entire history of Soviet society as an era of darkness. Instead, it was necessary to demonstrate that the people were strangers to "skepticism, lack of will and weakness, pessimism, and a nihilistic attitude toward reality."[107]

Khrushchev revisited the consequences of the opinion expressed by Yevtushenko on 17 December 1962 that there might or might not be a "Jewish question" in the country. His persistence in attacking the poet—commented the international press—certainly came from the fact that his verses about Babi Yar had had a great resonance among the younger generation, giving voice to "moral indignation" for political behaviors perceived as a violation of the regulatory principle of community life: truth telling.[108] However, there was also a conviction that an opaque attempt at instrumentalization was under way. In the early drafts of the report, dictated by Khrushchev on 18 and 19 February 1963, Yevtushenko was even accused of being a pawn of the "Zionists" due to his "political immaturity."[109] It was acknowledged that the poet had so far composed "good verses" that were greatly appreciated "by both young people and adults" and that denoted nothing "counterrevolutionary" or "anti-Soviet." With "Babi Yar," however, he had taken a "wrong turn" that happened to result in the unhappy "focus on events irrelevant as to both time and place," although the poem included real elements of history. The problem was that the interpretation of events might indeed be the result of inexperience ("a youthful sin"), but it might also have been inspired by "experienced people" who pursued "a more specific and harmful political goal: . . . reviving the Zionist rat under the pretext of fighting antisemitism." Yevtushenko's fault was not having understood the situation and therefore allowing himself to get entangled in "Zionist plots."[110] In the speech that Khrushchev delivered in public, the poet was scolded primarily for having failed to mention the many nationalities that had fallen victim to Nazi violence. He had, therefore, implied that Jews and Jews alone had been exterminated during the Nazi occupation, making people believe—with judgments that revealed a lack of "political maturity" and a distinct "ignorance of historical facts"—that ancient Judophobia had been preserved in the Soviet Union. In opposition to the *words* of the poem, the head of the Communist Party adduced the *things* of socialism. If antisemitism was a product of the class struggle, there could be no material basis for it in a classless society.[111] Confirming the validity of the party's official position through historical examples and personal reminiscences, Khrushchev also recalled that "different individuals behaved differently during the Great Patriotic War against the invaders," and after citing episodes of heroism even among Jews, he dwelled on "cases of treason by people of different nationalities." To support his thesis, he then told the story of the arrest of a certain Kogan, a member of the Komsomol in Kyiv who had allegedly worked during the war as an interpreter at the headquarters of Field Marshal Friedrich Paulus. Khrushchev's intention was to highlight the fact that, even among Jews, there had been collaborators and that, consequently, people's actions should always be judged "not from the point of view of national affiliation but rather from that of class affiliation." It would have been absurd "to blame the Russian people for the dirty provocations of the Black Hundreds," just as it would have been absurd "to attribute to the entire Jewish people the responsibilities of nationalism and Zionism" at various moments in the country's history.[112]

Khrushchev's decision to highlight a Jew's disloyalty to the homeland, in response to Yevtushenko, should be viewed in the context of the state's system for the communication of antisemitism.[113] This was on a par with the emerging anti-Jewish production in the literary field. The figure of the Jewish traitor Kogan indeed appears, in a "documentary" mode, in a story by writer Porfiry P. Gavrutto published in 1963 and reissued in 1965.[114] In the second publication, the character, whom the author declared to be real and not fictitious, was even better defined: he was allegedly a former Komsomol member who had handed over members of the Kyiv underground network to the Nazis and had served Friedrich Paulus for almost two years, cooperating in the interrogations of Soviet prisoners of war and even participating in the executions of compatriots.[115] The contradictions of the story (an "absurd fabrication") were denounced a few years later by a journalist and writer active during the war in the resistance whose husband had been murdered at Babi Yar. Ariadna G. Gromova managed to ascertain that there had never been a Kogan responsible for the fight against the Ukrainian resistance to the Nazis. The "real person" had left Kyiv together with the Red Army, and Paulus had not used any Jewish interpreter. Therefore, Gavrutto's book was to be considered "not only a failure," if it was meant to be a documentary work, "but also a danger, because," as Gromova commented, "it misleads readers and misinforms them."[116]

When Khrushchev trotted out the story of the Jewish traitor, an antisemitic and anti-Zionist campaign launched by a pamphlet published in Ukrainian by the Ukrainian Academy of Sciences titled *Iudayizm bez prykras* (Judaism without embellishment) was already under way.[117] The intention of the author, Trochym K. Kychko, was to reveal the reactionary, obscurantist, and inhuman essence of the Jewish religion.[118] If that was the goal, one might be led to think of any of the many violent antireligious propaganda manuals that had been compiled—some of them, incidentally, even by Jewish militant atheists. Instead, Kychko's pamphlet contained something more than just a description of the antireligious struggle that had been reactivated from 1958 on. The pamphlet was radically different from the state programs of atheism: accompanying the text with vulgar caricatures of Judophobic content (the work of M. O. Savchenko), it combined in a highly performative discourse the entire array of assertions to which the Soviet press, borrowing them from prerevolutionary culture, had occasionally resorted in order to cast a sinister light on Jews.[119] The oldest of those themes concerned the inextricable correlation between Judaism and money; the relatively more modern theme developed out of elements largely derived from *The Protocols of the Elders of Zion*, updated in light of more recent historical developments. It was not only a matter of connecting the oldest series of statements that amounted to the international Jewish conspiracy and the trope of Jewish wealth with the new series constituted by Zionism, the state of Israel, and capitalism. No, the pamphlet also involved the swapping out of actors (just as Khrushchev had done in the meeting with the representatives of letters and arts) on the classical stage set up immediately after liberation of collaboration with the enemy. On one page of Kychko's pamphlet, the image stands out of a Jew bowing to kiss a German soldier's boot, directly evoking the idea of Jewish collusion with the Nazis.[120]

Kychko's monograph caused international consternation.[121] The Ukrainian diaspora, well aware that the sentiments unveiled in *Iudayizm bez prykras* could be attributed to its people, turned the accusation of antisemitism back onto the Soviet state and the Communist policies of denationalizing its components.[122] For their part, Western Communist Parties, in a highly unusual procedure, disapproved of the publication's authorization.[123] That was especially noteworthy, given the fact that the book had been endorsed by the highest Soviet scientific institution, effectively forcing the Soviet authorities to take action.[124] In April 1964 the Ukrainian Ministry of Foreign Affairs forwarded to Petro Shelest, the first secretary of the Central Committee of the Communist Party of Ukraine, protests from the United Nations Human Rights Commission and criticisms from various Communist organizations. The ideological commission of the Central Committee of the Communist Party of the

Soviet Union was thus forced to officially issue sanctions against the volume for "its erroneous statements and illustrations," which risked "offending the feelings of believers" and could "be interpreted in the spirit of antisemitism."[125] However, the condemnation was formulated very vaguely, as the text was never placed under accusation. Indeed, its usefulness for the antireligious campaign was emphasized.[126] Neither was the author accused of violating article 66 of the Ukrainian criminal code, which protected the equality of citizens without distinction of race, nationality, or religion.[127]

A "Collective Human Tragedy"

Anatoly V. Kuznetsov was born in Kyiv in 1929 to a Ukrainian mother and a Russian father. He spent the years of the occupation in a house located in the immediate vicinity of Babi Yar. He did small jobs to ensure better odds of survival for himself and his family and twice escaped the deportation of teenagers to Germany as forced laborers. After the war, he developed a series of stories partly derived from this experience and in 1946 won a prize in a literary competition. For some time, he devoted himself to dance and drama, then worked as a theatrical extra, carpenter, and factory worker, but he also continued to write and won two more prizes. In 1957 the magazine *Yunost* published "Prodolzhenie legendy" (The legend continues), a story about a young man about to enter adulthood. The story brought him considerable renown. He then established himself as one of the main representatives of a literary current that adopted the Rousseauian model, tackling the prose of intimate personal life (*ispovedal'naja proza*, or "confessional prose").[128] Kuznetsov's novels and stories, translated into over thirty languages, had a total circulation of at least seven million copies in the Soviet Union alone.

His book *Babi Yar* was completed after Khrushchev's fall. It was a "documentary novel" that did not have properly artistic motivations and was conceived "without thinking about any method, power, boundary, censorship, or national prejudice." Kuznetsov had begun to imagine it during the war when, at the age of fourteen, he started recording in a large notebook descriptions of the bloodshed that occurred in the place where he lived: "I noted everything I saw or heard about Babi Yar. I had no idea why I was doing it, but it seemed necessary."[129]

The writer's correspondence with the literary scholar Shlomo Even-Shoshan, though we should take it with a grain of salt inasmuch as it was subjected to the oversight of state censorship, helps us to reconstruct some phases of the novel's preparation.[130] On 16 August 1964 Kuznetsov informed his Israeli translator that he had not yet started writing because he was aware of dealing with "something too complex and of great responsibility."[131] In a

letter a few months later, he mentioned having "only the first drafts." He had
recently returned to Kyiv to visit his mother and had ventured near the
ravine again, where he observed some significant changes, as he noted with
a touch of bitter irony: "The place is unrecognizable now; massive construction of new residential buildings is under way, while the ravine has been
covered up, and people say there will be a park or a stadium. Our little house
(or rather, what's now my mother's house) still stands but is only waiting to
be demolished at any moment. Life goes on optimistically, and it's not ex
cluded that on my next visit, I'll find my mother in an apartment in a nine-
story building with a view of the Dnipro or Podol while a soccer game is
played at Babi Yar."[132]

For the writing of the novel-documentary, the author also gathered sup-
plementary material (daily press, ordinances) and interviewed survivors and
other witnesses.[133] Among his most important interlocutors was Dina Pronicheva. After testifying at the 1946 Kyiv trial, Pronicheva began concealing
her experience as a survivor and even minimized her origins to protect herself against growing antisemitism. Kuznetsov managed with great difficulty
to persuade her to recount the story of her escape and rescue. The narrative,
"lasting several days and interspersed with heart attacks," unfolded "in an
old, ramshackle room" in the same house that Dina had left to go to Babi
Yar.[134] Another interlocutor, Vladimir Yu. Davydov, was one of the protagonists of the 29 September 1943 escape. In the novel, Kuznetsov focused in
particular on the fact that Davydov was arrested, in the "simplest and most
banal of fashions," by a Ukrainian policeman named Zhora Puzenko, an old
schoolmate with whom Davydov had long been acquainted. Davydov asked
the man whether he wasn't ashamed of the work he did, but the man just
shrugged and replied that he was paid to do it and then took Davydov to
Gestapo headquarters.[135] Meeting with people who had crawled "out from
under corpses" to escape the ravine greatly undermined the writer's physical,
mental, and emotional equilibrium. "The things they told me were so frightening that I lost sleep," he wrote in a letter dated 17 May 1965. "For that
entire month in Kyiv, my sleep was tormented by nightmares. I was so
exhausted that I was forced to leave without finishing the work. I turned to
other pursuits just to 'recover.'"[136] A subsequent letter dated 2 June reveals
an even deeper state of prostration:

> Now I am very ill. Something strange happened. In Kyiv I so damaged and
> tested my nerves, I so deeply took to heart everything that I encountered while
> gathering material for *Babi Yar*, that now I am undergoing intensive therapy and
> cannot work. It's too bad. I never expected that nightmares out of the past, more

than twenty years old, could upset me so deeply. For now, I have been prescribed a month-long course of treatment to rebalance my nervous system. I take strong medications that dull my perceptions a bit, and my mind doesn't really function very well. It's a challenge to sit down at the typewriter.[137]

Kuznetsov would always remember the phase when he was frequently forced to interrupt his work due to the "cries of thousands of people being killed in his ears." That was, after all, the dream that had long tormented him, jolting him constantly: "Now I saw myself lying down, and I was being shot in the face, the chest, the back of the head; and now I stood some way apart with a notebook in my hand, waiting for it all to start, but they weren't shooting, they were on lunch break, making a bonfire of books, pumping filthy water, and I just waited and waited for anything to happen so I could note down everything very conscientiously."[138]

Babi Yar appeared in serial form in 1966 in the widely circulated magazine *Yunost*, with accompanying drawings by the architect and graphic artist Savva G. Brodsky.[139] Shortly thereafter, it was printed as a book in its own edition.[140] It is the first documentary novel about the German occupation of Kyiv, except for the work of the author Dokia K. Humenna, who published from outside the country.[141]

Kuznetsov felt no hesitation in stating that the victims selected by the Germans for the Babi Yar massacre were Jews. But he certainly hadn't intended to overlook the other tens of thousands of Ukrainians and Russians murdered by the Nazis. He writes to that effect in his introductory chapter, recalling his return to Babi Yar with a friend after the liberation:

> As we went to the ravine, we saw a ragged old man crossing it with a sack on his shoulder. From his confident stride, we could tell that he must live nearby and that this had hardly been the first time he'd come here.
>
> "Grandfather," I asked, "is this where they shot the Jews, or is it farther on?"
>
> The old man stopped, looked me up and down, and said, "And how many Russians were killed here, and Ukrainians, and people of every nationality?"
>
> And then he walked away.[142]

During his visit to the place, the future writer had encountered children who were breaking up and crushing chunks of charcoal, then sifting them carefully in search of gold (earrings, teeth, rings). He himself had taken away one of those chunks weighing about two kilos: "It contained the ashes of a great many people in which everything had mixed together, a sort of international ash."[143] The objective had been, from the beginning, to give the broadest possible vision of the massacre. If Yevtushenko seemed to have found at Babi Yar "only the mass grave of people belonging to the Jewish nation," Kuznetsov saw "a common grave of thirty thousand Jews, thirty thousand Russians, twenty thousand Ukrainians, and so on."[144] No one could hope to calculate how many different nationalities were buried there: almost all the bodies had been burned, and the ashes were by and large scattered. The story, therefore, had to be developed "from the only true point of view, the internationalist one": the destruction of the Jewish people was "only a part of a larger collective human tragedy."[145] Hence the decision to do more than limit the narrative to a reconstruction of the massacre of 29–30 September 1941—as Yevtushenko had done, recalling in his verses only "the very first days of Babi Yar, when the Germans were killing the Jewish population"—and indeed to extend it to encompass the entire 778-day span of Kyiv's occupation.[146] Kuznetsov firmly stated this choice in a letter to his Israeli correspondent. Kuznetsov was concerned about the possibility of a "biased" Jewish translation, that is, one that would "highlight only what concerns the Jewish nation, leaving out everything else." The most important thing was that "when he wrote" he felt "neither Russian, nor Ukrainian, nor Jewish, nor Indian, nor Chinese but first and foremost a human being."[147]

"Cut, Modified, and Annotated"

The novel published in *Yunost* seemed entirely consistent with the canons of Soviet ideology, but the reader could not possibly guess that the text had undergone a radical editorial revision. According to an account that Kuznetsov provided a few years later when he had already emigrated, negotiations with the magazine's editorial office had been exhausting. The manuscript, delivered at the end of 1965, was immediately (and "one might say, to my horror") returned to him. With it came the advice that he show it to no one until it had been cleansed of the "anti-Soviet" content noted in the margins. Kuznetsov then presented a "toned-down version" in which the work's meaning "was somewhat understated, though it could still be inferred." Entire passages—on the destruction of Khreshchatyk, the main thoroughfare of Kyiv, which had been occupied by the German army and mined by the Communist security services before their retreat; the explosion of Pechersk Lavra, also ensured by the retreating security services; the collapse of the dam and the consequent catastrophe of 1961; and so on—had disappeared. Circulated in an even more condensed form, stripped of other challenging chapters, the novel managed to pass the scrutiny of several party filters until it reached the Central Committee, which authorized its publication. The novel was mainly considered a useful tool to "debunk Yevtushenko's famous poem."[148]

The actual censorship efforts conducted by *Yunost*'s editorial staff began immediately after that in the hopes of creating a version that matched what had been approved by the party organs. The reviewers "cut, modified, and annotated so extensively that in places the original text was no longer visible under their multicolored corrections."[149] Kuznetsov barely managed to hold on to the title. He had been ordered categorically to change it lest it suggest associations with Yevtushenko's verses. References critical of Stalin and the cult of personality, the terror of the 1930s, and the Communist system in general, as well as any allusion, even tacit, to the weakness of the Soviet military apparatus in comparison with the German juggernaut, were all eliminated. All of Kuznetsov's previous works had been subject to revisions, but in the case of *Babi Yar*, the writer was faced with the elimination of one-quarter of the novel, to the extent that "its meaning was completely reversed." At that point, he declared that he refused to publish it under those conditions and demanded the return of his manuscript.[150] But "something completely unexpected" happened: the text was not returned to the author ("as if it was no longer my property") and after further cuts and revisions, it was sent to print with a tiny, barely legible footnote: "editorial product [*zhurnal'nyj variant*]."[151]

Kuznetsov still hoped there could be a substantial revision of the work in the transition from magazine publication to a book edition, and he immediately began negotiations with the Molodaya Gvardiya publishing house. On 29 December 1966 he announced to Even-Shoshan the imminent release of a "much more complete" version. He had recently been to Babi Yar, where a solemn laying of a granite cornerstone announcing a future commemorative monument had taken place.[152] A few days later, announcing that he had begun the revision, he laid out "a series of additions" that the *Yunost* editorial office had previously dismissed as an "unnecessary luxury." He hoped to reach an agreement with the publisher regarding those additions of text soon.[153] Instead, Kuznetsov quickly found himself in a quandary: not only did the publishing house not agree to a review of new additions, but it actually demanded further cuts. Meanwhile, the first translations of the adapted version that had appeared in the magazine were getting under way abroad, while numerous requests for clarification had arrived concerning passages of the text that had been rendered incomprehensible by the censors' incoherent interventions. Official requests to view the unabridged text began coming into the Mezhdunarodnaya Kniga agency, which had been mentioned in the footnote concerning the "editorial product." The publisher was therefore authorized to start work anew on the manuscript. About thirty pages were selected that were considered "out of context" and judged to have "an innocuous bent." The approval of the censors, along with the crucial support of the Writers' Union's foreign commission, was obtained for these pages, if only to "show foreigners that a complete text did exist." That process proved largely useless, as translations had already begun to be published based on the severely abridged text published by *Yunost*. Nevertheless, Kuznetsov attempted to include the chapters authorized for foreign publication as part of the Russian edition being prepared for release in book form, but he enjoyed little success. After repeated refusals, he finally managed to secure the restoration of a few chunks of original text, but only in exchange for the softening of "other passages" and the addition, in a sort of balancing act, of "new and ideologically impeccable paragraphs," the content of which had been literally "dictated by the editors."[154] He later learned from authoritative sources that when the volume actually did come out, it was only in the nick of time: if it had come out only a few months later, the changes in the internal political situation would certainly have prevented it entirely.

Publication caused quite a sensation. The future psychiatrist and dissident Semyon F. Gluzman recalled that in his family, "for several weeks, we talked about nothing else." His parents talked about the novel among themselves or with visiting friends, and they did so with lively emotional involvement, discussing "details of the text that were incomprehensible to me."[155] Kuznetsov soon found himself inundated with messages from readers who wanted to express the depth of their emotion, which struck him as "the greatest possible reward for all the sleepless nights and days of hard work."[156] There were reviews that showed strong approval.[157] Still, negative reactions from the highest ranks of the party were not long in coming, casting the decision to authorize publication as a serious mistake. As a result, it was forbidden to publish the new work, and distribution of the book to libraries was embargoed.[158]

In July 1969, under the pretext of work on a new book to celebrate the centennial of Lenin's birth, Kuznetsov obtained permission to spend some time in London for research; there he was expected to gather material on the Bolshevik leader's stay as well as the Second Congress of the Russian Social Democratic Labour Party. Once there, he applied for and was accorded political asylum.[159] In a public statement released a short while later, he explained the reasons for his defection, which might have seemed incomprehensible to many, inasmuch as Kuznetsov enjoyed great popularity, honors, and privilege in his homeland:

> I could no longer live in the Soviet Union. It was an impulse stronger than me.
> I just couldn't go on. If I were forced to return, I would simply go mad. If I
> hadn't been a writer, maybe I could have endured it. But as a writer, it's

impossible for me. Writing is the only occupation in this world that I truly enjoy. When I write, I have the illusion that my life has some meaning. To me, the idea of not writing is more or less the same as the idea of not swimming would be for a fish. I have always written. I have been a published author for twenty-five years now. During those twenty-five years, not one of my works has been printed in the USSR exactly as I wrote them. For political reasons, Soviet censorship and editors cut, twist, and pervert my works, rendering them completely unrecognizable. Or else they simply forbid their publication. As long as I was young, I could still hope for something. Each new publication is a black day on the calendar for me, not a cause for celebration. Because my work comes out in a misrepresented, falsified, and altered form, I am ashamed to look people in the eye. In the USSR, writing a good book is still a very easy thing to do. No, the real torment begins afterward, when you to start to think about publishing it. In the last ten years, I have lived in a relentless state of contradiction, in utter darkness, with no way out. My shoulders slumped, and I could feel it. As I wrote my last novel, *Fire*, my soul felt petrified, empty of faith or hope. I already knew without a doubt that, even if they printed it, they would be sure to ruthlessly eliminate everything human about it; that, at best, they would publish another piece of "ideological" garbage (and, in fact, that is exactly what they did). I have reached the point where I can no longer write, can no longer sleep, can no longer breathe.[160]

The artist had the task of bringing the "unexplored" to light; he had the duty "to be honest, objective"; he had a mission "to create freely." These three activities were entirely precluded to him. After trying to find a compromise between servile subjugation and open rebellion, he concluded that every attempt to preserve even a minimal level of creative freedom had failed. His printed work was neither true literature nor a miserable lockstep with the party line but "the product of an inconceivable transaction between censorship and the author's conscience."[161] Having chosen exile, he knew full well that his books would be banned, and so he preferred, all things considered, to hasten the impending punishment:

I pray for all of my publications to be entirely destroyed. Since they are not what I actually wrote, not what I wanted to convey to the public, they are books that don't belong to me! I renounce them myself: "Publicly and forever, I renounce everything that has been printed under the name 'Kuznetsov' in the USSR or released as a translation of a Soviet edition in any other countries on Earth. I hereby formally declare that Kuznetsov is a dishonest, conformist, cowardly author. I renounce my surname." At long last, I want to be an honest man and an honest writer. All the works I publish from today forward will be signed with the name A. Anatol [Anatoly]. Please consider only those books as mine.[162]

The writer also confessed to having agreed to collaborate with the Soviet security services in order to win authorization for the trip to London.[163] And so he had provided false information about Yevtushenko and other freedom-minded artists (the writers Vasily P. Aksyonov and Anatoly T. Gladilin, the actors Oleg N. Yefremov, Oleg P. Tabakov, and Arkady I. Raikin), claiming that they had come up with the idea of preparing an underground newspaper.[164]

In addition to what he had published for the Soviet Union market, Kuznetsov had written "other things, freely, 'for himself,' stored underground to escape searches."[165] In anticipation of his defection, he had transferred all his works to microfilm and brought them with him, including the complete text of *Babi Yar*. It was under his new name of A. Anatoly that the novel was reprinted the following year in Russian by Posev editions in Frankfurt. In the preface to his readers, the author—after first reconstructing the vicissitudes that the text had faced—summarized the trials facing every Soviet writer: "I always had to fight for every sentence, haggling and adding ideological rub-bish. In the Soviet Union, given its Jesuitically minded publishing industry, everything is entangled, needlessly complicated, every book grows layer upon layer, chasms of censorship open wide. You publish in a magazine when you are able, and then, in the book version, you try to add something on the sly, and a little bit more in the second edition, but then, suddenly, the situation changes, and what was easily permitted before now becomes horrendous sedi-tion, and vice versa."[166]

Readers should always take these tribulations into account, he explained in a special preface for the Israeli translation of the (*unabridged*) novel: "When reading any book by a Soviet author, it takes enormous intellectual effort, factoring in the censorship, to identify the idea hidden between the lines, to reconstruct what has been deleted."[167] In the new version, in order to unveil and reveal the hidden idea, that layering was made visible by alternating the original's roman typeface with italics for parts that had been suppressed by the censors. Additions made between the Soviet and the Frankfurt editions were inserted in square brackets. Conceived this way, the book offered, and still offers now, "invaluable, concrete material concerning the methods, psychol-ogy, and even prejudices of editors and censors."[168]

The most important deletions concerned the participation of the city's population in the liquidation of the Jews and, more generally, the wide-spread adherence to Judophobic attitudes, anti-Soviet sentiments, or even sympathies for the occupier (episodes of turning informant, the looting of

Jewish property, violence by the Ukrainian police); portrayals of Soviet soldiers whose behavior contradicted the myth of heroism; and the persistence
of Judophobia after the war and its presence at all levels of the social hierarchy. Of the three chapters on burned books (in 1937 at the time of the Stalinist purges, in 1942 during the occupation of Kyiv, and in 1946 during the
phase of reconstruction), the censorship had allowed only the second chapter to appear. The last chapter, which told of state-sponsored antisemitism
and "no longer [spoke] of the Germans' attempts to remove Babi Yar from
history but instead of Soviet ones," almost cost the author "the right to publish the entire volume."[169] Indeed, the censors zealously removed anything
that might suggest that antisemitism was still alive in the Soviet Union. This
is evident, for instance, in a fragment of the chapter "The Ordinance,"
where Kuznetsov described the procession of Kyiv's Jews, which he had
witnessed:

> In a state of feverish excitement, I ran from group to group, listening to conver-
> sations, and the closer I got to Podol, the more people I saw in the streets. The
> residents watched from doorways and entrances, sighed, *chuckled, or shouted
> insults at the Jews. Suddenly, a bilious old woman with a filthy shawl ran into the
> street, snatched a suitcase from an old Jewish woman, and fled back into the court-
> yard. The Jewish woman started to scream, but some burly, mustached men barred
> her way at the gate. She sobbed, cursed, and lamented, but no one came to her
> defense, and the crowd passed by, heads down. I peeked through a crack and saw that
> there was already a good pile of stolen clothes in that courtyard. I caught some voices
> on the fly: they said that somewhere nearby, a coachman hired to transport the lug-
> gage of several families had whipped the horse and fled into an alley—and they
> hadn't been able to catch up with him.*[170]

Kuznetsov had also wanted to discuss the Soviet government's responsibility for having signed the Molotov-Ribbentrop Pact. The consequences had
been fatal for the Jewish population, which was kept in the dark about the
antisemitic policies adopted by their German ally for reasons of state. The
removal of the bracketed passage in the following quote is an excellent example of the sort of self-censoring technology that transforms the text into a
statement insinuating collusion between Germans and Jews:

> [When the ordinance was published, nine out of ten Jews had never heard of
> Nazi atrocities against Jews. Until the war broke out, Soviet newspapers only
> praised and exalted Hitler, the best friend of the Soviet Union, and gave no news
> about the situation of Jews in Germany and Poland. Among Kyiv's Jews, one

could even find enthusiastic admirers of Hitler, who was considered a talented statesman. Moreover,] the old people said that when the Germans were in Ukraine in 1918, they hadn't touched the Jews; on the contrary, they had treated them quite well because of the similar language, and so on.[171]

Other deletions concerned the decision of the Soviet security services to blow up several buildings along Khreshchatyk, effectively leaving Kyiv's Jews at the mercy of the Germans. These actions of sabotage had certainly caused military damage to the occupiers, but they also provoked a ruthless retaliation with little or no concern for the consequences visited upon the population at large: "[The Germans made their response to Khreshchatyk known five days later, on 29 September 1941.] No, they didn't make any official statement regarding Khreshchatyk and didn't publicly execute anyone. [But they became grim and angry, the smiles disappeared completely. It was terrifying to behold them, sooty black and sternly busy, as if they were preparing something.]"[172]

Naturally, all passages suggesting similarities between Nazism and Stalinism were expunged from the Soviet edition, including, for example, the words with which the author recalled the day when, during the occupation of Kyiv, he felt "the first stirrings of my too early coming of age." He was at the market at dusk, "unhappy and angry," still waiting for some chance customer willing to pay him to polish their shoes:

I looked around in astonishment, and the dusty, gray veil finally fell from the world. I saw . . . that on earth *there was neither intelligence, nor good, nor common sense, only* violence. Blood. Hunger. Death. That I didn't know why I lived and sat there under the awning with my brushes. *That there was no hope, not the slightest glimmer of hope in justice. There was no expectation of it anywhere or from anyone; it was one vast, immense Babi Yar. Two forces had clashed and were colliding against each other, like the hammer and the anvil, and in between stood the poor devils, and there was no way out, and everyone just wanted to live, didn't want to be beaten, wanted to eat, and everyone was screaming, squealing, grabbing each other by the throat in horror, and I, a lump of soft jelly,* sat in the middle of that black world—what for, why, who had made all this? There was nothing to hope for! Winter. Night.[173]

Profane, Erase, Redeem

In 1962 the ravine of Babi Yar was filled in with tons and tons of earth. Anatoly Kuznetsov, reconstructing the steps that led to the "elimination of the ashes," recalled the great expenditure of machinery ("excavators, bulldozers, dump trucks, tractors") employed to move and level the ground.[1] Where the Syrets concentration camp once stood, an urban agglomeration was built that was "constructed, one might say, on bones." During the excavations, human remains were repeatedly found, "sometimes intertwined with wire." In fact, "the balconies of the first row of those buildings directly overlooked the places where the mass executions of Jews took place in 1941."[2]

In June of that year, the executive committee of the Soviet of Deputies of the City of Kyiv adopted a resolution ordering the liquidation of the Lukyanivka Jewish cemetery, including the small and separate Karaite section. The decision also concerned other burial sites and was part of the relocation of interred bodies initiated in the 1950s to accommodate new urban development. Despite limited attempts at preservation, which mainly affected the graves of prominent figures from various communities, many cemeteries— and not only Jewish ones—were dismantled to make way for new neighborhoods, parks, and major roads.[3]

"A Thicket of Shrubs and a Forest of Wild Trees"

The Lukyanivka Jewish cemetery, located in the immediate vicinity of Repyakhiv Yar and Babi Yar, was opened in 1894. Over the years, it came to occupy an undeveloped area of just under twenty-five hectares. A significant part of its perimeter was marked by a brick wall, while the entrance included an elegant arched gate. The meticulous arrangement of the necropolis, compared to the neglect of the adjacent Orthodox cemetery, aroused animosity in antisemitic circles in the early twentieth century. In the 1930s part of the wall was demolished and taken for use as building materials elsewhere; it was replaced with a wooden fence. In 1937 burials were halted due to lack of space. With the German occupation of Kyiv, the systematic destruction of graves was undertaken. In particular, as we have seen, in August and September 1943 hundreds of stone tombstones and metal fences were used as bases for the pyres of newly exhumed corpses.[4]

After the war, the cemetery remained in a state of neglect for a long time. There was certainly no encouragement to protect it implicit in the government's attitude toward graphic symbols of Jewish culture. This is made evident, for instance, in a report dated 13 March 1953 sent by delegate P. Vilkhovy to the chairman of the Council for Religious Cults, Ivan V. Polyansky, and the secretary of the Central Committee of the Communist Party of Ukraine, Ivan D. Nazarenko. "Some new (and also a number of old) funeral monuments" in Jewish necropolises displayed "Zionist emblems, such as the Shield of David, the six-pointed star, and others." Similar depictions were also found in the Kyiv synagogue, even after its renovation in 1950, and in other Jewish places of worship. Vilkhovy asked for explanations and urged official guidelines on the matter with a series of questions whose grotesque nature should not be overlooked. Did the stonemasons who worked on the tombstones have the right to place Zionist emblems on them? Could the religious authorities of the Jewish community be required to manually remove such ornaments from the *aron* (the ark in a synagogue), prayer shawls, and other sacred objects, and exactly how ought this to be done? What should be the role and responsibilities of the Council for Religious Cults? The informant explicitly believed that before the creation of the State of Israel, these symbols could evoke "a 'religious' symbolism," but afterward, they had assumed "a purely Zionist character"—that is to say, a political nature—against which it was necessary to "fight resolutely."[5]

The final dismantling of the Lukyanivka Jewish cemetery was decided on 26 June 1962. Based on a decree of the State Planning Commission of the Ukrainian Soviet Socialist Republic "concerning burials and the maintenance of cemeteries in inhabited areas" (28 July 1958), it was established that the territory of the Jewish necropolis and the Karaite cemetery, covering a total area of 26.9 hectares, would now be assigned to the entity responsible for managing the green areas of the capital to create a public park. The decision referred to the fact that "most of the graves" had been destroyed during the German occupation and that the place had become "a thicket of shrubs and a forest of wild trees." The press was to inform the population to allow those interested in doing so to "remove the funereal monuments placed on the graves of their relatives." From 1 January 1963 everything that remained "unclaimed," that is, "monuments, slabs, fences," would be "removed and inventoried."[6]

Reburial, once initiated, posed numerous political and administrative problems for the authorities. An official of the local Council for Religious Cults, A. Sharandak, noted in a report sent to party leaders that as of 1 December 1962 about fifteen hundred human remains had been transferred from the Jewish and Karaite cemeteries to readied and fully equipped cemeteries. The transport of those remains was conducted "in an unorganized manner and without the necessary oversight by the office responsible for funeral services." Only the "lack of supervision" could explain how religious Jews had managed, quite independently, to move the remains of two zaddikim and other personalities "especially revered by believers." Buried in the Jewish cemetery alongside any number of notable community members who had been accomplished in religious, economic, and professional fields were certain important figures of Russian Zionism (Max E. Mandelstamm, Ber Borochov, Nachman S. Syrkin). Hence the concern that "in the situation that had meanwhile developed," the relocation of their remains, considered entirely "inappropriate," would be carried out by "nationalistic elements."[7]

On 10 January 1963 another official of the Religious Cults at the Council of Ministers of the Ukrainian Soviet Socialist Republic, K. F. Polonik, informed the deputy minister of foreign affairs that in execution of previous instructions, Kyiv's cemeteries were being shut down because "of the exhaustion of their capacity or the needs of urban redevelopment." To eliminate structures that were no longer in use, deadlines had been set that took into account the "period of mineralization" of the bodies: "For cemeteries with dry sandy soils, silty-clayey and slightly clayey soils, fifteen to twenty years from the day of the last burial; for cemeteries with clayey soils, twenty-five to thirty years." Population growth and new housing needs had led not only to the dismantling of the Jewish and Karaite cemeteries, as well as that of the Christian cemetery in Kopylovo, but also to the closure of seven other necropolises that had completely exhausted their capacity. For the removal of the bodies—an urgent step that had been announced to the population through the local press—"manpower and transportation resources" would be provided; graves were to be opened, and the remains were to be transferred "in the presence of relatives of the deceased."[8]

The redevelopment of the entire area would create not only a number of civic buildings but also a public park; the Avangard sports complex, equipped with two halls and a swimming pool; and a modern television station with a 385-meter-high antenna.[9] During the preliminary surveys, the "high density of Jewish burials," which, to judge by the tombstones, had continued until 1939 (thus after the site's official closure date), was confirmed. Consultations were also initiated with municipal offices responsible for funeral services and health and epidemiological controls. It was further ordered that removal of all tomb monuments and reburial of all bodies must be completed by the start of redevelopment work.[10]

However, the destruction of the Lukyanivka Jewish cemetery was not carried out in accordance with the antiseptic description proffered in the political and administrative decrees. In the summer of 1965, Anatoly Kuznetsov wrote by night and went to watch the machinery at work during the day: "The way they worked was sloppy and haphazard, and the freshly deposited soil sank and was undermined." The image of thousands of shattered tombstones and desecrated bodies is encapsulated in these few, terse words: "The bulldozers set to work, uprooting graves and slabs and upending skeletons and zinc coffins as they went."[11]

Viktor Nekrasov glimpsed—in the violation of bodies that had "been laid to eternal rest behind the stone wall of the ancient cemetery" and whose names had been entrusted to the eternity of carved tombstones—a determination to erase all traces of the Jewish presence in Kyiv in that twenty-five-hectare span. Lukyanivka lay adjacent to Babi Yar, the immense mass grave that, between 29 and 30 September 1941, had swallowed up 33,771 Jews, erasing their names from the city's history. Babi Yar might be gone now, but Lukyanivka was gone now too: "Neither the wall nor the cemetery existed anymore; there was only crumbled marble and granite in the shade of century-old linden and chestnut trees, along with scattered ruins of tombs desecrated with inscriptions." The "sacrilege" had begun with the Germans. They had destroyed—in their characteristically meticulous fashion—all the monuments on the main avenue, shattering slabs and obelisks. But even the Germans hadn't touched the side avenues, where tens of thousands of graves remained intact. Who had "completely" demolished them, given that "not a single stela" had been preserved in Lukyanivka? Nekrasov could not establish exactly when this had happened, but he knew the cemetery had already disappeared by the late 1950s: "Several tens of thousands of tombstones had been knocked down, smashed, shattered, and upended, while the small oval porcelain photos . . . had been broken with pickaxes or hammers. Without exception. The blind fury of destruction had passed through all the tombs, sparing none."[12]

Standing among the cemetery's ruins, Nekrasov wondered who could have been responsible for the devastation and what powerful "hatred" could have led to such "outrage." It was not the work of a single individual or a few savagely wielded clubs. To carry out such a "massively destructive undertaking," considering that almost all the temple-shaped tombs had been built on solid foundations that were designed to last for centuries, "hundreds of laborers" would have been required. It was likely that vandals in a state of drunkenness had attacked several dozen tombs, "but who destroyed the others? And with what tools of demolition? Bulldozers? Tractors? Dynamite? When did it happen: at night, during the day? And how long had it taken: a week, two weeks, a month? I could find no explanation then, and still I can't."[13]

Nekrasov evoked the old image of Lukyanivka as a suburb that had long been considered one of Kyiv's most beautiful: small houses dotting the greenery and broad patches of lilacs and jasmines. It was true, he added, that not everything had always been idyllic: In the old czarist days, the area was inhabited by the most reactionary and backward portions of the population, and it was there that the infamous case of Menahem Mendel Beilis, a Russian Jew accused of ritual murder in 1911, originated. Over the years, however, the neighborhood had become more civilized and less isolated. So how had this devastation come about?

> I wandered through the promenades, down narrow paths overgrown with dense shrubbery. I read the inscriptions on the shattered slabs—some, lying flat to prevent them from being overturned again, had been cemented into the fallen columns and walls, and flowers were placed beside them. I glanced inside the few preserved crypts and read the antisemitic slogans and the insults of hooligans defacing the walls (the marble had been torn away, and the writing was directly on the mortar). I stood for a long time overlooking the deep ravine at the bottom of which, heaped up one atop another, lay the funeral stelae that had been dumped there. (Only a few were broken; it was too much trouble to drag and push them down.) I kept wondering, and kept finding no answers.
>
> Even now, I find none. I can acknowledge, but I can't explain.
>
> Now the cemetery is relatively orderly. The traces of desecration persist, but most of the shattered granite and marble has been hauled away. An uninformed person might simply think that the cemetery is just one more abandoned location—sadly, we have hundreds and thousands of those. . . .
>
> There is no explanation. . . . And no one will offer one. . . . But there must be someone who knows. Because someone did all this. And it wasn't just one person. . . . All this happened in the second half of the twentieth century in the city of Kyiv, with a population of half a million. . . .
>
> It is difficult, it is shameful, to live in such a time.[14]

The writer would rework these initial reflections a few years later in a text he published while living abroad, laying even greater emphasis on the desecration of a place dedicated to preserving the memory and dignity of the deceased:

And here is another tragedy.

Perhaps even more terrible than death: the desecration of death. A savage, shameful, atrocious, incomprehensible desecration. . . .

I walk down a shady pathway. The place is silent, deserted; I hear leaves rustling beneath my footsteps. But all around me . . . all around me are thousands, tens of thousands of overturned, destroyed, mutilated funeral monuments. . . .

We are in the old Jewish cemetery. . . .

I turn down another pathway, then a third, a fourth. . . . The same scene. Granite or marble monuments weighing many tons, broken into a thousand pieces, scattered in the dust. Small oval portraits shattered, pounded with stones. And so for a long stretch of time . . . I have no idea what to say. All the monuments, without exception, have been destroyed. Countless . . . fifty thousand, a hundred thousand . . . a city of the dead. In the mausoleums and crypts, the marble has been ripped away. There are inscriptions on the walls . . . best not to read them at all.

It is a well-known fact that the Germans, in a frenzy of blind rage, devastated the central avenue. But they lacked the strength and the determination to destroy all the rest. That devastation was visited at a later date.

By whom?

No one knows, or if they do, they prefer to remain silent.

Drunken hooligans? But even supposing they'd been equipped with pickaxes and sledgehammers, they could only have tackled a dozen or two dozen monuments at the very most. Because those monuments were solidly built, designed to last for centuries, made with lead-reinforced concrete.

No, it wasn't a rabble of hooligans. It was a systematic, conscientious task. Carried out with judiciously chosen technical means. No one could have done this without bulldozers or tractors, perhaps even a tank.

I keep on walking. . . . Not a single monument has been preserved. At the bottom of the ravine, piles of debris. They took the trouble to drag them there and hurl them down. You couldn't do it in a day or two. It took weeks, months. . . .

And this is not in the wilderness. This is the heart of a city. The trolleybus runs right past here, at the far end of Herzen Street. (That's right, Alexander Herzen!) Just half a kilometer from the cemetery is the dacha where Khrushchev lived. . . .

I discovered all this in the late 1950s. By pure chance, while out walking. . . . And I was speechless. No one had ever told me about it. Even though years had passed. And to think how many people had buried their parents and grandparents there! It means they went there regularly. And not only did they go. Some of the monuments, not many—a hundred, two hundred at most—have been cemented to the ground, even in the upside-down position they were in, to prevent their utter destruction. . . .

No one speaks about it. Everyone remains silent. I questioned the people who live in the house at the cemetery entrance. Perhaps they were the old caretakers. "We don't know, we don't know. . . . We know nothing. . . ." They avoid meeting your gaze.

For the hundredth, for the thousandth time, I wonder: Who did this? Who authorized it? Who gave instructions? Who carried them out? How many of them were there? When did they do it? Where does this terrible anger, this hatred, this coarseness *come* from?

Or is it instead the product of calm, icy reckoning: Today, from here to there; tomorrow, from here to that other monument over there, and we'll be finished by the twentieth of the month. . . .

All this in the second half of the twentieth century, in the glorious city of Kyiv, before the eyes of one and all. . . .

I recently went back. Shortly before my departure. Fifteen years later . . . The cemetery is overgrown with shrubbery. The overturned monuments have been hauled off elsewhere. Not all of them, though. Here and there, among the weeds and thickets, you can glimpse the remains of pedestals, steps, fragments of marble and labradorite.

There are bulldozers, too. Clattering and thundering, they are constructing a road in place of the main avenue leading who knows where. . . . The place is deserted. Empty. Dead. . . . And horrifying.[15]

End of an "Unnatural Oblivion"

On 11 August 1965 the Council of Ministers of the USSR, responding to a request from Ukrainian authorities, approved the construction of two monuments "in memory of Soviet citizens and Red Army soldiers and officers who died at the hands of Nazi-Fascist invaders during the occupation of Kyiv."[16] A closed competition was then announced, asking participants to conceive and submit works intended to depict, "in artistic form," the heroism and will of the Soviet people to affirm "the Communist ideal," defend "the honor and freedom of the homeland," and proclaim "courage and valor in the face of death." Contestants were faced not only with the challenge of presenting their proposals on tight deadlines but also with the fact that the area designated by the authorities for the installation did not actually correspond to the site of the shootings. The creators of the proposals that were selected would have no decision-making power over the design of the memorial complex itself, which would be erected not at Babi Yar—which no longer existed—but instead in the "Shevchenko district of the city of Kyiv."[17]

Despite the limitations and restrictions established on any creative ideation, the competition nonetheless stood as a major critical event. In an extensive report published by the most important decorative arts journal of the period, Viktor Nekrasov recalled that Kyiv now had a "generation" of men and women for whom everything that had taken place at the site of the massacre represented "a distant history." In place of what had once been Babi Yar there was now "a vast, desolate, flat terrain covered with weeds." Around it, houses had sprung up, "an entire modern neighborhood," and there was nothing ("not an obelisk, not a stone") to commemorate the tragedy that had unfolded there: Only "an empty space" remained. The competition for the monument thus represented an opportunity to put an end an "unnatural oblivion."[18]

Even though it was strictly closed to all but a select group of professionals, the competition attracted the notice of architects, sculptors, and painters who had not been officially invited to participate. Quite unexpectedly, according to the recollections of one of the contestants, by the deadline for submission (20 December 1965), ninety-two professional projects had been submitted and registered; taken together with proposals submitted by nonprofessionals, the total exceeded one hundred.[19] Among those that attracted the most attention was a memorial complex designed by architect Josyp Yu. Karakis in collaboration with painter Zinovy Sh. Tolkachov and sculptors Yakiv S. Razhba and Yevgeny Zhovnirovsky.

Karakis was one of the most important architects and urban planners of Kyiv. The designer and builder of a substantial number of buildings considered exemplary for their innovative style, as well as an active defender of historical monuments, he can be regarded as a prominent figure of the brief period in which Ukrainian constructivism flourished.[20] After the war, he worked at the State Urban Planning Institute of Kyiv; he held the chair of architectural design at the Institute of Engineering and Construction; he led the Art Industry Institute of the Ukrainian Academy of Architecture. In the early 1950s he was involved, along with his colleague Yakiv A. Shteynberg, in the anticosmopolitan campaign. His dismissal triggered a strong reaction among the students, about thirty of whom signed a letter to the academic authorities stating that the measure deprived the architecture school of one of its most distinguished educators and thus basically marked its end.[21] He was rehabilitated after Stalin's death.

The idea behind Karakis's project was to transform the Babi Yar area into a space where no one should set foot. The site where the executions had taken place would be covered with red gravel or planted with poppies in order to symbolize the blood of the victims. Visitors would be welcomed in the central part of the park, an area bordered on three sides by chasms crossed by foot-bridges and designated for use in commemorative ceremonies. Three variants were considered. The first envisioned a tree-shaped monument with a split trunk, inside of which there would be a museum, partially underground. From the gallery that would house commemorative documentation, visitors would then climb a spiral staircase to an elongated, rectangular room with frescoes by Tolkachov depicting the triumph of life. The second variant proposed a sculptural group by Razhba: a majestic statue of grief with scenes of heroism, suffering, and death carved in relief, like so many still-gaping wounds. The third variant involved the installation of a concrete block about ten meters high perforated by the stylized figure of a man. This enormous stela would be topped by an eternal flame. On the right side, the walkway leading to the monument would be flanked by a concrete wall 3–3.5 meters high covered with mosaic panels depicting the massacre.[22] Whatever the choice of the commemorative sculpture to be placed in the center, the intent was that it should stand out on the horizon, with a suspended, sloping ramp of steps to be followed by visitors approaching the monument. The ramp's low, broad steps would naturally slow the pace of visitors' approach, suggesting a funeral march and a feeling of mourning for those descending into the ravine.[23]

Architect Avraam M. Miletsky had lost his mother and grandmother in the massacre. His memorial complex, which included a granite stela inscribed with "Babi Yar" in multiple languages, would extend with a wall running the entire perimeter of a precipice and then spreading out into a series of symbolically designed branches: In one there would be a depiction of a broken stroller and an umbrella, in another there would be a violin, in a third there would be a ball, and so on.[24] The project presented by sculptor Ada F. Rybachuk and architect Volodymyr Volodymyrovych Melnychenko proposed a high wall of massive stone blocks, which—in the impressions described by philosopher Karl M. Kantor—was intended to "enclose, embrace, protect the burial site of the people who had been executed." Particularly effective was the way in which the artists sought to "revive the sand-covered ravine," which seemed to materialize before the viewer's eyes. This project also envisioned a sloping path reconstructed in Kantor's mind as follows:

> Descending the wide steps toward the Urn with the "ashes" of the victims, you are not merely observing a monument from the outside, but it is as if you are retracing the path of those who were once thrown into the ravine. The stone blocks of the wall along which you walk suddenly come to life. It is the same line

of Jews resignedly walking toward death. And you walk with them. The stones of which the wall is made begin to move at first in a rhythmic cadence; then the pace becomes irregular, the rhythm breaks; the stones start to crack, crumble, and fall. They are the people struck down by bullets who are falling. The stones press painfully on the soul; you almost physically feel the sharp corners of the stones piercing the body, the head.[25]

Despite every attempt to avoid highlighting the competition (the director of the House of Architects, where the exhibition was held, Josyp R. Kailik, was even instructed not to post notices of the invitation of the candidates to attend), the discussion of the submissions on 23 January 1966 was very lively and followed by a large audience. The exhibition of sketches prompted strong reactions among the visitors, who had patiently waited for hours to enter the halls. Most of the works presented had nothing in common with the official artistic standards. According to one of the participants in the competition, architect Aleksandr Ya. Shteinberg, the jury consisted of only a very few professionals, whereas there was ample representation of party notables and government officials.[26] Architect Anatoly F. Ignashchenko recalled just how hesitant the commission was in its judging: They "could not (or would not) decide which submission to favor." Among those who spoke in the debate, he was particularly struck by the words of film director Sergei I. Parajanov and Viktor Nekrasov, both of whom favored preserving the site as much as possible. Parajanov argued that the exhibited works were "a mass of sculptures" and not "a memorial in the deepest sense of the term," meaning "something sacred." He pointed to the preservation of the ruins of the Armenian temple of Zvarnotz, near Yerevan, which was protected by the state as a national treasure and a symbol for reflecting "on the essence of things." Babi Yar could represent something similar; that was why it should "remain as it is, a place of tragedy." Nekrasov spoke "in more concrete terms." He had traveled extensively and had visited numerous sites that had been the scene of "crimes against humanity, against peoples." More than anything else, he had been impressed by Treblinka: "There are no gigantic sculptures, no elaborate compositions; to [commemorate] the number of dead, stones have been placed. . . . I see each victim."[27]

The commission concluded that none of the projects met the "essential conditions" of the competition and that the participants had "mostly" failed to meet the "main requirement": representing "the heroism and unyielding will of our people in the struggle for the victory of the great ideas of Communism, for the honor and freedom of the homeland." Instead, they had focused only on "themes of sorrow." For this reason, the commission instructed only the authors of the commissioned projects to revise their proposals, giving them just over a month (by 31 March 1966) to present their results. The other participants were not even informed of the decision.[28] The second round, however, also yielded no results.[29]

At the time of the public debate concerning the first round of the competition, Nekrasov had predicted that no candidate would pass the selection and that, in the end, the authorities would commission "some Vuchetich" to create a sculpture depicting "a brave soldier with a flag in one hand and a rifle in the other."[30] In other words, he had confided to Lazar Lazarev, the project chosen would be "the most mediocre," something that "had not been admitted to the exhibition" and "had not been submitted to the jury."[31] In a letter sent to an acquaintance on 28 May 1966, the writer revealed that he had managed, "secretly," to view the models of the second round, "kept under lock and key." Their quality was far inferior: "The two worst projects—women with resolute faces and outstretched arms—have been selected for construction. But if you ask me, nothing will come of it. At best, there will be a stone [with the inscription]: 'Coming Soon.'"[32]

Details "Impressed in Memory"

Since the late 1950s, Nekrasov had criticized the grandiose exaltation of heroism, that is, the rhetorical structure, the bombastic pathos of speeches and commemorative expressions, the taste for the monumental that had shaped the monotonous uniformity of Soviet art.[33] His vision was largely influenced by the ideas of Konstantin S. Stanislavsky, of whom he had been a pupil, concerning the "small truths [*malen'kie pravdy*] without which the great Truth cannot be built."[34] These ideas were very similar to those that had made *Front-Line Stalingrad* one of the most interesting and celebrated works of postwar realism.[35] How great an impression that novel had made was suggested by Ukrainian director Les Tanyuk, who had chanced upon the book as a student, still shaken by a childhood spent in a German concentration camp. For that reason, he couldn't stand reading anything about the war and had a special aversion to stories of valor and bravery: "and suddenly an unusually dry, hard prose about a man in a terrible conflict, where some lose their personalities, while others find them, where you believe every word and feel as if you are in the trenches yourself."[36]

Stanislavsky believed that the secret of his method was not to consider "physical actions in and of themselves" but only to consider them inasmuch as they help us "to feel the truth within us and believe it." In some cases, it was enough for an "instant of truth" to burst unexpectedly into an ordinary performance, producing an "unexpected gesture," alive and real, a "jarring truth" that stood out sharply from habitual conduct: "Like a draft of fresh air in a stuffy room, the 'unexpected' suddenly bursts from normal reality into the conventional atmosphere of the stage, revivifying the stale, stereotypical acting." Those moments, distilled from the concrete material of life, could invigorate the action depicted and perhaps even an entire theatrical performance. The result could be a kind of "thrust" that, in its turn, might prove capable of triggering a new creative impulse: "It is clear that a series of small truths in logical and coherent succession will allow us to feel and believe the truth for an extended time in a lengthy action. Truth will strengthen conviction, and conviction will support truth. Never overlook small physical actions. Learn to use them in the service of truth in order to believe that what you do onstage is real. . . . Each small truth will lead to a greater one, this one to that even greater one, and so on."[37]

To Stanislavsky's chain of "small truths," Nekrasov added the chain of "details" that continually burst into the narrative scheme, endowing it with meaning when linked together: "There are details that remain impressed in the memory for a lifetime. And not only do they remain impressed: though small and seemingly insignificant, they take root, they infiltrate into you, so to speak, they begin to grow, they germinate, and they develop into something significant, absorbing into themselves the essence of what is happening, becoming a kind of symbol."[38] Building a "conventional procedural situation" did nothing to produce any sense of connection with art in the viewer. Quite to the contrary, doing so ran the risk of overwhelming the characters (the "heroes"), turning them into "banal men, symbolizing fixed ideas, doing very little but talking a great deal or perhaps thinking out loud in the author's ordinary publicity-minded language." What undermined art most was the solemnity and bombast of heroes, whose sincerity was so very difficult to believe.[39]

To those who claimed the need for "great words" to accomplish "great deeds," it was necessary to oppose a style of moderation and simplicity: "There is another language, passionate but not bombastic, truthful but not prosaic, spoken by ordinary people, the same people who sometimes accomplish great deeds." Simple human language was far more moving than "fiery words that leave the heart cold and fail to stir the mind."[40] These were the principles Nekrasov had tried to apply to the screenplay of the film *Soldaty* (Soldiers), inspired by *Front-Line Stalingrad* and directed in 1956 by Aleksandr G. Ivanov. However, the Ministry of Defense had weighed in with the Central Committee of the Communist Party, forwarding a request to ban the film due to the "distorted" image it gave of the war, particularly of the defense of Stalingrad, by diminishing the role of the party in favor of the role played by an armed populace.[41] That it was not an easy language to convey or accept in an era when weakness or disability was subject to stigma and social isolation is demonstrated by an exchange of opinions Nekrasov had concerning that screenplay with a veteran at a literary event.[42] The veteran addressed him in these terms: "What were you thinking when you depicted the retreat? And to do it in that fashion, what's more." By which he meant images "devoid of appeal," filled with "barefoot soldiers, ragged, disorderly, a disorganized mob." Nekrasov had tried to explain to his interlocutor that the Battle of Stalingrad had been all the more epic because victory had come after the terribly difficult days of July 1942. That's why the Soviet army had been depicted in disarray in that way in the film. He couldn't know whether the veteran himself had taken part in the retreat, but it seemed to him that, if he had, that made matters even more serious, because the man *knew* the truth:

> I received an indignant response: "Yes, I retreated. And I know what it's like. But I don't want my teenage son to know it, to know that his father retreated the way you depicted in that scene. . . ."
>
> As strange as it may seem, even now, twenty years after the start of one of the most dreadful wars humanity has endured, it is possible to hear similar opinions. That we should not remember! Difficult years, retreats, the mass destruction of civilians by the Fascists, Majdanek, Auschwitz, Babi Yar . . . We should not remember.
>
> No, it is necessary to remember! And that this unknown young man should know all this. He must know how his father retreated, how he advanced, how he won, who his father's enemies were, and what they were capable of. All this must be told in the language of art: our great victories, the heroism and self-sacrifice of the people, their deeds, and their terrible sufferings.[43]

"In the language of art," Nekrasov wrote. To supplement his point, he included some sketches by Zinovi Tolkachov ("people, people, people—living and dead, tortured and survivors, elderly, women, children") created right after the liberation of Auschwitz in the pages of a notebook from the camp Kommandantura. From those sketches, the artist would later create some of his pictorial cycles on the extermination of European Jews. The preparatory sketches had then been put aside, only to be rediscovered by the artist himself, fifteen years later, among other old drawings kept since the war:

> Now I look at these sheets and ask myself: Why, despite being worn, yellowed, in some places torn, they make an even stronger impression than the finished series, why is it even more difficult to break free of them? Precisely because they

are sheets of paper. Because in these sheets the boundary between the artist's narration and the document [*dokumental'nost'*] almost disappears. Because they bear the stamp of the concentration camp commandant's office and even the phone number—65. Because on this sheet of paper depicting girls singing, there might just as well have been written the order to destroy these same girls. . . . This is the strength of these wrinkled, time-yellowed pages: in their truth, in their anger, in the overwhelming reliability of the source.[44]

"Almost Absolute Truth in Summary"

Nekrasov's intent becomes even clearer if we read his notes on contemporary architectural trends published in the early 1960s. Constructivism was presented as a model for its ability to exalt the components of structure, functionality, and purity within the formal organization of space. If the principle of *constructio* (to use the Latin) was respected, "neither war nor fire" could challenge it. This was demonstrated by works, diverse in era, vision, and context, that had shared something fundamental, "a constructiveness so strongly marked that the structure itself, from the perspective of the art of building, is the most advanced of its time." This principle constituted "a means to express a specific conception" and "a stimulus to create a new form, that is, a style." True architecture was immortal even when only ruins of its works remained because "thought, idea, and concept" were not lost. The constructivist movement—despite the renewal of materials and depictions—had respected the basic elements of the architectural act. Alongside this aspect was a way of conceiving beauty that was closely linked to functionality rather than decorative ornament and was based on the essential quality of lines: "Architecture is an art that uses volumes. At its base are the cube, the parallelepiped, the cone, the hemisphere, the pyramid. The logical union of these forms, the combination of faces and planes, creates a perfect architectural composition. Any kind of ornament hinders the perception of the main forms, corrupts them; it is rubbish that must be thrown away."[45]

In his youth as an architecture student, in the heat of discussion about the desired synthesis of the arts to be found in the constructivist method, Nekrasov, along with some fellow students, corresponded with Le Corbusier, who once summarized his thoughts on the renunciation of ornamentation as follows:

I cannot conceive of either sculpture or painting as ornament. I admit that both can evoke profound emotions in the observer similar to those produced in us by music and theater—it all depends on the quality of the work—but I am decidedly opposed to ornamentation. On the other hand, observing an architectural work and especially the space on which it is erected, we see that certain points belonging to the building itself or around it present themselves as precise intensive mathematical points, which are nothing but the key to the proportions of the work and its environment. These are the points of highest strength, and precisely in them can the architect's purpose be realized, whether in the form of a basin, a block of stone, or a statue. It can be said that at this junction point are all the conditions to articulate a discourse, a plastic discourse with everything that plasticity can develop that is both elevated and subjective.[46]

A few years before Le Corbusier's death, Nekrasov had suggested a reflection on the aesthetic and ethical consequences that the condemnation of constructivism as "formalism" had had in the Soviet Union. What followed the great experiments of the 1920s and 1930s? "Pomp, splendor, wealth." Cities began to fill "beyond measure with columns, pseudoclassical pediments, decorative arches and loggias, facades clad in polished granite." The surface of the walls was so frequently infested with superfluous elements that it sometimes seemed as if the building had been "corroded by some sort of skin disease." It was an escalation of "excesses" that did not adhere to the principle of "functionality" and that were certainly not placed at the service of the common man. While acknowledging some limits of the constructivist mentality (above all, the "dogmatism"), Nekrasov invited its embrace in open opposition to the idea of "majesty" and "monumentality," which in his view presented "antidemocratic" aspects. It was necessary to avoid the temptation to "astonish with size, height, and a costly, inexpressive grandiloquence"; instead, architects should seek what was "simple, clear, comfortable, friendly, in other words, human-sized."[47]

The 1965 competition offered the writer, who reported on it in the magazine *Dekorativnoe iskusstvo SSSR* (Decorative art of the USSR), an opportunity to revisit the lessons of constructivism.[48] The regulations of the competition called for a monument that, as we have seen, would reflect "in an artistic manner the heroism, indomitable will, courage, and valor of our people in the face of death at the hands of German executioners" and express "the mourning of the entire nation for the thousands of unknown heroes." To Nekrasov, it seemed that if he had to compete by meeting the required criteria (heroism, will, courage, valor), he would find himself "in a dead end." Since a "tragedy" had taken place at Babi Yar, the guidelines of the competition seemed completely out of place. If followed, they would not only subvert the actual features of the event but also change its meaning.[49]

The notion of "tragedy" introduced here by Nekrasov clearly recalls the invitation proffered by Stanislavski, his acting teacher, to be satisfied with "small realistic gestures, small physical truths"; to cling to "something real, stable, tangible"; to avoid falling into "pure craft, emphatic acting, excessive muscular tension." For the stage director, an actor needed to know how to "take advantage of the fact that small gestures, performed in a serious circumstance, acquire a huge function" in the art of conveying the most intense experiences. They have the prerogative of being able to create "an immediate correspondence between body and soul, between action and feeling, so that exterior action helps inner creation, and inner creation provokes exterior action." Especially in drama, it was necessary to act in a way that did not "milk the feeling," avoiding "representing passion for passion's sake, 'tear[ing] a passion to tatters' [William Shakespeare, *Hamlet*, act III, scene 2]."[50] For Nekrasov, along the same lines, it was necessary to represent violence against the defenseless without emphasis. The monument to the Warsaw Ghetto commemorated "an insurrection, a revolt, and a valiant death." That of Darnytsia was to be erected "to soldiers savagely executed, to fighters, to men captured with weapons in hand, to men largely young and strong." But Babi Yar was "a tragedy of the defenseless and the elderly."[51] The term "tragedy" was used repeatedly in the text and was emphasized "in a completely conscious manner." It was not only a "word" but also a "conception" that, for some reason, was feared. When invoked, it was coupled with the idea of "heroism and resistance." But what if neither was present, and one was faced only with "barbarity, blood, and death"?

> Among the competitors, many—aware of how difficult it is to tackle such a task—chose another path, adopting the tone of protest: "No!—their monuments affirm—This must not happen again! This cannot happen again!" Here before us are groups of executed people with clenched fists and arms raised toward the sky; here are mothers with children clinging to them, and again the same outstretched arms, as if to say: "We will not allow it!" Here before us are faces that always cry out this same: "No! Enough! Enough blood!"
>
> At first glance, the procedure adopted seems to convey the truth, but, as strange as it may seem, while you stand in front of these monuments, you begin to feel a sort of unease, embarrassment. You get the impression that this "No!" is directed at you, it is you who are not allowed to come closer. And so you step back. . . . You are afraid. Someone might tell me: So much the better if one is afraid: what happened here was terrifying. I agree, it was terrifying, but one should not forget that here we are also in a cemetery, and in a cemetery one wants to focus, collect oneself, reflect, remember.
>
> And, in any case, I do not wish to have emotions suggested to me. And not in such a direct, frontal way. Emotions should arise spontaneously, without compulsion.[52]

Some applicants, proposing "abstract" monuments, managed to evoke "emotions without putting rhetorical pressure" on the eye. What remained figurative was shifted, "in the form of relief, high or barely suggested, in some single detail or element of the sculpture, and blended with the architecture." Nekrasov referred to those projects that defined space or followed the course of the ravines with stone walls: "In principle, these are walls—straight or in the form of huge spirals, regular and smooth, or, on the contrary, broken, disorganized, literally collapsed by a bombardment; sometimes they are only granite columns with a hint of some face, or a gigantic torch on the ravine, where the path to reach it symbolizes the final part of the journey toward the execution."[53]

These projects were, on the whole, much more interesting than the others. There was "more thought, more imagination, one might even say more feeling," and "more space for personal thoughts." In other words, there was "greater freedom."[54] Nekrasov had long pondered how to evoke the sense of truth, how to touch emotions gradually, without forcing them, letting them develop in a natural yet complete manner:

> I examined about thirty projects. I saw symbols and allegories pass before me, women protesting, muscular and half-naked men of great realism, and more conventional figures, lines of people walking toward execution. . . . I saw stairs, stylobates, a mosaic, flags, barbed wire, footprints. I saw many things full of talent, made with heart and soul (I believe this is one of the most interesting competitions I have ever attended), and suddenly I understood one thing: places where the greatest tragedies have occurred do not need words. Literal symbolism pales in comparison to the events themselves, allegory is powerless.
>
> When I come to pay homage to the ashes of the victims, there is no need to tell me how they died. I already know. And there is no need to shout in my place: "No, we will not allow it!" I know where and when to shout, and perhaps not just shout, without being told. All I want is to come and lay flowers on the mass grave and stay there for a moment, alone and in silence.[55]

Stanislavski had been the master of "acting without anything." He taught his pupils to concentrate on "physical actions without objects," a technique that allowed the actor's attention, previously dispersed throughout the theater, to be gathered and focused, forcing it into a monitoring of oneself and one's movements, in other words, "logic and coherence." Doing exercises without objects meant learning to strengthen within oneself the sense and conviction of the truth. Where this happened, physical actions acquired "order, harmony, proportion," losing instinctive mechanicity and gaining authenticity and functionality.[56] Nekrasov shifted the system's focus from the theatrical gesture, devoid of matter, to the event celebrated in its purest form:

> I have seen many monuments to the victims of Fascism. Ugly and beautiful. Thunderous and silent. But none impressed me as much as the monument of Treblinka. There are only stones. Nothing but stones. Hundreds, thousands of stones. Of different size and shape. Pointed, blunt, worn, asymmetrical. Only stones. As if they were sprouting from the earth.
>
>   . . . Perhaps what comes closest to what I am talking about, to the issue I am trying to solve, is the proposal for a monument presented by unknown authors under the name *Black Triangle*: two gigantic prisms, one slightly inclined toward the other. Nothing more. I could not now explain why—and perhaps this is precisely the essential—but I suddenly found myself at the feet of these dolmen-prisms that dominated the entire site and felt them, though devoid of the gift of speech, speaking to me powerfully of something terrible and unforgettable.
>
> A powerful voice?
> Perhaps it was only a whisper. And perhaps it is I who say to someone:
> Stop and bow your head.
> Here men were shot.
> A hundred thousand.
> At the hands of the Nazis. The first volley was fired on 29 September 1941.[57]

Thus, in the event, the "I am" of Stanislavski resonated, "the almost absolute truth in summary," leading "to emotion, to feeling, to reliving the part."[58]

6

Claiming the Place

On the night of 8–9 March 1964, a group of artists, including Opanas I. Zaly-
vacha, Alla O. Horska, Lyudmyla M. Semykina, Halyna S. Sevruk, and Halyna O. Zubchenko, created the monumental stained glass *Shevchenko-Mother*
in the vestibule of the Red Pavilion at Kyiv University. The poet and writer
Taras H. Shevchenko, the 150th anniversary of whose birth was being celebrated, was depicted holding a grieving woman (Ukraine) to his chest with
one hand while holding a book aloft in the other. The image was surrounded
by an inscription reproducing a fragment from Shevchenko's *Imitation of
Psalm 11*:

For the poor, the destitute . . . I'll exalt

Those mute and lowly slaves!

And beside them as a sentry

I will place the word.[1]

Without even being evaluated by the arts commission, the stained glass was
immediately destroyed by order of the academic authorities, who deemed it
"nationalistic" in orientation.[2]

This demonstrative action took place during a period of significant intellectual ferment. In Ukraine as elsewhere, the de-Stalinization process had
brought to the fore a school of artists pressing for a loosening of state control
over creative work. The *shistdesyatnyky* (literally, "sixties," referring to the 1960s
generation) did not form a unified movement either aesthetically or ideologically. Although they often invoked national sentiment in advocating for the

preservation of the Ukrainian language and culture against the government's Russification policies, they did not draw inspiration from wartime (or prewar) nationalism but acted on an embryonically universalistic plane. They primarily shared the aspiration to promote democratization of knowledge, affirm social justice, ensure civil rights, and guarantee religious freedom.[3] Among the first significant initiatives were gatherings and literary evenings to commemorate prominent figures of the Ukrainian intelligentsia: Les Kurbas and Taras Shevchenko in 1962, Ivan Franko and Lesya Ukrainka in 1963.[4] In Kyiv the monument to Shevchenko, located near the main building of the university, became one of the symbols of protest.[5]

"The Feeling of Injustice"

The site of the extermination of Jews also became a place of public mobilization.[6] On 24 September 1966 a banner appeared on the only remaining wall of the destroyed Lukyanivka Jewish cemetery. It read in large letters in Russian on the left and Hebrew on the right, "Babi Yar"; at the bottom, centrally placed, "September 1941–1966"; and at the top, in smaller letters, to seal Babi Yar as a fragment of annihilated European Jewry, "Itzkor [Remember]—6 million." One of the young organizers of the gathering, Emmanuel (Amik) Diamant, explained the choice of that date, stating that although they were "completely ignorant" of national culture, the organizers believed that "Jewish anniversaries should be celebrated according to the Jewish calendar." The Nazis had begun the massacre "on the eve of Yom Kippur, which in 1941 fell on 29 September; in 1966 it fell on 24 September."[7]

At the point marking the entrance to the old cemetery, fifty or sixty people spontaneously gathered and stood in silence. The security services' intervention was very discreet, and the agents limited themselves to photographing the attendees. Among them was Viktor Nekrasov, who urged a gathering on 29 September to place "some kind of monument, even if temporary, made of wood or plywood." An inscription in Yiddish, entrusted to writer Itzik Kipnis and translated into both Russian and Ukrainian, was prepared.[8] No commemorative work was installed, but in the afternoon of 29 September, hundreds of people, including several representatives of the Moscow intelligentsia, writers and poets, journalists, and civil rights defenders, came to Babi Yar. Among them were Vladimir N. Voinovich, Pëtr I. Yakir, Yuli Ch. Kim, Feliks G. Svetov, Viktor S. Fogelson, and Vladimir N. Kornilov.

The reasons for the participation of so many Russian and Ukrainian intellectuals in a Jewish demonstration can be understood by following the evolution of literary critic Ivan M. Dziuba, already a significant figure in the Ukrainian national movement at the time. His notoriety was mainly linked to his treatise

Internatsionalizm chy rusyfikatsiya? (Internationalism or Russification?), which had been circulating since December 1965. Dziuba sent it attached to an open letter addressed to Petro Shelest, first secretary of the Central Committee of the Communist Party of Ukraine, and Volodymyr V. Shcherbytsky, chairman of the Council of Ministers of the Republic, to protest against the arrest of dozens of intelligentsia members. The essay spread widely in samizdat form (literature copied by hand or typewriter and distributed illegally) and became a sort of manifesto of nonconformist thought. The author argued that Soviet institutions, using internationalism as a shield, had arbitrarily abandoned Leninist policies of nationality in favor of forced cultural assimilation processes, thus betraying the spirit of Marxism-Leninism. In particular, Dziuba criticized Russification methods and any form of national discrimination, as well as the use of Ukrainophobic sentiments to assert Russian expansionism and chauvinism.[9]

Internationalism or Russification? greatly influenced the younger generation. For dissident Leonid I. Plyushch, it was a real revelation, one that made him understand the need to protect Ukrainian culture and taught him the meaning of the right to self-determination. From that moment forward, even though he had a very limited Ukrainian vocabulary, he began to express himself in his mother tongue and gradually developed a sense of "national pride"— "exactly as Soviet Jews became Zionists due to 'anticosmopolitan' or 'anti-Zionist' propaganda." For her part, his wife, "half Jewish and half Russian," realized upon reading the treatise that "as long as antisemitism existed, she could not help but remain Jewish, even though she was completely ignorant of Jewish language and culture, except for the works of Sholem Aleichem and Peretz Markish."[10]

Dziuba later recalled encountering prejudice and chauvinistic intolerance for the first time in the early 1950s, when, at just over twenty years old, he followed the progress of the campaign against "Zionism" and "Jewish bourgeois nationalism," which culminated in the "doctors' plot."[11] At that point, it suddenly became clear to him just how "defenseless Jews were against the most senseless accusations" and, consequently, how political their "vulnerability" really was. The realization that there was such a thing as a "Jewish question" gradually and haltingly took root in his mind, assisted by a useful analogy: "If the history of the Ukrainian people had been falsified, well, then, the history of the Jewish people and its culture had been erased." It was, in fact, as if "that people and culture had never existed." Moreover, "even the bureaucratized insult uttered against 'Ukrainian bourgeois nationalists'" served, in its fixity and repetitiveness, "to cast a shadow over the entire Ukrainian people and create the sensation of some offense" against a higher idea of belonging, namely, Soviet citizenship. It was "the feeling of injustice" to which Jews had blatantly fallen victim that aroused in Dziuba the feeling of injustice that Ukrainians suffered just as grievously. He then realized that no "theoretical preparation" was required to understand discrimination: It was sufficient to possess "a mind free of disquiet and wrath." The contribution of the *shistdesjatnyky*, the future dissidents, was undoubtedly essential in imposing a tradition of thought. But only "ideals of democracy and humanitarianism" could make it possible to cross the threshold of the private and the individualistic. That was why "Ukrainians involved in that larger movement openly opposed antisemitism, while our Jewish friends did exactly the same against Ukrainophobia."[12]

This was hardly an isolated stance. A comparable civic commitment can be found in the petition that poet and translator Svyatoslav J. Karavansky wrote in prison on 10 April 1966 to denounce policies aimed at discriminating against nations and the frequent abuses that weakened the ties of friendship among the various peoples of the USSR.[13] The document focused primarily on "Jewish victims" and outlined a map of the policies aimed at their marginalization

Firstly, allow me to draw your attention to the discrimination against the Jewish population. I raise this issue first because a society's behavior towards its Jewish population is the litmus test indicating the level of that society's multinational consciousness. The closure of Jewish cultural institutions (newspapers, schools, theaters, publishing houses); the execution of various representatives of Jewish culture; the discrimination in admission of Jews to institutions of higher and secondary education—these are all practices that developed during the period of the cult of personality. One might have assumed that a condemnation of that cult should also end these blatant injustices, but such was not the case. In order to satisfy foreign public opinion, Nikita Khrushchev (who paid little enough notice to Soviet public opinion) was forced to "rehabilitate" the innocent representatives of Jewish culture who'd been executed under Stalin. But he went no further than that.

Where are the Jewish theaters, newspapers, publishing houses, and schools now? In Odessa, there are about 150,000 Jews, but not a single Jewish school. And what about admission to higher education institutions? In Odessa, where 25 percent of the population is Jewish, Jews make up only 3–5 percent of the student body in those institutions. This is the unofficial quota adhered to in admission procedures. But Jewish students applying to higher education institutions in other cities are told: "You have a school in Odessa—go to 'your' school." Students from the Urals, Siberia, Moscow, Tula, and Saratov (all places that possess their own large and well-established universities) can study in Odessa, where dormitories are built specifically for them, while local Jewish students (as well as local Ukrainians and Moldovans) face strong restrictions on their right to higher education.

Practices of this kind can only lead Jews to the awareness that, in the Soviet Union, they belong to an inferior and unequally protected national group, pushing them towards Zionism. It must be admitted that Zionism has never been as popular among the Jewish population as it is today, and this is the direct consequence of discriminatory practices against the Jewish minority.[14]

"As a Ukrainian, I Am Ashamed"

Nekrasov urged Dziuba through mutual acquaintances to come to his house on the morning of 29 September. It immediately became clear to Dziuba why he had been invited, as that was "a special day in the lives of many Kyiv residents." At the appointed hour, he encountered a number of employees of the film studios at the host's house, preparing to film the gathering, convinced that, unless prohibitions stood in the way, the event could take on "a ritual significance."

> When we arrived at Babi Yar, we were stunned by what we saw. All the surrounding hills and heights were teeming with numerous groups of people, at first isolated. This spontaneous movement, however, seemed as if it were a single living being. On each individual face, pain was frozen, eyes were lost in the void: everyone looked back into the depths of time and saw the terrible image of what, for them, was not even past. The shadow of ancient horror and some strange bewilderment of the human hovered over Babi Yar; thousands of silent people faced with their trauma seemed to embody the silent lament of an entire people.
>
> All the people stood silent. But it was a questioning silence. They wanted to hear, they wanted to know. And when word spread that "the writers had arrived," the crowd rushed at us, pulled us aside, so that each of us was surrounded by a group of people asking, "Say, say something! . . ." I had no chance to hear what Viktor Platonovich said because I was surrounded by others, but there was no mistaking the fact that for him, a famous writer and former soldier, it was easier to find the words that those people so desperately needed. Then those words were passed from mouth to mouth, supplemented and commented upon.[15]

There are various accounts of participation in that event. Dissident writer Vladimir Voinovich, who had come from Moscow at Nekrasov's invitation, found himself facing a crowd that had gathered without any public announce-ment (Babi Yar was a "semiforbidden topic"). His reaction was that this was perhaps "the first truly spontaneous gathering in many years of Soviet power."[16] Nekrasov spoke "very little, in a calm and even voice."[17] According to his own recollections, he began by recalling what Anatoly V. Lunacharsky had written in the late 1920s to define the essence of antisemitism. Then, seeing all those people who, on that day of remembrance and mourning, "cried, sobbed, knelt, kissed the ground, and picked up handfuls of it to take away with them," he felt obliged to address them with "words of comfort and hope." He said there would be "a monument," and it could not "be otherwise."[18] Poet and physician Ion L. Degen recalled that those words evoked the classical vision of the writer's role. A writer who knows how to express feelings reopens the circle of popular narrative and can thus materially nourish memory. Degen had the impression that—despite the absence of noise throughout the area—Nekrasov's calm voice could not possibly be "perceived by people whose faces were barely distinguish-able in the distance." Yet "they heard, absorbed, remembered."[19]

Leonid Plyushch struggled to find the place where a "crowd of four to five hundred people, constantly renewed by continuous arrivals and departures," had already gathered, breaking up into smaller discussing groups, then reuniting when speeches were made. From what he could tell, one of the principal needs driving the impromptu speakers was to curb hostility toward Jews. For example, he heard writer Borys D. Antonenko-Davydovych, a survivor of the Stalinist labor camps, say that some Ukrainian intellectuals had managed to get Trochym Kychko's *Iudayizm bez prykras* (Judaism without embellishment, 1963) banned.[20] In his speech, architect Zachariy Belotserkovskiy drew the attention of those present to the contradiction between the "space of mourning" that brought them together and the "legacy" of a "still vibrant and flourishing hatred in soci-ety," in other words, "the ingrained antisemitism that one encountered when queuing up, riding the trolleybus, looking for a job, and even simply enrolling at university" with the full connivance of the authorities. Hence, he proposed a radical solution: "Demand that the state adopt a resolution to repress antisemi-tism, very similar to the recently passed law on hooliganism. As long as the state fails to recognize antisemitism as an antisocial phenomenon, no one will be protected, in daily life and at work, from offenses against national dignity, offenses completely devoid of accountability."[21]

Dina Pronicheva also spoke briefly.[22] But the words that aroused the most emotion were undoubtedly those spoken by Ivan Dziuba.[23] His nonconformist public speeches (e.g., at the Kyiv premiere of Sergei I. Parajanov's film *Tini zabu-tykh predkiv* [Shadows of forgotten ancestors] in September 1965 or at the House of Writers in January 1966) were so popular that they had long placed him under the close surveillance of the security services.[24] At Babi Yar he made it clear how important it was to hear "a single sincere, conscious word, coming from the heart," which had not been "planned, edited, or approved [in advance] by anyone" but instead had been "born from thought, from the soul, and at the moment, not by directive and order."[25] Nekrasov was impressed by the emotion felt by all those in the presence of this man who expressed "a feeling of shame" at being forced to recognize that enmity and distrust between peoples—namely, between Ukrainians and Jews, between Jews and Ukrainians—had not yet been completely eradicated. Dziuba conveyed this sentiment "with suffering and with no attempt to conceal his own personal discomfort" while calling for reconciliation and mutual understanding between two communities that had both suffered equally from intolerance.[26] This is how his speech began:

There are things, there are tragedies, before whose immensity all words are powerless, the best response to which is silence, the great silence of thousands of people. Perhaps it would have been better if we too had refrained from words and simply reflected in silence on what had brought us here. But silence is eloquent only once everything that *can* be said already *has* been said. When, on the contrary, many things have not yet been said, when *nothing* has yet been said, then silence becomes complicit in lies and slavery. That is why we speak, and we must speak, whether we can or we cannot, taking advantage of all the opportunities that so rarely come our way.

I too want to say a few words, a mere thousandth part of what I think today and would like to say here. I want to address you as brothers in humanity. I want to speak to you, as Jews, as what I am, a Ukrainian, a proud member of the Ukrainian nation.

Babi Yar is a tragedy that concerns all humanity, but it occurred on Ukrainian soil. Therefore, a Ukrainian, like a Jew, has no right to forget it. Babi Yar is a tragedy that we have in common, something that concerns, first and foremost, the Jewish people and the Ukrainian people.

Fascism brought this tragedy to our peoples.

But we must never forget that Fascism neither begins nor ends with Babi Yar: It begins with a lack of respect for our fellow men, and it ends with the destruction of our fellow men, with the destruction of peoples, not necessarily with a form of destruction like that of Babi Yar.[27]

The level of civilization of a society was not to be measured by technical or economic achievements but by the role given "to human dignity and conscience." That is why, on that day, it seemed so necessary to feel the duty to remember not only those who were murdered at Babi Yar but also the other

victims of Fascism: an "infinity of lost lives, vanished hopes, unfulfilled aspirations." But there was an issue that Dziuba addressed without any reticence,
even though he knew full well that he was being listened to by the security
service men sent to monitor the event:

> Are we deserving of this memory? Apparently not, if even today, among us,
> there is room for various forms of hatred toward our fellow man, including
> what we call—with an overused, now banal, but still terrible word—
> antisemitism. Antisemitism is an international phenomenon, and it has existed
> and still exists in all societies. Unfortunately, our society is no exception. In
> this, perhaps, there would be nothing surprising, since antisemitism is the fruit
> of a lack of culture and freedom, the principal and inevitable product of politi-
> cal despotism, and overcoming it on the scale of entire societies is neither easy
> nor quick. But what is most surprising is the fact that, in the postwar decades,
> no effective struggle has been conducted against it; indeed, it has often been
> artificially fueled.[28]

There had been frequent attempts to exploit "mutual prejudices" between
Ukrainians and Jews, feeding, on the one hand, the slogans of "Jewish bourgeois
nationalism" and "Zionism" and, on the other, those of "Ukrainian bourgeois
nationalism" and "separatism." These campaigns, "skillfully designed," had caused
enormous damage to both communities and had added further poison to the "bitter memory" of the history of their relations:

> As a Ukrainian, I am ashamed that even within my nation—as within other
> nations—there is antisemitism, there are those ignoble phenomena, unworthy
> of man, that we sum up with the word antisemitism. We Ukrainians must fight,
> within ourselves, against any manifestation of antisemitism or lack of respect for
> the Jew, against the underestimation of the Jewish problem.
>   You Jews must fight, from within, against those who do not respect the
> Ukrainian, the Ukrainian culture, the Ukrainian language, against those who
> wrongly see in every Ukrainian a latent antisemite.
>   We must free ourselves from all forms of hatred toward man, overcome all
> kinds of misunderstanding, and consolidate true brotherhood throughout
> our lives.[29]

Dziuba mentioned the names of many representatives of Jewish culture
(Sholem Aleichem, Yitskhok L. Perets, Mendele Mocher Sforim) and Ukrai-
nian culture (Taras Shevchenko, Lesya Ukrainka, Ivan Franko, Borys D.
Hrinchenko, Stepan V. Vasylchenko) who, in the past, on the basis of shared

ideals of justice and freedom for all peoples, had invested their beliefs in mutual understanding and fraternal coexistence. Sometimes they had even called for cooperation in the national liberation struggle (Vladimir E. Zhabotinsky). But the "noble tradition of solidarity" within differences seemed to have been shattered by the ideal of Communism's transcendence of national cultures and histories:

> The path to authentic, unforced brotherhood lies not in self-contempt but in self-awareness. Not in denying oneself and conforming to others but in being oneself and respecting others. Jews have the right to be Jews, Ukrainians have the right to be Ukrainians, in the fullest, deepest meaning of these words and not merely some formal sense. Let Jews know their history, culture, and language and be proud of them. Let Ukrainians know their history, culture, and language and be proud of them. Let each know the other's history and culture, the history and culture of various other peoples. Let them appreciate themselves and appreciate others as brothers.[30]

It would prove difficult to defeat social ignorance and hatred of others, but committing to that direction was the only alternative to indifference, assimilationism, and conformism. It was owed to the "victims of despotism," to the "finest representatives of the Ukrainian people and the Jewish people," to the "Ukrainian land on which they were called to live together," to "all humanity."[31]

Dziuba's speech enjoyed wide circulation in samizdat form.[32] Six years later, "distorted beyond recognition," it was presented as a charge against him. It was alleged that he had promoted "the union of Zionists with Ukrainian nationalists," a fact that violated criminal laws of the USSR.[33] The indictment was meticulously prepared from the speech delivered at Babi Yar, carefully reviewed for internal KGB use by an informant who showed notable skill in playing text against subtext:

> The *text* of the speech consists of six typewritten pages and begins with the words "There are things that are a tragedy . . . ," ending with the words ". . . it is our duty to humanity." In addition to calling for friendship between the Ukrainian and Jewish peoples and rejecting antisemitism and Fascism, the speech contains, so to speak, a *subtext* aimed at defaming our Soviet reality. On page 1, speaking of the tragedy of Babi Yar caused by Fascism, the author meaningfully notes: "However, we must not forget that Fascism does not begin with Babi Yar, nor does it end with it. Fascism begins with contempt for human beings and ends with the destruction of human beings, with the destruction of

peoples—though not necessarily solely with a form of destruction like that of Babi Yar." The author then, in essence, seeks to somehow identify [this] with the characteristics of the existing socialist system in our country. On the one hand, he argues that space conquest, economic and technical development, a brilliant and "prosperous" society could also have been created by Hitler, if Fascism had won. Therefore, it is necessary "to judge a particular society not by its technical progress, but by the role occupied by human beings and what worth is assigned to human dignity and conscience in it" (p. 2). Farther down, [the author] begins to talk about the fact that there are forms of hatred among us toward other humans, such as antisemitism; that during Stalin's time, an attempt was made to exploit mutual prejudices between Ukrainians and Jews; and that, after World War II, the fight against antisemitism was interrupted; that national issues in our country do not possess a public character; that no true and effective international education is conducted.

This *subtext* gives the speech an anti-Soviet orientation. 20.IV.1972.[34]

"Demagogic Public Actions"

The film director Rafaïl A. Nachmanovych and the cameraman Eduard L. Timlin, employees of the Ukrainian Documentary Film Studio (Ukrkinochronika), filmed footage of the demonstration, but all the material was confiscated by the militia.[35] The same treatment was given to the film crew of Mosnauchfil'm, who were on site to collaborate on a film by Israeli director and producer Margot Klausner about the life of Soviet Jews.[36] The security services mostly limited themselves to identifying some of the demonstrators and seizing the wreaths whose ribbons bore inscriptions in Hebrew from among the heaps of flowers scattered on the ground.[37]

The first secretary of the Kyiv city party committee, Oleksandr P. Botvyn, in a report addressed to the Central Committee, provided extensive detail about the assembly ("mainly young people") at the "site of the massacre of Soviet citizens by the Fascist occupiers." He reported that speeches were delivered that expressed not only sorrow for the victims but also dissatisfaction with the absence of local government representatives, disappointment over the lack of a commemorative monument, and concern over the resurgence of antisemitism. Several speakers denounced the discrimination inflicted on Jews, who no longer had schools, theaters, or newspapers. Some members of the Union of Writers of Ukraine highlighted the danger of Judophobia and advocated the need for Jews and Ukrainians to unite their efforts to "preserve their respective national cultures."[38] The report, referring to information received from the Council for Religious Cults of the Kyiv region and city, also insinuated that there had been premeditation in organizing the rally: The day before, some young people had gone to the synagogue to invite members of the congregation to participate and, upon their refusal, had labeled the community leaders as "enemies of the Jewish people." It would thus be safe to conclude that the gathering was "planned by Jewish and Ukrainian nationalists to incite nationalist tendencies among the Jewish population." In any case, an investigation was initiated to identify the agitators and take strict measures against those who had actively participated in the assembly. The Union of Writers of Ukraine had already launched an internal investigation at the request of that same committee to gather more detailed information about Nekrasov (a member of the Communist Party), Dziuba, Antonenko-Davydovych, and Belotserkovskiy and to impose appropriate sanctions. The executives at Ukrkinochronika immediately condemned Nachmanovych and Timlin for filming without authorization and for using state-owned equipment and film, warning them that they would be fired if they ventured to repeat the offense.[39]

The party administration's concerns about the spread of spontaneous gatherings also emerge from a subsequent document. The city committee met on 12 October and more emphatically decried the demonstration's "nationalistic" nature, having determined that on 29 September certain members of the intelligentsia (Dziuba, Lina V. Kostenko, Yevhen O. Sverstyuk, Mykola H. Plakhotniuk, and others) had gathered in the Bajkove cemetery and placed flowers on the grave of Mykhailo S. Hrushevsky ("Ukrainian nationalist and bourgeois historian") on the occasion of the one hundredth anniversary of his birth. The commitment of the local party offices, the report concluded, should be to "strengthen ideological and educational work among the collectives of the Union of Writers of Ukraine . . . ; demonstrate the groundlessness of the ideologically hostile nationalistic conceptions of the aforementioned individuals . . . ; and proclaim the inadmissibility of their demagogic public actions."[40]

The repressive measures primarily targeted Ukrkinochronika. Its director, Nikolai I. Kozin, was dismissed despite having no role in filming the demonstration—he was entirely unaware of it.[41] Film director Gely I. Snegiryov, also present at the assembly, and cameraman Eduard Timlin were downgraded to performing the humble tasks of subordinates. During a closed-door party meeting held on 24 February 1967, Snjehir'ov denounced the arbitrary nature of the sanctions leveled against him.[42] He also denied that the rally could possibly be viewed as a seditious initiative and claimed the right for non-Jews like him to visit Babi Yar: "It is a disgrace that a Kyiv resident for many generations has never once gone to the site of that immense tragedy."[43] Nekrasov was accused of "violating party discipline."[44] He issued a detailed statement at the request of the party committee of the Union of Writers of Ukraine, reiterating many arguments from his previous addresses:

> For many years, I have gone to Babi Yar on 29 September. I go not only because this place has become the mass grave of people I knew before the war. For me, as for many others, Babi Yar is a symbol of the monstrous essence of Fascism, the place where one of the darkest and indelible tragedies in history occurred.
>
> Over the past fourteen years, a place that the world should remember has been used as a city dump. Then they started "covering it up." I don't delve into the design issues related to the construction of a new urban development in the Babi Yar district. Whatever the justification for such construction, it is hard to explain the effort to level this place, both literally and figuratively. (First, Babi Yar was renamed Syretsky Yar, then, when it was flattened, it began to be called in official documentation "the site of the shooting of victims of Fascism in the Shevchenko district.")
>
> It is hard to understand why there is still no monument in this place, while Lidice, Oradour-sur-Glane, Oświęcim, Treblinka, Mauthausen, Dachau exist, and the bell of Buchenwald rings incessantly over Europe.
>
> On 29 September of this year, twenty-five years had passed since the mass shootings began at Babi Yar. That day, as always, I went to commemorate the innocent victims of the Fascists. Frankly, I hoped to see representatives of local authorities and social organizations there. To my astonishment and chagrin, I found none of them. At the site of the massacre, people whose relatives and friends lie in the ground of Babi Yar arrived, as did the few who managed to escape the Fascist bullets. Many came with flowers they scattered on the ground, as there was neither a monument nor a stone on which to place them. Many wept.
>
> That day, in that place, driven by the same feelings that led me in 1959 to write in the *Literaturnaya gazeta* about the fate of Babi Yar, I felt the need to say a few words to those who, like me, had come to honor the memory of the dead.
>
> I had not prepared a speech, I had written nothing; it sprang out spontaneously at the mass grave of thousands of tortured people. I simply said that—in the place where Fascism implemented its cruel, unprecedentedly vast, racist, antisemitic, and inhuman theorem, where our brothers and sisters now lie—a monument should be built. I felt it was my duty to speak, the duty of a man, a citizen, a Communist, a writer, to speak to those who had gathered there, many of whom expressed painful embarrassment that the site of a tragedy remains marked in no way, even on its twenty-fifth anniversary.

No one appointed me to speak. I spoke personally, and I believe that anyone who has a heart that has not completely hardened and turned to stone would have acted exactly as I did.[45]

The eloquent plea had no effect. From that moment forward, the writer was subjected to a long series of intimidations and harassment, accused of organizing a "Zionist gathering" at Babi Yar. The personal consequences of what has been described as "the most important episode of the sixties in the struggle of civil society against the party apparatus" have been summarized by Nekrasov himself.[46]

My God, how many times from then on would they remind me of this Babi Yar. In the meetings that fate held in store for me with countless party investigators, party commissions of inquiry, in the offices of the provincial, city, regional party committees . . . "Tell us what happened at Babi Yar!" But nothing at all had happened, I merely did what you—provincial committees, city committees, central committees—should have done on the twenty-fifth anniversary of the destruction of thousands, as you now call them, of "Soviet citizens": come and say what I said in your place—here there will be a monument!—what Dziuba said—it is time to end this shameful hostility [between nationalities]. You did not come—intentionally or out of forgetfulness—and we were forced to act in your place.[47]

The accusation of "Zionism" against a non-Jew should come as no surprise. The authorities had incorporated the place "Babi Yar" into "Zionism" so that—as Nahum Korzhavin aptly wrote—"the real meaning of the words" dissolved "into fantastic interpretations."[48] The noun "Zionist" progressively covered an increasingly broad spectrum of meanings: "Not only *any* Jewish personality but [more] simply any person of Jewish origin . . . who did not sit well, at a given moment, with the Soviet authorities." At the same time, the adjective "Zionist" was used to define not only all things Jewish but also what seemed to recall "the Elders of Zion or something similar" in a sort of contemporary revisitation of conspiracy theories.[49]

The pressure exerted by the September 1966 demonstration also had another outcome: Ukrainian leaders were forced to resume state memorial projects. On 20 October a resolution was adopted sanctioning the immediate laying of the first stones for a monument "in the territory of Babi Yar" and another in the Darnytsia area. The task of preparing a sketch for the two monuments and preparing the land for their placement was assigned to the Kyïvproekt Institute, represented by architect Mykola K. Shylo.[50] Shortly afterward, a simple granite stone was installed near Babi Yar with an inscription announcing a commemorative work: "Here a monument will be erected to Soviet citizens who were victims of Fascist crimes during the temporary occupation of Kyiv in 1941–43."[51] The intervention hinted at an opening of institutions to civil society. In a private letter, Ilya Ehrenburg even favorably commented on the placement of that stone and expressed confidence in the commitment, although nothing was yet known about the "artistic and moral merits" of the monument.[52]

On 3 November 1968 a memorial was inaugurated at the site of the Darnytsia concentration camp to honor Soviet citizens, soldiers, and officers of the Red Army. The artists were sculptor Valentyn I. Znoba and architects Oleksandr I. Malinowskyi and Yuri B. Moskaltsov. The central part, located in a forest clearing, consisted of a massive granite block five and a half meters high carved with the muscular torsos and stern faces of the camp prisoners. The complex was accessed along a short path marked at its start by an iron pole with broken barbed wire and a massive slab with an epitaph. However, no work had started at Babi Yar. In the concluding chapter of the revised and updated version of his novel, Anatoly Kuznetsov described the neglected state of the area. He was convinced that the neglect was a deliberate choice: "The stadium project remained unbuilt. Now, nothing is being done in the cursed place. Between the residential complex where the Syrets camp once stood and the television studios where the cemetery once lay, there is a vast abandoned stretch of land, overrun by thistles and brambles. Thus, on the third attempt, Babi Yar disappeared after all, and I believe that the Nazis, if they had had the time and machinery, could not have come up with anything better."[53]

"Defamation of Soviet Reality"

The national Jewish movement in the USSR initially focused on legal actions aimed at obtaining emigration visas: individual letters or collective appeals to various institutions, public demonstrations and hunger strikes, assemblies or gatherings, and dissemination of material abroad.[54] The movement had a powerful radicalizing effect partly due to the Arab-Israeli War of 1967 and partly due to the Jewish community's growing vulnerability to antisemitism because of the constant fueling of that fire by state anti-Zionism, so that it became less and less hesitant to show itself, and Jews were left without any protection.

Babi Yar was becoming not only a place of private or collective remembrance but also a symbolic space to assert a distinct Jewish national consciousness that gave new depth to the right to immigrate to the Jewish state. After the informal gathering to commemorate the twenty-fifth anniversary of the massacre, the city authorities, in order to undermine the initiative shown by the intelligentsia in envisioning a cultural alliance between the Jewish and Ukrainian nations, decided to give formal status to the commemorations at Babi Yar, which indeed officially began in September 1968.[55] Engineer Boris L. Kochubievsky, present at the ceremony, openly criticized the speakers, because instead of reiterating that Jews had been murdered there solely for being Jews, the speakers instead merely evoked the massacre of generic Soviet citizens, using the event to censure Israeli policy in the Middle East. For that reason, he was accused of defaming the Soviet order.[56]

Kochubievsky had moved closer to the Zionist movement during the Six-Day War and had previously challenged the accusation of "Israeli aggression" made by a party activist during a conference on the international situation at his workplace. In May 1968 he was forced to resign, a measure that was also taken against his Russian wife. That month, he wrote "Why I Am a Zionist," an article widely circulated through samizdat publications, explaining why the most active sectors of Jewish youth raised and educated in the USSR, largely atheistic and entirely ignorant of Jewish culture and language, now felt a strong sense of national identity and unity. He attributed this mainly to anti-semitism, both in its old configuration, which still thrived in the most backward circles of Soviet society, and in its more refined and recently established form: anti-Zionism. Evidence of this, in his view, was the vitality of the old battle cry of the Black Hundreds, once used in the fight against Communism: "Beat the Jews, save Russia!" now echoed with the slogan "Beat the Zionists!," then being invoked to defend Communism itself. Although the age of pogroms and of Babi Yar was probably gone forever, the oppression of Jews, led from above, was still the order of the day. It was felt in various forms: the absence of Jewish schools, religious persecution, challenges in finding jobs or accessing higher levels of education, "in short, at almost all levels of public life." These policies had particularly harsh consequences for the new generations: "We copy and memorize "Babi Yar" by Yevtushenko and similar poems. But few, even among the most educated young Jews, know there was a great Jewish poet named Chaim Nachman Bialik—one of us. This too is an example of the discrimination of our culture: young people have no opportunity to study and discover."[57]

During the summer of 1968, Kochubievsky applied to immigrate to Israel with his wife. Initially, his visa was denied for "lack of diplomatic relations," but in November he was suddenly informed that the request had been approved. On the same day that the couple was invited to the Department of Visas and Registration (Otdel viz I registracii, OVIR), however, their apartment was searched, some documents were seized, and they were placed under house arrest.[58] Adopting a strategy that philosopher Abraham J.

Heschel described as "the simple rhetoric of essential humanity,"[59] Kochubievsky then addressed an open letter to the Communist Party's general
secretary, Leonid I. Brezhnev, and the Ukrainian Communist Party's secretary, Petro Shelest:

> I am a Jew. I want to live in the Jewish State. It is my right, just as it is the right
> of a Ukrainian to live in Ukraine, the right of a Russian to live in Russia, the
> right of a Georgian to live in Georgia.
>   I want to live in Israel.
>   This is my dream; this is the goal not only of my life but also of the lives of
> hundreds of generations before me, of my ancestors driven from their land.
>   I want my children to study in a Hebrew school, I want to read Hebrew
> newspapers, I want to go to a Hebrew theater. What's wrong with that? What is
> my crime?[60]

Kochubievsky recalled that many of his relatives, including his father and
paternal grandparents, were killed during the war and that if they were still alive,
they would undoubtedly be by his side as his wife now was, since she had
rejected all their attempts to make her file for divorce. He believed he had the
right not to be involved in the affairs of a state where he felt like "a stranger" and
reiterated that he would continue to do everything in his power to emigrate.
Regarding the accusation against him—"defamation of Soviet reality"—he
really didn't even know what to think:

> In what does this defamation consist? Is it perhaps a defamation that in the
> multinational Soviet state, the Jewish people alone are not allowed to educate
> their children in Jewish schools? Is it perhaps a defamation to say that there is no
> Hebrew theater in the USSR? Is it perhaps a defamation to say that there are no
> Hebrew newspapers in the USSR? . . . Is it a defamation that for over a year, I
> have been unable to obtain permission to immigrate to Israel? Or is it a defama
> tion that no one wants to talk to me, that there is no one to appeal to? No one
> responds.[61]

At the beginning of December, Kochubievsky was arrested on charges of
violating article 187/1 of the penal code of the Ukrainian Socialist Soviet
Republic. By asserting that the state oppressed Jews, he had slandered the
Soviet political and social order in both oral and written form. On 20 January
the investigation was deemed concluded, and the case was referred to the
court, which requested additional investigation, finding insufficient evidence
for prosecution. The trial, closely followed by dissenting circles, finally took

place from 13 to 16 May 1969. Kochubievsky was charged with making a critical statement after a conference on "Israeli aggression" held at his factory, giving two speeches at Babi Yar on the anniversary of the massacre and Yom Kippur (29 September and 2 October 1968), writing a draft letter to the Ministry of the Interior protesting the denial of his emigration visa, and having some conversations with coworkers during which he allegedly expressed "defamatory" views on Soviet reality. The trial was supposed to be public, but only prescreened individuals were admitted to the courtroom, leading some excluded listeners to file a complaint with the Kyiv city prosecutor for violating article 20 of the Ukrainian code of criminal procedure. However, thanks to reports from several civil rights activists, it was possible to learn that the court displayed a prejudiced attitude and created an atmosphere of intolerance toward both the summoned witnesses and the defendant.[62] Both the public prosecutor and the judge repeatedly intervened with statements that displayed aggressive anti-Zionist tones, while the defense was clearly compromised by the investigating and judicial authorities.[63]

One of the main points supporting the prosecution, represented by prosecutor Surkov, was the critical comment made at Babi Yar on the anniversary of the massacre, a comment that the court considered as nationalist and Zionist propaganda.[64] As for the assertion that Jews were oppressed in the USSR, the prosecutor argued that there had indeed been cases of antisemitism in the country, but they were isolated incidents, and the law had always addressed them. The defendant's opinions, formed under Western influence, were therefore deemed entirely unfounded, driven by "nationalist sentiments" and a "superiority complex."[65]

In his final statement, Kochubievsky, who continued to assert his right to immigrate to Israel with his family, denied ever preaching "national enmity" or speaking of "state antisemitism"; instead, he only drew attention to individual hostility toward Jews. He also tried to evoke Yevgeny Yevtushenko's poem "Babi Yar," with which he felt fully aligned, but he was reprimanded by the judge, who ordered him not to "digress into history and literature."[66] The trial ended with a sentence of three years of corrective labor, upheld on appeal in June 1969. The engineer finished serving his sentence on 4 December 1971, and a few days later, he was allowed to leave the Soviet Union to move to Israel.

"An Almost Surreal Scene"

Starting from 1967, not only did national Jewish sentiment explode, but the campaign for aliyah (the immigration of Jews to Israel) intensified as well.[67] The resolution of migration issues in a country where there were no legal bases for granting or denying exit visas, nor was there any acknowledgment of an individual's free choice in the case of expatriation or repatriation, was left to the discretion of the OVIR officials and other administrative bodies, whose decisions were usually issued without explanation and orally. The absence of legislation regulating the "right to emigrate," denounced by members of the Moscow Helsinki Group (Moskovskaja Chel'sinskaja gruppa), meant that thousands of people considered "almost as semicriminals, if not traitors," found themselves "exposed to persecutions and abuses." They were indeed "forced to resign from their jobs, excluded from educational institutions, and often brought to trial based on false accusations."[68]

Viktor Nekrasov presented one of the many "personal cases" of those years in a short story published in 1976. Abram Lazarevich Jufa, a former combatant, an engineer, a model worker, and a party member, at almost sixty years old requests a visa to immigrate to Israel: "Why did he decide such a thing? He couldn't answer, exactly. He just wanted to. Although in early childhood he had studied in the heder of Uman', and his father regularly attended synagogue, he had never shown any inclination for the Jewish religion, nor for religion in general. He had studied in a Ukrainian vocational school and gone to university. He barely knew Yiddish. He had forgotten it. He had friends who were Russian, Ukrainian, and Jewish. But just what their nationality might have been, he couldn't say, at that time he didn't pay attention."[69]

Abram Lazarevich had never been a victim of antisemitic acts, although since 1949 he had felt the weight of the anticosmopolitan campaign, which had affected several of his friends and acquaintances. But after the Six-Day War, in the face of attacks against "Zionists, aggressors, and occupiers," his feelings of affiliation changed. It was true that, in the Soviet Union, citizens of Jewish nationality enjoyed the same rights as other nationalities: the rights to work, rest, education, and security in their old age. So what else did he want? "Not much. The freedom to make his own decisions." He didn't blame anyone for anything, neither the party nor the government. He was only asking for permission to immigrate to Israel. Why? It was "a personal matter."[70]

When the protagonist of the short story is subjected to a hearing, he presents his request for emigration before the party members, shifting from a purely personal matter to one that touches on the malaise afflicting much of Soviet Jewry:

> To many, it may seem strange—and I perfectly understand—that a man born in this land, a man who defended it during the Great Patriotic War, who studied and worked before the war and went on working for another twenty-five years after the war; a man who barely reads Yiddish and knows no Hebrew at all,

suddenly wants, in his old age, to move to a country inhabited by complete strangers who speak an unknown language, a country where other laws are in effect and where, in fact, there is a state of ongoing conflict being fought not to defend *your* interests but those of foreign individuals. I understand that all this may seem strange. But only at first glance. Let me repeat: only at first glance.

. . . Let me be frank with you. I have nothing to hide. And there is no reason to. (And here he begins to speak in a louder voice.) Personally, I feel no mark of antisemitism upon me. But does that really mean there is no such thing? Antisemitism exists. (Noise in the hall. Baruzdin taps the carafe with a pencil: "Order, order.") Yes, it exists. And the problem is not what we sometimes hear on the radio or the fact that there are no Jewish schools or Jewish newspapers, that there are very few synagogues . . . (A voice from the hall: "So does this mean you listen to the BBC?") That's not the point. And it's not even in the fact that someone, perhaps in a state of drunkenness or perhaps without even being drunk, might say "dirty Jew." No, the point has to do with something that cannot be spoken about, even though everyone is well aware of it: the limited number of Jews in universities and other institutions; my son's teacher who, having seen Israeli stamps in his album, orders him to throw them away immediately; books in Hebrew that are confiscated; the man who wanted to lay a wreath next to the stone at Babi Yar and who was first asked to translate the Hebrew inscription on the wreath and then prevented from laying the wreath anyway. The third day at OVIR, for example, at the visa office, it was explained to me clearly when I went in to get forms, a major with a medal on his chest said: "If it were up to me, I would gather you all together in one big pile and without much fuss kick you out—and good riddance . . . Enough sitting around here, muddying the waters, causing provocations. . . ." What should we call all this? Friendship of peoples? And the fact that, after such words, said right to your face, your desire to go to a small country that is building its life, where no one, drunk or sober, will ever call you "dirty Jew," that this desire should be called treason to the homeland and that you should be suspected of wanting to sell something to someone . . . That is the most offensive thing.[71]

According to data from the Ministry of Internal Affairs of the Ukrainian SSR, in the second half of the 1960s, 5,762 applications for departure were submitted by citizens of Jewish nationality residing mainly in Kyiv; in the period 1970–73, the number of requests grew to over 11,000 and continued to swell in the years that followed.[72] Babi Yar, put at the center of international interest by artists and writers, became the place where the civil disobedience of Jews was proclaimed.[73] The activity around the monumental stone block took on an increasingly marked affiliation with identity.[74] Many of those who took part in the demonstrations commemorating 29–30 September 1941 began to familiarize themselves with the Hebrew language by deciphering the letters in the inscriptions on the wreaths of flowers and memorizing the Kaddish even though they didn't understand the words.[75] Year after year, despite repressive interventions (arrests, beatings, fines, detentions, dismissals), attendance increased: fifty to seventy people in 1968, three to four hundred in 1969, seven to eight hundred in 1970.[76] "Each time," pointed out the main newsletter of the dissenters, "people are more courageous, more determined. The national self-awareness of those whose families and relatives lie in the soil of Babi Yar grows."[77]

Paid provocateurs from the security services often infiltrated the crowd to loudly assert the heroic role of the Russian people who fought to save the Jews and to diminish the symbolic significance of Babi Yar. This is what happened after the official demonstration in 1969, when two large wreaths were laid at the foot of the memorial stone—the first wreath made of white flowers, the second of blue flowers—in a rather original shape: triangles with equal sides (measuring about two meters) that, joined diagonally, formed a Magen David, a Star of David.[78] Leonid Plyushch, arriving with his wife late in the evening, found himself facing "an almost surreal scene":

> Faces of inspired young Jews and a crowd of "comrades" in plainclothes. The plainclothes people were of two types. Some looked like agents, that is, criminals with evasive eyes and a doglike expression. For some reason, you didn't see them as persecutors but as persecuted, hunted animals. The second category comprised individuals who looked bloated with contentment, carefully clean shaven, with snakelike eyes and a stupidly self-satisfied air.
>
> The plainclothes people tried to pick fights: What are you doing here? Why are you lighting candles? The answer was "to commemorate the victims." Everyone gathered around the stone that bears the promise to erect a monument—a stone covered in flowers.
>
> Two young people brought triangular wreaths of yellow flowers [*sic*] and placed them one on top of the other to form a Star of David. Scandal. The plainclothes people began to get agitated, shouting that the people buried here were not only Jews but also Communists. Someone responded: "No one forbids you from coming with a cross if you consider yourselves Russians, and there is also a right to place a five-pointed star [if you consider yourselves Communists]. . . ."
>
> An old Jew joined in with the chorus of plainclothes people, arguing that the enemies had imposed the yellow star on Jews, that the Fascists had branded them with it. They reminded him that once the five-pointed star was carved on the bodies of Bolsheviks. The young people began to tell the old man the history of the Star of David. Gradually the discussion switched to Yiddish. At last, the

old man put forward his conclusive argument: "But they will close our last syna-gogue." It turned out he was its caretaker. I felt sorry for him. But the young people showed no mercy and gave him the final blow: "What do we need a syna-gogue for, if it denies the history of the Jews and the Star of David?" The old man fell silent.[79]

The "surreal" nature of the event, according to Plyushch, lay in the fact that it was a clash between the descendants of the old Red commissars and their latter-day heirs: "The descendants were rebelling again, while the heirs contin-ued the work of the czarist police. With one difference: their victims were no longer called Judeo-Masons, Judeo-Cadets, Judeo-Communists, but Zionists."[80] Some young people were identified and detained by members of the security services, who had learned in advance about the intended details of the demon-stration and, in particular, the intention to lay "a wreath in the shape of a six-pointed star."[81] A similar attempt was made the following year, which seemed to confirm to the authorities the stubborn vitality of Zionist intrigues.[82] The law enforcement officials engaged in genuine "exercises of literary science," conduct-ing a careful inspection of bouquets and wreaths of flowers: "The militia and the cohort of plainclothes men backing them carefully check their ribbons and, in case of doubt ('in what language is it written? Translate, please'), there are police vans nearby ready to take away the young people carrying the wreaths. Older people and those with small bouquets are allowed through the double barrier without difficulty. At worst, a few get their pictures taken."[83]

Meanwhile, the operating theory of a collusion between Zionism and Nazism, a thesis with reliable popular appeal applied by Ukrainian collabora-tors in the immediate postwar period, was reaffirmed in Soviet language and gained increasing strength.[84] In March 1970 much attention was given to a letter sent to *Pravda* by self-proclaimed Soviet citizens of Jewish origin resid-ing in Ukraine. It stated that the tragedy of Babi Yar would forever remain "the incarnation not only of the fierce cruelty [*kannibalizm*] of the Nazis but also of the indelible infamy of their accomplices and followers, the Zionists" who had collaborated in the extermination of the peoples of the USSR.[85] This prompted Anatoly Kuznetsov to assert that Ukrainian Jews were "subjected to such intimidation that they were ready to sign anything."[86] Viktor Nekrasov also indignantly claimed that those who spoke at Babi Yar during official gath-erings had the gall to condemn not only the Nazis but also "their Zionist accomplices, hands stained with the blood of executed Kyivans."[87]

In 1971, the thirtieth anniversary of the massacre, the official commemora-tion comprised about five hundred people.[88] The informal one, held immedi-ately afterward, brought together over a thousand. A group of civil rights activists from Kharkiv was blocked by the police and ordered off the train before arriving in Kyiv. This did not prevent delegations from various cities (Moscow, Leningrad, Sverdlovsk, Tbilisi) from attending, laying about forty wreaths of flowers with inscriptions in Russian and Yiddish. The militia and agents of the security services, particularly numerous that day, photographed the participants and intervened harshly to seize or destroy any object that could be traced back to Jewish identity (yarmulkes or kippahs, black funeral ribbons, etc.).[89]

Demonstrative gatherings were not only held on the anniversaries of the massacre but also on other occasions. Activist Anatoliy (Alik) Feldman described one organized on 22 April of the same year to celebrate Yom HaShoah, the day of remembrance of the Holocaust established in the State of Israel. On the eve, he was summoned to the local KGB office along with some friends and subjected to a long interrogation. He was accused of conducting propaganda activities in favor of immigration to Israel and of organizing an *ulpan* (intensive Hebrew language course). The advice given to him was to change his attitude to avoid the risk of being sent back to a labor camp. Part of the conversation concerned the planned celebration for the following day. The detailed dialogue, reconstructed by Feldman himself, makes the ongoing clash clear:

What action have you planned for tomorrow?

We haven't planned any action. If you're interested in knowing what I personally intend to do tomorrow, I can say that I want to go to Babi Yar and lay a wreath in memory of the Jews who died there in 1941.

Why do you only commemorate the memory of the Jews, since there are Soviet citizens and other nationalities buried there?

But only the Jews were killed because they belonged to a specific people. It was genocide. Silencing this means justifying the Fascist murderers. Also, when we go to a cemetery, we go to the graves of our family members. Does that mean we disrespect the other graves? We mourn all the victims of the Nazis, but we don't hide that our souls suffer especially for the Jews who died. Isn't that natural?

Why did you choose tomorrow for the funeral ceremony when the entire Soviet people celebrate the anniversary of V. I. Lenin's birth? It may seem like a provocation.

It's a coincidence. The Hebrew calendar is lunar, and this year Yom HaShoah falls on 22 April.

And in the future will it be 1 May?

No, on 11 April.

Why didn't you celebrate this day last year?

When you're right, I can't help but agree with you. It was indeed our oversight. I can assure you it won't happen again.

We do not advise you to go to Babi Yar tomorrow. The act of laying wreaths with inscriptions in an unknown language and, more generally, your provocative behavior may provoke a counterreaction from the non-Jewish population. Aren't you afraid of that?

No, we're not afraid. I know that without your precise orders, nothing will happen. And excesses are not in your interest at this moment.

A police officer or a voluntary guard, or any Soviet citizen, doesn't know what's written on the wreath. What if it's an anti-Soviet slogan?

There are 150,000 Jews in Kyiv. You could have a helper who knows the Hebrew language.

In any case, we do not advise you to go. Besides the laws, there is the Soviet order. We will not allow anyone to violate it and organize religious orgies in a public place.

We don't need your advice. If you can, prohibit us from going to Babi Yar.

We can't prohibit it, but we warn you to use good sense.

Thanks for the warning, and let me warn you: Since you are aware that we want to lay wreaths, the responsibility for any possible incident will fall on you.[90]

The following day, the demonstration took place without incident. A few months later, Feldman was among the organizers of a hunger strike to protest more forcefully ("more dramatic forms of struggle were necessary") against the unwarranted refusal to grant immigration visas to Israel. It was decided that the protest would take place on 1–2 August during Tisha B'Av, a day of mourning in the Jewish religious calendar that involves a fast of just over twenty-four hours. On 1 August eleven people began the demonstration after notifying the chairman of the presidium of the Supreme Soviet of the USSR, Nikolai Podgorny, by telegram. The activists sat at the foot of the memorial stone. After about three hours, they were arrested by the police, and the next day, ten of them were sentenced by a people's court to fifteen days of detention for "petty hooliganism [melkoe chuliganstvo]"; one protester was fined.[91]

On 7 September 1972 several activists attempted to lay wreaths in memory of the eleven Israeli athletes killed at the Munich Olympics.[92] They were met by police patrols and KGB members in plain clothes, some of whom were well known for repeatedly participating in actions against Jewish dissent, particularly near the Kyiv synagogue. Twenty-seven people were arrested, eleven of whom were sentenced to fifteen days of detention, while five were fined. On 29 September that year, the official commemoration began later than usual.

The speaker focused on the "Israeli aggression against the Arabs," then, as usual, mentioned that Soviet citizens of various nationalities were killed at Babi Yar. The hundreds of people who came for the informal commemoration found the area heavily guarded. Wreaths with inscriptions in Hebrew or blue and white ribbons were not allowed, and the area was cleared quickly.[93]

The gathering held in 1973 was the subject of a report sent to the Central Committee of the Soviet Communist Party by the first secretary of the Central Committee of the Communist Party of Ukraine, Volodymyr Shcherbytsky. He reported on the official commemoration attended by about two thousand workers and the attempt by "a group of Jewish extremists from Kyiv," already authorized to immigrate to Israel, to "exploit the presence of a significant number of citizens, including Jews," to stage "a provocation against the community" with accomplices from Moscow, Odessa, and Novosibirsk. After the ceremony, about twenty "Zionists" approached the memorial stone to lay wreaths and flowers with white and blue ribbons, as well as to light candles. Moreover, they had pinned "yellow six-pointed paper stars and the image of the Israeli flag" on their clothes. This provoked the "indignation" of those present and led to a verbal altercation that ended with the detention of "Zionist I. S. Goldfarb," who was accused of "defamation," and three other activists, who defended him and refused to identify themselves. Shcherbytsky assured that appropriate measures had been taken to "strengthen the ideological work of party organizations among workers, educating them in the spirit of friendship among peoples, Soviet patriotism, and proletarian internationalism, as well as unmasking Zionism and Jewish bourgeois nationalism." He also assured that measures would be taken "to monitor the behavior of Jewish extremists and prevent their hostile and antisocial acts."[94]

In May 1974 a ceremony was organized to commemorate the massacre at Ma'I, a small town in northern Israel, on 15 May. About twenty Jews, mostly visa applicants, notified the authorities by telegram of their intention to hold a peaceful demonstration at Babi Yar. They were met by about two hundred uniformed and plainclothes officers who tried in every way, in a state of great agitation, to hinder the movements of the "pilgrims." However, no demonstrator was arrested. A silent stop was allowed near the granite boulder, but laying wreaths was forbidden, so they were taken to the nearby Jewish cemetery. Reporting the event, Gely Snegiryov used dark tones to depict the authorities' agitation:

> The dying hydra thrashes its tail, destroying aimlessly. And again, I ask myself the same senseless questions. Why these two hundred against twenty? They know this will make noise abroad. They understand that this ceremony poses no

threat to order and power. And not just the security service members, as they must undoubtedly have informed the secretary of the Central Committee of Ukraine, Shcherbytsky, and he must have issued orders. They know and understand, while the hydra, to its own detriment, thrashes its tail senselessly and aimlessly. Where will it turn tomorrow, who will it strike down tomorrow? In the face of its madness, what guarantee is there that, from one day to the next, trucks [*voronki*] labeled "Meat" won't start running through the streets, houses, and apartments? What to expect when there is no common sense?[95]

In 1974 the thirtieth anniversary of Ukraine's liberation from Nazi occupation was observed. The authorities deemed it unnecessary to hold an official commemoration at Babi Yar at the end of September as usual, focusing instead on an initiative involving "all memorial sites associated with the events of the Great Patriotic War." However, they took care to prevent "any illegal actions by extremist elements" with the help of "municipal administrative bodies."[96] Shortly before that day, eighty-six Jews from various cities had sent a petition to the Central Committee of the Soviet Communist Party lamenting the absence of a commemorative monument and proposing the creation of a special fund for its construction: "Are construction materials insufficient, perhaps? Given the current scale of construction work in the country, it's a drop in the bucket. Are financial resources insufficient? But a monument costs much less than one of the thousands of tanks that have been continuously supplied to Arab countries for twenty years. If, nevertheless, there is not even the possibility of setting aside even one tank's worth of funds, there is no doubt that Soviet Jews are ready to raise the necessary resources to build the monument."[97]

The pressure exerted by this initiative is evidenced by the fact that local Communist Party organizations felt the need to intervene promptly to respond to the "so-called refuseniks" and their announced "public committee for fundraising," entrusting the daily newspaper *Vechirniy Kyiv* with the publication on the eve of 29 September of "material concerning the monument project and its construction," which had already been ratified.[98] The preparation of the petition was closely monitored by the security services of the Ukrainian republic, as indicated by a special report sent by the chairman of the committee representing them at the Council of Ministers, Vitaliy Fedorchuk, to Volodymyr Shcherbytsky on 21 September. It highlighted that "Zionist extremists in the city of Kyiv" had taken to "using Jewish religious holidays and certain commemorative dates, including 29 September," to organize "nationalistic and anticommunity demonstrations with provocative intent." The report detailed the surveillance activities conducted by KGB agents against several activists. Agents had monitored the movements of activists to Moscow to ensure wide participation in the thirty-third anniversary commemoration, prepare a broadly agreed upon petition, and guarantee the transmission of information to the foreign press about the worsening situation of the "refuse-niks" (*otkazniki*) and the likely preparation of new trials against them. Fedor-chuk, while trying to downplay the numerical significance of those involved and thus highlight the effectiveness of the "preventive-prophylactic measures" adopted in recent times, stressed the need for a comprehensive "action plan to ensure security and social order in the Babi Yar district on 29 September." Plans were developed to deploy all operational means to ascertain the actual intentions of the "extremists," identify the initiators and instigators of the demonstration, put them under strict surveillance, hinder their movements, and prevent their presence at the commemoration by any means. It was also necessary to reinforce the presence of KGB personnel, militia, and security services at the site to prevent the "Zionists" from approaching the memorial stone.[99]

"They Stole from Me an Unfinished Work"

On 17–18 January 1974 Nekrasov's residence was subjected to a thorough search, lasting forty-two hours, in a quest for "literature of an anti-Soviet and defamatory nature," as stated in the warrant.[100] Seven sacks of books, newspa-pers, manuscripts, letters, photographs, a tape recorder and tapes, a typewriter, and two cameras were taken away, nearly the writer's entire personal archive, including documentation collected and compiled for Babi Yar, with an album of snapshots taken there. The officials focused particularly on the photo-graphic material, as detailed in the investigation record: "Album of photo-graphs with a white polyethylene cover: 24.5 × 17.3 × 1.5 cm, with the text 'Babi Yar' handwritten in black ink on the front. On the first page of the album, a clipping of V. Nekrasov's text titled 'Why Wasn't It Done?' is pasted. In the fifteen pages of the album, photographs of city outskirts landscapes and cem-etery snapshots with toppled monuments are pasted. At the end of the album are fifteen images with similar cemetery landscapes."[101]

The apartment was entirely ransacked, and "the writer's whole life was offended and vilified."[102] It was a true act of intimidation, followed by a long series of weekly interrogations to induce him to correct his mistakes or even emigrate, thereby depriving an entire generation of readers of access to his books.[103] From those interrogations with the KGB investigating judge, Nekra-sov retained, above all, a sense of dishonor: "The shame of going into details, of giving the impression that one was justifying oneself for something, or simply responding, but, above all, acting as if nothing had happened. . . . That feeling still haunts me. An older man, a professional writer, must prove that he has the right to read books."[104] A few weeks later, Nekrasov wrote an article, published in mid-April by a Russian émigré magazine, reflecting on the nature of the search ("the extreme extent of the state's distrust toward one of its citizens") and the meaning of the inquisitorial questions he had been subjected to ("an offensive and outrageous intrusion into your intimate life"):

> Perhaps a writer may not even be published, but he still cannot help writing, he cannot remain silent. It is his obligation, his duty. But how can he fulfill it when, at any moment, nice polite people can come to you with an order, seize the freshly inked pages of what you were writing, and take them away?
>
> They stole from me an unfinished work—small but very important to me—about Babi Yar, the 1941 tragedy, the way they leveled a forty-meter-deep ravine after the war, covered it up, and almost forgot it—then, how they placed a simple stone at the massacre site; and yet there is still no monument; about how people come every year on 29 September with wreaths and flowers, and about what happens there.
>
> And so they took away my manuscript and the album with my photographs of Babi Yar in all its stages of erasure. As well as the film . . . Will they return them? I don't know . . . I will reconstruct the manuscript. They will come again and take it again. And then? Always like this? And the film? Will they burn it?[105]

On 20 May Nekrasov wrote to Leonid Brezhnev, stating that he had decided, driven by recent events, to take an extreme step. His living conditions had become so complicated that he was "completely deprived of the possibility of working" and forced to acknowledge that the path to reaching readers was now "closed." The authorities had not only prevented him from publishing; they had found other measures of "pressure and punishment," all because he had always tried to defend "personal principles and convictions." The extensive incursion among his papers in January had resulted in the confiscation of drafts that he hadn't even typed yet. The range of actions taken against him, from the most significant to the most trivial, formed "the chain of a single process, offensive to human dignity," aimed solely at preventing him from "living and acting with serenity." Therefore, unable to "endure further offenses," he sought permission from the country's highest authority ("recognizing the evident hostility of the designated bodies") for a measure he would never have wished for in another context: "authorization to leave the country for two years." He was aware of the gravity of the choice, especially due to his deep connection to the land where he'd been born and raised, where he had studied and worked, and for whose defense he had received two war wounds.

But he had no other way out: "A writer cannot work knowing that, at any moment, they can come to him and take away what he has written and never return it."[106] The next day, the Kyiv section of the Union of Writers expelled Nekrasov for "anti-Soviet behavior incompatible with the requirements of the union's statute" and for "dishonoring the high title of Soviet writer with his activities and amoral behavior."[107]

On 10 July Nekrasov formally requested a three-month exit visa for himself and his wife. The first secretary of the Central Committee of the Communist Party of Ukraine, Volodymyr Shcherbytsky, immediately reported this to the highest authorities. The report summarized the contents of previous investigations and exaggerated the potential danger posed by the accused. It outlined the intellectual biography of the writer, emphasizing the "serious ideological errors" he had committed, the "distortion of Soviet reality" and the "idealization of the capitalist world" present in many of his works from the 1950s and 1960s. According to Shcherbytsky, Nekrasov had subsequently "fully adopted positions opposed to the Soviet system." For many years, he had exerted a "corrupting influence on ideologically immature youth and other people in his environment"; he had established "systematic relations with foreigners working in foreign ideological centers" and had provided them with "defamatory information" about the Soviet Union; he had turned his apartment into "a meeting place for anti-Soviet elements—Zionists and other extremists," with whom he discussed how to make the activities of the "so-called 'movement for democratization in the USSR'" more effective, preparing "provocative demonstrations." The writer was even thought to be in line to potentially assume a future role as "leader of the so-called 'democrats'" if Andrei D. Sakharov were to emigrate. The reeducative and coercive measures taken on several occasions had proved to be in vain, emphasized the first secretary. Nekrasov persisted in his "provocative" behavior and remained wedded to "hostile positions." Regarding the visa application, there was information suggesting that he intended to use that visa to travel abroad and never return to his homeland. In conclusion, given that he was a "morally depraved personality" and incapable of playing "a significant role in the anti-Soviet émigré community," it was deemed a waste of time and effort to attempt to hinder his request. The issue of a possible return to the Soviet Union would be addressed in due time "in accordance with his behavior outside the borders."[108]

On 27 July 1974 Nekrasov received a temporary visa allowing him to travel to Switzerland for ninety days. On 12 September he left the Soviet Union forever. This was, in effect, a sentence of exile.[109] From that date, he would be an emigrant. The project about Babi Yar would never be completed, despite all his good intentions to reconstruct the confiscated material.[110]

Those Days Known to All

Nekrasov had already been definitively expelled from the party on 24 May 1973. From that moment, "as a writer, that is, as a man who not only writes but also publishes his writings," he ceased "to exist."[111] Among the works that did not reach publication in the Soviet Union were the essays known as the "Gorodskie progulki" (City walks), composed in 1969–70. This collection, dedicated to the city of Kyiv, devoted considerable space to Babi Yar. The author brought to completion here the genre of travel narratives transformed into a "free reflection on life, on oneself, on art, and on history." His thoughts moved freely between topics, memories, impressions, observations, from the small to the large and vice versa, without submitting to any "conventional plot," because he intended to reflect only the "internal logic of the narrator." It was a form of writing born of the experience of realistic wartime storytelling (or of the "diary") and now freed from the "artistic 'lie'" of Soviet literature.[112] It was also the assertion of a model of life as a quest for truth based on a few solid principles, respected in all the major phases of life, "whether he was fighting on the Mamaev Kurgan, where there were five to twelve hundred fragments of shrapnel and bullets concentrated in a square meter of land; or when he later described the reality of battles in Stalingrad; or when, as a free man, he recounted his impressions abroad; or when he refused to back down and yielded not at all in spite of pressure from literary leaders and party leadership, the press, and the KGB."[113]

Nekrasov had proposed that "Gorodskie progulki" be published by *Novy mir*, which was the most liberal of the Soviet literary magazines and to which he had long been a contributor. But the manuscript, after undergoing the usual editorial treatment ("corrected, supplemented, reread, rewritten"), was embargoed just before going to print. The editor in chief suggested revising a substantial part of the text, specifically "the chapter on Babi Yar." But since it had already been sufficiently "shortened" and the author had no intention of making a "new revision," no agreement could be found to permit the publication of the entire text.[114] This interrupted the literary path Nekrasov had undertaken in his country ("writing and publishing") and ended his hope that the moderate work plan formulated in the introduction ("to take a walk, observe with curiosity, and evoke memories") would allow him "to offend no one," passing unscathed through the mesh of censorship "so that all my explorations in childhood and youth, the flow of reflections—having sidestepped every obstacle—would finally reach the reader."[115] "Gorodskie progulki" would see the light only after he emigrated, integrated into a text titled "Zapiski zevaki" (Reflections of a wanderer).[116]

In the essay on Babi Yar, unacceptable to the censor, Nekrasov began with a description that seemed to emphasize above all the anonymous aspect to which the territory of the genocide had been reduced:

> A small mound of flowers. Wreaths. Large, small, medium. Simple bouquets of flowers. On the wreaths, ribbons with inscriptions: "To our father, to our mother, to our grandfather from the children, daughters, grandchildren"; "To our children, who were not allowed to grow up"; ["From the Jews of Sverdlovsk"]; "To the victims of the Fascist executioners"; ["From the Jews of Minsk to those who were tortured in Babi Yar"].
>
> Under the wreaths, a gray granite stone (no longer visible). It states that a monument will be built here. Around it, a clearing: grass, small firs, and young birches, all very clean and orderly. Behind the stone, a grove; between the stone and the road, a path of concrete slabs, some steps, two poles with spotlights.
>
> Out front, on the asphalt road, cars, buses, and trolleybuses speed by. A hundred meters farther on, a colorful and translucent shelter: "Trolleybus stop Shcherbakovsky Department Store." On the other side, the television tower, still under construction. Beyond the asphalt road, a thicket of shrubs and, in the distance, the new buildings of the Syrets district. Turning your back to the stone, you can glimpse on the right of the abandoned land a kind of embankment covered with older shrubs. It is the upper edge of the Yar, which no longer exists. Here the machine guns were placed. And there were also machine guns on the other side of the Yar.
>
> Today the Yar has disappeared. It has been leveled. An asphalt road crosses it. Thirty years ago, this road did not exist. But there was a chasm extending in depth as much as fifty meters. Increasingly wide and less deep, it stretched to Podol, to Kurenivka. It was the outskirts of Kyiv, Syrets. There were no houses here. Closer to the city, bordered by a brick wall, was the Jewish cemetery. It, too, has disappeared.[117]

Nekrasov did not find it necessary to dwell on these events, as it was "a known tragedy." He merely emphasized that "never before had men consciously destroyed so many of their kind in such a short time." He did not, however, hesitate to highlight, once again, that the victims were "elderly, women, children, defenseless people." Only later in that place would "stronger, younger individuals, and not only Jews" lose their lives.[118] The traces of the destruction had now been definitively erased, and the people buried remained "nameless": "In Prague there is a synagogue whose walls are inscribed with the names of Jews who died during the occupation. In Stalingrad the marble walls of the Pantheon bear the names of those who defended the Mamaev Kurgan. . . . At Babi Yar no one knows who was killed. Only the children and grandchildren know the names of fathers, grandfathers, and great-grandfathers. Those few who miraculously managed to escape from that hell remain ignorant of the names of those who groaned and gasped next to them."[119]

In the following years, whenever Nekrasov returned to Babi Yar, he focused not on the history of the massacre, about which he felt he had nothing more to add, but on the consequences of its manipulation. On 7 March 1979, in a talk on Radio Liberty prompted by the release of the film *Holocaust*, he stated that the way in which "efforts were made to erase from human memory everything concerning and recalling the tragic events" was "equally terrible, even if theoretically without victims or blood":

> If you go to the city of Kyiv today, where everything happened thirty-eight years ago in the early days of the German occupation, the Intourist guide will obligatorily take you, after a visit to the Cathedral of Saint Sophia and the Pechersk Lavra, to the outskirts of Syrets. And there they will show you an imposing and rather spectacular monument depicting powerful, seminude, angry people carved in stone. And they will explain: "Here, the Nazi-Fascist barbarians killed about one hundred thousand innocent Soviet citizens." "Jews?" you will ask. "Elderly, women, children . . . and prisoners of war of all nationalities," the guide will answer without looking you in the eyes.
>   . . . Thirty years ago, there was nothing here but a dump. A tiny crooked plaque, prohibiting the dumping of waste under the threat of a 300-ruble fine, was submerged in a sea of all kinds of garbage: crates, rusty buckets, troughs, beds, half-rotten rags, and at the bottom of the ravine, men crawling in search of metal containers, rings, and gold earrings. . . . Only every autumn, at the end of September, other people would arrive on the shrub-covered cliffs and stand silently amid all the garbage, wiping away tears.[120]

"Nowhere Have I Felt So Much Anger"

The monument Nekrasov referred to was inaugurated on 2 July 1976. It was an imposing work about fifteen meters tall created by sculptors Mykhailo H. Lysenko, Oleksandr P. Vitryk, and Viktor V. Suchenko and architects Anatoliy F. Ignashchenko, Mykola K. Ivanchenko, and V. M. Ivanchenkov. A bronze plaque bore an inscription in Ukrainian without any reference to the Jews: "Here, in 1941–1943, the German Fascist occupiers shot more than 100,000 citizens of

Kyiv and prisoners of war." There was no mention of the Jews during the crowded official ceremony, held on a date with no relation to the events. The press reported that tens of thousands of "peaceful citizens of Kyiv, including many children, women, and elderly," were dragged into the massacres at Babi Yar and that "Russians, Ukrainians, Jews, Belarusians, Poles" were killed there.[121] The sculptural complex was not placed in the area where the shootings had occurred; on the contrary, it was deliberately located at a significant distance.[122] But most importantly, it depicted not victims but a defiant resistance fighter; fearless soldiers with clenched fists; a sailor defending an elderly woman; a young man who, as he fell, refused to bow his head. The work was crowned by the figure of a mother, symbolizing the triumph of life over death. Even the grass and flowers in the basin below were intended as testimony to the "immortality of life."[123] How had the monument come to be completed? According to sculptor Oleksandr Vitryk, who worked on the project, a new competition was announced in 1968, and it was won by a team led by Mykhailo Lysenko, a professor at the State Art Institute of Kyiv and creator of representative Soviet monumental works.[124] Others argue that the assignment was not made after a comparative evaluation.[125]

Nevertheless, the design process extended over many years and encountered several difficulties, including the death of Lysenko in 1972.[126] In 1975 the construction of the "monument to Soviet citizens and soldiers and officers of the Soviet army prisoners of war killed by German Fascist occupiers in the Syrets district of Kyiv" was finally approved, allocating the plot of land (about seven hectares) and the necessary funds.[127] The memorial was conceived as a complex of many figures. The first project envisioned a sort of funeral procession that Lysenko explained by appealing to the concepts of both heroism and suffering: "The people have raised, with their powerful arms, the remains of thousands of brave Soviet citizens who died in the most inhumane suffering. With great sorrow, workers and soldiers, women with children and sailors, young girls and elderly people, all without exception march with banners to pay the final tribute to the fallen. Eternal grief. Gusts of fresh, free wind make the mourning flags wave. The entire group is imbued with struggle and victory—light over darkness. In the funeral grandeur, the feelings of human dignity are expressed."[128]

Initially, it seems, the front of the composition was supposed to feature a family of Jews (an old man wearing the tallit, a young mother nursing her child, an old woman covering the eyes of her grandson with her hand) in the foreground with respect to the other figures (a sailor, a soldier, a partisan).[129] However, the instructions of the commissioning patron were stringent. The memorial was not for the victims but for the fighters who protected them: "The Jews who were shot had not defended the homeland and went to their death with resignation.

Therefore, the figures in the memorial must include soldiers, athletes, Communists, and partisans. Jews should not be shown."[130] Despite the ideological convergence of the authors in favor of a heroic representation, they still tried to include in the ensemble an old Jew over whom a young woman wept. But the party's control organs were unyielding. Problems also arose when someone noticed that the ravine, echoed in its natural form as a decorative motif at the base of the complex, had six branches that would form a Star of David. Architect Ignashchenko had to cover part of the excavations.[131]

The monument inaugurated in 1976 as we see it today can be considered the only representation that Soviet power could accept of the history of Babi Yar. The setting was to be completed with the construction of a cultural and recreational park in the Shevchenko district. The project included an open-air theater for a thousand seats, a summer cinema, pavilions for reading and chess, cafés, and commercial kiosks. The "active recreation" area was to feature playgrounds and attractions. The sports sector was to include a stadium with five thousand seats, athletic facilities, and many sports fields.[132] These structures were not built, but the conversion of the entire area into public green space was nonetheless completed in 1980, covering a total area of 118 hectares and definitively concealing the ravine, of which only a small upper portion remained intact. "Thanks to the rational use of the steep terrain (Babi Yar) and existing green spaces (Kyrylivsky haj)—read a classic repertoire on the urban transformations of the capital—wonderful landscapes open up from panoramic terraces arranged in a descending form."[133]

After the inauguration of the sculptural complex, Jewish commemorations of the anniversary continued to take place where Babi Yar merged into the Lukyanivka cemetery. The authorities primarily sought to hinder the arrival of delegations from other cities. In 1976 some activists were preemptively summoned by the city committee of the party and informed that there would be no obstacles, but all those who intended to come from Moscow would be blocked. Dissident Anatoly B. (Natan) Sharansky was detained a few hours before departure and subjected to a lengthy interrogation that prevented him from being physically present at the demonstration.[134] The following year, about forty Jews awaiting emigration visas addressed the Supreme Soviet, expressing the hope that there would be no obstacles to commemorative actions. In Kyiv other activists requested permission for a funeral ceremony with prayers and wreath laying. However, since wreaths were only allowed without any inscriptions in Hebrew characters, the activists filed a complaint and declared—in protest—a hunger strike. Many activists were detained in Moscow and Kyiv or summoned to various law enforcement agencies to hinder their movements.[135]

One of the first critical reactions to the monument inaugurated in July 1976, published two months later by the émigré press, came from Nahum Korzhavin. The poet informed his readers that, "next to the site of the events," an "obelisk [*sic*!]" had been built to celebrate the death of generic Soviet citizens "without specifying their nationality". It was true that not "only Jews" had died at Babi Yar and that everyone had "the right to be remembered," but the Jews had been killed there "solely because of their national identity."[136] A much more elaborate intervention came from a member of the Moscow Helsinki Group, mathematician Naum N. Meiman. Emphasizing the difference between a monument and a memorial, he noted that the monument was not erected "to perpetuate the memory of the event," as a memorial sign should, "but to alter it." The client knew that "human memory is ephemeral," while the monument is enduring. The client knew that the population, in the face of the permanence of "cement, granite, bronze," would forget the "meaning" of the place engraved in a simple inscription. Meiman reiterated what *everyone* knew: Children, the elderly, and women were killed not "as Soviet citizens or enemies of Germany but because and only because they were Jews." Those who, for whatever reason, found themselves in the crowd and could prove they were not of Jewish nationality escaped execution. Any attempt to "mask and blur" the racial character of the genocide should be considered an act of "extreme contempt" toward the victims. At Auschwitz, Treblinka, and the Warsaw Ghetto, "not monuments but memorials" had long been installed. Their significance was not just to "express grief for the deceased." It was to remind "the living" more than the dead, "the peoples of the countries where the crimes were committed" more than the Jews. Memorials had a function of "purification" of the territories contaminated by the massacres.[137] It was precisely this purification of the place that had been thwarted at Babi Yar.

In the choice of Babi Yar as the site of death, there was, for Meiman, the "intentional transparency of the crime" that the Germans were about to commit: "an open place of destruction" located just "beyond the barbed wire and unique in size." While the deportation of Jews in Western and Central Europe ended in concentration camps, where the extermination was made invisible, in the occupied Soviet territories, the elimination was conceived as an immediate "public act": Between the city and the ravine, there was just a long and symbolic iron rod with spikes that forbade passage but allowed a glimpse of what was happening. Babi Yar thus represented a kind of "boundary in the moral and material history of humanity."[138] Its mere presence would constitute a memorial. But the presence had been removed. It is true that a trace ("admirable representation") of the tragedy had been preserved in the prose, poetry, and music of various artists, but it was also true that Kuznetsov's story had been withdrawn from libraries, Yevtushenko's verses were no longer reprinted, and Shostakovich's symphony had been eliminated from concert repertoires.[139]

Meiman performed an exemplary reconstruction of the chronology of the erasure. First, he recalled how Nekrasov had managed in the late 1950s to prevent the "shame" of building a stadium and other recreational facilities at Babi Yar. This was followed by a "rather unusual procedure to honor the victims" when it was decided to flood the ravine, causing a catastrophe. Even more rapid and decisive was the action in the adjacent Jewish cemetery where, "without informing the population," bulldozers and perhaps even heavier equipment were used to destroy and dump every grave monument into the chasm before leveling the ground. If it weren't for Nekrasov's account of that "outrage against the dead" in "Zapiski zevaki," Meiman himself would not have known about the "desecration" of his father's grave. Finally, after placing a provisional commemorative stone and undergoing the "tragicomic adventures" of an architectural competition whose projects were repeatedly altered, they arrived, ten years later, at the inauguration of an imposing monument to Soviet soldiers' heroism that was placed "even farther from Babi Yar" than the previous granite block.[140]

Why should one not stop at the "place" of the death of tens of thousands of people? What kind of "tribute to the memory" of the deceased could be spoken of if the point of extermination was not only unmarked but also kept secret? Meiman had no doubts: the "topography" of the area had been "artfully" altered to prevent visitors from orienting themselves and ultimately make the event evanescent in its representation. Furthermore, the statuary complex bore an inscription ("in Ukrainian") that did not even consider the linguistic identity of the victims of those two days in September: Jews who spoke Russian and Yiddish ("the languages of Kyiv Jewry"), many of whom, "in their last agonizing moments," surely prayed in Hebrew. The ones who spoke in Ukrainian were the German accomplices. The monument was merely "a voluminous, pompous materialization of the lie"—a lie that was producing and would continue to produce "poisonous fruits." In reality, Kyiv's citizens were aware of the systematic extermination of Jews that occurred in 1941. The monument, with its "official deceit cast in iron and carved in marble," would inevitably lead them to draw "precise conclusions" about the event.[141]

An even more radical reaction came from Elie Wiesel, who in August 1979 arrived in Kyiv at the head of a delegation of the President's Commission on the Holocaust, established the previous year in the United States at the behest of Jimmy Carter. It was an opportunity to visit Babi Yar again. As we have

seen, Wiesel had been there for the first time in 1965 and remembered well the
sensations of that visit: "Nowhere have I felt so much anger and helplessness."
At that time, he was convinced that Babi Yar was beyond the city, "in the heart
of the forest," far from human eyes. He could not even remotely conceive that
the massacre had taken place in the immediate vicinity of the capital. He was
wrong:

> The inhabitants had heard the gunshots, they had seen the victims parade by;
> they had seen the earth open up to swallow their Jewish neighbors, their Jewish
> comrades, their Jewish colleagues. . . . The massacre took place almost before
> their eyes, but they closed their eyes to work and sleep and live and wait as if it
> had nothing to do with them. Why did the city do nothing to protect its Jewish
> inhabitants? Why did it do nothing to hide a few children, a few elderly people
> here and there? The facts are evident, and they are terrible because they are true
> and accusatory: there are fewer survivors from Babi Yar than from any other
> similar place. That year in Kyiv, I met one: a woman broken and mute. And
> crazy.[142]

Wiesel had to overcome a lack of interest in Babi Yar, disinformation about
Babi Yar, and the denial of Babi Yar. At the time of his first visit, faced with the
"absence of a tombstone, an inscription," he had a furious reaction: "Anger
against the murderers, but also against their accomplices and the local spectators who let them do it," as well as "anger against the regime that in 1965,
despite external pressures, refused to allow a monument to be erected in memory of the victims swallowed by hatred and indifference." He had written *The
Jews of Silence: A Personal Report on Soviet Jewry* in 1966 as a "book of hope,"
as an "appeal to solidarity and faith." But in the chapter on Babi Yar, he wanted
to convey "the opaque, atrocious, inhuman silence, in short, the hostile and
suffocating silence." The anger he felt lasted a long time. But "could I have
foreseen that it would resurface, even more violently, on the occasion of a new
visit to the same place?"[143]

In his later memoirs, Wiesel still retained "fragments of images" from his
first experience: "The terrified old men in the synagogue. The mute woman
and her sealed memories." It seemed incomprehensible to him that for entire
days, Jews were massacred without any chance to escape or find a hiding place
while the rest of the population did nothing to help a neighbor, a friend, an
acquaintance. The impact at the moment of the second trip was similar: "Kyiv,
or officialized oblivion. Kyiv, or outrage. How can a Jew not feel anguish in
this place?" The mission was carried out in an official form and followed, on
tight schedules, the classic rituals of Soviet ceremonial with conventional

speeches and screenings of documentaries about the genocide and with details that were unfortunately unknown to the general public. The worst moment, however, was in front of the monument:

> Military band, bouquets of flowers of all colors. All the Ukrainian authorities and media are present. They are proud of themselves, the political leaders of Kyiv. They can no longer be blamed for the absence of a monument at Babi Yar. Here it is, the monument. So, they seem to ask us, are you happy now?
>
> The immense monument, in Stalinist style, is grandiose, pompous, flashy, and frankly vulgar. Its dimensions and ugliness produce an oppressive effect. Bah, I tell myself, it's their business. It's not up to me to accuse them of a lack of taste, but I can, I must, blame them for their lack of tact, decency, honesty, their willingness to distort historical truth, in short, their taste for lying.
>
> The fact is that the word "Jew" does not appear on the monument. The inscription presents the victims as Soviet citizens murdered by the Fascists. . . .
>
> The anger that fills me ends up overflowing. I tell the Ukrainian authorities that I had felt pained and offended when in 1965, in this cursed place, there was only emptiness hiding what remains of the victims: their memory. But it was nothing compared to what I feel now.[144]

What he felt in 1979 ("fury and despair"), Wiesel aligned chaotically in a crescendo of invectives: "How dare they falsify the truth to this extent? Who allowed, who ordered this sacrilege? The Jews who were killed, *why* were they killed? Because they were Ukrainians, or Soviets, or Communists?"[145]

"Outside the Law"

The early 1980s saw an intensification of the efforts of the refuseniks: appeals to the authorities, public petitions, hunger strikes.[146] Among the most determined and radical were also the Jews of Kyiv. The OVIR systematically denied exit visas, and only a few dozen people were authorized to reunite with close relatives (parents or children) in Israel or other countries. In an "appeal to the Jewish people" (26 April 1980), it is written: "Kyiv is the only city in the Soviet Union that has responded with protests and mass collective actions to the mass refusals of emigration. For this, it will be the first city where mass repressions will fall on the families of the refuseniks."[147]

Retaliations took the form of dismissals and steep obstacles to finding employment suitable to people's skills, arbitrary and threatening summonses to police offices or security services headquarters, administrative arrests (up to fifteen days) for trivial reasons or judicial proceedings based on false accusations, impediments to free movement within the territory, and roundups in stations and airports to hinder travel to the capital to file appeals and applications.[148] And these are just some of the countless abuses and harassments committed against those who wanted to leave the Soviet Union. All this happened, as noted, not only in the absence of regulations and laws governing migration issues and protecting citizens from institutional arbitrariness but also in violation of the Universal Declaration of Human Rights and the International Covenant on Civil and Political Rights, as well as the Helsinki Final Act of the Conference on Security and Cooperation in Europe (Helsinki Accords), also signed by the Soviet government.[149] The most severe punishments, according to the testimony of physicist Mark Ya. Azbel, were reserved for those who, believing that the "monument" had left room for "memorials," made "pilgrimages" to places where, under German occupation, Jews had been massacred. Those who annually tried to express their condolences to the dead were subjected, in increasing numbers, to restrictive measures. This too showed that "the state was determined to erase the memory of the massacres" with unprecedented energy.[150]

On 20 September 1981 twenty-one Kyiv refuseniks addressed a letter to the presidium of the Supreme Soviet of the USSR, reminding them that forty years earlier, Babi Yar had been the scene of the extermination of "thousands of elderly people, women, and children, killed only because they were Jews." That act of genocide was unmistakably a direct result of Nazism. But there should be no underestimation of the fact that the conditions enabling it had been initially dictated by a gradually increasing "restriction of rights" that began as something of only "the slightest significance." The signatories to the document—even while acknowledging that "violations of legality, initially insignificant," did not necessarily have to turn into a "tragedy"—considered it appropriate to draw attention to the "possibility of their evolving growth." The signatories, therefore, were demanding an end to the "violations of the law" that had been increasingly frequent in Kyiv over the previous two years. The precarious situation in which many Jews found themselves was intolerable—and that was even before submitting, "based on the right to choose their place of residence," an application to emigrate. Many of them had been "illegally" denied that opportunity, primarily on the flimsy pretext that they had no close relatives in Israel. Experience also showed that the label of refusenik variously exposed a person to discrimination both at work and in a job search, prevented a person from obtaining adequate education and professional qualifications, failed to ensure that a person's children could receive an education corresponding to their abilities, and prevented the elderly from receiving the necessary social assistance. The refusenik label invariably aroused "distrust and suspicion" among local authorities, as evidenced by the "constant monitoring" exercised by the police and security services. Essentially, a true "ostracism" was in place. But that was not all: from time to time, someone might be stripped of the relatively preferable "epithet of refusenik" and instead pinned with the label of "petty hooligan, slanderer, delinquent, drug addict, weapons carrier, or parasite," thus rendering them even more vulnerable. This was evidenced by certain cases of heavy prison sentences (Valery M. Pilnikov, Kim B. Fridman, Vladimir S. Kislik, Stanislav A. Zubko), to say nothing of the fact that administrative arrests had become a full-blown "system of persecution." If the supposed acts of "illegality" were not immediately halted, then other labels from the criminal code could easily be added: "anti-Soviet, profiteer, illegal trafficker, rapist, or thief." It was no longer necessary to "physically destroy people"; instead, "moral pogroms, incessantly implemented," might prove every bit as lethal.[151]

The measures implemented to prevent any gathering at Babi Yar were a litmus test for any understanding of the dimensions of the "lack of rights and humiliation" of which the Jewish refuseniks were victims. On 27 September 1981, for example, significant police forces in uniform and plain clothes stood by all day in the vicinity. All access roads to the area were guarded, as were train stations and the airport, and at various points in the city, activists from Kyiv or other locations such as Moscow, Odessa, and Leningrad were blocked. Some were charged with "petty hooliganism" and sentenced to penalties provided for administrative offenses (ten to fifteen days of arrest); others were forcibly put on trains and escorted by police back to the location of their departure. Those who managed to reach Babi Yar despite the strict controls were allowed to approach only if they formed small groups of about eight people led by militia agents. On 3 October twenty-nine Jewish Zionists from Moscow addressed an "open letter" to the Central Committee of the Communist Party of the Soviet Union:

> What do all these people have in common? Why does the mere intention of honoring the memory of the victims of the Nazi genocide, the memory of their grandparents and parents, put them in a position to be subjected to persecution and repression, threats, and insults? The answer was given by the KGB men: "We will not allow nationalists to lay wreaths at Babi Yar!" The "nationalists" are, in the language of the KGB, Jews who want to immigrate to Israel. That is, all of us. Thus, they compare us to neo-Fascists and, with the promise of punishments, forbid us from going to the graves of our loved ones. . . . We are not asking you for anything, we do not want anything. We are merely informing you

of what has happened. For us, this is not a revelation. It is yet another confirmation that we Jews who wish to leave the Soviet Union for Israel have been placed outside the law.[152]

About a month later, Elena G. Bonner, Sofiya V. Kalistratova, and Naum N. Meiman, members of the Moscow Helsinki Group, commemorated the fortieth anniversary of the Babi Yar massacre, noting that only "thanks to the persistent demands of public opinion" had a monument been erected in a place long ago turned into a "dump." The eventual construction of the sculpture, devoid of any reference to the genocide of Jews, however, would do nothing to curb the determination to strengthen the sense of identity of the Jews of Kyiv and other cities, who continued to gather periodically—as Jews—to commemorate the victims at the one location where they had always gathered, at a theoretical point of intersection between the area where the firing had taken place and the "house of eternity" (*bet olam*). That year, official countermeasures had prevented most of the attendees from approaching ("all access roads were barred by militia and plain-clothes 'volunteer guards'"), thus confirming that the state meant not only to repress any requests for permission to emigrate and "erase from people's consciousness the memory of Babi Yar" but also to eliminate from Ukrainian history the history of its Jewish population.[153] This was also the disconsolate observation of Mark Azbel, who had emigrated a few years earlier: "Nothing remains. Not only is the recent memory of the slaughtered Jews wiped out, but of the many centuries of Jewish culture in that country nothing remains. No museums, no documents, no objects of art, not a photograph. It would be much harder to restore this [Jewish] culture in Russia than to reconstruct the culture of ancient Egypt or Greece or the Mayan people."[154]

Reflecting on the reasons that led to the erasure of Babi Yar, Nekrasov always insisted on the intentionality of government policies. In his view, that choice not only was due to the desire to minimize the genocide of the Jews, absorbing it into the more general persecutions and sufferings of Soviet citizens during the war; but also demonstrated the rooted stereotype that most Jews had fled to Tashkent or other protected locations far from the front. The choice not only expressed the claimed necessity of defending against an alleged aggressive Jewish nationalism but also was the direct consequence of a veto placed on the memory of the defenseless, motivated by prejudices about the victims' inability to resist:

"Why go there? What's there to remember? Heroes? There are no heroes here! People came voluntarily and were shot. It was their fault. There was no reason to show up. . . ." Yes, that's exactly what was said. And many years later, the party "leaders" repeated the same thing to me when I mentioned a monument. "A monument to whom? To cowards who voluntarily showed up for execution? But do you understand what you're proposing? No, we must forget! Erase it from the face of the earth! And find names to remove! There's Syretsky Yar and that's it. There's no Babi Yar. There is and was none. . . . Forget it!"[155]

First, the area was renamed in official documents; then, it was turned into a public dump. It was then decided to level the ravine using powerful pumps that for months "furiously" filled it with new detritus, a liquid mixture of sand and clay: "The chasm disappeared. Babi Yar was eliminated. In its place an abandoned plot of land took form. Weeds." The only reason that the project to create a park, a stadium, and other entertainment facilities had failed to proceed was the collapse of the dam erected at the mouth of the basin in the spring of 1961. Then, five years later, a spontaneous public demonstration succeeded in bringing to light the "infamy" that, twenty-five years after, there was not a single marker to commemorate the extermination of Kyiv's Jews: "Neither a monument nor a plaque—a desolate wasteland, weeds . . . and underneath, human bones." After the temporary appearance of a stone with an inscription, the construction of a group of sculptures of "powerful, proud, and unyielding fighters" finally arrived, standing at the very spot where "old, sick, and defenseless Jews" had died. The conclusion of this umpteenth narrative reconstruction of the event by Nekrasov may sound almost paradoxical: "I believe that not even Hitler and Goebbels together could have devised something similar—on the site of a nonexistent Babi Yar, erect a monument to the lasting and indestructible force of antisemitism."[156]

In reality, that observation was the result not of a paradox but of a constant and coherent analysis that, focusing repeatedly and unhurriedly on the prohibitions, had become more and more complex over time, burrowing its way to the very heart of the methodology for constructing oblivion, understood as a lasting condition of the nullification of word and feeling. That is why Nekrasov had come to the conclusion, expressed in 1975 in "Zapiski zevaki," that there was no longer any need for a monument at Babi Yar. The simple commemorative plaque that the authorities had introduced after the 1966 democratic gathering was actually *better*:

No, there's no need for a monument!

The best monument is the stone currently there. It has everything: thirty years of oblivion, the secrecy, the long stereotypical inscription in journalistic style that is devoid of any emotion, the promise ("There will be a monument. Why are you agitating?"), no shouting, no excitement. But above all, a place to lay flowers. Lay flowers and stand for a while in silence. . . .

In Darnytsia, however, there are three robust, seminaked, muscular young men full of anger and hatred. It's just not clear why, strong and well fed as they are, they didn't break their chains to attack the Germans. Such guys would have put an entire patrol to flight.[157]

In an unpublished preparatory text likely dating back to 1973 and frequently cited here, the writer offered a better explanation of his idea without resorting to irony of any sort. The existence of that modest marker was the "best solution," not so much because there were no adequate architectural skills in the country but because the stone, in its "melancholic insignificance and sobriety," as well as in the "bureaucratic" nature of the inscription, expressed much greater "grief and tragedy" than any sculptural group of seminaked and indomitable athletes with "clenched jaws and fists." At the same time, Nekrasov clearly explained the reasons for what he defined as true and proper harassment of the victims:

They ordered us to forget Babi Yar. Actually, they didn't even order it. Someone simply said somewhere: "A monument? Why a monument? To people who voluntarily went to their deaths? Without resistance, without protest, like a rabbit into a boa's jaws? No, sorry, we don't erect monuments to cowards. . . ." By whom and when exactly this was said it's not so important, one can only guess, but the seeds fell on fertile ground. On different occasions, from different people, mostly endowed with power, I heard these words: "They didn't resist." The word "Jews" was never pronounced. It would have been vulgar for anyone to do so, one couldn't speak like that, but it was implied. And so it was ordered—we will now say so—to forget Babi Yar.[158]

Writing from exile, Nekrasov often returned in his memory to the city of Kyiv, dwelling on its architectural novelties. He could now judge them only indirectly due to the wall that divided him from his homeland: "Finally, after thirty years, a monument at Babi Yar. Difficult to understand from a photograph what they have done: something heroic, muscular, looking confidently to the future. To the victims of the 'temporary occupation.' Not a word about their identity."[159]

In August 1991 Ukraine declared its independence. On 29 September of that year President Leonid M. Kravchuk inaugurated a bronze menorah monument, the work of architect Yuri A. Paskevych, in collaboration with sculptors Yakym D. Levych and Oleksandr Ya. Levych and the contribution of engineer Borys Giller. Due to a misinterpretation of documents and testimonies, however, the sculpture was placed in a part of the territory where no Jews at all had been shot. From that moment, a new phase began for the history of Babi Yar in a complex interplay of proposals and controversies, public demonstrations and acts of reconciliation, academic conferences and publications, the creation of public committees and research centers, but above all in a growing fragmentation of commemorative markers. Today, on the territory of what was Babi Yar, there are about thirty monuments and plaques commemorating the slaughter of both Jews and non-Jews—Ukrainian nationalists, Orthodox clerics, patients from the psychiatric hospital, athletes, Soviet or German prisoners of war who died in captivity, detainees in the Syrets camp, Roma, children, and people who died in the Kurenivka disaster. Not all the victims died at Babi Yar, but the "ravine" was chosen as a symbol for their tragic demise, and the entire area has become an object of competition among groups and communities.[160]

An initiative by the nongovernmental organization Babi Yar Holocaust Memorial Center planned to build a center for documentation, commemoration, and education, but construction work has been temporarily suspended due to the Russian invasion.[161]

Epilogue

Nahum Korzhavin's "Poema sushchestvovaniya" (Poem of existence) (1970) was circulated through the samizdat under the title "Babi Yar." "It is not an easy poem to read," wrote the author in presenting it for the first time in print. He did not feel proud of this; he would have preferred clearer and more straightforward verses, but the theme did not lend itself to simplicity: "I would have had to sidestep the thought and the emotion." It was even plausible to say that "if it had been possible to write the poem easily, then it might not have been written at all: the motive would have disappeared." The text, Korzhavin added, "is read, must be read, slowly." A man stunned and oppressed by a great weight wants "to understand what to do with himself and remember why he is alive." This was not usually the function attributed to verse, but the twentieth century could in no way be considered a time that fit the norm of things: "And only for this reason could I open myself to poetry."[1]

> I have come to you, Babi Yar.
> If pain has an age,
> Then I am incredibly old,
> It cannot be counted in centuries.
>
> I stand here on the earth and pray:
> If I manage not to go mad,
> I will listen to your voice, Earth,
> Speak.
>
> What a din in your breast!
> I will understand nothing.

Is it water that resounds underground
Or the souls that lie in the *yar*?

I ask the maples: Answer,
Let me partake—you are witnesses.
Silence.
Only the wind
Among the leaves.

I turn to the sky: Tell me,
You, indifferent to the outrage.
There was life. There will be life.
But I see nothing on your face.
Perhaps the stones will answer?
No . . .

(Lev Ozerov, "Babi Jar," 1946)

~

On the road that runs alongside Babi Yar
They are laying asphalt.
In a slow swirl
The tar bubbles, and the dirty
and resolute workers feel the heat.

From now on, thanks to the efforts
Of the fathers of this glorious city,
A straight and majestic road
Will pass here without dips or potholes.

. . . .

Unfortunately, the one who went from here
One day toward death in the silent crowd
Injured the soles of his feet on the clods of dirt
And stumbled in despair. . . .

Perhaps, it would have been easier for him to bear

The pain, taking the last steps,
If the dips or potholes had not exhaled
Before time, a sepulchral sleep.

Oh, better that the splendor of the asphalt coatings
Had not covered the ditches and hollows,
Had not appeased those who still suffered
And did not soothe the wounds on the road of affliction!

May the young walk that path
And sometimes stumble into the holes
So as not to forget the grim terror
That then struck the columns of the condemned!

. . . I myself love the new road,
Covered with chestnuts in autumn,
The freshly cut grass in the gardens,
The beauty of the poplars, and the elegance of the pines.

But suddenly the old wall appears
And you read eagerly, as on a page,
Those tragic characters
That you will not recognize on the asphalt. . . .

(Sava Holovanivsky, "Vulytsya Melnykova" [Melnykova Street], 1968)

~

Babi Yar. It was . . . I remember . . . September . . . forty-one.
I was there and I stayed. I had just forgotten.
Or rather, I remembered something, but I thought: My nerves will not
sustain me.
And now it is clear: It is the plain truth. I am dead.

Suddenly I began to choke and remembered suddenly with trembling:
The heaviness of the bodies . . . me in the blood . . . me lying there . . . me
getting up with difficulty . . .
It's a private matter. But there's also much in common.
It concerns everyone, even if not everyone was killed that day.

It always concerns everyone! Because the soul does not live disconnected
From the arisen world, where men are angry with God.
Yes, I lived among you. Forgetting it would be fatal for you.
I also do not have the right to forget.

(Nahum Korzhavin, "Poema sushchestvovaniya" [Poem of existence], 1975

Notes

Preface

1. This is the official German data, reported in report no. 101 (2 October 1941) on the activity of Einsatzgruppe C in Soviet territory: Klaus-Michael Mallmann, Andrej Angrick, Jürgen Matthäus, and Martin Cüppers, eds., *Die "Ereignismeldungen UdSSR" 1941: Dokumente der Einsatzgruppen in der Sowjetunion* [The "USSR Event Reports" 1941: Documents from the operational groups in the Soviet Union] (WBG, 2011), 615.

Introduction

1. Mordechai Altshuler, ed., *Distribution of the Jewish Population of the USSR 1939* (Centre for Research and Documentation of East-European Jewry, Hebrew University of Jerusalem, 1993), 20; Altshuler, *Soviet Jewry on the Eve of the Holocaust: A Social and Demographic Profile* (Centre for Research and Documentation of East-European Jewry, Hebrew University of Jerusalem, 1998), 225. See also Aleksandr I. Kruglov, ed., *Sbornik dokumentov i materialov ob unichtozhenii nacistami evreev Ukrainy v 1941–1944 godach* [Collection of documents and materials on the destruction of Jews of Ukraine by the Nazis in 1941–1944] (Institut Iudaiki, 2002), 82.

2. "Special'noe soobshchenie o polozhenie v gorode Kieve posle okkupacii ego protivnikom" [Special report on the situation in the city of Kyiv after the occupation by the enemy], 4 December 1941, in *Istochnik: Dokumenty russkoj istorii*, no. 3 (1995): 137. The report, submitted to Nikita Khrushchev by the commissioner for internal affairs of the Ukrainian Soviet Socialist Republic, Serhiy Savchenko, was transmitted to Joseph Stalin on 7 December 1941.

3. See the eyewitness account in a letter sent from Kyiv on 28 July 1945: "Pis'mo D. F. Oksanicha, A. N. Babad-Koval'chika, I. N. Zlatkovskoj Il'e Erenburgu" [Letter from D. F. Oksanich, A. N. Babad-Koval'chik, I. N. Zlatkovskaja to Ilya Ehrenburg], in *Babiy Jar: K pjatidesjatiletiyu tragedii 29–30 sentjabrja 1941 goda* [Babi Yar: On the fiftieth anniversary of the tragedy of 29–30 September 1941], ed. Shmuel Spector and M. Kipnis (Biblioteka-Alija, 1991), 41. Concerning the capture of Kyiv and the events that immediately followed, see Karel C. Berkhoff, *Harvest of Despair: Life and Death in Ukraine Under Nazi Rule* (Belknap Press of Harvard University Press, 2004), 24–33.

4. The bibliography on Babi Yar is now vast. Here I will go no further than to refer to Karel Berkhoff's fundamental works, in particular, *Harvest of Despair*, 59–88; "Babyn Jar: Misce najmasshtabnishoho rozstrilu jevreïv nacystamy v Radjans'komu Sojuzi" [Babi Yar: The site of the largest massacre of Jews by the Nazis in the Soviet Union], in *Babyn Jar: Masove ubyvstvo i pam'jat' pro n'oho; Materialy mizhnarodnoï naukovoï konferenciï 24–25 zhovtnja 2011 r., m. Kyïv* [Babi Yar: Mass murder and memory of it; Proceedings of the International Scientific Conference, Kyiv, 24–25 October 2011], ed. Mykhailo Tyahlyi and Vitaly Nachmanovych (Ukraïns'kyj centr vyvchennja istorii Holokostu, Hromads'kyj komitet dlja vshanuvannja pam'jati zhertv Babynoho Jaru, 2012), 8–20; "Babi Yar," in *Online Encyclopedia of Mass Violence: Case Studies*, 27 May 2015, https://www.sciencespo.fr/mass-violence-war-massacre-resistance/en/document/babi-yar.html; "'The Corpses in the Ravine Were Women, Men, and Children': Written Testimonies from 1941 on the Babi Yar Massacre," *Holocaust and Genocide Studies* 29, no. 2 (2015): 251–74; "The Dispersal and Oblivion of the Ashes and Bones of Babi Yar," in *New Directions in Holocaust Research and Education*, ed. Wendy Lower and Lauren Faulkner Rossi (Northwestern University Press, 2017), 256–76.

5. Testimony of I. S. Yanovych given to the bodies of the People's Commissariat for Internal Affairs (hereafter NKVD), 15 November 1943, in *Babiy Jar: Chelovek, vlast', istoriya; Dokumenty i materialy* [Babi Yar: The man, the power, the history; Documents and materials], vol. 1, *Istoricheskaja topografiya: Chronologiya sobytiy* [Historical topography: Chronology of events], ed. Tatiana Evstafeva and Vitaly Nachmanovich (Vneshtorgizdat Ukrainy, 2004), doc. 15, p. 230.

6. The Darnytsia POW camp was created immediately after the occupation of Kyiv (with the official name Kiew-Ost) and remained active until 28 September 1943. From January 1942 it was renamed Stalag 339 Kiew-Darniza. It occupied an area of approximately 1.5 × 1 kilometers and was fenced with barbed wire to a height of 3.5–4 meters. According to military investigations conducted after the liberation, about three hundred thousand people passed through it, and about sixty-eight thousand prisoners died there. See the report of the Extraordinary State Commission for Investigation of Nazi War Crimes of 18 December 1943, in *Prestupnye celi—prestupnye sredstva: Dokumenty ob okkupacionnoj politike fashistskoj Germanii na territorii SSSR (1941–1944 gg.)* [Criminal goals—criminal means: Documents on the occupation policy of Nazi Germany in the territory of the USSR (1941–1944)] 2nd ed. (Izdatel'stvo politicheskoj literatury, 1968, doc. 95, pp. 186–92.

7. Mikhl Tanklevski, "Der kiever khurbn" [The destruction in Kyiv], *Eynikayt*, 5 April 1943, 2, translated in Boris Czerny, "Témoignages et oeuvres littéraires sur le massacre de Babi Yar 1941–1948," *Cahiers du monde russe* 53, no. 4 (2012): 554. See Arkady Zeltser, "Tema 'Evrei v Bab'em Jaru' v Sovetskom Sojuze v 1941–1945 godach" [The theme "Jews in Babi Yar" in the Soviet Union in 1941–1945], in Tyahlyi and Nachmanovych, *Babyn Jar*, 87.

8. See Hans-Adolf Jacobsen, "Kommissarbefehl und Massenexekutionen sowjetischer Kriegsgefangener," in *Anatomie des SS-Staates* [Anatomy of the SS state], ed. Hans Buchheim, Martin Broszat, Hans-Adolf Jacobsen, and Helmut Krausnick (Walter-Verlag AG, 1965), 2:163–279.

9. Concerning the activities of the underground groups led in Kyiv by Ivan D. Kudrya, see *Kievshchina v gody Velikoj Otechestvennoj vojny 1941–1945 gg.: Sbornik*

dokumentov [The resistance in Kyiv during the Great Patriotic War, 1941–1945: Collection of documents] (Kievskoe obl. knizhno-gazetnoe izd-vo, 1963), 215–24.

10. Concerning the significance of the explosions in Kyiv from the point of view of the German military command, see the testimony of General Alfred Jodl before the Nuremberg tribunal, 4 June 1946, in *Trial of the Major War Criminals Before the International Military Tribunal: Nuremberg, 14 November 1945–1 October 1946; Official Text* (Government Printing Office, 1947–49), xv, 329.

11. Testimony of D. I. Budnik given to the Prosecutor's Office, 14 February 1967, in Evstafeva and Nachmanovich, *Istoricheskaja topografiya*, doc. 50, p. 300.

12. Report no. III (12 October 1941) on the activity in Soviet territory of Einsatzgruppe C, in *The Einsatzgruppen Reports: Selections from the Dispatches of the Nazi Death Squads' Campaign Against the Jews in Occupied Territories of the Soviet Union, July 1941–January 1943*, ed. Yitzhak Arad, Shmuel Krakowski, and Shmuel Spector (Holocaust Library, 1989), 184–85; Kruglov, *Sbornik dokumentov*, 86–87; Mallmann et al., *Die "Ereignismeldungen UdSSR" 1941*, 672–73.

13. Irina Khoroshunova, "Kievskie zapiski, 1941–1944" [Kyiv notes, 1941–1944], in *Die Schoah von Babi Yar: Das Massaker deutscher Sonderkommandos an der jüdischen Bevölkerung von Kiew 1941 fünfzig Jahre danach zum Gedenken* [The Shoah of Babi Yar: The massacre of the Jewish population of Kiev by German Sonderkommandos in 1941, commemorated fifty years later], ed. Erhard R. Wiehn (Hartung-Gorre Verlag, 1991), 282.

14. Dokia K. Humenna, *Chreshchatyj Jar (Kyïv 1941–43): Roman-chronika* [Chreshchatyj Jar (Kyiv 1941–43): Novel-chronicle] (Slovo, 1956), 174–75.

15. For the killings of Jews in Kyiv before 29 September, see Vitaly Nachmanovich, "Rasstrely i zachoroneniya v rajone Bab'ego Jara vo vremja nemeckoj okkupacii g. Kieva 1941–1943 gg.: Problemy chronologii i topografii" [Executions and burials in the Babi Yar area during the German occupation of Kyiv: Problems of chronology and topography], in Evstafeva and Nachmanovich, *Istoricheskaja topografiya*, 94–98.

16. Aleksandr Kruglov, "'Schießt ihn Tot': Rol' shtaba Ekel'na i podchinënnych emu podrazdeleniy v istreblenii evreev Ukrainy letom i osen'ju 1941 g." ["Schießt ihn Tot ("Shoot him dead")": The role of Jeckeln's headquarters and his subordinate units in the execution of Ukrainian Jews in the summer and autumn of 1941], *Problemy istorii Holokostu*, no. 3 (2006): 45; Kruglov, *Tragediya Bab'ego Jara v nemeckich dokumentach* [The tragedy of Babi Yar in German documents] (Tkuma, 2011), 22–23.

17. Nachmanovich, "Rasstrely i zachoroneniya v rajone Bab'ego Jara," 102.

18. Testimony of M. S. Lutsenko given to the KGB, 2 June 1980, in Evstafeva and Nachmanovich, *Istoricheskaja topografiya*, doc. 57, p. 315.

19. See the observations of Nachmanovich, "Rasstrely i zachoroneniya v rajone Bab'ego Jara," 96–97.

20. Testimony of N. T. Gorbacheva given to the NKGB, 28 November 1943, in *Prestupnye celi—prestupnye sredstva*, doc. 67, pp. 148–49; Evstafeva and Nachmanovich, *Istoricheskaja topografiya*, doc. 22, pp. 242–43.

21. Testimony of N. F. Petrenko given to the NKGB, 28 November 1943, in Evstafeva and Nachmanovich, *Istoricheskaja topografiya*, doc. 21, p. 241.

22. Report no. 97 (28 September 1941) on the activities in Soviet territory of Einsatzgruppe C, in Arad et al., *The Einsatzgruppen Reports*, 165; Spector and Kipnis,

Babiy Jar, 18; Kruglov, *Sbornik dokumentov*, 77. A subsequent report (no. 106, 7 October 1941) recorded a Jewish population prior to the outbreak of the war amounting to about three hundred thousand people (Arad et al., *The Einsatzgruppen Reports*, 172).

23. Shmuel Spector, "Tragediya v Bab'em Jaru" [The tragedy of Babi Yar], in Spector and Kipnis, *Babiy Jar*, 11.

24. Berkhoff, "Babi Yar."

25. CDAHO Ukraïny, f. 1, op. 23, spr. 121, ark. 2.

26. Report no. 106 (7 October 1941) on the activities in Soviet territory of Einsatzgruppe C, in Arad et al., *The Einsatzgruppen Reports*, 173; Spector and Kipnis, *Babiy Jar*, 19–20; Kruglov, *Sbornik dokumentov*, 80.

27. Testimony from July 1945, in Spector and Kipnis, *Babiy Jar*, 42–43.

28. CDAHO Ukraïny, f. 1, op. 23, spr. 121, ark. 7. See Vitaly Nachmanovych, "Do pytannja pro sklad ucasnykiv karal'nych aktsiy v okupovanomu Kyjevi (1941–1943)" [On the question of the composition of punitive squads in occupied Kyiv (1941–1943)], in *Druha svitova vyjna i dolja narodiv Ukraïny: Materialy 2-ï Vseukraïns'koï naukovoï konferenciï, m. Kyïv, 30–31 zhovtnja 2006 r.* [The Second World War and the fate of the peoples of Ukraine: Proceedings of the Second Pan-Ukrainian Scientific Conference, Kyiv, 30–31 October 2006] (Zovnishtorgvydav, 2007), 227–62; Nachmanovych, "Bukovyns'kyj kurin' i masovi rozstrily jevreïv Kyjeva voseny 1941 r." [The Bukovina Regiment and the mass shootings of Kyiv Jews in the autumn of 1941], *Ukraïns'kyj istorychnyj zhurnal* 3, no. 474 (2007): 76–97.

29. See the testimony of the poet and playwright Nahum M. Korzhavin, *V soblaznach krovavoj epochi: Vospominaniya v dvuch knigach* [Temptations of a bloody era: Memoirs in two books] (Zacharov, 2007), 1:107–9, on the torture inflicted on his uncles by the caretaker of the building where they lived in the ten days preceding their death at Babi Yar.

30. "Kiev, Babiy Jar," in *Chernaja kniga o zlodejskom povsemestnom ubiystve evreev nemecko-fashistskimi zachvatchikami vo vremenno okkupirovannych rajonach Sovetskogo Sojuza i v lagerach Pol'shi vo vremja vojny 1941–1945 gg.* [The black book of the wicked and systematic murder of Jews by German Fascist invaders in the temporarily occupied territories of the Soviet Union and in the camps of Poland during the war of 1941–1945], ed. Vasily Grossman and Ilya Ehrenburg (Yad, 1993), 20; Italian translation: *Il libro nero: Il genocidio nazista nei territori sovietici, 1941–1945* [The black book: The Nazi genocide in Soviet territories, 1941–1945] (Mondadori, 1999), 27.

31. Report no. 126 (27 October 1941) on the activities in Soviet territory of Einsatzgruppe C, in Arad et al., *The Einsatzgruppen Reports*, 211; see also report no. 128 (2 November 1941), in Arad et al., *The Einsatzgruppen Reports*, 217; Spector, *Babiy Jar*, 21; Kruglov, *Sbornik dokumentov*, 94.

32. Regarding the complex issues of the evacuation of the Jewish population in the Soviet Union, see Dov Levin, "The Fateful Decision: The Flight of the Jews into the Soviet Interior in the Summer of 1941," *Yad Vashem Studies* 20 (1990): 115–42; Mordechai Altshuler, "Escape and Evacuation of Soviet Jews at the Time of the Nazi Invasion: Policies and Realities," in *The Holocaust in the Soviet Union: Studies and Sources on the Destruction of the Jews in the Nazi-Occupied Territories of the USSR, 1941–1945*, ed. Lucjan Dobroszycki and Jeffrey S. Gurock (M. E. Sharpe, 1993), 77–104; Vadim

Dubson, "On the Problem of the Evacuation of Soviet Jews in 1941 (New Archival Sources)," *Jews in Eastern Europe* 3, no. 40 (1999): 37–56.

33. Testimony of E. Gorodetskaya, in *My choteli zhit'*. . . : *Svidetel'stva i dokumenty* [We wanted to live . . . : Testimonies and documents], ed. Boris Zabarko (Duch i Litera, 2013), 1:219.

34. Korzhavin, *V soblaznach krovavoj epochi*, 1:17.

35. Neli Melman, "Tol'ko fakty: Antisemitizm na puti k obrazovaniyu i nauke" [Only facts: Antisemitism on the way to education and science], *Evrejskaja starina* 2, no. 61 (2009), http://berkovich-zametki.com/2009/Starina/Nomer2/Melman1.php. Neli's father's older brother managed to escape after the arrest; upon returning to his home, he was recognized by another elderly family maid, the wife of a policeman, who reported him. He also died at Babi Yar.

36. See Mordechai Altshuler, "The Distress of Jews in the Soviet Union in the Wake of the Molotov-Ribbentrop Pact," *Yad Vashem Studies* 36, no. 2 (2008): 73–114.

37. Grossman and Ehrenburg, *Chernaja kniga*, 21; Italian translation, 29 (modified). Tamara Mikhaseva's testimony was collected by Rafaïl Skomorovsky, "Kryvavyj Jar: Ne zabudemo, ne prostimo" [The bloody ravine: We will not forget, we will not forgive], *Radjans'ka Ukraïna*, 9 January 1945; see Zeltser, "Tema 'Evrei v Bab'em Jaru,'" 94–95.

38. "Rasskaz nauchnogo sotrudnika Ierusalimskogo Universiteta Konstantina Miroshnika, kotorom v 1941 godu bylo shestnadcat' let" [Story of the scientific associate of the University of Jerusalem Konstantin Miroshnik, who was sixteen years old in 1941], in *Babiy Jar*, ed. Efrem Baukh (Izdanie Sojuza zemljachestv-vychodcev iz SSSR, 1981), 10, ellipsis added; Ilya Levitas, ed., *Pamjat' Bab'ego Jara: Vospominaniya, dokumenty* [Memory of Babi Yar: Recollections, documents] (Evreijskij sovet Ukrainy—Fond "Pamjat' Bab'ego Jara," 2001), 120. Having arrived in the village of Bilogorodka with his tutor, the adolescent was handed over by her to the *starosta* (mayor), who ordered the police to send him back to Kyiv. From there, he fled and survived.

39. Deposition of S. S. Tauzhnyansky given to the KGB, 20 May 1980, in Evstafeva and Nachmanovich, *Istoricheskaja topografiya*, doc. 53, p. 307.

40. Deposition of G. Ya. Batasheva given on 15 July 1980, in Bogdan Ya. Martynenko, "Tragediya Bab'ego Jara: Rassekrechennye dokumenty svidetel'stvujut" [The tragedy of Babi Yar: Testimonies from declassified documents], in Khoroshunova, "Kievskie zapiski," 364–65. The neighbor was Nikolai A. Soroka.

41. Shelya Polishchuk, "My vyderzhali vsë . . ." [We endured everything . . .], in *Zhivymi ostalis' tol'ko my: Svidetel'stva i dokumenty* [Only we survived: Testimonies and documents], ed. Boris Zabarko (Zadruga, 1999), 309–10.

42. Deposition of E. E. Borodyanskaya-Knysh given to the NKVD, 2 March 1944, in Evstafeva and Nachmanovich, *Istoricheskaja topografiya*, doc. 27, p. 257.

43. "Svjashchennik Glagolev: Soobshchenie I. Minkinoj-Egorychevoj" [Priest Glagolev: Message from I. Minkina-Egorycheva], in Grossman and Ehrenburg, *Chernaja kniga*, 373; Italian translation, 595 (modified). The text was prepared for publication by Rachel A. Kovnator. The witness was actually named Izabella N. Mirkina-Egorycheva, not Minkina-Egorycheva. She was rescued and saved by the Orthodox priest Aleksey A. Glagolev and his family. Glagolev wrote a personal testimony in 1945, which essentially presents this same text attributed to Mirkina-Egorycheva: Aleksey

Glagolev, *Za drugi svoja* [For my friends], ed. Pavel G. Protsenko, *Novyj mir*, no. 10 (1991): 132.

44. Grossman and Ehrenburg, *Chernaja kniga*, 21; Italian translation, 28; A. Anatoly [Anatoly Kuznetsov], *Babiy Jar: Roman-dokument* [Babi Yar: Documentary novel] (Posev, 1970); Italian translation, *Babiy Jar: Romanzo-documento* (Adelphi, 2019), 97; letter from Evsei Lantsman from the archive of Ilya Ehrenburg, in Spector and Kipnis, *Babiy Jar*, 70.

45. *Iz dnevnika uchitel'nicy gor Kieva L. Nartovoj* [From the diary of the teacher from Kyiv L. Nartova], CDAHO Ukraïny, f. 1, op. 22, spr. 347, ark. 2 (recorded on 29 September).

46. Kuznetsov, *Babiy Jar*, 93; Italian translation, 95.

47. Grossman and Ehrenburg, *Chernaja kniga*, 21; Italian translation, 28 (modified).

48. "Svjashchennik Glagolev," in Grossman and Ehrenburg, *Chernaja kniga*, 373; Italian translation, 596. See also Glagolev, *Za drugi svoja*, 132.

49. Testimony of D. M. Pronicheva in the version collected by Kuznetsov, *Babiy Jar*, 100–101; Italian translation, 101–2, ellipsis added.

50. From the diary of the teacher from Kyiv L. Nartova, CDAHO Ukraïny, f. 1, op. 22, spr. 347, ark. 1 (recorded on 28 September).

51. Fedir Pihido-Pravoberezhnyj, *Velyka Vitchyznjana viyna* [The Great Patriotic War] (Novyj Shljach, 1954), 108.

52. Kuznetsov, *Babiy Jar*, 93; Italian translation, 95.

53. From the diary of the teacher from Kyiv L. Nartova, CDAHO Ukraïny, f. 1, op. 22, spr. 347, ark. 1–2 (recorded on 29 September).

54. Grossman and Ehrenburg, *Chernaja kniga*, 21; Italian translation, 28–29 (modified).

55. Deposition given on 27 August 1959, in *"Bei tempi": Lo sterminio degli ebrei raccontato da chi l'ha eseguito e da chi stava a guardare* ["Good times": The extermination of the Jews told by those who carried it out and by those who watched] (Giuntina, 1990), 54; original edition, *"Schöne Zeiten": Judenmord aus der Sicht der Täter und Gaffer* ["Beautiful times": Murder of the Jews from the perspective of the perpetrators and onlookers], ed. Ernst Klee, Willi Dressen, and Volker Riess (Fischer, 1988). For other depositions of German soldiers collected during criminal proceedings, see Kruglov, *Tragediya Bab'ego Jara*, 29–33.

56. Feliks Levitas and Mark Shimanovsky, *Babiy Jar: Stranicy tragedii* [Babi Yar: Pages of a tragedy] (Sled, 1991), 23–24, which includes the testimony of Dina Pronicheva, "V Bab'em Jaru" [In Babi Yar], *Pravda Ukrainy*, 13 January 1946, ellipses added.

57. In the version reported by Kuznetsov, *Babiy Jar*, 105; Italian translation, 106.

58. Deposition of G. Ya. Batasheva given to the KGB, 15 July 1980, in Evstafeva and Nachmanovich, *Istoricheskaja topografiya*, doc. 62, pp. 321–22. See also Martynenko, "Tragediya Bab'ego Jara," 366.

59. Deposition given on 27 August 1959, in Klee et al., *"Bei tempi,"* 55. The procedure referred to by Höfer is that of *Sardinenpackung* (sardine packing system), promoted by Friedrich Jeckeln to make large-scale killing more efficient. See Raul Hilberg, *La distruzione degli ebrei d'Europa* (Einaudi, 1995), 330; original definitive edition, *The Destruction of the European Jews* (Holmes and Meier, 1985).

60. Deposition of K. Werner given on 28 May 1964, in Klee et al., *"Bei tempi,"* 56–57, ellipses added.

61. "O razrusheniyach i zverstvach sovershënnych nemecko-fashistskimi zachvatchikami v gorode Kieve" [On the destructions and atrocities committed by the German Fascist invaders in the city of Kyiv], *Izvestia*, 29 February 1944; *Sbornik soobshcheniy Chrezvychajnoj gosudarstvennoj komissii o zlodejaniyach nemecko-fashistskich zachvatchikov* [Collection of reports of the Extraordinary State Commission on the Atrocities of the German Fascist Invaders] (Gospolitizdat, 1946), 161.

62. Grossman and Ehrenburg, *Chernaja kniga*, 22; Italian translation, 30 (modified).

63. Protocol of the deposition of D. M. Pronicheva at the Kyiv trial, 12 January 1946, in Evstafeva and Nachmanovich, *Istoricheskaja topografiya*, doc. 37, pp. 278–79, ellipsis added. Dina Mironivna Pronicheva (1911–77), a theater actress, managed to escape again during a transfer. She would become one of the main witnesses of the postwar period. The figure of this survivor and the various versions of her testimonies have been extensively studied by Karel C. Berkhoff, "Dina Pronicheva's Story of Surviving the Babi Yar Massacre: German, Jewish, Soviet, Russian, and Ukrainian Records," in *The Shoah in Ukraine: History, Testimony, Memorialization*, ed. Ray Brandon and Wendy Lower (Indiana University Press, in association with the United States Holocaust Memorial Museum, 2008), 291–317.

64. Grossman and Ehrenburg, *Chernaja kniga*, 22–23; Italian translation, 30–31 (modified). See also the deposition given to the NKVD, 2 March 1944, in Evstafeva and Nachmanovich, *Istoricheskaja topografiya*, doc. 27, p. 257.

65. Testimony of S. I. Lutsenko reported by Aleksandr Avdeyenko and Pyotr Olender, "Babiy Jar," *Krasnaja zvezda*, 20 November 1943, 3, ellipsis added.

66. Testimony of M. S. Lutsenko given to the NKVD, 15 November 1943, in Evstafeva and Nachmanovich, *Istoricheskaja topografiya*, doc. 16, p. 232.

67. Testimony of M. S. Lutsenko given to the KGB, 2 June 1980, in Evstafeva and Nachmanovich, *Istoricheskaja topografiya*, doc. 57, p. 315.

68. Testimony of I. S. Yanovich given to the NKVD, 15 November 1943, in Evstafeva and Nachmanovich, *Istoricheskaja topografiya*, doc. 15, p. 231. Yanovich added that "he had heard that some were killed by electric current."

69. Testimony of A. M. Yevgenyev given to the KGB, 14 February 1967, in Evstafeva and Nachmanovich, *Istoricheskaja topografiya*, doc. 52, pp. 305–6. In a subsequent deposition given to the KGB on 9 June 1980, the same witness described the stages of undressing and killing that he could clearly observe, albeit from a distance (see Evstafeva and Nachmanovich, *Istoricheskaja topografiya*, doc. 60, p. 318).

70. Testimony of L. I. Zavorotnaya given to the Prosecutor's Office, 11 February 1967, in Evstafeva and Nachmanovich, *Istoricheskaja topografiya*, doc. 45, p. 294. See also a later testimony given to the KGB on 5 June 1980, in Evstafeva and Nachmanovich, *Istoricheskaja topografiya*, doc. 59, p. 317. In her testimony, Zavorotnaya recalled with precision the nature of the order issued by the German high command for the Jews of Kyiv to assemble in the cemetery district. See testimony given to the NKVD, 9 November 1945, in Evstafeva and Nachmanovich, *Istoricheskaja topografiya*, doc. 30, p. 264, where the assembly date is erroneously indicated as 24 September 1941.

71. Report no. 101 (2 October 1941) on the activity of Einsatzgruppe C in Soviet territory, in Arad et al., *The Einsatzgruppen Reports*, 168; Spector and Kipnis, *Babiy Jar*,

19; Kruglov, *Sbornik dokumentov*, 77; Mallmann et al., *Die "Ereignismeldungen UdSSR" 1941*, 615. For further information, see Kruglov, "'Schießt ihn Tot,'" 45–47; Kruglov, *Tragediya Bab'ego Jara*, 34–35.

72. Report no. 106 (7 October 1941) on the activity of Einsatzgruppe C in Soviet territory, in Arad et al., *The Einsatzgruppen Reports*, 173; Spector and Kipnis, *Babiy Jar*, 19–20; Kruglov, *Sbornik dokumentov*, 80; Mallmann et al., *Die "Ereignismeldungen UdSSR" 1941*, 640–42, ellipsis added.

73. Khoroshunova, "Kievskie zapiski," 292–93.

74. Khoroshunova, "Kievskie zapiski," 293–94.

75. Aleksandr I. Kruglov, *Unichtozhenie evreyskogo naseleniya Ukrainy v 1941–1944 gg.: Chronika sobytiy* [The destruction of the Jewish population of Ukraine in 1941–1944: Chronicle of events] (Mogilëv-Podol'skaja rajtipografija, 1997), 26.

76. Kuzma K. Dubina, *Zlodejaniya nemcev v Kieve* [German atrocities in Kyiv].

77. Deposition of A. Heidborn given on 1 November 1963, in Klee et al., *"Bei tempi,"* 57.

78. Victor Klemperer, *Testimoniare fino all'ultimo: Diari 1933–1945* [Witnessing to the last: Diaries 1933–1945] (Mondadori, 2000), 525; original edition, "Ich will Zeugnis ablegen bis zum letzten" [I will bear witness to the last day], in *Tagebücher 1933–1945* [Diaries 1933–1945] (Aufbau, 1995).

79. Kruglov, "'Schießt ihn Tot,'" 50.

80. Based on German sources, Aleksandr Kruglov believes that, in the period between the end of September and the first half of October 1941, thirty-seven to thirty-eight thousand Jews were exterminated in Kyiv, and during the entire period of occupation, thirty-nine to forty thousand were exterminated (*Tragediya Bab'ego Jara*, 39). See also Kruglov, "'My povynni buly vykonuvaty brudnu robotu . . .': Znyshchennja jevreïv Kyjeva voseny 1941 r. u svitli nimec'kych dokumentiv" ["We had to do the dirty work . . .": The destruction of Kyiv Jews in the fall of 1941 in the light of German documents], in Tyahlyi and Nachmanovych, *Babyn Jar*, 117–56.

81. Concerning the complexity of the chronology and localization of the Kyiv massacres, see the contribution of Nachmanovich, "Rasstrely i zachoroneniya v rajone Bab'ego Jara," 84–163.

82. Tetjana Jevstaf'jeva, "Trahediya Babynoho Jaru u 1941–1943 rr. (za dokumentamy Haluzevogo derzhavnogo archivu Sluzhby bezpeky Ukraïny)" [The tragedy of Babi Yar in 1941–1943 (based on documents from the Sectoral State Archive of the Security Service of Ukraine)], *Z archiviv VUChK-GPU-NKVD-KGB* 1–2, no. 22–23 (2004): 354–55; "Tragediya Bab'ego Jara (1941–1945)," in *Druha svitova viyna i dolja narodiv Ukraïny*, 278.

83. Joseph Goebbels, *Die Tagebücher von Joseph Goebbels*, ed. Elke Fröhlich (Sauer, 1994), II/2:142, in Jeffrey Herf, *The Jewish Enemy: Nazi Propaganda During World War II and the Holocaust* (Belknap Press of Harvard University Press, 2006), 116.

84. Report no. 112 (13 October 1941) on the activity in Soviet territory of Einsatzgruppe C, in Arad et al., *The Einsatzgruppen Reports*, 187–88.

85. The publications of the collaborationist newspaper began on 21 September in Zhytomyr. Dismantled in December 1941, it was replaced by *Novoe ukrains'ke slovo* and continued to perform its function. See Yulia Smilyanskaya, "Istoriya odnoj redakcii (gazety 'Ukrainskoe slovo' e 'Novoe ukrainskoe slovo')" [History of an editorial office

(the newspapers *Ukraïns'ke slovo* and *Novoe ukraïns'ke slovo*)], in *Ten' Cholokosta: Materialy II mezhdunarodnogo simpoziuma "Uroki Cholokosta i sovremennaja Rossiya," Moskva 4–7 maja 1997 g.* [The shadow of the Holocaust: Proceedings of the Second International Symposium "The Lessons of the Holocaust and Contemporary Russia," Moscow, 4–7 May 1997], ed. Ilya A. Altman (Cholokost, 1998), 140–45; Altman, "Otrazhenie Cholokosta v presse okkupacionnovo perioda na territorii Ukrainy" [The reception of the Holocaust in the press of the occupation period in Ukrainian territory], in *Katastrofa jevropejs'kogo jevrejstva pid chas Drugoï svitovoï viyny: Materialy VII naukovoï konferenciï* [The massacre of European Jews during World War II: Proceedings of the Seventh Scientific Conference], ed. Ilya A. Altman (Instytut Judaïky, 2000), 300–304; Altman, *Zhertvy nenavisti: Cholokost v SSSR, 1941–1945* [Victims of hatred: The Holocaust in the USSR, 1941–1945] (Fond Kovcheg, 2002), 50.

86. Khoroshunova, "Kievskie zapiski," 275.

87. The relevance of his activity had already been highlighted by Dubina, *Zlodejaniya nemcev v Kieve*, 8–9; Kuznetsov, *Babiy Jar*, 219; Italian translation, 210.

88. "Malen'kyj budynok" [The small house], *Ukraïns'ke slovo*, 9 October 1941.

89. Shmuel Spector, "The Holocaust of Ukrainian Jews," in *Bitter Legacy: Confronting the Holocaust in the USSR*, ed. Zvi Gitelman (Indiana University Press, 1997), 47; Spector, "Tragediya v Bab'em Jaru," 12–13.

90. Aleksandr Prusin, "Ukrainskaja policiya i Cholokost v general'nom okruge Kyiv, 1941–1943: Dejstviya i motivacii" [The Ukrainian police and the Holocaust in the Kyiv General District, 1941–1943: Actions and motivations], *Holokost i suchasnist'* 1, no. (2 (2007): 35. Concerning the debate, see, in particular, Marco Carynnyk, "Foes of Our Rebirth: Ukrainian Nationalist Discussions About Jews, 1929–1947," *Nationalities Papers* 39, no. 3 (2011): 315–52; John-Paul Himka, "The Lviv Pogrom of 1941: The Germans, Ukrainian Nationalists, and the Carnival Crowd," *Canadian Slavonic Papers / Revue canadienne des slavistes* 53, no. 2/4 (2011): 209–43; Gabriel N. Finder and Alexander V. Prusin, "Collaboration in Eastern Galicia: The Ukrainian Police and the Holocaust," *East European Jewish Affairs* 34, no. 2 (2004): 95–118; Per A. Rudling, *The OUN, the UPA and the Holocaust: A Study in the Manufacturing of Historical Myths* (Center for Russian and East European Studies, University of Pittsburgh, 2011).

91. Prusin, "Ukrainskaja policiya i Cholokost," 37–41.

92. Prusin, "Ukrainskaja policiya i Cholokost," 43–49.

93. Polishchuk, "My vyderzhali vsë . . . ," 311–12.

94. These are Evdokia G. Mikhailova, Anna G. Morozova, Grigory T. Buvajlik, Varvara G. Stepanovich, Taisiya S. Dobosh, Raisa M. Shelestovskaja, Polina, and Maria and Leonida Levchuk. They were all named Righteous Among the Nations of Babi Yar in 1992 and Righteous Among the Nations in 1994. See Ilya M. Levitas, ed., *Babiy Jar: Spasiteli i spasënnye* [Babi Yar: Rescuers and rescued] (Stal, 2005), 122–24.

95. Testimony of D. M. Pronicheva reported by Kuznetsov, *Babiy Jar*, 100; Italian translation, 102.

96. Viktor Nekrasov, "Zapiski zevaki" [Reflections of a wanderer], *Kontinent*, no. 4 (1975): 73. See also Nekrasov, "Mama: Memuarnyj ocherk" [Essay in memory of my mother], *Novoe russkoe slovo*, 7–8 October 1980.

97. Testimony of E. Gorodetskaya in Zabarko, *My choteli zhit'* . . . , 1:221.

98. Testimony of E. Gorodetskaya in Zabarko, *My choteli zhit'* . . . , 1:221.

99. Grossman and Ehrenburg, *Chernaja kniga*, 22; Italian translation, 30.

100. Grossman and Ehrenburg, *Chernaja kniga*, 23; Italian translation, 31.

101. The members of the Grigorenko family have been awarded the title of Righteous Among the Nations of Babi Yar. Valentina Ya. Litvinenko was declared Righteous Among the Nations in 1992. See Levitas, *Babiy Jar*, 105.

102. Revekka Shvarcman, "Ja plakala i prosila Boga, chtoby Bog pomog nemeckomu soldatu . . ." [I cried and begged God to help the German soldier . . .], in Zabarko, *Zhivymi ostalis' tol'ko my*, 488–89; Zabarko, *My choteli zhit'* . . . , 2:505–6; Levitas, *Babiy Jar*, 173. The members of the Radchenko, Nechay, and Taraday families have been recognized as Righteous Among the Nations of Babi Yar.

103. Testimony of G. Ya. Batasheva given to the KGB, 15 July 1980, in Evstafeva and Nachmanovich, *Istoricheskaja topografiya*, doc. 62, p. 322; Levitas, *Pamjat' Bab'ego Jara*, 89–90; Levitas, *Babiy Jar*, 107–8. It has been hypothesized that the German soldiers might have been Paul Wörzberger and Johann Koller. See Aleksandr Kruglov, "Uchastie nemcev v spasenii evreev v Ukraine v 1941–1944 gg." [The participation of Germans in the rescue of Jews in Ukraine in 1941–1944], in *Cholokost na territorii SSSR: Materialy XIX mezhdunarodnoj ezhegodnoj konferencii po iudaike* [The Holocaust in Soviet territory: Proceedings of the Nineteenth International Annual Conference on Judaic Studies] (Moscow Centr nauchnych rabotnikov i prepodavatelej iudaiki v VUZach "Sefer," 2012), 1:49–50; Kruglov, "'My povynni buly vykonuvaty brudnu robotu . . . ,'" 148–50. The neighbor who helped the two fugitives was Nikolai A. Soroka, killed by the Gestapo in 1943.

104. Mikhail V. Koval, "Tragediya Bab'ego Jara: Istoriya i sovremennost'" [The tragedy of Babi Yar: History and present], *Novaja i novejshaja istorija*, no. 4 (1998): 28; Prusin, "Ukrainskaja policiya i Cholokost," 51–52. The savior "Gordon" is Roman-Osyp Bida, a member of the Organisation of Ukrainian Nationalists (OUN-M), killed at Babi Yar in February 1942.

105. On Aleksey Aleksandrovich Glagolev (1901–72) and his family, see Leonid Yaskevich and Magdalina Glagoleva-Pal'jan, "Svetil'nik very i blagochestiya" [Lamp of faith and devotion], *Vestnik russkogo christjanskogo dvizheniya*, no. 181 (2000): 88–102; Magdalina A. Glagoleva-Pal'jan, "Vospominaniya ob Aleksandre Aleksandroviche Glagoleve" [Recollections of Aleksandr Aleksandrovich Glagolev], *Egupec*, no. 8 (2001): 311–38; Konstantin B. Sigov, "Svideteli Neopalimoj Kupiny: Sem'ja Glagolevych" [Witnesses of the burning bush: The Glagolev family], *Vestnik russkogo christjanskogo dvizheniya* 185, no. 1 (2003): 311–25. Aleksey Glagolev wrote a personal testimony in 1945 at the request of the official ecclesiastical authorities and sent it to the then secretary of the Central Committee of the Communist Party of Ukraine, Nikita Khrushchev. It was made public in the early 1990s. See Glagolev, *Za drugi svoja*, 130–39. His father, Aleksandr Aleksandrovich Glagolev (1872–1937), was called as a consultant by the defense committee of Mendel Bejlis, accused of ritual murder, in 1913.

106. Dmytro Pasichny, hidden behind a tombstone in the Jewish cemetery, witnessed the shootings at Babi Yar as well as other violence committed against Jews in the city. See Grossman and Ehrenburg, *Chernaja kniga*, 23; Italian translation, 31–32.

107. "Svjashchennik Glagolev," in Grossman and Ehrenburg, *Chernaja kniga*, 374–75; Italian translation, 597–98. Father Aleksey Glagolev, his wife, Tatiana, and their

daughter, Magdalina Pal'jan, were recognized as Righteous Among the Nations on 12 September 1991.

108. Walter Laqueur, *Il terribile segreto: La congiura del silenzio sulla "soluzione finale"* (Giuntina, 1983), 112–13; original edition, *The Terrible Secret: Suppression of the Truth About Hitler's "Final Solution"* (Weidenfeld and Nicolson, 1980).

109. "Nazis Drive Jews in Ukraine to Unknown Destination" and "Kyiv Made 'Judenrein,'" *JTA Daily News Bulletin*, 21 October 1941. See, for a broader context, Yitzhak Arad, "The Holocaust as Reflected in the Soviet Russian Language Newspapers in the Years 1941–1945," and Dov-Ber Kerler, "The Soviet Yiddish Press: 'Eynikayt' During the War, 1942–1945," both in *Why Didn't the Press Shout? American and International Journalism During the Holocaust*, ed. Robert M. Shapiro (Yeshiva University in association with Ktav, 2003), 199–220, 221–49; Karel C. Berkhoff, "Total Annihilation of the Jewish Population: The Holocaust in the Soviet Media, 1941–45," *Kritika: Explorations in Russian and Eurasian History* 10, no. 1 (2009): 61–105; Berkhoff, *Motherland in Danger: Soviet Propaganda During World War II* (Harvard University Press, 2012), 116–66; Mordechai Altshuler, "The Holocaust in the Soviet Mass Media During the War and in the First Postwar Years Re-Examined," *Yad Vashem Studies* 39, no. 2 (2011): 121–68.

110. Letter dated 28 September 1941 cited in Sven Oliver Müller, "Nationalismus in der deutschen Kriegsgesellschaft 1939 bis 1945" [Nationalism in German wartime society 1939 to 1945], in *Die Deutsche Kriegsgesellschaft 1939 bis 1945: II: Ausbeutung, Deutung, Ausgrenzung* [The German war society 1939 to 1945: II: Exploitation, interpretation, exclusion], ed. Jörg Echternkamp (Deutsche Verlags-Anstalt, 2005), 84; Peter Fritzsche, *Life and Death in the Third Reich* (Belknap Press of Harvard University Press, 2008), 152; Italian translation, *Vita e morte nel Terzo Reich* (Laterza, 2010), 147. For further details, see also Fritzsche, "Babi Yar, but Not Auschwitz: What Did Germans Know About the Final Solution?," in *The Germans and the Holocaust: Popular Responses to the Persecution and Murder of the Jews*, ed. Susanna Schrafstetter and Alan E. Steinweis (Berghahn Books, 2015), 85–104.

111. Annotation dated 11 October 1941, in Willy Cohn, *Als Jude in Breslau, 1941* [As a Jew in Breslau, 1941], ed. Joseph Walk (Bleicher, 1984), 106; Fritzsche, *Life and Death*, 197; Italian translation, 190.

112. "Nazis Execute 52,000 Jews in Kyiv; Smaller Pogroms in Other Cities," *JTA Daily News Bulletin*, 16 November 1941.

113. "Zverstva nemcev v Kieve" [The atrocities of the Germans in Kyiv], *Pravda* and *Izvestia*, 19 November 1941.

114. Fedor D. Sverdlov, ed., *Dokumenty obvinjajut: Cholokost; Svidetel'stva Krasnoj Armii* [The documents accuse: Holocaust; The testimonies of the Red Army] (Cholokost, 1996), 46.

115. Pyotr Stepanenko, "Chto proischodit v Kieve" [What is happening in Kyiv], *Krasnaja zvezda,* 28 November 1941, reprinted in *Pravda,* 29 November 1941. According to Berkhoff, "The Corpses," 255–56, the name of the author might be fictitious.

116. *Special'noe soobshchenie o polozhenie v gorode Kieve,* in *Istochnik. Dokumenty russkoj istorii,* no. 3 (1995): 140–41.

117. "O povsemestnych grabezhach, razorenii naseleniya i chudovishchnych zverstvach germanskich vlastej na zachvachennych imi sovetskich territoriyach" [On the

widespread looting, ruin of the population, and monstrous atrocities by the German authorities in the Soviet-occupied territories], *Pravda*, 7 January 1942. See also *Noty narodnogo komissara inostrannych del tov: V. M. Molotova* [Notes of the people's commissar for foreign affairs: V. M. Molotov] (Gospolitizdat, 1942), 29–30; *Soviet War Documents (June 1941–November 1943)* (Embassy of the USSR, 1943), 97.

118. "O povsemestnych grabezhach."

119. See "O provodimom gitlerovskimi vlastjami istreblenii evreyskogo naseleniya Evropy" [On the extermination of the Jewish population of Europe carried out by the Hitlerian authorities], *Pravda*, 18 December 1942; *Vneshnjaja politika Sovetskogo Sojuza v period otechestvennoj vojny* [Foreign policy of the Soviet Union during the Great Patriotic War] (Ogiz, 1946), 1:328–29.

120. "Ob osushchestvlenii gitlerovskimi vlastjami plana istrebleniya evreyskogo naseleniya Evropy" [On the implementation of the plan for the extermination of the Jewish population of Europe by the Hitlerian authorities], *Pravda*, 19 December 1942; *Vneshnjaja politika Sovetskogo Sojuza*, 1:329–37.

121. On this controversial figure, see Shimon Redlich, "Sheptyts'kyi and the Jews During World War II," in *Morality and Reality: The Life and Times of Andrei Sheptyts'kyi*, ed. Paul R. Magocsi (Canadian Institute of Ukrainian Studies, University of Alberta, 1989), 145–62; Redlich, "Metropolitan Andrii Sheptyts'kyi and the Complexities of Ukrainian-Jewish Relations," in Gitelman, *Bitter Legacy*, 61–76; Zhanna Kovba, ed., *Mytropolyt Andrei Sheptytsky: Dokumenty i materialy 1941–1944* [Metropolitan Andrei Sheptytsky: Documents and materials] (Duch i Litera, 2003); John-Paul Himka, "Christianity and Radical Nationalism: Metropolitan Andrei Sheptytsky and the Bandera Movement," in *State Secularism and Lived Religion in Soviet Russia and Ukraine*, ed. Catherine Wanner (Woodrow Wilson Center Press with Oxford University Press, 2012), 93–116; John-Paul Himka, "Metropolitan Andrey Sheptytsky and the Holocaust," *Polin: Studies in Polish Jewry* 26 (2014): 337–59.

122. Pierre Blet, Robert A. Graham, Angelo Martini, and Burkhart Schneider, eds., *Actes et documents du Saint Siège relatifs à la seconde guerre mondiale* [Acts and documents of the Holy See relating to the Second World War] (Libreria Editrice Vaticana, 1967), vol. 3, doc. 406, p. 625 (29–31 August 1942), ellipsis added.

123. Ivan F. Stadnyuk, *Ispoved' stalinista* [Confession of a Stalinist] (Patriot, 1993), 101–5; Berkhoff, "The Dispersal," 257.

124. Shmuel Spector, "*Aktion* 1005—Effacing the Murder of Millions," *Holocaust and Genocide Studies* 5, no. 2 (1990): 158.

125. Concerning this operation, see Spector, "*Aktion* 1005," 157–73; Yitzhak Arad, *The Holocaust in the Soviet Union* (University of Nebraska Press—Yad Vashem, 2009), 347–56; Andrej Angrick, "Operation 1005: The Nazi Regime's Attempt to Erase Traces of Mass Murder," in *Killing Sites: Research and Remembrance*, ed. International Holocaust Remembrance Alliance (Metropol Verlag, 2015), 47–59.

126. In the Syrets concentration camp and its immediate vicinity, over twenty-five thousand prisoners of war and civilians perished. See Stanislav Aristov, "Next to Babi Yar: The Syrets Concentration Camp and the Evolution of Nazi Terror in Kyiv," *Holocaust and Genocide Studies* 29, no. 3 (2015): 431–59.

127. Grossman and Ehrenburg, *Chernaja kniga*, 24; Italian translation, 33 (modified).

128. *Sbornik soobshcheniy Chrezvychajnoj gosudarstvennoj komissii*, 162. This is the testimony of former Syrets prisoners L. K. Ostrovskiy, V. Yu. Davydov, Ya. A. Steyuk, and I. M. Brodskiy, who were employed to erase the mass graves of Babi Yar. Other testimonies of former prisoners involved in the operation in Evstafeva and Nachmanovich, *Istoricheskaja topografiya*, 222–30, 234–36, 243–56, 291–93, 295–97, 300–304, 309–14, 319–21.

129. Spector, "Tragediya v Bab'em Jaru," 14. For this reason, there is still a significant variation in the number of cremated corpses according to Lev Elbert, "Babiy Jar—proshloe i sovremennost" [Babi Yar—the past and the present], in Baukh, *Babi Yar*, 55. Referring to estimates by the surviving group of grave diggers, it would be about 110,000 bodies.

130. Affidavit of Paul Blobel, NO-3947, Nuremberg, 18 June 1947, in Yitzhak Arad, ed., *Unishtenie evreev SSSR v gody nemeckoj okkupacii (1941–1944): Sbornik dokumentov i materialov* [The annihilation of Soviet Jews during the years of Nazi occupation (1941–1944): Collection of documents and materials] (Yad Vashem, 1992), 275–76; Arad, Israel Gutman, and Abraham Margaliot, eds., *Documents on the Holocaust: Selected Sources on the Destruction of the Jews of Germany and Austria, Poland, and the Soviet Union* (University of Nebraska Press—Yad Vashem, 1999), 472. Paul Blobel was sentenced to death for crimes against humanity at Nuremberg in 1948 at the conclusion of the trial against the leaders of the Einsatzgruppen and was executed in Landsberg-am-Lech prison on 7 June 1951. For a profile of him, see Hilary Earl, *The Nuremberg SS-Einsatzgruppen Trial, 1945–1958: Atrocity, Law, and History* (Cambridge University Press, 2009), 124–25, 127, 163–67.

131. Grossman and Ehrenburg, *Chernaja kniga*, 24; Italian translation, 33.

132. Testimony of I. S. Yanovych given to the NKVD, 15 November 1943, in Evstafeva and Nachmanovich, *Istoricheskaja topografiya*, doc. 15, p. 231. See also the testimony of M. S. Lutsenko given during the same investigation and on the same day, in Evstafeva and Nachmanovich, *Istoricheskaja topografiya*, doc. 16, p. 232.

133. Vasily Grossman, "Ukraina" [Ukraine], in *Gody vojny* [Years of war] (Ogiz, 1945), 354 (previously published in *Eynikayt*, 12 October 1943; absent from the contemporary correspondence in *Krasnaja zvezda*, 12 October 1943). See also Grossman, *A Writer at War: Vasily Grossman with the Red Army 1941–1945*, ed. Antony Beevor and Luba Vinogradova (Pantheon Books, 2005), 249–50; Italian translation, *Uno scrittore in guerra* (Adelphi, 2015), 290. See also John Garrard and Carol Garrard, *Le ossa di Berdichev: La vita e il destino di Vasiliy Grossman* (Marietti, 2009), 241–43; original edition, *The Bones of Berdichev: The Life and Fate of Vasily Grossman* (Free Press, 1996).

134. Testimony in Aleksandr Shlaen, *Babiy Jar* (Abris, 1995), 30. The "geological layering" of human bodies is also mentioned in Boris N. Polevoy, *V konce koncov: Njurnbergskie dnevniki* [In the end: Nuremberg diaries] (Sovetskaja Rossija, 1969), 201–2, where the author—in addition to evoking the "stench" and "dizziness"—expressed his conviction that one day in that place a monument would be erected to future memory. Boris Polevoy provided one of the first accounts of the Auschwitz camp: "Kombinat smerti v Osvencime (Ot voennogo korrespondenta 'Pravdy')" [The death factory at Auschwitz (From the war correspondent of *Pravda*)], *Pravda*, 2 February 1945.

135. Among the accounts of soldiers and correspondents, the most significant is probably Avdeyenko and Olender in Levitas, *Babiy Jar*.

136. Mykola Bazhan, "Jar" [Ravine], in *V dni viyny: Poeziy* [In the days of war: Poetry] (Vijs'kove vyd-vo NKO, 1945), 63–65; and Bazhan, *Tvory v chotyriokh tomakh* [Works in four volumes] (Dnipro, 1984), 1:291–93, ellipsis added. Mykola Platonovych Bazhan (1904–83), whose second marriage was to a Jewish woman, Nina Volody-myrivna Lauer, had philosemitic positions. He had an excellent knowledge, among other things, of Yiddish and Hebrew. In the early postwar years, he was a member of the Central Committee of the Communist Party of Ukraine and was deputy chairman of the Council of Ministers of the republic.

137. Bill Downs, "Blood at Babii Yar: Kyiv's Atrocity Story," *Newsweek*, 6 December 1943, 22, reprinted in Robert H. Azbug, *America Views the Holocaust, 1933–1945: A Brief Documentary History* (Bedford and St. Martin's Press, 1999), 163–64.

138. William H. Lawrence, "50,000 Kyiv Jews Reported Killed," *New York Times*, 29 November 1943, 3. The American journalist soon changed his mind, particularly after visiting the Majdanek camp, as he recalled in his memoirs: Bill Lawrence, *Six Presidents, Too Many Wars* (Saturday Review Press, 1972), 90–95, 100–103. Lawrence's skepticism was not shared by most of the correspondents present at that meeting. See the analysis of the American press conducted by Deborah E. Lipstadt, *Beyond Belief: The American Press and the Coming of the Holocaust, 1933–1945* (Free Press, 1986), 245–47.

139. The commission was established on 2 November 1942. See Kiril Feferman, "Soviet Investigation of Nazi Crimes in the USSR: Documenting the Holocaust," *Journal of Genocide Research* 5, no. 4 (2003): 587–602; Feferman, *Soviet Jewish Stepchild: The Holocaust in the Soviet Mindset, 1941–1964* (VDM Verlag Dr. Müller, 2009), 28–42; Marina Sorokina, "People and Procedures: Toward a History of the Investigation of Nazi Crimes in the USSR," *Kritika: Explorations in Russian and Eurasian History* 6, no. 4 (2005): 797–831; Nathalie Moine, "La commission d'enquête soviétique sur les crimes de guerre nazis: Entre reconquête du territorie, écriture du récit de la guerre et usages justiciers" [The Soviet commission of inquiry into Nazi war crimes: Between reconquest of territory, writing of the story of the war and vigilante practices], *Le mouvement social* 1, no. 222 (2008): 81–109; Niels Bo Poulsen, "Rozsliduvannja voen-nych zlochyniv 'po-sovets'ky': Krytychnyj analiz materialiv Nadzvychajnoï derzhavnoï Komisiï" [Investigating war crimes "the Soviet way": Critical analysis of the materials of the Extraordinary State Commission], *Holokost i suchasnist'* 1, no. 5 (2009): 27–45.

140. For information on the activities of the Kyiv Commission, see Feferman, "Soviet Investigation," 587–602; Feferman, *Soviet Jewish Stepchild*, 38–42.

141. "O razrusheniyach i zverstvach sovershënnych nemecko-fashistskimi zachvat-chikami v gorode Kieve" [On the destruction and atrocities committed by the German Fascist occupiers in the city of Kyiv], in *Izvestia* and *Krasnaja zvezda*, 29 February 1944, and *Pravda*, 1 March 1944. See also *Sbornik soobshcheniy Chrezvychajnoj gosudarstven-noj komissii*, 151–65. The report was also published in booklet form in Ukrainian: *Pro rujnuvannja i zvirstva, zapodiyani nimets'kofashysts'kymy zaharbnykamy v m. Kyjevi* [On the destruction and atrocities committed by the German Fascist occupiers in the city of Kyiv] (Ukrainian State Publishing House, 1944).

142. See *Sbornik soobshcheniy Chrezvychajnoj gosudarstvennoj komissii*, 152, 160–65.

143. *Sbornik soobshcheniy Chrezvychajnoj gosudarstvennoj komissii*, 164.

144. The final version was approved by the chairman of the Extraordinary State Commission, N. M. Shvernik, and its members M. T. Rylsky, P. H. Tychyna, and A. N. Tolstoy. See Lev A. Bezymenskiy, "Informaciya po-sovetski" [Information in the Soviet way], *Znamya*, no. 5 (1998): 191–99. See also Ilya Altman and Claudio Ingerflom, "Le Kremlin et l'Holocauste. 1933–2001," in *Avant et après Auschwitz*, by Vasily Petrenko (Flammarion, 2002), 260–61; original edition, *Do i posle Osvencima* [Before and after Auschwitz] (Fond Cholokosta, 2000); Altman, *Zhertvy nenavisti*, 397–98. Even before it was included in the report of the Extraordinary State Commission, the expression "peaceful Soviet citizens" was used in various official interventions or war correspondence after the liberation of Kyiv. See Serhy Yekelchyk, "The Civic Duty to Hate: Stalinist Citizenship as Political Practice and Civic Emotion (Kyiv, 1943–53)," *Kritika: Explorations in Russian and Eurasian History* 7, no. 3 (2006): 534–37; Yekelchyk, *Stalin's Citizens: Everyday Politics in the Wake of Total War* (Oxford University Press, 2014), 11–13.

145. Yekelchyk, "The Civic Duty," 537; Yekelchyk, *Stalin's Citizens*, 14.

146. See Leonyd M. Abramenko, ed., *Kyïvs'kyj proces: Dokumenty ta materialy* [The Kyiv trial: Documents and materials] (Lybid', 1995).

147. N. S. Khrushchev to I. V. Stalin, 8 November 1943, CDAHO Ukraïny, f. 1, op. 23, spr. 577, ark. 11–12; Nikita Khrushchev, "Tovarishchu Stalinu: Polozhenie v Kieve" [To Comrade Stalin: The situation in Kyiv], *Pravda*, 9 November 1943, 1.

148. "Osvobozhdenie ukrainskich zemel' ot nemeckich zachvatchikov i ocherednye zadachi vosstanovleniya narodnogo chozajstva Sovetskoj Ukrainy" [The liberation of Ukrainian lands from German occupiers and the immediate tasks of restoring the national economy in Soviet Ukraine], *Pravda*, 16 March 1944, 2.

149. Testimony of Róża Hudes in Léon Leneman, *La tragédie des Juifs en URSS* (Desclée De Brouwer, 1959), 179; Joseph B. Schechtman, *Star in Eclipse: Russian Jewry Revisited* (Thomas Yoseloff, 1961), 80, ellipsis added. Later, to the writer Ilya Ehrenburg—who had sent a letter pleading with him to intervene with the authorities in Kyiv to oppose the project of building a market on the site of Babi Yar—Nikita Khrushchev replied to "not interfere" in matters that did not concern him, suggesting that he "limit himself to writing good stories." See Abraham Sutskever, "Ilia Erenburg: A kapitl zikhroynes fun di yoren 1944–1946" [Ilya Ehrenburg: A chapter of memories from the years 1944–1946], *Di goldene keyt*, no. 61 (1967): 30; and Yehoshua A. Gilboa, *The Black Years of Soviet Jewry, 1939–1953* (Little, Brown and Company, 1971), 36.

150. The quote "our people" is from "Osvobozhdenie ukrainskich zemel' ot nemeckich zachvatchikov."

151. Feferman, *Soviet Jewish Stepchild*, 36.

152. *Izvestija CK KPSS*, no. 7 (1990): 211. In Russian the word *židy* is derogatory.

Chapter 1. Form and Truth

1. Paul Celan, introduction to a selection of Mandelstam's poems in German translation, in Celan, *The Truth of Poetry: "The Meridiano" and Other Prose*, ed. Giuseppe Bevilacqua (Einaudi, 1993), 40.

2. Among the rare exceptions are the works of the historian Kuzma K. Dubina, *Zlodejaniya nemcev v Kieve* [German atrocities in Kyiv] (Ogiz, 1945); Dubina, *778 trahichnych dniv Kyjeva* [The 778 tragic days of Kyiv] (Ukraïns'ke derzhavne

vydavnyctvo, 1945). See also Dubina, *V gody tjazhelych ispytaniy* [In years of severe trials] (Obl. kn.-gaz. izd-vo, 1962), which, based on the findings of the Extraordinary State Commission for Investigation of Nazi War Crimes, made brief references to the massacres at Babi Yar, albeit with contradictions regarding the location of the executions. Dubina did not omit the fact that the Germans initially used the site to exterminate Jews, subsequently highlighting the elimination of many other groups.

3. See Maxim D. Shrayer, "Jewish-Russian Poets Bearing Witness to the Shoah, 1941–1946: Textual Evidence and Preliminary Conclusions," in *Studies in Slavic Languages and Literatures (ICCEES Congress Stockholm 2010 Papers and Contributions)*, ed. Stefano Garzonio (Portal on Central Eastern and Balkan Europe, 2011), 59–119; Borys Chornyj, "Literaturni svidchennja masovogo znyshchennja jevreïv u Babynomu Jaru" [Literary testimonies of the mass extermination of Jews at Babi Yar], and Luba Jurgenson, "Spadshchyna Babynoho Jaru v literature" [The legacy of Babi Yar in literature], both in *Babyn Jar: Masove ubyvstvo i pam'jat' pro n'oho; Materialy mizhnarodnoï naukovoï konferencii 24–25 zhovtnja 2011 r., m. Kyïv* [Babi Yar: Mass murder and memory of it; Proceedings of the International Scientific Conference, Kyiv, 24–25 October 2011], ed. Mykhailo Tyahlyi and Vitaly Nachmanovych (Ukraïns'kyj centr vyvchennja istorii Holokostu, Hromads'kyj komitet dlja vshanuvannja pam'jati zhertv Babynoho Jaru, 2012), 198–210, 211–20; Boris Czerny, "Témoignages et oeuvres littéraires sur le massacre de Babi Yar 1941–1948" [Testimonies and literary works on the massacre of Babi Yar 1941–1948], *Cahiers du monde russe* 53, no. 4 (2012): 523–70; Annie Epelboin and Assia Kovriguina, *La littérature des ravins: Écrire sur la Shoah en URSS* [Ravine literature: Writing about the Shoah in the USSR] (Robert Laffont, 2013); Catherine Coquio, *La littérature en suspens: Écritures de la Shoah; Le témoignage et les oeuvres* [Literature in suspense: Scriptures of the Shoah; The testimony and the works] (L'Arachnéen, 2015), 97–172.

4. Ilya Lvovich Selvinsky, "Ja eto videl!" [I saw it!], *Krasnaja zvezda*, 27 February 1942, 3, and *Oktjabr'*, no. 1–2 (1942): 65–66. Ilya Lvovich Selvinsky (1899–1968) volunteered during World War II and participated in military operations in his native Crimea and in Kuban in the North Caucasus. A direct witness to the extermination, he dedicated other significant compositions to it during the war, such as "Sud v Krasnodare" [Trial in Krasnodar], "Kerch," and "Kandava." For more on Selvinsky, see Maxim D. Shrayer, *I SAW IT: Ilya Selvinsky and the Legacy of Bearing Witness to the Shoah* (Academic Studies Press, 2013).

5. Selvinskiy, "Ja eto videl!"

6. Evdokia Olshanskaya, "Mne zhizn' podarila vstrechi s poetom" [Life gave me meetings with the poet], *Zerkalo nedeli*, 24 April 1998; Shrayer, "Jewish-Russian Poets," 68. Olshanskaya later wrote "Ballada o materi" [Ballad about the mother, 1956], celebrating the rescue by a Ukrainian woman of a child who was thrown into the ravine but escaped death. See Ilya M. Levitas, ed., *Babiy Jar: Spasiteli i spasënnye* [Babi Yar: Rescuers and rescued] (Stal, 2005), 491.

7. Levitas, *Babiy Jar*, 534.

8. Published in the first brief poetry collection of Olga Anstei, *Dver' v stene: Stichi* [A door in the wall: Verses] (no publisher, 1949), comprising verses composed between 1930 and 1948. Kyrylivskyi Yari is one of the other names used to refer to the area adjacent to Babi Yar and distributed around the Kyrylivskyi Monastery. Olga

Nikolaevna Anstei (born Steinberg, 1912–85) was one of the most famous poets of the "second wave" of Russian emigration (1943–45). Originally from Kyiv, a city that would become one of the central themes of her work, she left the Soviet Union in 1943 with her husband, the poet Ivan Venediktovich Elagin (real surname, Matveyev, 1918–87), who had a Jewish mother. She lived briefly in Prague, then for a long time in Germany (the experience in the displaced persons camp in Schleissheim is prominent in her verse and prose). In 1950 she immigrated to the United States. See Tatiana Fesenko, "Ol'ga Nikolaevna Anstej: Lyusha," *Novyj zhurnal*, no. 161 (1985): 128–37.

9. Anstei, *Dver' v stene*, 23–24.

10. Myroslav Shkandrij has drawn attention to the most eminent Ukrainian literary figures who, even during the war, explicitly referenced the persecution of Jews in their works; see *Jews in Ukrainian Literature: Representation and Identity* (Yale University Press, 2009), 173. Tychyna's verses were first published without a title in *Literatura i mystectvo*, 20 September 1942 (the date of composition was indicated by the author: 15–16 August 1942); then Pavlo H., "Tychyna, Jevrejs'komu narodovi" [To the Jewish people], in *Poeziï (1941–1944)* [Poems (1941–1944)] (Ukraïns'ke derzhavne vydavnyctvo, 1945), 66–68; the Russian version is *Evrejskomu narodu* [To the Jewish people], in *Izbrannoe* [Selected works] (Ogiz, 1946), 303–5.

11. Maksim Ryl'skij [Maksym Tadeyovych Rylsky], "Evrejskomu narodu" [To the Jewish people], in *Slovo o materi rodine* [A word about the motherland] (Goslitizdat, 1943), 29–30. These verses circulated only in Russian translation; the original "Jevreis'komu narodu" [To the Jewish people] was published in 1988.

12. Ilya Ehrenburg, "Brodjat Rachili, Chaimy, Lii" [Rachel, Chaim, Lea roam], in *Vernost' (Ispaniya. Parizh): Stichi* [Fidelity (Spain. Paris): Verses] (Gosudarstvennoe izdatel'stvo chudozhestvennoj literatury, 1941), 52.

13. See his memoirs in Ilya Ehrenburg, "Lyudi, gody, zhizn" [People, years, life], in *Sobranie sochineniy v vos'mi tomach* [Collected works in eight volumes] (Chudozhestvennaja Literatura, 2000), 7:65–70; Italian translation, *Uomini, anni, vita* [Men, years, life] (Editori Riuniti, 1961), 2:82–90. Concerning the figure of the writer Ilya Grigoryevich Ehrenburg (1891–1967), see Aleksandr I. Rubashkin, *Publicistika Il'i Erenburga protiv vojny i fashizma* [Ilya Ehrenburg's journalism against war and Fascism] (Sovetskij Pisatel', 1965); Rubashkin, *Il'ja Erenburg: Put' pisatelja* [Ilya Ehrenburg: The writer's path] (Sovetskij Pisatel', 1990); Anatol Goldberg, *Ilya Ehrenburg: Writing, Politics and the Art of Survival* (Weidenfeld and Nicolson, 1984); Ewa Bérard, *La vie tumultueuse d'Ilya Ehrenbourg: Juif, russe et soviétique* [The tumultuous life of Ilya Ehrenburg: Jew, Russian, and Soviet] (Ramsay, 1991); Julian L. Laychuk, *Ilya Ehrenburg: An Idealist in an Age of Realism* (Lang, 1991); Joshua Rubenstein, *Tangled Loyalties: The Life and Times of Ilya Ehrenburg* (Basic Books, 1996); Boris Ya. Frezinskiy, *Ob Il'ie Erenburge (Knigi, ljudi, strany): Izbrannye stat'ja i publikacii* [Ilya Ehrenburg (books, people, countries): Selected articles and publications] (Novoe literaturnoe obozrenie, 2013).

14. Ilya Ehrenburg, "25 sentjabrja 1941 goda" [25 September 1941], in Ehrenburg, *Letopis' muzhestva* [Chronicles of courage], 2nd ed. (Sovetskij Pisatel', 1983), 46; Ehrenburg, "Kyiv," *Krasnaja zvezda*, 27 September 1941, 3; Ehrenburg, *Vojna 1941–1945* [War 1941–1945] (Astrel', 2004), 102, 106. A few days later, Ehrenburg clarified that the decision to remain silent about the "fall of Kyiv" was entirely incomprehensible to him: "Everyone talks about it, in factories, in military units, on the streets. One cannot

remain silent about events of such importance for the country." See Ehrenburg to
A. S. Shcherbakov, S. A. Lozovskiy, and G. F. Aleksandrov, 7 October 1941, in *"Na
cokole istorii . . .": Pis'ma 1931–1967* ["At the base of history . . .": Letters 1931–1967], ed.
Boris Ya. Frezinskiy (Agraf, 2004), 293.

15. On Ehrenburg's relationship with Judaism, see Shimon Markish, "Tri primera"
[Three examples], *Vestnik evrejskoj kul'tury* 3, no. 6 (1990): 18–27, and 4, no. 7 (1990):
42–53; Anatol Goldberg, "Ilya Ehrenburg," in *Jews in Soviet Culture*, ed. Jack Miller
(Transaction Books, 1984), 183–213; Boris Paramonov, "Portret evreja: Erenburg" [Por-
trait of a Jew: Ehrenburg], *Zvezda*, no. 1 (1991): 132–50; and especially Mordechai
Altshuler, "Erenburg i evrei (Nabrosok portreta)" [Ehrenburg and the Jews (sketch of
a portrait)], in *Sovetskie evrei pishut Il'e Erenburgu, 1943–1966* [Soviet Jews write to Ilya
Ehrenburg, 1943–1966], ed. Mordechai Altshuler, Icchach Arad, and Shmuel' Krakovs-
kiy (Centr po issledovaniju i dokumentacii vostochnogo-evropejskogo evrejstva—Yad
Vashem, 1993), doc. 14, pp. 9–105. See also Antonella Salomoni, *L'Unione Sovietica e la
Shoah: Genocidio, resistenza, rimozione* [The Soviet Union and the Shoah: Genocide,
resistance, removal] (Il Mulino, 2007), 111–23.

16. Ilya Ehrenburg, "Svideteli" [Witnesses], *Krasnaja zvezda*, 13 December 1941, 3;
Ehrenburg, *Vojna 1941–1945*, 158–59.

17. Ilya Ehrenburg, "Armiya palachej" [The army of executioners], *Krasnaja zvezda*,
3 April 1942, 3.

18. Ilya Ehrenburg, "Kyiv," *Krasnaja zvezda*, 27 September 1942, 4; Ehrenburg,
Vojna II: Aprel' 1942–mart 1943 [The war: April 1942–March 1943] (Gospolitizdat,
1943), 141.

19. Ilya Ehrenburg, "Opravdanie nenavisti" [The justification of hatred], *Pravda*,
26 May 1942; Ehrenburg, *Vojna 1941–1945*, 217.

20. Ilya Ehrenburg, "Orda na Donu" [The horde on the Don], *Krasnaja zvezda*,
12 July 1942, 3, ellipses added.

21. Ilya Ehrenburg, "Evrei" [Jews], *Krasnaja zvezda*, 1 November 1942, 3; Ehrenburg, *Vojna 1941–1945*, 317–18, ellipsis added.

22. Ilya Ehrenburg, "Undzer ort" [Our place], *Eynikayt*, 25 June 1943, 4; Ehrenburg,
"Nashe mesto" [Our place], *Birobidzhanskaja zvezda*, 11 August 1943; Ehrenburg,
Vojna 1941–1945, 457–59. Ehrenburg had already published a report on Babi Yar:
"Gebentshte erd" [Blessed earth], *Eynikayt*, 15 October 1942, 2.

23. Ilya Ehrenburg, "Kyiv zhdët" [Kyiv waits], *Za schast'e rodiny*, 9 October 1943,
and *Znamya rodiny*, 10 October 1943; Ehrenburg, *Vojna 1941–1945*, 489. See also
Ehrenburg, "Pered Kievom" [Before Kyiv], *Krasnaja zvezda*, 14 October 1943.

24. I. Ehrenburg to Aleksandr F. Morozov, 24 October 1943, in Ehrenburg, *"Na
cokole istorii . . . ,"* 325.

25. Ilya Ehrenburg, "Delo sovesti" [A matter of conscience], *Pravda*, 29 October
1943; Ehrenburg, *Vojna 1941–1945*, 501, 505.

26. Ilya Ehrenburg, "Di daytshishe fashistn torn nit lebn blaybn!" [German Fascists
must not live!], *Eynikayt*, 4 November 1943, 2; Ehrenburg, "Nemeckie fashisty ne dol-
zhny zhit'" [German Fascists must not live], *Birobidzhanskaja zvezda*, 26 November
1943; Ehrenburg, *Vojna 1941–1945*, 506–7.

27. Ehrenburg, *Vojna 1941–1945*, 507, ellipsis added.

28. Ilya Ehrenburg, "Svideteli" [Witnesses], *Krasnaja zvezda*, 19 December 1943, 4; Ehrenburg, *Voina (aprel' 1943–mart 1944)* [War (April 1943–March 1944)] (Gosudarstvennoe izdatel'stvo chudozhestvennoj literatury, 1944), 160. Drobyc'kyj Jar is the place near Kharkiv where, between mid-December 1941 and early January 1942, the Germans killed sixteen to twenty thousand people, mostly Jews.

29. Ilya Ehrenburg, "Dychanie rebënka" [The breath of the child], *Krasnaja zvezda*, 2 March 1944, 3; Ehrenburg, *Voina (aprel' 1943–mart 1944)*, 123.

30. Ilya Ehrenburg, "Spravedlivost'" [Justice], *Krasnaja zvezda*, 19 December 1943; Ehrenburg, *Voina (aprel' 1943–mart 1944)*, 165. See also, in a softened version, Ehrenburg, "Spravedlivost'" [Justice], *Vojna i rabochiy klass*, no. 12 (1944): 7–11. The Krasnodar trial was held between 14 and 17 July 1943; the Kyiv trial took place, as mentioned, between 17 and 28 January 1946. For an updated overview of studies on Soviet judicial procedures of the time, see Franziska Exeler, "Nazi Atrocities, International Criminal Law, and War Crimes Trials: The Soviet Union and the Global Moment of Post–World War II Justice," in *The New Histories of International Criminal Law: Retrials*, ed. Immi Tallgren and Thomas Skouteris (Oxford University Press, 2019), 189–219.

31. The image is present in a letter sent to Ehrenburg by one of his correspondents, Evsei Lantsman, where the writer dwells on the fate of children who, at Babi Yar, were mostly thrown into the ravine alive or barely stunned: letter from Evsei Lantsman from the archive of Ilya Ehrenburg, in *Babiy Jar: K pjatidesjatiletiyu tragedii 29–30 sentjabrja 1941 goda* [Babi Yar: On the fiftieth anniversary of the tragedy of 29–30 September 1941], ed. Shmuel Spector and M. Kipnis (Biblioteka-Alija, 1991), 70 (the letter is undated).

32. Ilya Ehrenburg, "Oni k nam prishli—oni ot nas ne ujdut" [They came to us—and they will not escape], *Na razgrom vraga*, 6 February 1944; *Bloknot agitatora krasnoj armii*, no. 4 (1944): 26–28; Ehrenburg, *Vojna 1941–1945*, 562–63.

33. Ilya Ehrenburg, "Pomnit'!" [Remember!], *Pravda*, 17 December 1944; Ehrenburg, *Vojna 1941–1945*, 680, ellipsis added. The theme of children in Ehrenburg's prose was already present in the article "2 marta 1942 goda" [2 March 1942], first published in *Vojna 1941–1945*, 195–97. Although it includes several factual errors, it is also strongly emphasized in the official statement "Ob osushchestvlenii gitlerovskimi vlastjami plana istrebleniya evreyskogo naseleniya Evropy" [On the implementation of the plan for the extermination of the Jewish population of Europe by the Hitlerian authorities], *Pravda*, 19 December 1942, as noted by Ilya Altman, *Zhertvy nenavisti: Cholokost v SSSR, 1941–1945* [Victims of hatred: The Holocaust in the USSR, 1941–1945] (Fond Kovcheg, 2002), 395.

34. Ilya Ehrenburg, "Narodoubiycy" [The murderers of nations], *Znamya*, no. 1–2 (1944): 185; Ehrenburg, *Vojna 1941–1945*, 572, 579.

35. Ilya Ehrenburg, "Narodoubiycy" [The murderers of nations], in *Chernaja kniga* [The black book], ed. Vasily Grossman and Ilya Ehrenburg (Interbuk, 1991), 2:241–42 (and later Tarbut, 1980); available in English as Ilya Ehrenburg and Vasily Grossman, *The Complete Black Book of Russian Jewry*, trans. David Patterson (Routledge, 2003). Reports sent by partisan movement commands record the data of children and elderly people buried alive at Babi Yar. See, for example, the report prepared by Sergeant Bobyr, 1 December 1942, CDAHO Ukraïny, f. 62, op. 1, spr. 210, ark. 7.

36. Ilya Ehrenburg, "Oni otomstjat za vsë" [They will avenge everything], *Komsomol'skaja pravda,* 2 April 1944; *Evrejskiy narod v bor'be protiv fashizma: Materialy III antifashistskogo mitinga predstavitelej evreyskogo naroda i III plenuma evreyskogo anti-fashistskogo komiteta v SSSR* [The Jewish people in the fight against Fascism: Materials of the Third Antifascist Meeting of Representatives of the Jewish People and the Third Plenum of the Jewish Anti-Fascist Committee in the USSR] (Ogiz-Der emes, 1945), 38; Ehrenburg, *Vojna 1941–1945,* 596–97.

37. Ilya Ehrenburg, "Zapomni etot rov" [Remember this ditch], in *Derevo: Stichi 1938–1945 gg.* [The tree: Verses, 1938–1945] (Sovetskij Pisatel', 1946), 51.

38. Ehrenburg, "Zapomni etot rov," 51.

39. Alexander Werth, *Russia at War, 1941–1945* (Dutton, 1964); Italian translation, *La Russia in guerra, 1941–1945* (Mondadori, 1966), 411–12.

40. See the analysis of the entire cycle in Shrayer, "Jewish-Russian Poets," 73–85; Maxim D. Shrayer, "Ilya Ehrenburg's January 1945 'Novy Mir' Cycle and Soviet Memory of the Shoah," in *Eastern European Jewish Literature of the 20th and 21st Centuries: Identity and Poetics,* ed. Klavdia Smola (Verlag Otto Sagner, 2013), 191–209.

41. Rubenstein, *Tangled Loyalties,* 210.

42. Ilya Ehrenburg, "K chemu slova i chto pero . . ." [What meaning do words and the pen possess . . .] (1944), *Novyj mir,* no. 1 (1945): 16; then in Ehrenburg, *Derevo,* 45–46. See Shrayer, "Jewish-Russian Poets," 75.

43. For other testimonies on the trauma of return and the difficulty of recognizing Kyiv after the occupation, see Victoria Khiterer, "We Did Not Recognize Our Country: The Rise of Antisemitism in Ukraine Before and After the Second World War, 1937–1947," *Polin: Studies in Polish Jewry* 26 (2014): 361–79.

44. Rubenstein, *Tangled Loyalties,* 209.

45. Ilya Ehrenburg, "Lyudi, gody, zhizn'," in Ehrenburg, *Sobranie sochineniy,* 7:69; Italian translation, *Uomini, anni, vita,* 2:88 (modified).

46. Ilya Ehrenburg, "O tom zhe" [Again on that], *Krasnaja zvezda,* 10 January 1945, 3; Ehrenburg, *Vojna 1941–1945,* 690–91. In 1947 Ehrenburg published in the magazine *Novyj mir* (nos. 4–8) the long novel *Burja* [The storm], in which, through the fate of the Al'per family, he recounts the history of Jews during World War II and focuses on the massacre of Babi Yar, described with strong attention to the specificity of the victims. See Ehrenburg, *Burja* (Sovetskij Pisatel', 1948); Italian translation, *La tempesta,* 2 vols. (Macchia, 1950–52), a work conceived, by his own admission, as "a succession of meetings, conversations, spectacles, emotional states, linked to personal memories" (Ehrenburg, "Lyudi, gody, zhizn'," in *Sobranie sochineniy,* 7:649; Italian translation, *Uomini, anni, vita,* 5:7). He later wrote a continuation (*Devjatyj val* [The ninth wave] [Sovetskij Pisatel', 1953]), in which the protagonist, Major Osip Al'per, returns to visit Babi Yar, where his mother and daughter are buried.

47. Pavel Antokolsky, "Syn" [Son], *Znamya,* no. 7–8 (1943): 1–12; see the first, reduced version: "Syn: Povest' v stichach" [Son: Story in verse], *Smena,* no. 4 (1943): 10–12. The poem won the Stalin Prize of the second class in 1946.

48. Quoted in Maxim D. Shrayer, "Pavel Antokolsky as a Witness to the Shoah in Ukraine and Poland," *Polin: Studies in Polish Jewry* 28 (2016): 545.

49. Pavel Antokolsky, "Lager' unichtozheniya" [Extermination camp], *Znamya,* no. 10 (1945): 34. Antokolsky wrote the verses while he was under the strong impressions he

received while crossing the Sobibór region. Based on the materials collected during that trip, Antokolsky also wrote, together with Veniamin A. Kaverin [Veniamin Zilber], the essay "Vosstanie v Sobibore" [The Sobibór uprising], *Znamya*, no. 4 (1945), then included in Grossman and Ehrenburg, *Chernaja kniga*, 420–31; Italian translation, 671–87.

50. Pavel Antokolsky, "Nevechnaja pamjat'" [Noneternal memory], *Znamya*, no. 7 (1946): 64–65. The distribution of that work was long blocked following its first publication. The poem was not reissued in the USSR until 1966: "Nevechnaia pamiat'" [Noneternal memory], in *Izbrannoe* [Selected works] (Chudozhestvennaja Literatura, 1966), 2:170–74. In a subsequent edition (*Sobranie sochineniy* [Collected works] [Chudozhestvennaja Literatura, 1971], 2:152–55), references to Judaism were omitted or softened, fundamentally changing the meaning of the poem. See Levitas, *Babiy Jar*, 373–74. Pavel Grigoryevich Antokolsky (1896–1978), poet, playwright, and translator, organized theatrical performances for soldiers at the front during the war and worked as a war correspondent. He is the author of the autobiographical story "Moi zapiski" [My memoirs], written in July 1953, shortly after Stalin's death. See Pavel Antokolsky, *Daleko eto bylo gde-to . . . Stichi. P'esy. Avtobiograficheskaja povest'* [It was far away, somewhere . . . Verses. Plays. Autobiographical story], ed. Andrei Toom and Anna Toom (Dom-muzej Mariny Cvetaevoj, 2010), 227–405. Concerning his wartime work related to genocide, see Shrayer, "Jewish-Russian Poets," 90–95, 101; Shrayer, "Pavel Antokolsky as a Witness," 539–56.

51. Leonid Pervomayskiy, "V Babynim Jaru" [At Babi Yar], in *Tvory v semy tomach* [Works in seven volumes] (Dnipro, 1985), 1:373; Levitas, *Babiy Jar*, 508. Leonid Solomonovych Pervomayskyi (pseudonym of Illya Shlyomovych Hurevych, 1908–73), a writer and poet working in the Ukrainian language, was born into a Jewish family of bookbinders. Abandoning Jewish culture and the Yiddish language, he chose to write not in Russian but in Ukrainian. A war correspondent during the war, his collections of verses *Den' narodzhennja* [Birthday] and *Zemlja* [The earth] earned him wide acclaim and the second-class Stalin Prize in 1946. He managed to evacuate his closest family from Kyiv before the city was occupied by the Germans. In 1949 he was sucked into the anticosmopolitan campaign along with other Ukrainian Jewish writers and accused of nationalistic tendencies. Jewish themes occupy a significant place in his work. See Yohanan Petrovsky-Shtern, *The Anti-Imperial Choice: The Making of the Ukrainian Jew* (Yale University Press, 2009), 165–227; Shkandriy, *Jews in Ukrainian Literature*, 125–36, 208–10.

52. Leonid Pervomayskiy, "Voskresy mene, majbutnje" [Revive me, future], in *Chaj lishajet'sja vohon': Z neopublikovanoï spadshchyny; Poeziï, proza, notatky, lysty* [Let the fire remain: From the unpublished heritage; Poetry, prose, notes, letters] (Radjans'kyj Pys'mennyk, 1983), 27–29. The poet more explicitly touches on the theme of Babi Yar in the short story "Vulytsya Melnykova" [Melnykova Street] (1970), in Pervomayskiy, *Tvory v semy tomach*, 3:416–29, set in Kyiv on the eve of the massacre. See Petrovsky-Shtern, *The Anti-Imperial Choice*, 202–3, 221.

53. Lev Ozerov, "Babiy Jar," *Oktjabr'*, no. 3–4 (1946): 160–63. The poem was reprinted in Lev Ozerov, *Liven'* [The shower] (Molodaya Gvardiya, 1947), 25–32; later in Ozerov, *Lirika: 1931–1966* [Lyrics: 1931–1966] (Sovetskij Pisatel', 1966), 57–62. See Ananij Rochlin, *O poeme L'va Ozerova "Babiy Jar"* [On Lev Ozerov's poem "Babij

Yar"], *Novoe russkoe slovo*, 27–28 September 1997; Shrayer, "Jewish-Russian Poets," 85–90; Maxim D. Shrayer, "Lev Ozerov as a Literary Witness to the Shoah in the Occupied Soviet Territories," in *The Holocaust: Memories and History*, ed. Victoria Khiterer, Ryan Barrick, and David Misal (Cambridge Scholars Publishing, 2014), 176–87. Lev Adolfovich Ozerov, pseudonym of Lev Eisikovich Goldberg (1914–96), was a poet, translator, and literary critic who was born in Kyiv. During World War II he was a correspondent for the army newspaper *Pobeda za nami*. Involved in the anticosmopolitan campaign, after the war he was excluded from teaching and editorial work.

54. Lev Ozerov, "Terpen'e—muzhskaja rabota" [Patience is a man's job], in *O Viktore Nekrasove: Vospominaniya (Chelovek, voin, pisatel')* [About Viktor Nekrasov: Memoirs (man, warrior, writer)] (Ukraïns'kyj Pys'mennyk, 1992), 231–32; Ozerov, "Malenkaja povest' o Viktore Nekrasove" [A brief story about Viktor Nekrasov], *Strelec* 1, no. 73 (1994): 240, recalling how Ehrenburg later asked his permission to use the information he had gathered for the novel *Devjatyj val*.

55. Lev Ozerov, "Ob ukrainskoj poezii voennych let" [On Ukrainian poetry of the war years], *Znamya*, no. 1–2 (1944): 299–300. See the denunciation report by A. M. Egolin and M. T. Iovchuk to the secretary of the Central Committee of the Communist Party, A. S. Shcherbakov, 4 April 1944, in *"Literaturnyj front": Istoriya politicheskoj cenzury, 1932–1946 gg.; Sbornik dokumentov* ["The literary front": History of political censorship, 1932–1946; Collection of documents], ed. Denis L. Babichenko (Enciklopedija rossijskich dereven, 1994), doc. 63, p. 130.

56. Lev Ozerov, "Kiev, Babiy Jar," in Grossman and Ehrenburg, *Chernaja kniga*, 17–25; Italian translation, 23–34. See "Ne zabudem, ne prostim . . . Materialy, sobrannye L'vom Ozerovym" [We will not forget, we will not forgive . . . Materials collected by Lev Ozerov], in Spector and Kipnis, *Babiy Jar*, 75–94.

57. See note 38. For an introduction to the history of *The Black Book*, see Salomoni, *L'Unione Sovietica e la Shoah*, 161–71.

58. These words, placed at the end of the essay, were removed from the version prepared for printing along with explicit references to the Jewish identity of the victims. This can be easily seen in the version of the volume published in 1993, which restores in square brackets the expunged passages: "Kiev, Babiy Jar," in Grossman and Ehrenburg, *Chernaja kniga*, 24–25; Italian translation, 34; see also Spector and Kipnis, *Babiy Jar*, 94 (with some variations).

59. Shimon Redlich, ed., *Evrejskiy antifashistskiy komitet v SSSR, 1941–1948: Dokumentirovannaja istoriya* [The Jewish Anti-Fascist Committee in the USSR, 1941–1948: A documented history] (Mezhdunarodnye Otnoshenija, 1996), doc. 136, pp. 259–60 (Jewish Anti-Fascist Committee to the Central Committee of the Communist Party, 28 November 1946, signed by S. M. Mikhoels, I. S. Fefer, V. S. Grossman, and I. G. Ehrenburg).

60. Redlich, *Evrejskiy antifashistskiy*, doc. 137, pp. 261–62 (note by G. F. Aleksandrov to A. A. Zhdanov, 3 February 1947); Dzhachangir G. Nadzhafov and Zinaida S. Belousova, eds., *Stalin i kosmopolitizm, 1945–1953: Dokumenty Agitpropa CK* [Stalin and cosmopolitanism, 1945–1953: Documents of the agitprop of the Central Committee] (Mezhdunarodnyj Fond Demokratija—Materik, 2005), doc. 33, pp. 103–5. On 7 October 1947 the press division of the propaganda department communicated to

Zhdanov the final condemnation of the volume for its "serious political errors" (Redlich, *Evrejskiy antifashistskiy*, doc. 139, p. 263).

61. See Salomoni, *L'Unione Sovietica e la Shoah*, 250–51.

Chapter 2. Return, Reconstruction, Recognition

1. Concerning the difficulties of returning, the persistence of antisemitic attitudes, and the complex issue of restitution rights, denied to the displaced and even more so to Jews, see Mordechai Altshuler, "Antisemitism in Ukraine Toward the End of World War II," in *Bitter Legacy: Confronting the Holocaust in the USSR*, ed. Zvi Gitelman (Indiana University Press, 1997), 77–90; Altshuler, "The Pain of Homecoming: Soviet Jews Return to the Ukraine in the Wake of the Holocaust," in *Moreshet: Journal for the Study of the Holocaust and Antisemitism*, no. 12 (2015): 275–325; Yaacov Ro'i, "The Reconstruction of Jewish Communities in the USSR, 1944–1947," in *The Jews Are Coming Back: The Return of the Jews to Their Countries of Origin After WWII*, ed. David Bankier (Berghahn Books—Yad Vashem, 2005), 186–205; Rebecca Manley, "'Where Should We Resettle the Comrades Next?': The Adjudication of Housing Claims and the Construction of the Post-War Order," in *Late Stalinist Russia: Society Between Reconstruction and Reinvention*, ed. Juliane Fürst (Routledge, 2006), 233–46; Manley, *To the Tashkent Station: Evacuation and Survival in the Soviet Union at War* (Cornell University Press, 2009), 238–69; Martin J. Blackwell, *Kyiv as Regime City: The Return of Soviet Power After Nazi Occupation* (University of Rochester Press, 2016), 159–67.

2. Arkady I. Vaksberg, *Stalin protiv evreev* [Stalin against the Jews] (Liberti, 1995), 213–14; Vaksberg, *Iz ada v raj i obratno: Evrejskiy vopros po Leninu, Stalinu i Solzhenitsynu* [From hell to paradise and back: The Jewish question according to Lenin, Stalin, and Solzhenitsyn] (Olimp, 2003), 272–73.

3. Nahum M. Korzhavin, *V soblaznach krovavoj epochi: Vospominaniya v dvuch knigach* [Temptations of a bloody era: Memoirs in two books] (Zacharov, 2007), 1:697.

4. Report of 13 September 1944, in Gitelman, *Bitter Legacy*, 300–307 (published earlier in *Jews in Eastern Europe* 3, no. 22 [1993]: 52–62); Vladimir Khanin, ed., *Documents on Ukrainian Jewish Identity and Emigration, 1944–1990* (Frank Cass, 2003), doc. 1, pp. 41–50; Mikhail Mitsel, *Evrei Ukrainy v 1943–1953 gg.: Ocherki dokumentirovannoj istorii* [The Jews of Ukraine in 1943–1953: Essays of documented history] (Duch i Litera, 2004), doc. I.2, pp. 42–53. Concerning the frequent antisemitic disturbances in Kyiv in June and August 1944, see a detailed report by the head of police Komarov, 8 September 1944, in Mitsel, *Evrei Ukrainy*, doc. I.1, pp. 36–41.

5. Report of 28 September 1944, in *Gosudarstvennyj antisemitizm v SSSR: Ot nachala do kul'minacii, 1938–1953* [State antisemitism in the USSR: From the beginning to the peak, 1938–1953], by Gennady V. Kostyrchenko (Mezhdunarodnyj Fond Demokratija—Materik, 2005), doc. 2–13, p. 40, ellipsis added.

6. Kostyrchenko, *Gosudarstvennyj antisemitizm*, doc. 2–13, p. 41.

7. Kostyrchenko, *Gosudarstvennyj antisemitizm*, doc. 2–13, p. 43. See Mitsel, *Evrei Ukrainy*, doc. I.3, pp. 54–62; Khanin, *Documents on Ukrainian Jewish Identity*, doc. 1, pp. 53–58. As we will see, the reference was to the attempt by Dovid Hofshteyn to organize a commemoration at Babi Yar.

8. Iosif D. Rozenshtein was tried and sentenced to be executed on 1 October 1945 for the murder. See two reports sent on 5 and 8 September 1945 by the NKVD of

Ukraine to the secretary of the Central Committee of the Communist Party of Ukraine, Demyan S. Korotchenko, in Mitsel, *Evrei Ukrainy*, doc. I.4, pp. 63–64, and doc. I.5, pp. 65–66, and in Kostyrchenko, *Gosudarstvennyj antisemitizm*, doc. 3–1, pp. 62–63, and doc. 3–2, p. 64. Concerning the Kyiv pogrom, see Amir Weiner, *Making Sense of War: The Second World War and the Fate of the Bolshevik Revolution* (Princeton University Press, 2001), 192–93; Victoria Khiterer, "We Did Not Recognize Our Country: The Rise of Antisemitism in Ukraine Before and After the Second World War, 1937–1947," *Polin: Studies in Polish Jewry* 26 (2014): 370–71.

9. Kostyrchenko, *Gosudarstvennyj antisemitizm*, doc. 3–3, pp. 65–72. See Gennady V. Kostyrchenko, *V plenu u krasnogo faraona: Politicheskie presledovaniya evreev v SSSr v poslednee stalinskoe desjatiletie* [Prisoners of the red pharaoh: Political persecutions of Jews in the USSR in the last Stalinist decade] (Mezhdunarodnye Otnoshenija, 1994), 53–54; Kostyrchenko, *Tajnaja politika Stalina: Vlast' i antisemitizm* [Stalin's secret policy: Power and antisemitism] (Mezhdunarodnye Otnoshenija, 2001), 353–56.

10. Kostyrchenko, *Gosudarstvennyj antisemitizm*, doc. 3–3, p. 65, ellipses added.

11. Kostyrchenko, *Gosudarstvennyj antisemitizm*, doc. 3–3, p. 66.

12. Kostyrchenko, *Gosudarstvennyj antisemitizm*, doc. 3–3, pp. 67–68.

13. Kostyrchenko, *Gosudarstvennyj antisemitizm*, doc. 3–3, pp. 69–70.

14. Kostyrchenko, *Gosudarstvennyj antisemitizm*, doc. 3–3, p. 70, ellipsis added.

15. Kostyrchenko, *Gosudarstvennyj antisemitizm*, doc. 3–3, pp. 70–71. It seems that the four authors of the appeal were all arrested (Kostyrchenko, *Tajnaja politika Stalina*, 356).

16. Boris Slutsky, "Pro evreev" [About Jews], *Novyj mir*, no. 10 (1987): 175; Slutsky, *Sobranie sochineniy* [Collected works] (Chudozhestvennaja Literatura, 1991), 1:165. Officially published only after the author's death, these verses, probably written in the period 1952–56 and among the most quoted of all Slutsky's "Jewish" texts, circulated in the Jewish samizdat (literature copied by typewriter or by hand and distributed illegally). Concerning their significance, see Marat Grinberg, *"I Am to Be Read Not from Left to Right, but in Jewish: From Right to Left": The Poetics of Boris Slutsky* (Academic Studies Press, 2011), 139–41.

17. A celebratory model common to all the countries that emerged victorious from the war, as Weiner recalls, *Making Sense of War*, 232–33. For the Ukrainian case, see Serhy Yekelchyk, "The Leader, the Victory, and the Nation: Public Celebrations in Soviet Ukraine Under Stalin (Kyiv, 1943–1953)," in *Jahrbücher für Geschichte Osteuropas* 54, no. 1 (2006): 3–19; Yekelchyk, *Stalin's Citizens: Everyday Politics in the Wake of Total War* (Oxford University Press, 2014), 34–67.

18. Yekelchyk, "The Civic Duty to Hate: Stalinist Citizenship as Political Practice and Civic Emotion (Kyiv, 1943–53)," *Kritika: Explorations in Russian and Eurasian History* 7, no. 3 (2006): 536; Yekelchyk, *Stalin's Citizens*, 13.

19. Letter cited in Fedor Guber, "Pamjat' i pis'ma" [Memory and letters], *Daugava* 11, no. 161 (1990): 104–5; Vasily Grossman, *A Writer at War: Vasily Grossman with the Red Army 1941–1945*, ed. Antony Beevor and Luba Vinogradova (Pantheon Books, 2005), 254; Italian translation, *Uno scrittore in guerra* (Adelphi, 2015), 296.

20. Yuri Janovskij [Yanovsky], "Pis'ma iz Njurnberga" [Letters from Nuremberg], in *Sobranie sochineniy* [Collected works], vol. 2, *Rasskazy i ocherki* [Stories and essays] (Izdatel'stvo "Izvestia," 1960), 449.

21. I use Yakov Chelemsky, "Nikogda v etom gorode ne bylo pyli" [There was never dust in this city], in *Izbrannnye stichotvoreniya* [Selected poems] (Chudozhestvennaja Literatura, 1974), 96; Ilya M. Levitas, ed., *Babiy Jar: Spasiteli i spasënnye* [Babi Yar: Rescuers and rescued] (Stal, 2005), 552. Yakov Aleksandrovich (Ajzikovich) Chelemski (1914–2003), poet, writer, and translator, born in Ukraine, although exempt, volunteered and was a frontline correspondent for various army newspapers.

22. A. Anatoly [Anatoly Kuznetsov], *Babiy Jar: Roman-dokument* [Babi Yar: Documentary novel] (Posev, 1970), 18–19; Italian translation, *Babiy Jar: Romanzo-documento* (Adelphi, 2019), 25–26, ellipsis added.

23. Isaac Trachtenberg, "'Davajte v mir bylogo my dver' priotvorim': Iz zapisok kievskogo studenta-medika voennych let" ["Let's open the door to the world of the past": From the notes of a wartime Kyiv medical student], *Zerkalo nedeli*, 2 November 2007. Trachtenberg's perception of the place (*jar*) seems to echo Ilyz Ehrenburg, "Spravedlivost'," *Krasnaja zvezda*, 19 December 1943.

24. A preliminary analysis of these visits has been conducted by Karel C. Berkhoff, "The Dispersal and Oblivion of the Ashes and Bones of Babi Yar," in *New Directions in Holocaust Research and Education*, ed. Wendy Lower and Lauren Faulkner Rossi (Northwestern University Press, 2017), 261–63.

25. Sarah Kolchinskaya, "Iz pisem," in *Babiy Jar*, ed. Efrem Baukh (Izdanie Sojuza zemljachestv-vychodcev iz SSSR, 1981), 65. The identity of the soldier is indicated by Mordechai Altshuler, "Jewish Combatants of the Red Army Confront the Holocaust," in *Soviet Jews in World War II: Fighting, Witnessing, Remembering*, ed. Harriet Murav and Gennady Estraikh (Academic Studies Press, 2014), 34n35.

26. See M. Kipnis, "Posleslovie," in *Babiy Jar: K pjatidesjatiletiyu tragedii 29–30 sentjabrja 1941 goda* [Babi Yar: On the fiftieth anniversary of the tragedy of 29–30 September 1941], ed. Shmuel Spector and M. Kipnis (Biblioteka-Alija, 1991), 181–82; Spector, "Uroki Bab'ego Jara" [Lessons of Babij Yar], in *Pamjat' Bab'ego Jara: Vospominaniya, dokumenty* [Memory of Babi Yar: Recollections, documents], ed. Ilya Levitas (Evreijskij sovet Ukrainy—Fond "Pamjat' Bab'ego Jara," 2001), 226.

27. Kolchinskaya, "Iz pisem," 58.

28. Kolchinskaya, "Iz pisem," 59–60.

29. Aleksandr Burakovsky, "Pamjat' nuzhna ne mertvym . . ." [Memory is not needed by the dead . . .], *My zdes'*, 30 September–6 October 2010, http://newswe.com/index.php?go=Pages&in=view&id=2725; Aleksandr Burakovsky, "Holocaust Remembrance in Ukraine: Memorialization of the Jewish Tragedy at Babi Yar," *Nationalities Papers* 39, no. 3 (2011): 375.

30. Yuri Shcheglov, "V okopach Bab'ego Jara" [In the trenches of Babij Yar], *Kontinent* 1, no. 111 (2002): 295, ellipsis added. Concerning the first visit to Babij Yar with his mother after returning to Kyiv, see Shcheglov, *Evrejskiy kamen', ili Sobach'ja zhizn' Erenburga: Istoriko-filologicheskiy roman* [Jewish stone, or the dog's life of Ehrenburg: Historical-philological novel] (Mosty Kul'tury-Gesharim, 2004), 87.

31. Boris Shifman, "Pis'mo iz Izrailja" [Letter from Israel], in *Izhoj: Viktor Nekrasov u spohadach suchasnykiv* [Rebel: Viktor Nekrasov in the memories of contemporaries] (Duch i Litera, 2014), 118.

32. Shimon Kipnis, "A kristal vaz ful fun erd fun babi yar" [A crystal vase full of soil from Babij Yar], *Fraye naye prese* (Paris), 29 September 1973; Kipnis, "Vaza,

napolnennaja zemlej Bab'ego Jara" [A vase filled with soil from Babij Yar], in *Kniga pamjati* [The book of memory], ed. Iosif Vinokurov, Shimon Kipnis, and Nora Levin (Izd-vo Korporacii "Mir," 1983), 38–39; Nora Levin, *The Jews in the Soviet Union Since 1917: Paradox of Survival* (Tauris, 1990), 1:421–22. Founded in 1920, the State Jewish Theater (Gosudarstvennyj Evrejskij Teatr-Goset) was closed in 1949 as part of the anticosmopolitan campaign.

33. Minutes of the presidium of the Jewish Anti-Fascist Committee, 23 October 1945, in Joshua Rubenstein, "Night of the Murdered Poets," in *Stalin's Secret Pogrom: The Postwar Inquisition of the Jewish Anti-Fascist Committee*, ed. Joshua Rubenstein and Vladimir P. Naumov (Yale University Press, 2001), 39; Italian translation, *La notte dei poeti assassinati: Antisemitismo nella Russia di Stalin* [The night of the murdered poets: Antisemitism in Stalin's Russia] (SEI, 2009), 46. Solomon Michajlovich Mik-hoels (Vovsi) (1890–1948), actor and director, was the artistic director of the State Jewish Theater in Moscow from 1929. President of the Jewish Anti-Fascist Committee, he led it until his death. He was assassinated in January 1948 by agents of the Soviet security services.

34. Testimony of Lev A. Fink, *I odna—moja—sud'ba: Vospominaniya, razdum'ja, polemika* [And one—my—fate: Memories, reflections, polemics] (Tarbut, 1993), 235–36. See Leonid M. Leonov, *Zolotaja kareta* [The golden carriage] (VUOAP, 1946).

35. Account of Aleksandr M. Borshchagovskiy, *Zapiski balovnja sud'by* [Reflections of a favorite of fate] (Sovetskij Pisatel', 1991), 115. The author revisited the theme in Borshchagovskiy, "Damskiy portnoj" [The ladies' tailor], *Teatr*, no. 10 (1980): 142–67. Aleksandr M. Borshchagovskiy (1913–2006) was born in Bila Tserkva, a Ukrainian city about eighty kilometers from Kyiv that was the scene of one of the most significant massacres of September 1941. During the war, he fought at the front. In 1949, as part of the ideological campaign against "rootless cosmopolitanism," he was fired, expelled from the Communist Party, and deprived of the opportunity to publish because of his alleged participation in an "antipatriotic group of theater critics."

36. See Antonella Salomoni, "La seconda guerra mondiale e il fronte orientale: Spazio del genocidio e rovine ebraiche" [The Second World War and the Eastern Front: Space of genocide and Jewish ruins], in *Le guerre in un mondo globale* [Wars in a global world], ed. Tommaso Detti (Viella, 2017), 133–53.

37. Account of Major Ruvim M. Oksenkrug, 4 September 1944, from the Kherson region, in *Sovetskie evrei pishut Il'e Erenburgu, 1943–1966* [Soviet Jews write to Ilya Ehrenburg, 1943–1966], ed. Mordechai Altshuler, Icchach Arad, and Shmuel' Krakovskiy (Centr po issledovaniju i dokumentacii vostochnogo-evropejskogo evrejstva—Yad Vashem, 1993), doc. 14, p. 151. See also the letter of response from the secretary of a regional Communist Party committee admitting the authorities' shortcomings and assuring immediate action, also in Altshuler et al., *Sovetskie*, doc. 14b, pp. 155–56. And see Antonella Salomoni, *L'Unione Sovietica e la Shoah: Genocidio, resistenza, rimozione* [The Soviet Union and the Shoah: Genocide, resistance, removal] (Il Mulino, 2007), 199–200.

38. Shimon Redlich, ed., *Evrejskiy antifashistskiy komitet v SSSR, 1941–1948: Doku-mentirovannaja istoriya* [The Jewish Anti-Fascist Committee in the USSR, 1941–1948: A documented history] (Mezhdunarodnye Otnoshenija, 1996), doc. 41, p. 108 (letter

to S. M. Mikhoels, 4 December 1945). See Salomoni, *L'Unione Sovietica e la Shoah*, 200.

39. Altshuler et al., *Sovetskie*, 294–95.

40. See Mordechai Altshuler, "Jewish Holocaust Commemoration Activity in the USSR Under Stalin," *Yad Vashem Studies* 30 (2002): 271–96; Altshuler, *Religion and Jewish Identity in the Soviet Union, 1941–1964* (Brandeis University Press, 2012), 205–28.

41. On private commemoration efforts, see Rebecca L. Golbert, "Holocaust Sites in Ukraine: Pechora and the Politics of Memorialization," *Holocaust and Genocide Studies* 18, no. 2 (2004): 205–33; Golbert, "Holocaust Memorialization in Ukraine," *Polin: Studies in Polish Jewry* 20 (2007): 222–43.

42. Mikhail Mitsel, *Obshchiny iudejskogo veroispovedaniya v Ukraine (Kyiv, L'vov: 1945–1981 gg.)* [Jewish religious communities in Ukraine (Lviv: 1945–1981)] (Institut Iudaiki, 1998), 17–18; Ro'i, "The Reconstruction of Jewish Communities," 199.

43. Mikhail Mitsel, "Zapret na uvekovechenie pamjati kak sposob zamalchivaniya Cholokosta: Praktika KPU v otnoshenii Bab'ego Jara" [The ban on perpetuating memory as a method of silencing the Holocaust: The practice of the Communist Party of Ukraine regarding Babui Yar], *Holokost i Suchasnist'* 1, no. 2 (2007): 10; Mitsel, *Obshchiny iudejskogo veroispovedaniya*, 21–22; Khanin, *Documents on Ukrainian Jewish Identity*, doc. 13, pp. 86–87.

44. See a report from the Council for Religious Cults Under the Council of People's Commissars of the USSR, in Altshuler, *Religion and Jewish Identity*, 208.

45. Kolchinskaya, "Iz pisem," 63. See Altshuler, *Religion and Jewish Identity*, 209–11.

46. Abram Kagan, *Chto ja videl na evrejskom kladbishche okolo Bab'ego jara* [What I saw in the Jewish cemetery near Babi Yar], in Boris Czerny, "Témoignages et oeuvres littéraires sur le massacre de Babi Yar 1941–1948" [Testimonies and literary works on the massacre of Babi Yar 1941–1948], *Cahiers du monde russe* 53, no. 4 (2012): 556–57, ellipsis added. Abram Ya. Kagan (1901–65), writer, poet, and playwright, wrote a novel titled *Oyf undzer erd* (On our earth, 1944) about the events of war. From 1945 to 1948 he was a correspondent from Kyiv for *Eynikayt*. Arrested on 24 January 1949, he was sentenced to fifteen years of confinement. He returned to Kyiv after being rehabilitated in 1956.

47. Dovid Hofshteyn, "Kiev," *Eynikayt*, 11 November 1943, 3; Hofshteyn, *Ikh gleyb* [I believe] (Der Emes, 1944), 49–50. In these verses there is no mention of Babi Yar. Dovid Hofshteyn (Davyd Naumovych Gofshtejn) (1889–1952) was born in Korostyshiv, not far from Kyiv. He received a traditional Jewish education and composed verses in Hebrew, Yiddish, Russian, and Ukrainian even while still a child. He began publishing in Yiddish in 1917. After living and working for some time in Moscow, he went to Berlin in 1924 and visited Palestine in 1925; then in 1926 he returned to Kyiv. He was a member of the presidium of the Jewish Anti-Fascist Committee, and on 16 September 1948 he was the first of its leaders to be arrested by Ukrainian security services for "anti-Soviet activities." Sentenced to death during the trial against the Jewish Anti-Fascist Committee, he was shot on 12 August 1952.

48. Concerning these difficulties, see Altshuler, "Antisemitism in Ukraine," 78–80.

49. Altshuler, "Antisemitism in Ukraine," 80. See the denunciation of Hofshteyn's "active Zionist action" in the report, cited above, of the commission of inquiry on "anti-Semitic manifestations in Ukraine" (28 September 1944), in Kostyrchenko, *Gosudarstvennyj antisemitizm*, doc. 2–13, p. 43; Mitsel, *Evrei Ukrainy*, doc. I.3, p. 57. For an analysis of the methods of construction underlying the charges of nationalism, also directed at Hofshteyn, see Alexandre Bortchagovski, *L'holocauste inachevé, ou comment Staline tenta d'éliminer les Juifs d'URSS* [The unfinished Holocaust, or how Stalin tried to eliminate the Jews of the USSR] (Lattès, 1995), 59–66, 179–84, 218–24; original edition, Aleksandr M. Borshchagovskiy, *Obvinjaetsja krov': Dokumental'naja povest'* [Blood levels its accusations: Documentary history] (Progress-Kultura, 1994).

50. Kostyrchenko, *Gosudarstvennyj antisemitizm*, doc. 3–15, p. 102 (secret report by M. S. Popereka, deputy minister of state security of Ukraine, 27 May 1947, to L. M. Kaganovich on the activities of "Jewish nationalists" in the republic). See also Kostyrchenko, *Gosudarstvennyj antisemitizm*, doc. 3–28, p. 122; Redlich, *Evrejskiy antifashistskiy*, doc. 188, p. 362 (secret report by V. S. Abakumov, minister of state security, 26 March 1948, to the top leaders of the Council of Ministers of the USSR and the Central Committee of the Communist Party on the illegal activities of the Jewish Anti-Fascist Committee).

51. Testimony of Abram Kagan reported in Arkady Zeltser, "Tema 'Evrei v Bab'em Jaru' v Sovetskom Sojuze v 1941–1945 godach" [The theme "Jews in Babi Yar" in the Soviet Union in 1941–1945], in *Babyn Jar: Masove ubyvstvo i pam'jat' pro n'oho; Materialy mizhnarodnoï naukovoï konferencii 24–25 zhovtnja 2011 r., m. Kyïv* [Babi Yar: Mass murder and memory of it; Proceedings of the International Scientific Conference, Kyiv, 24–25 October 2011], ed. Mykhailo Tyahlyi and Vitaly Nachmanovych (Ukraïns'kyj centr vyvchennja istorii Holokostu, Hromads'kyj komitet dlja vshanuvannja pam'jati zhertv Babynoho Jaru, 2012), 90–91.

52. I make use of Itzik Kipnis, "Baby-Yar (Tsum dritn Yahrzeit)" [Babi Yar (third anniversary)], in *Untervegns un andere dertseylungen* [On the road and other short stories] (Yiddisher Kultur Farband, 1960), 347–52. The subsequent edition in Kipnis, *Tsum lebn: Dertseylungen* [Toward life: Short stories] (Sovetski pisatel, 1969), is reworked, particularly attenuating the theme of revenge. The first complete version in Russian is in *Holokost i suchasnist'* 4, no. 10 (2003): 1–2; extensive excerpts are in Spector and Kipnis, *Babiy Jar*, 165–69; and Baukh, *Babi Yar*, 71–74. See also the analysis by Czerny, "Témoignages et oeuvres littéraires," 537–42. Itzik Kipnis (Isaak Nuchimovich Kipnis) (1896–1974), poet and writer in Yiddish, was born in Slovechne, a Ukrainian village in the Volyn region (now Zhytomyr region). He published his first collection of poems in 1923. In 1926 the story "Khadoshim un teg" (Months and days), in which he described anti-Jewish pogroms and the experience of the revolution, was the target of severe criticism. He worked extensively as a children's writer and translator. After several collections of stories, in 1939 he published the novel *Di shtub* (The house). With the outbreak of the war, he joined the National Guard but was rejected due to his age and was evacuated from Kyiv, returning only in the spring of 1944. See his account of the difficulties of repatriation in liberated territories due to the hostility of the environment in Itzik Kipnis, *Tog un tog* [Day by day] (Y. L. Peretz, 1980), 403–4.

53. Kipnis, "Baby-Yar (Tsum dritn Yahrzeit)," 347.

54. Kipnis, "Baby-Yar (Tsum dritn Yahrzeit)," 347, ellipsis added. The poet Dovid Bergelson, in one of his articles on Kyiv in 1943, also invited people to take the route from Khreshchatyk to Podil "on foot rather than by public transport" (Dovid Bergelson, "Kiev," *Eynikayt*, 1 May 1943, 4).

55. Kipnis, "Baby-Yar (Tsum dritn Yahrzeit)," 348–49.

56. Kipnis, "Baby-Yar (Tsum dritn Yahrzeit)," 349.

57. Kipnis, "Baby-Yar (Tsum dritn Yahrzeit)," 350.

58. Kipnis, "Baby-Yar (Tsum dritn Yahrzeit)," 350–51.

59. Kipnis, "Baby-Yar (Tsum dritn Yahrzeit)," 351–52.

60. Kipnis, "Baby-Yar (Tsum dritn Yahrzeit)," 352. The feeling of revenge is also present in Itzik Kipnis, "Fun mayne togbikher," *Sovetish heymland*, no. 1 (1965): 117, cited in Harriet Murav, "Poetry After Kerch': Representing Jewish Mass Death in the Soviet Union," in Murav and Estraikh, *Soviet Jews in World War II*, 160. For a reflection on the feeling of revenge, see Antonella Salomoni, "La vendetta sul fronte orientale: Realtà, rappresentazioni, controversie" [Revenge on the Eastern Front: Realities, representations, controversies], in *Teatri di guerra: Rappresentazioni e discorsi tra età moderna ed età contemporanea* [Theaters of war: Representations and discourses between the modern and contemporary ages], ed. Angela De Benedictis (Bononia University Press, 2010), 297–318.

61. Kipnis, "Baby-Yar (Tsum dritn Yahrzeit)," 351.

62. For the summary of Kipnis's story, I used Yehoshua A. Gilboa, *The Black Years of Soviet Jewry, 1939–1953* (Little, Brown and Company, 1971), 144. One of the most important Yiddish texts dedicated to Babi Yar is the section "Etsemes khayaveshes" [Dry bones] from the poem by Peretz Markish, "Milkhome" [The war] (Der Emes, 1948) (Yiddisher kultur farband, 1956), 2:589–98, inspired by Ezekiel 37:1–14, and the poem by Arn Kushnirov, "Di muter Rokhl" [Mother Rachel], *Heymland: Literarish-kinstlerisher almanakh*, no. 5 (1948): 36–40; Kushnirov, *Geklibene lider* [Selected poems] (Sovetski pisatel, 1975), 60–66.

63. The story was published in Yiddish in Łódź by the organ of the Central Committee of Polish Jews, *Dos naye lebn*, on 19 May 1947.

64. This theme is especially evident in Itzik Kipnis, *Khadoshim un teg: A khronik* [Months and days: A chronicle] (Kooperativer farlag kultur-lige, 1926), a classic of Soviet Yiddish literature in which the author confronts the issue of pogroms during the Civil War: the months are the idyllic time of traditional life in the native shtetl of Slovechne, the days are the tragic time of anti-Jewish violence. See David G. Roskies, *Against the Apocalypse: Responses to Catastrophe in Modern Jewish Culture* (Harvard University Press, 1984), 183–85; Mikhail Krutikov, "Rediscovering the Shtetl as a New Reality: David Bergelson and Itsik Kipnis," in *The Shtetl: New Evaluations*, ed. Steven T. Katz (New York University Press, 2007), 214–21.

65. "Natsionalizm untern shleyer fun felker frayntshaft" [When nationalism hides under the veil of friendship among peoples], *Eynikayt*, 3 July 1947. This was followed by Leib Kvitko's attack, "Tsu naye ideyisher reynkayt fun undzer literatur" [The new ideological purity in our literature], *Eynikayt*, 5 July 1947. See Benjamin Pinkus, *The Soviet Government and the Jews, 1948–1967: A Documented Study* (Cambridge University Press, 1984), 149.

66. Doklad t. Zhdanova, "O zhurnalakh *Zvezda* i *Leningrad*" [The report from Comrade Zhdanov in *Zvezda* and *Leningrad*], *Bol'shevik*, no. 17–18 (1946): 4–19; *Pravda*, 21 September 1946.

67. The resolution that was published in *Kul'tura i zhizn'*, 20 August 1946, and *Pravda*, 21 August 1946, was abridged and did not include the final points. For the full version, see "Postanovlenie Orgbjuro CK VKP(b) 'O zhurnalach *Zvezda* i *Leningrad*'" [Resolution of the organizational bureau of the Central Committee of the VKP(b) "On the journals *Zvezda* and *Leningrad*"], in *"Literaturnyj front": Istoriya politicheskoj cenzury, 1932–1946 gg.; Sbornik dokumentov* ["The literary front": History of political censorship, 1932–1946; Collection of documents], ed. Denis L. Babichenko (Enciklopedija rossijskich dereven, 1994), doc. 91, pp. 221–25; Andrei N. Artizov and Oleg V. Naumov, eds., *Vlast' i chudozhestvennaja intelligentsiya: Dokumenty CK RKP(b)-VKP(b), VChK-OGPU-NKVD o kul'turnoj politike, 1917–1953 gg.* [Power and the artistic intelligentsia: Documents of the Central Committee of the RKP(b)-VKP(b), the VChK-OGPU-NKVD on cultural policy, 1917–1953] (International Democracy Foundation, 1999), sec. 7, doc. 19, pp. 587–91.

68. Kostyrchenko, *V plenu u krasnogo faraona*, 73; Babichenko, *"Literaturnyj front,"* doc. 91, p. 222; Artizov and Naumov, *Vlast' i chudozhestvennaja intelligentsiya*, sec. 7, doc. 19, p. 588.

69. Fedor Levin, "Zhizn' idët vperëd" [Life goes on], *Literaturnaya gazeta*, 5 October 1946, 3. Concerning the tasks of care entrusted to literature and the therapy of the word, see Anna Krylova, "Healers of Wounded Souls: The Crisis of Private Life in Soviet Literature, 1944–1946," *Journal of Modern History* 73, no. 2 (2001): 307–31.

70. See the analysis by Pinkus, *The Soviet Government*, 148–49.

71. See Serhy Yekelchyk, "Celebrating the Soviet Present: The 'Zhdanovshchina' Campaign in Ukrainian Literature and the Arts," in *Provincial Landscapes: Local Dimensions of Soviet Power, 1917–1953*, ed. Donald J. Raleigh (University of Pittsburgh Press, 2001), 255–75.

72. Lazar M. Kaganovich was appointed first secretary of the Communist Party of Ukraine on 27 February 1947 and was recalled to Moscow in December of the same year. See Kostyrchenko, *Tajnaja politika Stalina*, 357–61; Serhy Yekelchyk, *Stalin's Empire of Memory: Russian-Ukrainian Relations in the Soviet Historical Imagination* (University of Toronto Press, 2004), 72–87.

73. S. R. Savchenko, head of Ukrainian security services, to L. M. Kaganovich, summer 1947, in Kostyrchenko, *Gosudarstvennyj antisemitizm*, doc. 3–16, p. 103.

74. Report on the meeting in "Dokumenty z archivnoï kryminal'noï spravy I. Kipnisa" [Documents from the archive criminal file of I. Kipnis], *Z archiviv VUChK-GPU-NKVD-KGB* 3–4, no. 8–9 (1998): 277–304.

75. *Literaturna hazeta*, 25 September 1947, in Pinkus, *The Soviet Government*, 149.

76. Hryhoriy Polyanker and Matvii Talalayevsky, "Pro odne shkidlyve opovidannia" [On a harmful story], *Literaturna hazeta*, 18 September 1947, in Pinkus, *The Soviet Government*, 149.

77. Haim Loytsker, "Far ideyisher reynkayt fun undzer literatur" [For the ideological purity of our literature], *Der shtern* 2 (1948): 112, in Pinkus, *The Soviet Government*, 172. In this difficult context, another novella written in 1945–46 referencing Babi Yar remained unpublished: Itzik Kipnis, "Ven-nit-ven" [No matter when], in Kipnis,

Tsum lebn, 211–20. See the analysis by Harriet Murav, *Music from a Speeding Train: Jewish Literature in Post-Revolution Russia* (Stanford University Press, 2011), 245.

78. See "Dokumenty z archivnoï kryminal'noï spravy I. Kipnisa." Kipnis later reworked the text and published some excerpts in "Folksshtime" (Warsaw) in 1959. The full text was printed in the early 1970s: *Mayn shtetele Sloveshne* [My village of Slovechne], 2 vols. (I. L. Peretz, 1971). Concerning the role of the shtetl in Kipnis's work, in addition to Krutikov, "Rediscovering the Shtetl," see Murav, *Music from a Speeding Train*, 253–58.

79. Concerning the Kipnis case, see also Mordechai Altshuler, "Itsik Kipnis: The 'White Crow' of Soviet Yiddish Literature, the MGB File of 1949," *Jews in Russia and Eastern Europe* 53, no. 2 (2004): 68–167.

80. Redlich, *Evrejskiy antifashistskiy*, doc. 189, pp. 371–72 (resolution of the Politburo of the Central Committee of the Communist Party on the closure of the Jewish Anti-Fascist Committee, 20 November 1948); Kostyrchenko, *Gosudarstvennyj antisemitizm*, doc. 4–1, p. 138; Dzhachangir G. Nadzhafov and Zinaida S. Belousova, eds., *Stalin i kosmopolitizm, 1945–1953: Dokumenty Agitpropa CK* [Stalin and cosmopolitanism, 1945–1953: Documents of the agitprop of the Central Committee] (Mezhdunarodnyj Fond Demokratija—Materik, 2005), doc. 83, pp. 193–94. In addition to the suppression of the newspaper *Eynikayt*, the publishing house Der Emes was closed. See "Postanovlenie Politbjuro CK VKP(b) o zakrytii izdatel'stva 'Der Emes,' 25 nojabrja 1948 g." [Resolution of the Politburo of the Central Committee of the VKP(b) on the closure of the Der Emes publishing house, 25 November 1948], in Artizov and Naumov, *Vlast' i chudozhestvennaja intelligentsiya*, sec. 7, doc. 58, p. 643.

81. Vladimir P. Naumov, ed., *Nepravednyj sud: Posledniy stalinskiy rasstrel; Stenogramma sudebnogo processa nad chlenami Evrejskogo Antifashistskogo Komiteta* [Unjust judgment: The last Stalinist execution; Transcript of the trial against members of the Jewish Anti-Fascist Committee] (Nauka, 1994), 15.

82. See the documents on the liquidation of Jewish theaters published in Kostyrchenko, *Gosudarstvennyj antisemitizm*, 283–98.

83. "Ob odnoj antipatrioticheskoj gruppe teatral'nych kritikov" [On an unpatriotic group of theater critics], *Pravda*, 28 January 1949; Nadzhafov and Belousova, *Stalin i kozmopolitizm*, doc. 100, pp. 232–40. The article in *Pravda* was preceded by a report by writer Aleksandr A. Fadeyev in December 1948 during a plenum of the Union of Writers' leadership, explicitly equating "cosmopolitans" with Jews. See "O nekotorych prichinach otstavaniya sovetskoj dramaturgii" [On some causes of the backwardness of Soviet drama], *Literaturnaya gazeta*, 22 December 1948, 1. A. A. Zhdanov used the expression "rootless cosmopolitanism" for the first time in an official speech at the beginning of 1948. See *Soveshchanie dejatelei sovetskoj muzyki v CK VKP(b)* [Conference of Soviet music figures at the Central Committee of the VKP(b)] (Pravda Publishing House, 1948), 139–40. But it has been reported that Stalin had already used it in 1941 to designate enemy agents. See a note from Bulgarian politician Georgi M. Dimitrov, 12 May 1941, in Georgy I. Chernyavsky, "Dnevniki G. M. Dimitrova" [The diaries of G. M. Dimitrov], *Novaja i novejshaja istorija*, no. 5 (2001): 54.

84. Borshchagovskiy, *Zapiski balovnja sud'by*, 178.

85. Borshchagovskiy, *Zapiski balovnja sud'by*, 267. Concerning the specific meaning and use of the derogatory term *zhid* in Russian history and culture, see John D. Klier,

"'Zhid': Biography of a Russian Epithet," *Slavonic and East European Review* 60, no. 1 (1982): 1–15; Henrik Birnbaum, "Some Problems with the Etymology and Semantics of the Slavic 'Zid' 'Jew,'" *Slavica Hierosolymitana* 7 (1985): 1–11; Alessandro Cifariello, *L'ombra del 'kahal': Immaginario antisemita nella Russia dell'Ottocento* [The shadow of the "kahal": Antisemitic imagery in nineteenth-century Russia] (Viella, 2013), 27–42.

86. "Ob odnoj antipatrioticheskoj gruppe teatral'nych kritikov"; Nadzhafov and Belousova, *Stalin i kosmopolitizm*, doc. 100, p. 234.

87. See first and foremost the editorial articles "Do konca razoblachit' antipatrioticheskuju gruppu teatral'nych kritikov" [To thoroughly expose the unpatriotic group of theater critics], *Literaturnaya gazeta*, 29 January 1949, 1; "Na chuzhdych poziciyach: O proiskach antipatrioticheskoj gruppy teatral'nych kritikov" [On alien positions: The intrigues of the unpatriotic group of theater critics], *Kul'tura i zhizn'*, 30 January 1949, both in Nadzhafov and Belousova, *Stalin i kosmopolitizm*, doc. 101, pp. 242–50, and doc. 102, pp. 250–59.

88. Kostyrchenko, *Gosudarstvennyj antisemitizm*, doc. 4–32, pp. 233–34 (report from the propaganda and agitation section of the Central Committee of the Communist Party, signed by D. T. Shepilov, transmitted to J. V. Stalin no later than 3 February 1949); Nadzhafov and Belousova, *Stalin i kosmopolitizm*, doc. 105, p. 263 (resolution of the Politburo of the Central Committee of the Communist Party, 8 February 1949).

89. Nikolai M. Gribachev, "Protiv kozmopolitizma i formalizma v poezii" [Against cosmopolitanism and formalism in poetry], *Pravda*, 16 February 1949; Nadzhafov and Belousova, *Stalin i kosmopolitizm*, doc. 113, pp. 294, 297.

90. Nadzhafov and Belousova, *Stalin i kosmopolitizm*, doc. 113, pp. 294–96. The reference was to the pieces by Daniil Danin, "Preodolenie stradaniy" [Overcoming suffering], *Znamya*, no. 7 (1946): 179–84; Danin, "My chotim videt' ego lico" [We want to see his face], *Literaturnaya gazeta*, 27 December 1947, 3; Danin, "Strast', bor'ba, dejstvie! (O dramaticheskom nachale v poslevoennoj sovetskoj poeme)" [Passion, struggle, action! (On the dramatic principle in the postwar Soviet poem)], *Novy mir*, no. 10 (1948): 247–71.

91. See Efim Melamed, "Istochniki dlja istorii evrejskich nauchnych i kul'turnoprosvetitel'skych uchrezhdeniy 1920–1940-ch godov v archivach Ukrainy" [Sources for the history of Jewish scientific and cultural institutions of the 1920s–1940s in Ukrainian archives], in *Yiddish: Language and Culture in the Soviet Union*, ed. Leonid F. Katsis, Maria Kaspina, and David E. Fishman (RGGU, 2009), 234–37.

92. Part of the documents related to the judicial inquiry in *Z archiviv VUChK-GPU-NKVD-KGB* 3–4, no. 8–9 (1998): 83–335.

93. See the reports of the security services of the Ukrainian Soviet Socialist Republic (4, 16, 27–28 February and 3 March 1949) on reactions to the dismantling of the Jewish Anti-Fascist Committee, the arrests of "Jewish nationalists," and the "exposure" of the activities of "cosmopolitan critics," *Z archiviv VUChK-GPU-NKVD-KGB* 3–4, no. 8–9 (1998): 42–64.

94. Nadzhafov and Belousova, *Stalin i kozmopolitizm*, doc. 130, pp. 329–30 (report by the agitprop of the Central Committee to G. M. Malenkov regarding the withdrawal by Glavlit of books by "repressed authors," 24 March 1949).

95. See Lyubomir D. Dmiterko, "Sostojanie i zadachi teatral'noj i literaturnoj kritiki na Ukraine" [The condition and tasks of theatrical and literary criticism in

Ukraine], *Literaturnaya gazeta*, 9 March 1949, 2; Pinkus, *The Soviet Government*, 173–74.

96. CDAMLM Ukraïny (Central State Archives Museum of Literature and Arts of Ukraine), f. 727, op. 1, od. zb. 105, ark. 1, 5, 6.

97. "Za dal'nejshiy pod"ëm ukrainskogo sovetskogo izobrazitel'nogo iskusstva" [For the further growth of Soviet Ukrainian visual arts], *Pravda Ukrainy*, 25 May 1949, 1.

98. Speech by the chairman of the committee for the arts of the Ukrainian Soviet Socialist Republic, M. P. Pashchin, at the Fourth Plenum of the Union of Ukrainian Artists (1949), CDAMLM Ukraïny, f. 581, op. 1, od. zb. 126, ark. 18–19. Zinovi Shenderovych Tolkachov (1903–77), painter and graphic artist, came from a Jewish family in the Minsk governorate. On the eve of World War II, he was a professor at the Kyiv Art Institute. He went to the front as a volunteer and was very active as an artist during the war. His work progressively acquired an increasingly documentary character, finding a complete expression starting in the autumn of 1944, when he began working in a unit engaged on the First Ukrainian Front with the task of collecting evidence on German crimes in occupied territories. He was at Majdanek and Auschwitz immediately after the liberation of the two death camps. Deeply moved by what he had seen, he conceived and created graphic cycles collected in albums and exhibited, to wide repercussions and response, in many areas of liberated Poland. For his recent rediscovery, see *Zinovi Tolkachov: Tvory z muzejnych ta pryvatnych zbirok* [Zinovi Tolkachov: Works from museum and private collections] (Duch i Litera, 2005); Mirjam Rajner, "From the Shtetl to the Flowers of Auschwitz and Back: The Creation, Reception, and Destiny of Zinovii Tolkachev's Art," in *Images of Rupture Between East and West: The Perception of Auschwitz and Hiroshima in Eastern European Arts and Media*, ed. Urs Heftrich, Robert Jacobs, Bettina Kaibach, and Karoline Thaidigsmann (Winter University Press, 2016), 155–85.

99. Sava O. Holovanivsky to Ilya G. Ehrenburg, 2 February 1947, in *Ilya Ehrenburg's Mail: I Hear Everyone . . . 1916–1967*, ed. Boris Y. Frezinsky (Agraf, 2006), 232.

100. Speech by M. P. Pashchin, who defined the *tallit katan* as "the ritual garment of fanatical Jews." See Borshchagovskiy, *Zapiski balovnja sud'by*, 276–77.

101. Concerning the figure of Dmytro L. Klebanov (1907–87), composer, pedagogue, and conductor, see Irma Zolotovytska, *Dmytro Klebanov* (Muzychna Ukraina, 1980).

102. *Pervyj vsesojuznyj s'ezd sovetskich kompozitorov: Stenograficheskiy otchët* [First All-Union Congress of Soviet Composers: Stenographic report] (Publishing House of the Union of Soviet Composers of the USSR, 1948), 65. Concerning the anticosmopolitan campaign in the musical field between 1949 and 1953, see Kiril Tomoff, *Creative Union: The Professional Organization of Soviet Composers, 1939–1953* (Cornell University Press, 2006), 152–88.

103. "Za dal'nejshiy rascvet ukrainskoj sovetskoj muzyki: Na sobranii kompozitorov Ukrainy" [For the further development of Soviet Ukrainian music: The meeting of Ukrainian composers], *Pravda Ukrainy*, 19 March 1949; report by Pavel N. Gapochka, head of the propaganda office of the Central Committee of the Communist Party of Ukraine, to Nikita Khrushchev, 20 March 1949, in Mitsel, *Evrei Ukrainy*, doc. IX.1, p. 190. See Pinkus, *The Soviet Government*, 175.

104. Report by P. N. Gapochka, in Mitsel, *Evrei Ukrainy*, doc. IX.1, pp. 194–95.

105. See Irma Zolotovitsky, "Zufälliges und Nicht-Zufälliges in Schostakowitschs 'Jüdischen' Kompositionen" [Accidental and nonaccidental in Shostakovich's "Jewish" compositions], in *Dmitri Schostakowitsch und das jüdische musikalische Erbe = Dmitri Shostakovich and the Jewish Heritage in Music*, ed. Ernst Kuhn, Andreas Wehrmeyer, and Gunther Wolter (Kuhn, 2001), 109–10; and the interview with Igor Blazhkov conducted by Tatiana Frumkis: "Trudnosti udesjaterjali moju energiyu . . ." [Difficulties increased my energy tenfold . . .], *Evropa-Ekspress* (Berlin), 11 February 2008, http://web.archive.org/web/20130626045251/http://www.euxpress.de/archive /artikel_8402.html.

106. Kostyrchenko, *Gosudarstvennyj antisemitizm*, doc. 4–41, p. 255 (report on measures taken by the secretariat of the Union of Writers, 24 March 1953).

107. Kostyrchenko, *Gosudarstvennyj antisemitizm*, doc. 4–41, p. 257.

108. Kostyrchenko, *Gosudarstvennyj antisemitizm*, doc. 4–41, p. 257.

Chapter 3. Transforming Space

1. Resolution no. 378 of the Council of People's Commissars of the Ukrainian Soviet Socialist Republic and the Central Committee of the Communist Party of Ukraine, 13 March 1945, CDAVO Ukraïny (Central State Archives of Supreme Bodies of Power and Government of Ukraine), f. 2, op. 7, spr. 2103, ark. 22. See also resolutions no. 622 of 25 June 1945 and no. 449/42 of 2 October 1945 on allocations and preparatory work for the construction of the monument, DAK, f. R-1, op. 4, spr. 75, ark. 143 and 141.

2. Aleksandr Naiman, "Babiy Jar: Tragediya i pamjat'" [Babi Yar: Tragedy and memory], *Evrejskij obozrevatel'*, 3 April 2002, http://www.jewukr.org/observer /j007_26/p0104_r.html; Tatiana Evstafeva, "K istorii ustanovleniya pamjatnika v Bab'em Jaru" [On the history of the installation of a monument at Babi Yar], *Evrejskij obozrevatel'*, 5 June 2002, http://www.jewukr.org/observer/j011_30/p0102_r.html; Evstafeva, "Babiy Jar: Poslevoennaja istoriya mestnosti" [Babi Yar: Postwar history of the site], in *Babyn Jar: Masove ubyvstvo i pam'jat' pro n'oho; Materialy mizhnarodnoï naukovoï konferenciï 24–25 zhovtnja 2011 r., m. Kyïv* [Babi Yar: Mass murder and memory of it; Proceedings of the International Scientific Conference, Kyiv, 24–25 October 2011], ed. Mykhailo Tyahlyi and Vitaly Nachmanovych (Ukraïns'kyj centr vyvchennja istorii Holokostu, Hromads'kyj komitet dlja vshanuvannja pam'jati zhertv Babynoho Jaru, 2012), 22. See also press reactions: "Pamjatnik pogibshim v Bab'em Jaru" [A monument to those killed at Babi Yar], *Pravda*, 4 April 1945, 3; M. Ayzenshtadt, "A denkmol in Babi Yar" [A monument to Babij Jar], *Eynikayt*, 7 July 1945, 2, in Arkady Zeltser, "Tema 'Evrei v Bab'em Jaru' v Sovetskom Sojuze v 1941–1945 godach" [The theme "Jews in Babi Yar" in the Soviet Union in 1941–1945], in Tyahlyi and Nachmanovych, *Babyn Jar*, 93.

3. Explanatory note to the Plan for the Reconstruction and Development of the Economy of the City of Kyiv for 1948–1950, in *Babiy Jar: Chelovek, vlast', istoriya; Dokumenty i materialy* [Babi Yar: The man, the power, the history; Documents and materials], vol. 1, *Istoricheskaja topografiya: Chronologiya sobytiy* [Historical topography: Chronology of events], ed. Tatiana Evstafeva and Vitaly Nachmanovich (Vneshtorgizdat Ukrainy, 2004), doc. 101, pp. 401–2. After the war, a speech that Nikita

Khrushchev allegedly made at Babi Yar a few days after the liberation of Kyiv before a crowd of party members, military personnel, and surviving Jews who gathered there for the first time gained some traction. The words of the Ukrainian leader were reported as follows by Léon Leneman, *La tragédie des Juifs en URSS* (Desclée De Brouwer, 1959), 192: "Humanity must never forget the terrible massacre committed by the Germans at Babi Yar. Babi Yar must remain in history as a name that instills terror. To ensure this is never forgotten, Soviet authorities will erect a commemorative monument here—a gigantic luminous tower. We will bring people from all over the world to see and remember what was done to innocent Soviet Jews." The speech gained some resonance, as evidenced by the following writings: "Desecration and Neglect of Cemeteries," *Jews in Eastern Europe* 1, no. 1 (1959): 3; Patricia Blake, "New Agony for Russian Jews," *Life*, 7 December 1959, 73.

4. See Tatiana Evstafeva, "Babiy Jar vo vtoroj polovine XX v." [Babi Yar in the second half of the twentieth century], in Evstafeva and Nachmanovich, *Istoricheskaja topografiya*, 188–92.

5. See A. Anatoly [Anatoly Kuznetsov], *Babiy Jar: Roman-dokument* [Babi Yar: Documentary novel] (Posev, 1970), 19–20; Italian translation, *Babiy Jar: Romanzo-documento* (Adelphi, 2019), 26; Viktor Nekrasov, "Gorodskie progulki" [City walks], *Yunost*, no. 7 (1988): 21; Viktor Nekrasov, "Zapiski zevaki" [Reflections of a wanderer], *Kontinent*, no. 4 (1975): 76. The activity of "gold diggers" at massacre sites or Jewish cemeteries was common after the war throughout Eastern Europe and was vainly denounced by survivors and Jewish religious authorities. Concerning the extensive issue of greed toward Jewish property, see Jan T. Gross and Irena Grudzińska Gross, *Złote żniwa: Rzecz o tym, co się działo na obrzeżach zagłady Żyd.w* [Golden harvest: Events at the periphery of the Holocaust of the Jews] (Krakow: Znak, 2011); Italian translation, *Un raccolto d'oro: Il saccheggio dei beni ebraici* [A golden harvest: The looting of Jewish assets] (Turin: Einaudi, 2016). The essay quickly sparked a lively debate in Poland: see particularly *Wokół "Złotych żniw": Debata o książce Jana Tomasza Grossa i Ireny Grudzińskiej-Gross* [Around *Golden Harvest*: Debate on the book by Jan Tomasz Gross and Irena Grudzińska-Gross] (Znak, 2011); Marek J. Chodakiewicz, Wojciech J. Muszyński, and Paweł Styrna, eds., *Golden Harvest or Hearts of Gold? Studies on the Fate of Wartime Poles and Jews* (Leopolis Press, 2012).

6. Resolution no. 7/sr. of the Executive Committee of the Kyiv Workers' Council, 14 August 1946, DAK, f. R-1, op. 7, spr. 14, ark. 15.

7. Nekrasov, "Zapiski zevaki," 76. Even before the war, some parts of Babi Yar were used as a dump. See Tatiana Evstafeva and Vitaliy Nachmanovich, "Syrec, Luk'janovka i Babiy Jar v pervoj polovine XX v. (do nachala nemeckoj okkupacii 1941–1943 gg.): Istoriya zastrojki i problemy topografii" [Syrets, Lukyanovka, and Babij Yar in the first half of the twentieth century (up to the beginning of the German occupation, 1941–1943): History of construction and topography problems], in Evstafeva and Nachmanovich, *Istoricheskaja topografiya*, 69.

8. Roman Levin, "Babiy Yar," in *Pogoda na zavtra* [Weather for tomorrow] (Majdan, 1995), 138, in Annie Epelboin and Assia Kovriguina, *La littérature des ravins: Écrire sur la Shoah en URSS* [Ravine literature: Writing about the Shoah in the USSR] (Robert Laffont, 2013), 160.

9. Isaak Trabskiy, "Zhiznennyj podvig" [A vital feat], *Slovo/Word*, no. 61 (2009), http://magazines.russ.ru/slovo/2009/61/tr20.html, ellipsis added; Karel C. Berkhoff,

Babi Yar Site of Mass Murder, Ravine of Oblivion (United States Holocaust Memorial Museum, Center for Advanced Holocaust Studies, 2012), 10.

10. David Budnik and Yakov Kaper, *Nichto ne zabyto: Evrejskie sud'by v Kieve, 1941–1943* [Nothing is forgotten: The fates of Jews in Kyiv, 1941–1943] (Hartung-Gorre, 1993), 53.

11. Nekrasov, "Zapiski zevaki," 74.

12. Boris Slutsky, "Pamjatnik" [Monument], *Literaturnaya gazeta*, 15 August 1953, 3; Slutsky, *Pamjat': Kniga stichov* [Memory: Book of verses] (Sovetskij Pisatel', 1957), 7–9; Slutsky, *Sobranie sochineniy* [Collected works] (Chudozhestvennaja Literatura, 1991), 1:83–84.

13. Kuznetsov, *Babiy Jar*, 478–79; Italian translation, 449.

14. Lev Ozerov, "Snova u Bab'ego Jara" [Back at Babi Yar], in *Babiy Jar: Spasiteli i spasënnye* [Babi Yar: Rescuers and rescued], ed. Ilya M. Levitas (Stal, 2005), 489.

15. Yuri Kaplan, "Babiy Jar," in Levitas, *Babiy Jar*, 448. That feeling of guilt led Yu. Kaplan to collect for many years the verses that various authors had written about Babi Yar; these were subsequently included in the first significant poetic anthology, curated and published by Kaplan on the occasion of the fiftieth anniversary. See *Echo Bab'ego Jara: Poeticheskaja antologiya* [The echo of Babi Yar: Poetic anthology] (RIF, 1991); and *Vidlunnja Babynoho Jaru: Poetychna antolohiya* [The echo of Babi Yar: Poetic anthology] (Firma JuH-Instytut Judaïky, 2001). Among the subsequent collections of poetry, see also Ilya Levitas, ed., *Babiy Jar v serdce: Poeziya* [Babi Yar in the heart: Poetry] (Holovna specializovana redakcyja literatura movamy nacional'nych menshyn Ukraïny, 2001).

16. Nahum Korzhavin, "Konec veka" [End of the century] (1961), in *Vremena: Izbrannoe* [Times: Selected works] (Frankfurt am Main: Posev, 1976), 287. Regarding the composition of these verses, see Korzhavin, *V soblaznach krovavoj epochi: Vospominaniya v dvuch knigach* [Temptations of a bloody era: Memoirs in two books] (Zacharov, 2007), 2:593. Korzhavin was also the author of "Poema sushchestvovaniya" [Poem of existence], *Vremja i my*, no. 1 (1975): 115–26; *Vremena*, 311–37, which circulated in samizdat under the title *Babiy Jar*. Nahum M. Korzhavin (pseudonym of Nahum M. Mandel, 1925–2018), poet, playwright, and translator born in Kyiv, was arrested at the end of 1947 during the anticosmopolitan campaign and deported until 1954, when he was released due to an amnesty. He emigrated in 1973.

17. Shike Driz, "Luftbalonen" [Balloons], in *Di ferte strune* [The fourth melody] (Sovetski pisatel, 1969), 134.

18. Shike Driz, "Babi-iar," in Driz, *Di ferte strune*, 135–36.

19. See "Rasskaz Artistki Nechamy Lifshic o pesne Shiki Driza 'Kolybel'naja Bab'emu Jaru'" [The story of Nechama Lifshitz about Shike Driz's song "Lullaby for Babi Yar"], in *Babiy Jar*, ed. Efrem Baukh (Izdanie Sojuza zemljachestv-vychodcev iz SSSR, 1981), 95–98; *American Jewish Year Book* 62 (1961): 288; Joseph B. Schechtman, *Star in Eclipse: Russian Jewry Revisited* (Thomas Yoseloff, 1961), 98.

20. This is the artist's recollection reported by Yaacov Ro'i, "Nechama Lifshitz: Symbol of the Jewish National Awakening," in *Jewish Culture and Identity in the Soviet Union*, ed. Yaacov Ro'i and Avi Beker (New York University Press, 1991), 179.

21. A. Zhukova, "Vsegda boec" [Always a fighter], *Ogonëk*, 12 March 1961, 16; Vladimir A. Rudnyï, "Geroicheskiy talent" [Heroic talent] (1961), in *Dejstvujushchiy flot*

[Action fleet] (Voenizdat, 1965), 573–80; *Sovetish heymland*, no. 1 (1961): 49. B. I. Prorokov's cycle inspired the Symphonic Frescoes for Orchestra, op. 10 (1961), by Leonid O. Hrabovsky, a major representative of the Kyïvs'kyj Avangard and one of the first minimalist composers in the USSR. An attempt to perform the symphony in March 1963 under the direction of Igor Blazhkov led to Hrabovsky's expulsion from the Kyiv Conservatory. See Peter J. Schmelz, *Such Freedom, if Only Musical: Unofficial Soviet Music During the Thaw* (Oxford University Press, 2009), 35.

22. Aleksandr Tichomirov, *Pamjati nevinno ubiennych* [In memory of innocent victims], ed. Aleksandra Tichomirova (Majer, 2015); Valentina Byalik, "Cholokost glazami Aleksandra Tichomirova" [The Holocaust through the eyes of Aleksandr Tichomirov], *Russkoe iskusstvo*, no. 4 (2013): 158–61. Concerning the theme of Babi Yar in the works of other important artists such as Vadim Sidur, Josyp Vaysblat, Efim Simkin, and Mikhail Zvyagin, see Iryna Klimova, "Babyn Yar in Sculpture and Painting," in *Babyn Yar: History and Memory*, ed. Vladyslav Hrynevych and Paul R. Magocsi (Duch i Litera, 2016), 266–68.

23. Viktor Nekrasov, "Pochemu eto ne sdelano?" [Why wasn't it done?], *Literaturnaya gazeta*, 10 October 1959, 2.

24. Anna Berzer, "O Viktore Nekrasove" [About Viktor Nekrasov], *Druzhba narodov*, no. 5 (1989): 149.

25. Published first under the title *Stalingrad* in the journal *Znamya*, no. 8–9 (1946): 3–82, and no. 10 (1946): 38–146 (Moskovskij Rabochij, 1946); then under the title *V okopach Stalingrada* [Front-Line Stalingrad] (Sovetskij Pisatel', 1947); Italian translation, *Nelle trincee di Stalingrado* [In the trenches of Stalingrad] (Mondadori, 1964). The publication coincided with the dissemination of new party directives in the literary and artistic fields, widely acknowledged by the same magazine, *Znamya*, in issue no. 10. The story received mixed reactions from critics and, before being awarded the Stalin Prize, Second Class, was attacked for its lack of "ideality." For a reading of the work's *podtekst* (subtext), see Grigory Svirsky, *Na lobnom meste: Literatura nravstvennogo soprotivleniya, 1946–1976 gg.* [On the scaffold: Literature of moral resistance, 1946–1976], 2nd ed. (Kruk, 1998), 37–52 (original edition, Overseas Publications Interchange, 1979). A broad look at the topos of World War II in Russian and Soviet literature is found in Frank Ellis, *The Damned and the Dead: The Eastern Front Through the Eyes of Soviet and Russian Novelists* (University Press of Kansas, 2011).

26. See the recollections of architect Boris P. Zhezherin in *Architektura sovetskogo Kieva* [The architecture of Soviet Kyiv], by Boris L. Erofalov-Pilipchak (Izdatel'skij dom A+S, 2010), 79–80. Nekrasov was a student of Josyp Yu. Karakis, with whom he maintained close relations for a long time. See Sergei V. Babushkin, Dmitri Brazhnik, Irma I. Karakis, and Andrei Puchkov, eds., *Architektor Iosif Karakis: Sud'ba i tvorchestvo (Al'bom-katalog k stoletiyu so dnja rozhdeniya)* [Architect Iosif Karakis: Fate and work (album-catalog for the centenary of his birth)] (Informacionno-izdatel'skij centr "Simvol-T," 2002), 14.

27. Vladimir A. Potresov, ed., *Perepiska Viktora Nekrasova: "I vsë-taki ostalsja zhiv"; Frontovye pis'ma (1943–1944)* [Correspondence of Viktor Nekrasov: "And yet I remained alive"; Front letters (1943–1944)], http://nekrasov-viktor.com/Letters/Nekrasov-Letters -frontovie.aspx; "Frontovye pis'ma Viktora Nekrasova (1943–1944)" [Front letters of Viktor Nekrasov (1943–1944)], *Ogonëk*, no. 8 (1989): 18–20.

28. Karo Halabyan, "Kakim budet Stalingrad" [What will Stalingrad be like], *Stalingradskaja pravda*, 10 September 1944. On Stalingrad as a "monument-city," see Yulia V. Yanushkina, "Architekturnye obrazy poslevoennogo Stalingrada" [Architectural images of postwar Stalingrad], *Internet-vestnik VolgGAS U. serija politematicheskaja* 1, no. 25 (2013), http://vestnik.vgasu.ru/attachments/Yanushkina-2013_1(25).pdf.

29. Potresov, *Perepiska Viktora Nekrasova*. The letter from Karo S. Halabyan to V. Nekrasov, then given to his family, is dated 27 April 1944.

30. Viktor Nekrasov, "Spivajmo slavu peremozi" [Let's sing the glory of victory], *Radjans'ke mystectvo*, 13 May 1945, 3; Nekrasov, "Spoem slavu Pobede" [Let's sing the glory of victory], in Nekrasov, "P.S. k 'okopnoj pravde'" [P.S. to "trench truth"], ed. Aleksandr Parnis, *Nashe nasledie*, no. 73 (2005): 16–17.

31. Nekrasov, "Spivajmo slavu peremozi." For the second quote I rely upon Viktor Nekrasov, *Nelle trincee di Stalingrado* [In the trenches of Stalingrad] (Castelvecchi, 2013), 106, ellipsis added.

32. Nekrasov, "Spivajmo slavu peremozi." Nekrasov returned repeatedly to this issue, particularly after the construction of the monument that he later called the "monster-woman," in Viktor Nekrasov, "Mysli o Stalingrade" [Thoughts on Stalingrad], *Russkaja mysl'*, 7 August 1980, 7.

33. Nekrasov, "Spivajmo slavu peremozi." The competition for the reconstruction of Khreshchatyk was announced on 22 June 1944 and concluded in 1947 after three rounds. The rebuilding was completed in 1960. See Erofalov-Pilipchak, *Architektura sovetskogo Kieva*, 285–335. Nekrasov's interest in the urban redevelopment of Kyiv is also evidenced by the article "Razmyshleniya o Kreshchatike" [Reflections on Khreshchatyk], *Literaturnaya gazeta*, 5 June 1952, 2.

34. Lev Ozerov, "Terpen'e—muzhskaja rabota" [Patience is a man's job], in *O Viktore Nekrasove: Vospominaniya (Chelovek, voin, pisatel')* [Recollections of Viktor Nekrasov (man, warrior, writer)] (Ukraïns'kyj Pys'mennyk, 1992), 231–33; Ozerov, "Malenkaja povest' o Viktore Nekrasove" [A brief story about Viktor Nekrasov], *Strelec* 1, no. 73 (1994): 240–42.

35. Lazar Lazarev, "Iz ognja . . . : O Viktore Nekrasove" [From the fire . . . : About Viktor Nekrasov], in *Shestoj etazh, ili perebiraja nashi daty* [The sixth floor, or reexamining our anniversaries] (Knizhnyj Sad, 1999), 184–85; Lazarev, *Zapiski pozhilogo cheloveka: Kniga vospominaniy* [Reflections of an elderly man: Book of memories] (Vremja, 2005), 43. See also Lazarev, "Kak neoperabel'nyj oskolok" [Like an inoperable shard], *Lechaim* 7, no. 123 (2002), http://www.lechaim.ru/ARHIV/123/lazarev.htm.

36. Lazarev, "Iz ognja . . . ," 185–86; Lazarev, *Zapiski pozhilogo cheloveka*, 44. The article, as mentioned, was published in the 10 October 1959 issue of *Literaturnaya gazeta*; Yom Kippur fell on 12 October that year.

37. This was clearly highlighted in a news article about Nekrasov's article published by the international Jewish press: *Jews in Eastern Europe* 1, no. 3 (1960): 28–29. Nekrasov had begun with a reference to the official note issued by Vyacheslav Molotov on 6 January 1942 and to the report of the Extraordinary State Commission for Investigation of Nazi War Crimes in Kyiv, also produced during the Nuremberg trials, to remind readers of the human losses in the massacre. He also emphasized that the figures were conservative estimates.

38. Nekrasov, "Pochemu eto ne sdelano?" Nekrasov frequently visited Babi Yar, preferably on foot, as recalled by Yuri Shcheglov, "V okopach Bab'ego Jara" [In the trenches of Babij Yar], *Kontinent* 1, no. 111 (2002): 296–97.

39. Nekrasov, "Pochemu eto ne sdelano?" The international Jewish press, around the same time, drew attention to the fact that the site of the extermination of tens of thousands of Jews had become a grazing ground for livestock (*American Jewish Year Book* 61 [1960]: 259).

40. Ilya Ehrenburg, for example, fully shared Nekrasov's indignation in a letter to a certain K. Shargorodskaya, 30 November 1959, in which he emphasized the need to protect the burials of the "victims of Fascism" in the numerous "Babi Yars" scattered across the country. See Ilya Ehrenburg, *"Na cokole istorii . . .": Pis'ma 1931–1967* ["At the base of history . . .": Letters 1931–1967], ed. Boris Ya. Frezinskiy (Agraf, 2004), 474.

41. In particular, some war veterans residing in the district expressed their support for the writer's proposal to erect a monument at the site of the mass shootings "as soon as possible." However, they felt that some corrections were necessary: the ravine should not remain unchanged in its form. Considering Kyiv's urban planning needs, part of the area needed to be converted into a park with a sculpture dedicated to the "victims of Fascism" at its center. This was what had been done in Lidice, they wrote, where they had not been content to "preserve the ashes and the execution site" but had decided to plant a rose garden there. See "Pis'mo v redakciyu: Eto neobchodimo sdelat'" [Letter to the editor: This is necessary to do], *Literaturnaya gazeta*, 22 December 1959, 2. Indeed, in a letter from the deputy minister of culture of the Ukrainian SSR, L. Kuropatenko, to the deputy chairman of the Council of Ministers of the Republic, M. S. Grechukha, dated 22 January 1959, the hypothesis of "an obelisk with an appropriate inscription" had already been advanced. See CDAVO Ukraïny, f. 2, op. 9, spr. 6430, ark. 155. See also the subsequent proposal of 24 January 1959 in CDAVO Ukraïny, f. 2, op. 9, spr. 6430, ark. 153.

42. "Po sledam vystupleniya 'Literaturnoj gazety': 'Pochemu eto ne sdelano?'" [In response to the article in *Literaturnaya gazeta*: "Why wasn't it done?"], *Literaturnaya gazeta*, 3 March 1960, 2. See Schechtman, *Star in Eclipse*, 102; Benjamin Pinkus, *The Soviet Government and the Jews, 1948–1967: A Documented Study* (Cambridge University Press, 1984), 97.

43. "Soviets and Babiy Jar," *Jews in Eastern Europe* 1, no. 5 (1960): 7.

44. This is the case of André Blum (Blumel), former president of the Fédération sioniste de France and a prominent figure in the France-USSR Friendship Association, upon returning from a visit to the Soviet Union in the summer of 1962. See "Soviet Authorities Urged to Erect Monument to Jewish Martyrs," *JTA Daily News Bulletin*, 16 August 1962; *American Jewish Year Book* 64 (1963): 354.

45. Edward Crankshaw, *Khrushchev: A Career* (Viking Press, 1966), 155.

46. The report was published under the title "My Visit to Babi Yar," *Midstream* 5, no. 4 (1959): 49–57. I rely upon Schechtman, *Star in Eclipse*, 103.

47. Schechtman, *Star in Eclipse*, 100–101. Concerning the forced removal of the memory of Babi Yar, see also the report by journalist Boris Smolar for the American Jewish press, in Hasia R. Diner, *We Remember with Reverence and Love: American Jews and the Myth of Silence After the Holocaust, 1945–1962* (New York University Press, 2009), 282.

48. Patricia Blake, "New Agony for Russian Jews," *Life*, 7 December 1959, 63–73.

49. Blake, "New Agony," 71, 78.

50. Blake, "New Agony," 71, 73.

51. Blake, "New Agony," 73. The article by P. Blake aroused very negative reactions in the Ukrainian press outside of the country. See, for example, "Weapon of Anti-semitism," *Svoboda: Ukrainian Weekly*, 19 December 1959, 2; Lew Shankowsky, "Russia, the Jews and the Ukrainian Liberation Movement," in *Ukrainians and Jews: A Symposium* (Ukrainian Congress Committee of America, 1966), 76–78.

52. Essential points of the ten-year urban development plan in Kyiv (1951–60) are in Evstafeva and Nachmanovich, *Istoricheskaja topografiya*, doc. 106, pp. 407–11.

53. Kuznetsov, *Babiy Jar*, 479; Italian translation, 450.

54. For a reconstruction of the history of the catastrophe, see Oleksandr L. Anisimov, *Kurenivs'kyj apokalipsys: Kyïvs'ka trahediya 13 bereznja 1961 roku u fotohrafiyach, dokumentach, spohadach . . .* [The Kurenivka apocalypse: The Kyiv tragedy of 13 March 1961 in photographs, documents, memoirs . . .] (Fakt, 2000); Anisimov, *Kievskiy potop: Kurenevskaja tragediya 13 marta 1961 goda* [The Kyiv flood: The Kurenivka tragedy of 13 March 1961] (Kurch', 2003); Evstafeva, "Babiy Jar vo vtoroj polovine XX v.," 195–201; Evstafeva, "K 50-letiyu Kurenevskoj tragedii" [For the fiftieth anniversary of the Kurenivka tragedy], *Kyïv: Fotolitopys*, 10 March 2011, http://photohistory.kiev.ua/articles.php?a=1; "Kurenivs'ka tragediya 13 bereznja 1961 r. u Kyjevi: Movoju dokumentiv, ochima svidkiv" [The Kurenivka tragedy of 13 March 1961: Original documents, eyewitness accounts], in *Kurenivs'ka trahediya 13 bereznja 1961 r. u Kyjevi: Prychyny, obstavyny, naslidky; Dokumenty i materialy* [The Kurenivka tragedy of 13 March 1961: Causes, circumstances, consequences; Documents and materials], ed. Valeriy A. Smoliy et al. (Instytut istorij Ukrajny NAN Ukrajny, 2012), 6–18; Viktor O. Krupyna, "'Zhertv bahato, a v hazetach nichoho ne pyshut' . . .' (Kurenivs'ka trahediya 13 bereznja 1961 r. v Kyjevi)" ["Many victims, but nothing is written in the newspapers . . ."] (The Kurenivka tragedy of 13 March 1961 in Kyiv)], *Ukraïns'kyy istorychnyj zhurnal*, no. 4 (2012): 140–53.

55. Kuznetsov, *Babiy Jar*, 480; Italian translation, 451.

56. Petro Shelest, *"Spravzhniy sud istoriï shche poperedu": Spohady, shchodennyky, dokumenty, materialy* ["The real judgment of history is yet to come": Memoirs, diaries, documents, materials], comp. Volodymyr Baran et al. (Heneza, 2003), 137, in Smoliy et al., *Kurenivs'ka trahediya*, 8.

57. Sergei Tiktin, "Babiy Jar: Aprel' 1961" [Babi Yar: April 1961], in Baukh, *Babiy Jar*, 137.

58. Informative note no. 10 from the secretary of the Central Committee of the Communist Party of Ukraine, I. P. Kazanets, to the presidium of the Central Committee of the Communist Party of Ukraine, "On the Progress of the Work for the Elimination of the Consequences of the Floods and Destruction iIn Frunze Street, Podil District, Kyiv," 25 March 1961, in Smoliy et al., *Kurenivs'ka trahediya*, doc. 65, p. 163; Evstafeva and Nachmanovich, *Istoricheskaja topografiya*, doc. 132, pp. 461–62.

59. Transcript of the meeting of the state commission of experts to ascertain the causes of the incident in the Babi Yar area, 16 March 1961, intervention of O. L. Filaklhtov, in Smoliy et al., *Kurenivs'ka trahediya*, doc. 25, pp. 63, 65; Evstafeva and Nachmanovich, *Istoricheskaja topografiya*, doc. 133, pp. 466, 468.

60. Conclusions of the commission of experts on the reasons for the removal of the fluidized soil from the drains in Babi Yar, 20 March 1961, in Evstafeva and Nachmanovich, *Istoricheskaja topografiya*, doc. 136, p. 482; Smoliy et al., *Kurenivs'ka trahediya*, doc. 51, p. 135.

61. Informative note by V. Nikitchenko, head of the KGB, to the Central Committee of the Communist Party of Ukraine on the moods of the inhabitants of Kyiv after the Babi Yar disaster, 14 March 1961, in Smoliy et al., *Kurenivs'ka trahediya*, doc. 12, pp. 39–40.

62. Smoliy et al., *Kurenivs'ka trahediya*, doc. 12, pp. 40–41.

63. Oleksiy J. Davydov (1907–63) was chairman of the Kyiv executive committee from December 1947 until his death. He committed suicide on 20 October 1963, a little more than two years after the Kurenivka disaster. See Vitaly Nachmanovich, "Poslednjaja zhertva Bab'ego Jara" [The last victim of Babi Yar], *Ukraïna i svit s'ogodni*, 19 March 2006, http://www.kby.kiev.ua/komitet/ua/history/art00011.html.

64. For example, see the following reports by V. Nikitchenko, head of the KGB, to the Central Committee of the Communist Party of Ukraine, which collected oral information and correspondence excerpts on the moods of the inhabitants of Kyiv: 17 March 1961, in Smoliy et al., *Kurenivs'ka trahediya*, doc. 35, pp. 100–104; 18 March 1961, in Smoliy et al., *Kurenivs'ka trahediya*, doc. 40, pp. 108–12; 18 March 1961, in Smoliy et al., *Kurenivs'ka trahediya*, doc. 42, pp. 114–17; 3 April 1961, in Smoliy et al., *Kurenivs'ka trahediya*, doc. 80, pp. 203–4. Concerning the reactions of the people of Kyiv, see Tatiana Evstafeva, "Babiy Jar-2: Polveka spustja" [Babi Yar 2: Half a century later], *Ezhenedel'nik 2000* 10, no. 549 (2011), http://www.kby.kiev.ua/komitet/ru/history/art00063.html; Evstafeva, "K 50-letiyu Kurenevskoj tragedii."

65. Informative note by V. Nikitchenko, head of the KGB, to the Central Committee of the Communist Party of Ukraine on the moods of the inhabitants of the capital after the incident in the Podil district, Kyiv, 16 March 1961, in Smoliy et al., *Kurenivs'ka trahediya*, doc. 31, p. 96.

66. Testimony of Tiktin, "Babiy Jar: Aprel' 1961," 137. The idea of the "revenge of the Jews" enjoyed enormous circulation, in Sarra Tartakovskaya and Manya Guralnik, "Iz pisem," in Baukh, *Babiy Jar*, 60–61.

67. Informative note by V. Nikitchenko, head of the KGB, to the Central Committee of the Communist Party of Ukraine on the moods of the inhabitants of Kyiv after the incident in the Podil district, 17 March 1961, in Smoliy et al., *Kurenivs'ka trahediya*, doc. 35, p. 104.

68. News reported by *American Jewish Year Book* 63 (1962): 370.

69. *Vechirniy Kyïv*, 31 March 1961, 3, in Smoliy et al., *Kurenivs'ka trahediya*, doc. 77, p. 197.

70. Informative note by V. Nikitchenko, head of the KGB, to the Central Committee of the Communist Party of Ukraine on the reaction of the inhabitants of Kyiv to the dissemination, by the government commission, of the results of the investigation into the Kurenivka incident, 3 April 1961, in Smoliy et al., *Kurenivs'ka trahediya*, doc. 80, pp. 203–4. According to surveys attributable to the first secretary of the Central Committee of the Communist Party of Ukraine, P. Yu. Shelest, the death toll was 198 and the injured 250 (Shelest, "Spravzhniy sud istoriï shche poperedu," 137, in

Smoliy et al., *Kurenivs'ka trahediya*, 18), but unofficial data account for about fifteen hundred victims (Anisimov, *Kievskiy potop*, 13).

71. *Vechirniy Kyïv*, 31 March 1961, 3, in Smoliy et al., *Kurenivs'ka trahediya*, doc. 77, p. 197.

72. Evstafeva, "K 50-letiyu Kurenevskoj tragedii."

73. Ben Cion Goldberg, "Moï vidvidyny Ukraïny" [My visits to Ukraine], in *Ukraïnci i jevreï: Zbirnyk statej, dokumentiv ta eseïv* [Ukrainians and Jews: A collection of articles, documents, and essays], comp. Oleksandr Panchenko (Hadyach, 2006), 354–55, in Aleksandr Burakovsky, "Holocaust Remembrance in Ukraine: Memorialization of the Jewish Tragedy at Babi Yar," *Nationalities Papers* 39, no. 3 (2011): 374.

74. Michael Kaufman, "Visit to Babi Yar," in *The Unredeemed: Anti-Semitism in the Soviet Union*, ed. Ronald I. Rubin (Quadrangle Books, 1968), 264–68.

75. Concerning the interest in Babi Yar shown by foreign tourists between the mid-1950s and mid-1980s and the concerns this aroused among Soviet authorities, see Mikhail Mitsel, "Zapret na uvekovechenie pamjati kak sposob zamalchivaniya Cholokosta: Praktika KPU v otnoshenii Bab'ego Jara" [The ban on perpetuating memory as a method of silencing the Holocaust: The practice of the Communist Party of Ukraine regarding Babui Yar], *Holokost i Suchasnist'* 1, no. 2 (2007): 19–24.

76. Elie Wiesel, *Les juifs du silence: Témoignage* [The Jews of silence: Testimony] (Seuil, 1966), 40–41; Italian translation, *Gli ebrei del silenzio* [The Jews of silence] (Spirali, 1985), 38–39 (which I have modified).

77. Wiesel, *Les juifs du silence*, 42; Italian translation, 39–40, ellipsis added.

78. Wiesel, *Les juifs du silence*, 42; Italian translation, 40. Concerning the Soviet silence about Babi Yar, see also Jorge Semprún and Elie Wiesel, *Tacere è impossibile: Dialogo sull'Olocausto* [It is impossible to remain silent: Dialogue on the Holocaust] (Guanda, 1995), 32–33.

79. Wiesel, *Les juifs du silence*, 48; Italian translation, 45 (which I have modified).

80. Wiesel, *Les juifs du silence*, 4; Italian translation, 45.

Chapter 4. Acts of Justice in Poetry, Music, Prose

1. "US Rabbis Visit Babi Yar; Recite Prayer for 100,000 Killed Jews," *JTA Daily News Bulletin*, 27 July 1966.

2. Yevgeny Yevtushenko, *Autobiografia precoce* [Early autobiography] (Feltrinelli, 1963), 141, taken from the version published by the weekly *L'Express* from 21 February to 21 March 1963, later disavowed by the author. The English edition is *A Precocious Autobiography* (Dutton, 1963).

3. Yevgeny Yevtushenko, "Bratskaja GES" (1964–65), in *Bratskaja GES, stichi i poemy* [The Bratsk hydroelectric power station, verses and poems] (Sovetskij Pisatel', 1967), 179; Italian translation, *La centrale elettrica di Bratsk* (Rizzoli, 1965). Concerning the civic function of the poet, see Yevtushenko, *Autobiografia precoce*, 144–46, 149, and, more generally, the selection of texts in Yevtushenko, *Fatal Half Measures: The Culture of Democracy in the Soviet Union*, ed. Antonina W. Bouis (Little, Brown and Company, 1991), 193–211. For a broader context, see Evgeny Dobrenko and Ilya Kalinin, "Literary Criticism During the Thaw," in *A History of Russian Literary Theory and Criticism: The Soviet Age and Beyond*, ed. Evgeny Dobrenko and Galin Tihanov (University of Pittsburgh Press, 2011), 184–206.

4. Yevtushenko, *Autobiografia precoce*, 185. Concerning the Jewish theme in Yevtushenko's writings, see Dmitry Tsvibel, *Ot stancii Zima k Bab'emu Jaru: Evrejskie obertony tvorchestva Evtushenko* [From Zima Station to Babi Yar: Jewish overtones in Yevtushenko's work] (PIN, 2008).

5. Interview conducted by Mikhail Buzukashvili, "Evgeniy Evtushenko o 'Bab'em Jare'" [Yevgeny Yevtushenko on "Babi Yar"], *Chajka*, 16 January 2011, http://www.chayka.org/node/3104. See also the recollection of Anatoly Kuznetsov in A. Anatoly [Anatoly Kuznetsov], *Babiy Jar: Roman-dokument* [Babi Yar: Documentary novel] (Posev, 1970), 6; Italian translation, *Babiy Jar: Romanzo-documento* (Adelphi, 2019), 14. Yevtushenko first approached the tragedy of Babi Yar through the verses of Ilya Ehrenburg and Lev Ozerov. See Yevgeny Yevtushenko, *Ja prishël k tebe, Babiy Jar . . . Istoriya samoj znamenitoj sinfonii XX veka* [I came to you, Babi Yar . . . The story of the most famous symphony of the twentieth century] (Tekst-Knizhniki, 2012), 9.

6. Concerning the meaning of his "shame as a coauthor" in the composition of "Babi Yar," see Yevgeny Yevtushenko, *Volchiy pasport* (Vagrius, 1998), 432–35; Yevtushenko, *Ja prishël k tebe*, 30–35. The expression *volchiy pasport* (literally, "wolf passport") dates back to the prerevolutionary period. In czarist Russia, it indicated an identification document with a note warning of "subversivism," and it prevented access to state service and public institutions, including educational ones. In the Soviet era, it was an official attestation of demerit issued by a school, national institute, a trade union, a Komsomol (Communist Youth) cell, or the party. Yevtushenko received it at the age of fifteen following his expulsion from school.

7. Buzukashvili, "Evgeniy Evtushenko."

8. Concerning the "acute perception of time" that led Yevtushenko "to turn into a novella whatever he chose and to enchant an audience with his stories," see Vitaly Korotich, "Uchodjaschaja natura, ili Dvadcat' let spustja" [A quiet nature, or twenty years later], *Bul'var Gordona*, 15 February 2011.

9. Yevtushenko, *Autobiografia precoce*, 185–86, ellipsis added.

10. Ilya Levitas, "Istoriya odnogo stichotvoreniya" [The story of a poem], in *Babiy Jar: Spasiteli i spasënnye* [Babi Yar: Rescuers and rescued], ed. Ilya M. Levitas (Stal, 2005), 420–21.

11. Yevgeny A. Yevtushenko, "Babiy Jar," *Literaturnaya gazeta*, 19 September 1961, 4.

12. The description is from Elie Wiesel, *Les juifs du silence: Témoignage* [The Jews of silence: Testimony] (Seuil, 1966), 40; Italian translation, *Gli ebrei del silenzio* [The Jews of silence] (Spirali, 1985), 38. To understand the emotional impact aroused by the poem, see Matvei Geizer, "Evrejskaja muza Evgeniya Evtushenko" [The Jewish Muse of Yevgeny Yevtushenko], *Evrejskij obozrevatel'*, 24 September 2007, http://www.jew ukr.org/observer/eo2003/page_show_ru.php?id=2178; also in *Korni*, no. 51 (2011): 120–35.

13. Semyon Lipkin, *Le destin de Vasily Grossman* [The fate of Vasily Grossman] (L'âge d'homme, 1990), 50. A similar thought was expressed by the poet Aleksandr T. Tvardovsky, who, in the notebooks kept during a mission in Italy, wrote on 20 March 1962 after an evening spent with Mario Alicata and Giancarlo Pajetta, "We can also say that the verses of Babi Yar are simply mediocre, but we cannot say that there is no antisemitism among us." See Aleksandr T. Tvardovsky, *Den' byl polon novizny i uznavaniya (iz ital'janskoj zapisnoj knizhki)* [The day was full of newness and recognition

(from the Italian notebook)], *Vestnik Evropy*, no. 17 (2006), http://magazines.russ.ru
/vestnik/2006/17/tv27.html.

14. Yevgeny Yevtushenko, "Babiy Jar," in *Non sono nato tardi* [I wasn't born late],
trans. Ignazio Ambrogio (Editori Riuniti, 1962), 209–11. Among the translations of the
poem, the German one by Paul Celan stands out: "Jewgeniy Jewtuschenko, Babiy Jar,"
Sinn und Form, no. 5–6 (1962): 701; "'Babi Yar' in vier deutschen Fassungen" ["Babi
Yar" in four German versions], *Die Zeit*, 18 January 1963 (here together with translations of the same poem by Eckhart Schmidt and Alexander Kaempfe, Franz Leschnitzer,
and Anselm Hollo). The article accompanying the translations in *Die Zeit* under the
byline of critic Rudolf Walter Leonhardt (*Was bedeutet Jewtuschenko als Lyriker?* [What
does Yevtushenko mean as a poet?]) garnered a great deal of attention because it stated
that the massacre was carried out by Soviet troops. See the author's apologies in "Leh-
ren aus einem Besuch" [Lessons from a visit], *Die Zeit*, 25 January 1963. For Celan's
reaction, see a letter to his friend Tanya Adler-Sternberg (19 January 1963) in Ilana
Shmueli, *Di' che Gerusalemme è: Su Paul Celan, ottobre 1969–aprile 1970* [Say Jerusalem
is: On Paul Celan, October 1969–April 1970], ed. Jutta Leskien and Michele Ranchetti
(Quodlibet, 2002), 23–24; original edition, *Sag, dass Jerusalem ist: Über Paul Celan,
Oktober 1969–April 1970* (Edition Isele, 2000).

15. Yevtushenko, "Babiy Jar," 209–11.

16. "Desecration and Neglect of Cemeteries," *Jews in Eastern Europe* 1, no. 1 (1959):
3; Patricia Blake, "New Agony for Russian Jews," *Life*, 7 December 1959, 73.

17. Report by P. Vilkhovy, 28 October 1958, in Mikhail Mitsel, *Obshchiny iudejskogo
veroispovedaniya v Ukraine (Kyiv, L'vov: 1945–1981 gg.)* [Jewish religious communities in
Ukraine (Lviv: 1945–1981)] (Institut Iudaiki, 1998), doc. 20, pp. 98–99.

18. See Benjamin Pinkus, *The Soviet Government and the Jews, 1948–1967: A Documented Study* (Cambridge University Press, 1984), 96–97; Pinkus, *The Jews of the Soviet
Union: The History of a National Minority* (Cambridge University Press, 1988), 231, 233.

19. See "The Malakhovka Affair," *Jews in Eastern Europe* 1, no. 2 (1959): 9–13.

20. See the report of the first vice president of the KGB, Pyotr Ivanovich Ivashutin,
to the Central Committee of the CPSU, 3 November 1959, in Boris Morozov, *Documents on Soviet Jewish Emigration* (Frank Cass, 1999), doc. 6, pp. 43–45. The international press immediately highlighted the episode, starting with "American Traveller
Reports Synagogue and Caretaker's Cottage at Jewish Cemetery Fired in Malakhovka,"
New York Times, 13 October 1959.

21. Ilya Ehrenburg, "Lyudi, gody, zhizn'" [People, years, life], in *Sobranie sochineniy
v vos'mi tomach* [Collected works in eight volumes] (Chudozhestvennaja Literatura,
2000), 8:480.

22. "Malakhovka—a Soviet Admission," *Jews in Eastern Europe* 1, no. 3 (1960): 15;
see also Pinkus, *The Soviet Government*, 140–41.

23. The text of two leaflets is reported in "The Malakhovka Affair," 9–10. See
"Malachovka," *Socialisticheskij vestnik*, no. 12 (1959): 240–41; Pinkus, *The Soviet Government*, 139–40; Gennady V. Kostyrchenko, *Taynaya politika Khrushcheva: Vlast',
intelligentsiya, evreyskiy vopros* [The secret policy of Khrushchev: Power, intelligentsia,
Jewish question] (Mezhdunarodnye Otnoshenija, 2012), 213–14. An indirect testimony
of the climate of tension produced by the spread of antisemitic violence is found in the
antiutopian novel *Govorit Moskva* [Moscow speaks] (1960–61), by Yuli M. Daniel,

which tells of the introduction in the USSR, by decree of the presidium of the Supreme Council, of the Day of Public Murders (Den' otkrytych ubiystv). The Jew Volod'ka Margolis declares that this time, if there is a pogrom of all Jews, he will fight: "It won't be like Babi Yar. . . . I will shoot them, those disgusting reptiles!" See Nikolay Arzhak [Yuli M. Daniel], *Govorit Moskva* (B. Filippoff, 1962), 21; Italian translation, *Qui parla Mosca* (Bietti, 1966), 56, ellipsis added.

24. Patricia Blake and Max Hayward, eds., *Dissonant Voices in Soviet Literature* (Pantheon Books, 1962), 259.

25. See Yevgeny Yevtushenko, "Iz starych i novych tetradej: Stichi" [From old and new notebooks: Poems], *Znamya*, no. 4 (1987): 3–24. Concerning the meaning of the term *ochotnorjadec*, see the *Tolkovyj slovar' russkogo jazyka* [Explanatory dictionary of the Russian language], ed. Dmitri N. Ushakov, vol. 2 (Gosudarstvennoe izdatel'stvo inostrannych i nacional'nych slovarej, 1938).

26. Yevtushenko, *Autobiografia precoce*, 189.

27. Document cited in Yevgeny Zhirnov, "Ochen' svoevremennyj poet" [A very timely poet], *Kommersant': Vlast'*, 7 February 2005, http://www.kommersant.ru /doc/544964; Tsvibel, *Ot stancii Zima k Bab'emu Jaru*, 26.

28. Aleksey Markov, "Moj otvet" [My answer], *Literatura i zhizn'*, 24 September 1961. The magazine *Literatura i zhizn'* was the organ of the Union of Writers of the Russian Soviet Federative Socialist Republic.

29. Dmitri Starikov, "Ob odnom stichotvorenii" [About a poem], *Literatura i zhizn'*, 27 September 1961.

30. Starikov, "Ob odnom stichotvorenii." "It was difficult," commented Yevtushenko, "to imagine anything more monstrous and ridiculous than that accusation" (*Autobiografia precoce*, 193; Yevtushenko, *Ja prishël k tebe*, 45).

31. Yevtushenko, *Autobiografia precoce*, 193; Yevtushenko, *Ja prishël k tebe*, 45. Both A. Ya. Markov and D. V. Starikov belonged to the conservative and nationalist faction of the Union of Writers. See Nikolai Mitrokhin, *Russkaja partija: Dvizhenie russkich nacionalistov v SSSR, 1953–1985* [The Russian party: The movement of Russian nationalists in the USSR, 1953–1985] (Novoe Literaturnoe Obozrenie, 2003), 166. Concerning the intellectual and political climate of the time, see also Vladislav M. Zubok, *Zhivago's Children: The Last Russian Intelligentsia* (Belknap Press of Harvard University Press, 2009), 233–36.

32. Boris Frezinsky, ed., "'Ne otzvenelo nashe delo' (Boris Sluckiy v zerkale ego perepiski s druz'jami)" ["Our case still resonates" (Boris Slutsky in the light of his correspondence with friends)], *Voprosy literatury*, no. 3 (1999): 293–94; *Pochta Il'i Erenburga: Ja slyshu vse . . .* , 470. Writer Lev A. Kassil wrote to Ehrenburg on 8 October, saying he had resigned from the editorial committee of *Literatura i zhizn'*, of which he was a member, immediately after the publication of Markov's "shameful verses," thus before the "dishonest speculation" by Starikov, from which Kassil nevertheless dissociated himself, and he had officially communicated this decision to the direction of the Union of Writers (*Pochta Il'i Erenburga*, 471).

33. *Voprosy literatury*, no. 3 (1999): 295–96; Ilya Ehrenburg, *"Na cokole istorii . . .": Pis'ma 1931–1967* ["At the base of history . . .": Letters 1931–1967], ed. Boris Ya. Frezinskiy (Agraf, 2004), 505–7.

34. Ilya Ehrenburg, "Pis'mo v redakciyu" [Letter to the editor], *Literaturnaya gazeta*, 14 October 1961; Ehrenburg, *"Na cokole istorii . . . ,"* 504; *Sovetskie evrei pishut Il'e*

Erenburgu, 1943–1966 [Soviet Jews write to Ilya Ehrenburg, 1943–1966], ed. Mordechai Altshuler, Icchach Arad, and Shmuel' Krakovskiy (Centr po issledovaniju i dokumentacii vostochnogo-evropejskogo evrejstva—Yad Vashem, 1993), doc. 14, p. 487. Around that same time, at the Twenty-Second Congress of the CPSU, *Literaturnaya gazeta* was severely reprimanded by Nikolai M. Gribachev, who accused it of "irresponsibility" for dealing with "sensationalistic" publications. See *XXII s'ezd Kommunisticheskoj partii Sovetskogo Sojuza (17–31 oktjabrja 1961 goda): Stenograficheskiy otchët* [Twenty-Second Congress of the Communist Party of the Soviet Union (17–31 October 1961): Stenographic report] (Gosizdat, 1962), 2:512.

35. Ehrenburg, "Lyudi, gody, zhizn'," 480–81. Concerning the issue of the specificity of genocide highlighted by Yevtushenko's verses, see also the memoirs of a veteran of Stalinist camps: Isay L. Abramovich, *Vospominaniya i vzgljady* [Memories and views] (KRUK-Prestizh, 2004), 1:270–71.

36. Samuil Ya. Marshak, "Moj otvet" [My answer], in Levitas, *Babiy Jar*, 426; previously published in Aleksandr Donat, *Neopalimaja kupina: Evrejskie sjuzhety v russkoj poezii; Antologiya* [The burning bush: Jewish themes in Russian poetry; Anthology] (New York University Press, 1973). Among the poetic replies, there were also the verses of Konstantin M. Simonov, *Otvet Markovu* [Answer to Markov]. Anonymous supportive poetic compositions also circulated that were attributed to Margarita I. Aliger, Ilya Ehrenburg, and others. Despite all the promises, Yevtushenko did not obtain the public support of Mikhail A. Sholokhov, as detailed in Yevtushenko, *Volchiy pasport*, 285–91.

37. Moshe Decter, "Russian Art & Anti-Semitism: Yevtushenko vs. Khrushchev; A Speech by Mikhail Romm," *Commentary* 36, no. 6 (1963): 436, reprinted in *Khrushchev and the Arts: The Politics of Soviet Culture, 1962–1964*, ed. Priscilla Johnson and Leopold Labedz (MIT Press, 1965), 98–99. See the full version of the speech in Mikhail I. Romm, *Ustnye rasskazy* [Oral stories] (Vsesojuznoe tvorcesko-proizvodstvennoe ob'edinenie "Kinocentr," 1991), 175.

38. "Soviet Jewish General Reports in Paris on Situation of Jews in Russia," *JTA Daily News Bulletin*, 27 November 1961.

39. "Drognula sistema zamalchivaniya gitlerovskoj politiki istrebleniya evreev" [The system of concealing Hitler's policy of exterminating Jews has broken down], *Socialisticheskij vestnik*, no. 3 (1965): 76.

40. Buzukashvili, "Evgeniy Evtushenko"; Yevtushenko, *Autobiografia precoce*, 193–94. The poet reported receiving several thousand private letters of thanks and support (about thirty thousand!), while only thirty or forty had an aggressive tone (Yevtushenko, *Autobiografia precoce*, 194; Yevtushenko, *Ja prishël k tebe*, 45). A selection of reactions can be found in Yevgeny Yevtushenko, *Pervoe sobranie sochineniy v 8-i tomach* [First collection of works in eight volumes] (Pervaja Obrazcovaja Tipografija, 1998), 2:503–13.

41. "Soviet Liberalism and the Jews," *Jews in Eastern Europe* 2, no. 2 (1963): 43.

42. Patricia Blake, "New Voices in Russian Writing," *Encounter*, no. 115 (1963): 32. On that same evening, Yevtushenko, at the audience's insistent request, recited "Babi Yar" five times. Recently, the authorship of the verses has been disputed by the widow of the poet Yuri A. Vlodov, who accused Yevtushenko of plagiarism. For a

comprehensive refutation, see Feliks Rakhlin, "Pljaska na kostjach" [Dancing on bones], *My zdes'*, 5–15 June 2016, http://newswe.com/index.php?go=Pages&in=view &id=8882.

43. Testimony of Isaak Glikman in *Pis'ma k drugu: Dmitriy Shostakovich Isaaku Glikmanu* [Letters to a friend: Dmitri Shostakovich to Isaak Glikman], by Dmitriy Shostakovich (DSCH-Kompozitor, 1993), 173.

44. Solomon Volkov, ed., *Testimony: The Memoirs of Dmitri Shostakovich* (Faber and Faber, 1981), 140; Italian translation, Solomon Volkov, ed., *Testimonianza: Le memorie di Dmitriy Shostakovich* (Mondadori, 1979), 250–51.

45. Volkov, *Testimony*, 141–42; Italian translation, 253. The verses by Yevtushenko titled "Nasledniki Stalina" [The heirs of Stalin] were published in *Pravda*, 21 October 1962. They were composed in 1961, immediately after the Twenty-Second Congress of the CPSU, but were judged anti-Soviet, and for that reason, their publication was not immediately authorized. See Yevgeny A. Yevtushenko, *Posle Stalina: Nasledniki Stalina, Babiy Jar i drugie* [After Stalin: The heirs of Stalin, Babi Yar, and others] (Russian Language Specialties, 1962).

46. For a comprehensive discussion, I refer readers to the collection *Dmitri Schosta- kowitsch und das jüdische musikalische Erbe* [Dmitri Shostakovich and the Jewish heri- tage in music], ed. Ernst Kuhn, Andreas Wehrmeyer, and Günter Wolter (Ernst Kuhn Berlin, 2001).

47. Volkov, *Testimony*, 119–20; Italian translation, 220–22. Shostakovich visited Babi Yar in 1955 alone and without telling anyone. See Sofia Khentova, *Udivitel'nyj Shostakovich* [The extraordinary Shostakovich] (Variant, 1993), 45.

48. Volkov, *Testimony*, 120–21; Italian translation, 222–23 (which I have modified).

49. Volkov, *Testimony*, 118; Italian translation, 218–19 (which I have modified).

50. See the memoirs of Yevgeny A. Yevtushenko, *Rasskazyvaet poet Evgeniy Evtush- enko* [The poet Yevgeny Yevtushenko tells] (1987), recorded as an appendix to *Sin- foniya n. 13*, Melodija version A10 00285 000, conducted by Gennady N. Rozhdestven- sky, also in Elizabeth Wilson, *Shostakovich: A Life Remembered* (Faber and Faber, 2006), 413.

51. Dmitri Shostakovich to Isaak Glikman, 31 May 1962, in Shostakovich, *Pis'ma k drugu*, 172–73.

52. Concerning the structure and peculiarities of the symphony, see Wilson, *Shosta- kovich*, 401–3.

53. Verses published in Yevgeny Yevtushenko, *Vzmach ruki: Stichi* [A hand gesture: Verses] (Molodaya Gvardiya, 1962), 121–23, 109–10, 92–93; Italian translations of "L'umorismo" and "La carriera" in Yevtushenko, *Non sono nato tardi*, 188–90, 144–45.

54. D. Shostakovich to I. Glikman, 2 July 1962, in Shostakovich, *Pis'ma k drugu*, 175.

55. D. Shostakovich to I. Glikman, 9 July 1962, in Shostakovich, *Pis'ma k drugu*, 178.

56. The poem "Strachi," the only previously unpublished one used by Shostakovich in the symphony, was published for the first time in *Komsomolskaja pravda*, 21 October 1962, 4. Yevtushenko had initially titled it "Zakljat'e" [The oath]; it was Shostakovich who chose the new title.

57. Volkov, *Testimony*, 102–3; Italian translation, 193 (which I have modified). Con- cerning the importance of the relationship between word and music for Shostakovich,

used in order to express the feeling of fear unambiguously, see also Yevtushenko, *Volchiy pasport*, 438; Yevtushenko, *Ja prishël k tebe*, 50.

58. Yevtushenko wrote recently of having long regretted the "weak rhetoric" of three quatrains of the poem that were included in the original version to escape censorship; he was finally able, in the late nineties, to find a variant that could at least partly satisfy him. See the new version in Yevtushenko, *Ja prishël k tebe*, 74–75.

59. D. Shostakovich to E. Yevtushenko, 8 July 1962, in Yevtushenko, *Volchiy pasport*, 522, ellipses added; Yevtushenko, *Ja prishël k tebe*, 89–90; Dmitri Shostakovich, *Trascrivere la vita intera: Lettere 1923–1975* [Transcribing your entire life: Letters 1923–1975], ed. Elizabeth Wilson (Il Saggiatore, 2006), 363–64. Shostakovich proposed to Yevtushenko the creation of a symphony on the theme of *Muki sovesti* [The pains of conscience], but of that project, only the verses with the same title (1966), which the poet dedicated to the composer, remain. See Yevgeny Yevtushenko, "Geniy vyshe zhanra: K 70-letiyu so dnja rozhdeniya D. Shostakovicha" [A genius beyond genre: Concerning the seventieth anniversary of the birth of D. Shostakovich], *Yunost*, no. 9 (1976): 66; Yevtushenko, *Ja prishël k tebe*, 132–33.

60. Marietta Shaginjan, "Dmitriy Shostakovich" (1966), in *Raboty o muzyke* [Works on music], vol. 9 of *Sobranie sochineniy v 9-ti t.* [Collected works in nine volumes] (Chudozhestvennaja Literatura, 1975), 450.

61. Recollections of Yevtushenko on Shostakovich and Symphony No. 13 in Wilson, *Shostakovich*, 413–14.

62. Yevtushenko, "Geniy vyshe zhanra," 66; Yevtushenko, *Volchiy pasport*, 438–39; Yevtushenko, *Ja prishël k tebe*, 51; Yevtushenko, *Fatal Half Measures*, 294. At the same time as the creation of Dmitri Shostakovich's symphony in 1962, Yevtushenko's verses were set to music by the Moscow bard Aleksand A. Dulov, but this composition, for obvious reasons, did not have the same resonance.

63. Yevtushenko, *Volchiy pasport*, 428; Yevtushenko, *Ja prishël k tebe*, 22.

64. Recollections of K. P. Kondrashin in Vladimir G. Razhnikov, *Kirill Kondrashin rasskazyvaet o muzyke i zhizni* [Kirill Kondrashin tells about music and life] (Sovetskij Kompozitor, 1989), 184.

65. Concerning the defection of Mravinsky and the criticisms that this behavior aroused in musical circles, see Wilson, *Shostakovich*, 403, 406, 415–17; Laurel E. Fay, *Shostakovich: A Life* (Oxford University Press, 2000), 230, 233.

66. Concerning Kondrashin's relations with Shostakovich, see Gregor Tassie, *Kirill Kondrashin: His Life in Music* (Scarecrow, 2010), 207–43.

67. See D. Shostakovich to I. Glikman, 24 June 1962, in Shostakovich, *Pis'ma k drugu*, 174.

68. D. Shostakovich to B. Gmyrya, 19 June 1961, in Khentova, *Udivitel'nyj Shostakovich*, 55; Yevtushenko, *Volchiy pasport*, 520; Yevtushenko, *Ja prishël k tebe*, 88.

69. Letter from B. Gmyrya, in Khentova, *Udivitel'nyj Shostakovich*, 69. See also the testimony of I. Glikman in Shostakovich, *Pis'ma k drugu*, 174–75. During the war, B. R. Gmyrya was in the area occupied by the Germans and performed for the occupiers. For this reason, he should have been condemned as a collaborator, but he was pardoned by Nikita Khrushchev and continued his prestigious career. Concerning relations between Shostakovich and the Ukrainian bass, see Ganna Prynts, Marianna

Kopytsya, and Natalia Tsymbalista, *Gmyrya i Shostakovych* [Gmyrya and Shostakovich] (Fond Borysa Gmyri, 2006).

70. Concerning contacts with A. F. Vedernikov, see Galina Vishnevskaya, *Galina: Istorija zhizni* [Galina: Story of a life] (Nikeja, 2011), 373–74; Italian translation, *Galina* (Frassinelli, 1985).

71. Vishnevskaya, *Galina*, 374, 376.

72. Razhnikov, *Kirill Kondrashin*, 188; Wilson, *Shostakovich*, 409. Also see the testimony of the photographer Viktor Akhlomov, "V komande Shostakovicha: Vospominaniya fotokorrespondenta" [With Shostakovich's team: Recollections of a photo journalist], *Nashe nasledie*, no. 79–80 (2006): 170–75.

73. Testimony of I. Glikman in Shostakovich, *Pis'ma k drugu*, 183.

74. The campaign against "formalism" and "abstractionism" had just begun with the sudden visit of Khrushchev and other dignitaries on 1 December 1962 to the state exhibition at the Moscow Manege. See "Vyskazyvanija N. S. Chrushchëva pri poseshenija vystavki proizvedenij moskovskich chudozhnikov" [Statements by N. S. Khrushchev during the visit to the exhibition of works by Moscow artists], in *Nikita Sergeevich Chrushchëv: Dva cveta vremeni; Dokumenty iz lichnovo fonda N. S. Chrushchëva* [Nikita Sergeevich Khrushchev: The two colors of time; Documents from N. S. Khrushchev's personal archives] (Mezhdunarodnyj Fond "Demokratija," 2009), 2:522–33. For further insights, see Yuri Ya. Gerchuk, *"Krovoizlijanie v MOSCh," ili Chrushchëv v Manezhe 1 dekabrja 1962 goda* ["A hemorrhage in the Moscow Artists' Union," or Khrushchev at the Manege, 1 December 1962] (Novoe Literaturnoe Obozrenie, 2008). The impact of that event is well emphasized by Gian Piero Piretto, *Quando c'era l'URSS: 70 anni di storia culturale sovietica* [When there was the USSR: Seventy years of Soviet cultural history] (Cortina, 2018), 422–26.

75. "Stenogramma vstrechi rukovoditelej KPSS i sovetskogo pravitel'stva s dejateljami literatury i iskusstva" [Stenogram of the meeting of the CPSU leaders with representatives of literature and art], in *Nikita Sergeyevich Khrushchev: Dva cveta vremeni*, 2:546–47. For the report of the meeting in the press, see "Tvorit' dlja naroda vo imja kommunizma: Vstrecha rukovoditelej partii i pravitel'stva s dejateljami literatury i iskusstva" [Creating for the people in the name of Communism: Meeting of the party and government leaders with representatives of literature and art], *Pravda*, 18 December 1962. The speech by L. F. Ilyichev was reported instead in a summarized form in *Pravda*, 22 December 1962.

76. "Stenogramma," 2:547–48.

77. "So who benefits from the attempt to restore the justice of the past? Don't you see that it can feed specific nationalistic intentions? Do you think this applies only to Russians, Ukrainians, or Poles? Why shouldn't it also apply to Jews? What guarantee do we have? No, we are all equal, and we all can equally make a mistake and allow a wrong interpretation" ("Stenogramma," 2:549).

78. "Stenogramma," 2:565.

79. Decter, "Russian Art," 434; reprinted in Johnson and Labedz, *Khrushchev and the Arts*, 121.

80. Yevtushenko, "Geniy vyshe zhanra," 66; Yevtushenko, *Volchij pasport*, 428, 439; Yevtushenko, *Ja prishël k tebe*, 21, 52.

81. Razhnikov, *Kirill Kondrashin*, 188; Wilson, *Shostakovich*, 409–10.

82. Recollections collected in 1983 by Solomon Volkov, *Shostakovich and Stalin: The Extraordinary Relationship Between the Great Composer and the Brutal Dictator* (Alfred A. Knopf, 2004), 274; Italian translation, *Stalin e Šostakovič* (Garzanti, 2006), 326 (which I have modified), ellipsis added.

83. Yevgeny Yu. Sidorov, "Solo Evgenija Evtushenko" [A solo by Yevgeny Yevtushenko], *Oktjabr'*, no. 10 (1982): 190.

84. Yevtushenko, "Geniy vyshe zhanra," 66; Yevtushenko, *Volchij pasport*, 439; Yevtushenko, *Ja prishël k tebe*, 52; Yevtushenko, *Fatal Half Measures*, 295.

85. Yevtushenko, *Volchij pasport*, 429–30; Yevtushenko, *Ja prishël k tebe*, 24.

86. In particular, see Pyotr N. Pospelov, "Trinadcataja sinfonija Shostakovicha" [Shostakovich's Symphony No. 13], *Moskovskaja pravda*, 19 December 1962; "Dve prem'ery D. Shostakovicha: Trinadcataja sinfonija i opera 'Katerina Izmajlova'" [Two premieres by D. Shostakovich: Symphony No. 13 and the opera *Katerina Izmajlova*], *Leninskoe znamya*, 19 December 1962.

87. The 20 December performance was recorded by Radio Moscow, but the tape remained inaccessible for a long time. It was released in 1993 by the record company Russian Disc: Dmitri Shostakovich, *Symphony No. 13 "Babi Yar,"* Vitaly Gromadsky (bass), State Academic Choir, Yurlov Russian Choir, Moscow Philharmonic Orchestra, conducted by Kirill Kondrashin, audio CD 11 191.

88. "Vyrazhat' pomysly sovremennikov" [Expressing the thoughts of contemporaries], *Sovetskaja kul'tura*, 25 December 1962, ellipses added.

89. Leonid V. Maksimenkov, ed., *Muzyka vmesto sumbura: Kompozitory i muzykanty v Strane Sovetov, 1917–1991* [Music instead of chaos: Composers and musicians in the Soviet Union, 1917–1991] (Mezhdunarodnyj Fond "Demokratija," 2013), doc. 428, pp. 584–85.

90. Razhnikov, *Kirill Kondrashin*, 188.

91. Vishnevskaya, *Galina*, 377.

92. Maria Yudina, *Luchi bozhestvennoj ljubvi: Literaturnoe nasledie* [Beams of divine love: Literary heritage] (Universitetskaja Kniga, 1999), 521; Yudina, *Nereal'nost' zla: Perepiska 1964–1966 gg.* [The unreality of evil: Correspondence, 1964–1966] (Rosspen, 2010), 285. The reference was to *One Day in the Life of Ivan Denisovich* by Aleksandr I. Solzhenitsyn, published in November 1962, and the verses by Boris Pasternak, *Dusha* [Soul] (1956). Yudina did not send the letter to Shostakovich. It remained in her personal archives and was published in the 1990s in a version complemented by the author with further reflections on Symphony No. 13.

93. Maria Yudina to Pyotr P. Suvchinsky and Marianna L. Suvchinskaya, 28 December 1962, in Maria Yudina, *Duch dyshit, gde chochet: Perepiska 1962–1963 gg.* [The spirit blows where it wants: Correspondence, 1962–1963] (Rosspen, 2010), 397. Later, in a letter to the musicologist Fred K. Priberg dated 20 February 1963 hailing the "magnificent Symphony No. 13 by Shostakovich-Yevtushenko," the pianist referred to its "archaic patina," which she considered "intentional" (438). See also Grigory Hansburg, "Die Reaktion der Pianistin Maria Yudina auf Schostakowitschs Dreizehnte Symphonie," in Kuhn et al., *Dmitri Schostakowitsch*, 274–78.

94. Abram G. Yusfin, "Evrejskaja oficial'naja muzyka v epochi eë oficial'nogo nesushchestvovanija v Rossii" [Official Jewish music at the time of its official nonexistence

in Russia], in *Evrei v Rossii: Istorija i kul'tura; Sbornik nauchnych trudov* [Jews in Russia: History and culture; Collection of scientific works] (Peterburgskij evreijskij universitet, 1995), 3:203.

95. "Iz stenogrammy zasedanija Ideologicheskoj komissii pri CK KPSS 24 i 26 dekabrja 1962 g." [From the stenogram of the meeting of the ideological commission of the Central Committee of the CPSU, 24 and 26 December 1962], *Izvestia CK KPSS*, no. 11 (1990): 201. During that same period, the editor in chief of *Literaturnaya gazeta*, Valery A. Kosolapov, had been replaced, having been deemed guilty, among other things, of having consented to the publication of Yevtushenko's verses (Johnson and Labedz, *Khrushchev and the Arts*, 15). In more recent times, the poet dedicated to Kosolapov the verses *Krasivye glaza* [Beautiful eyes] (2004), describing the event. See Yevgeny Yevtushenko, "Tovarishch redactor" [Comrade editor], *Literaturnaya gazeta*, 9 June 2010; Yevtushenko, *Ja prishël k tebe*, 46–48. The ideological commission was a newly established body (23 November 1962) tasked with managing issues mainly related to the sphere of culture and organizing meetings with representatives of the intelligentsia to convey to them instructions on how to work in the spirit of the party.

96. Recollections from the poet on the reasons for his "compromise" in Yevtushenko, *Volchij pasport*, 440–41; Yevtushenko, *Ja prishël k tebe*, 53–56 (where it is hinted that Shostakovich would have agreed with the changes). A severe critique of Yevtushenko's opportunism and conformity is in Gennady V. Kostyrchenko, *Taynaya politika Stalina: Vlast' i antisemitizm* [Stalin's secret policy: Power and antisemitism] (Mezhdunarodnye Otnoshenija, 2001), 365–70.

97. Marietta Shaginjan, *50 pisem D. D. Shostakovicha* [Fifty letters from D. D. Shostakovich], *Novyj mir*, no. 12 (1982): 140. The press reported that Shostakovich had eliminated some verses of the poem to make it easier for the singers. See "Vzyskatel'nost' chudozhnika: Opera D. Shostakovicha 'Katerina Izmajlova' na scene" [The artist's intransigence: D. Shostakovich's opera *Katerina Izmajlova* onstage], *Pravda*, 10 February 1963. Concerning Shostakovich's negative reaction to the changes, see also Kondrashin's testimony in Razhnikov, *Kirill Kondrashin*, 188–89.

98. D. Shostakovich to I. Glikman, 28 January 1963, in Shostakovich, *Pis'ma k drugu*, 185. Yevtushenko's poem would be republished only in 1983 in a volume of selected works without the changes made to the text. See Yevgeny Yevtushenko, *Sobranie sochinenij v trëch tomach* [Collected works in three volumes], vol. 1, *Stichotvorenija i poemy, 1952–1964* [Verses and poems, 1952–1964] (Chudozhestvennaja Literatura, 1983), 316–19. However, it was accompanied by a note from the author: "Babi Yar is a ravine on the outskirts of Kyiv where the Nazis annihilated tens of thousands of Soviet citizens, including Jews, Ukrainians, Russians, and other inhabitants of Kyiv. At the time the verses were written, there was still no monument at Babi Yar. Now this monument to the victims of Fascism has been installed. Fascism adopted a policy of genocide toward the Jewish people. By a tragic paradox of history, the Israeli government has applied a policy of genocide toward the Palestinians, forcibly deprived of their land" (316). Yevtushenko returned to the entire affair, explaining in detail the reasons that led him to that statement, in Yevtushenko, *Volchij pasport*, 239–40.

99. *Le Monde*, 14 February 1963, in Johnson and Labedz, *Khrushchev and the Arts*, n. 41. Concerning the various interviews that Yevtushenko gave to the French press in those days, in which he reiterated his firm opposition to antisemitism in any form, see

"Soviet Liberalism and the Jews," 46–47. The poet soon became the target of new attacks inspired by party organizations. On 30 March 1963 *Literaturnaya gazeta* published the stenogram of the Fourth Plenum of the Union of Writers' Directorate, which took aim at him with various critiques. At the same time, he was targeted by Grigory Oganov, Boris Pankin, and Valentin Chikin, "Kuda vedët chlestakovshina" [Where does the *chlestakovshchina* lead], *Komsomol'skaja pravda*, 30 March 1963, and in a booklet titled *Vo ves' golos* [Not mincing words] (Pravda, 1963). The assaults reached such a point that a rumor spread in Moscow of his suicide, as recorded on 12 April 1963 by the writer Korney I. Chukovsky, *Dnevnik (1930–1969)* [Diary (1930–1969)] (Sovremennyj Pisatel', 1994), 2:340–41. Even in 1965, in the fourth issue of the journal *Oktjabr'*, an article by A. Dremov, "Nachalo polozheno: A dal'she? . . ." [The foundation has been laid: And then? . . .], was published, in which Yevtushenko's work was criticized, with particular attention to his verses on Babi Yar. See D. Shostakovich to I. Glikman, 23 April 1965, in Shostakovich, *Pis'ma k drugu*, 202.

100. Account by Vitaly V. Katayev, "'Umirajut v Rossii strachi': O tom, kak v marte 1963 goda v Minske ispolnjali 13-ju simfoniju Shostakovicha" ["Fears are dying in Russia": How in March 1963 Shostakovich's Symphony No. 13 was performed in Minsk], *Russkaja mysl'*, 24 October 1996, http://libelli.narod.ru/music/shostakovich/symph13 .html; see Katayev, "Umirajut v Rossii strachi" [Fears are dying in Russia], in *Shostakovichu posvjashchaetsja: Sbornik statej k 90-letiju kompozitora (1906–1996)* [In honor of Shostakovich: Collection of essays for the ninetieth anniversary of the composer (1906–1996)], ed. Elena B. Dolinskaya (Kompozitor, 1997), 169–75.

101. Yevtushenko, *Volchiy pasport*, 528; Yevtushenko, *Ja prishël k tebe*, 83.

102. Ariadna B. Ladygina, "Slushaja Trinadcatuju simfoniyu" [Listening to Symphony No. 13], *Sovetskaja Belorussiya*, 2 April 1963. For the specialized musical critique, see Viktor P. Bobrovsky, "Programmnyj simfonizm Shostakovicha: Stat'ja vtoraja, Trinadcataja simfoniya" [Shostakovich's programmatic symphonism: Second article, Symphony No. 13], in *Muzyka i sovremennost'* [Music and modernity], fasc. 5 (Muzgiz, 1967), 38–73.

103. Inessa F. Dvuzhilnaya, "Nezvuchashchie partitury: Tema Cholokosta v tvorchestve Mechislava Vajnberga" [Unplayed scores: The Holocaust theme in Mieczysław Weinberg's work], in *Cholokost na territorii SSSR: Materialy XIX mezhdunarodnoj ezhegodnoj konferencii po iudaike* [The Holocaust in Soviet territory: Proceedings of the Nineteenth International Annual Conference on Judaic Studies] (Moscow Centr nauchnych rabotnikov i prepodavatelej iudaiki v VUZach "Sefer," 2012), 1:113–14. For Weinberg's work, see Antonina Klokova, "'Meine moralische Pflicht': Mieczysław Weinberg und der Holocaust," *Osteuropa* 60, no. 7 (2010): 173–82.

104. "Vysokaja idejnost' i chudozhestvennoe masterstvo—velikaja sila sovetskoj literatury i iskusstva" [High ideological commitment and artistic mastery—the great strength of Soviet literature and art], *Pravda*, 10 March 1963. Khrushchev's speech was widely circulated and published as a booklet (Gos. izd-vo politicheskoj literatury, 1963). I will use the version in *Novyj mir*, no. 3 (1963): 3–33; Johnson and Labedz, *Khrushchev and the Arts*, 148–86.

105. "Vysokaja idejnost' i chudozhestvennoe masterstvo," 7; Johnson and Labedz, *Khrushchev and the Arts*, 152.

106. "Vysokaja idejnost' i chudozhestvennoe masterstvo," 10; Johnson and Labedz, *Khrushchev and the Arts*, 156.

107. "Vysokaja idejnost' i chudozhestvennoe masterstvo," 15; Johnson and Labedz, *Khrushchev and the Arts*, 163.

108. "Khrushchev's Pronouncement on the Jewish Question," *Jews in Eastern Europe* 2, no. 2 (1963): 19.

109. "Konspekt vystupleniya N. S. Chrushchëva na vstreche s predstaviteljami intelligencii" [Summary of N. S. Khrushchev's speech at the meeting with representatives of the intelligentsia], in *Nikita Sergeevich Chrushchëv: Dva cveta vremeni*, 2:607–8, 610. For Khrushchev's fear of Yevtushenko's "recruitment" by "Zionism," see Kostyrchenko, *Tajnaja politika Stalina*, 364–65.

110. "Dopolnenie k konspektu vystupleniya na vstreche s intelligenciej" [Supplement to the summary of the speech at the meeting with the intelligentsia], in *Nikita Sergeevich Chrushchëv: Dva cveta vremeni*, 2:626, ellipsis added.

111. "Vysokaja idejnost' i chudozhestvennoe masterstvo," 30; Johnson and Labedz, *Khrushchev and the Arts*, 181–82.

112. "Vysokaja idejnost' i chudozhestvennoe masterstvo," 31–32; Johnson and Labedz, *Khrushchev and the Arts*, 183–84. For the story of the traitor Kogan, see the "Konspekt vystupleniya N.S. Chrushchëva na vstreche s predstaviteljami intelligencii," 610–11.

113. For the spread of antisemitic and anti-Zionist literature in Ukraine during that period, see Nina Bibichkova and Mark Kipnis, "A List of Anti-Judaic and Anti-Zionist Books Published in the Ukrainian SSR in 1960–1984," *Jews and Jewish Topics in Soviet and East-European Publications*, no. 2–3 (1986): 47–58.

114. Porfiry Gavrutto, *Tuchi nad gorodom* [Clouds over the city] (Molodaya Gvardiya, 1963); Gavrutto, *Tuchi nad gorodom*, 2nd ed. (Moskovskij Rabocij, 1965); Gavrutto, *Tuchi nad gorodom*, 3rd ed. (Molodaya Gvardiya, 1968).

115. Gavrutto, *Tuchi nad gorodom*, 2nd ed., 175–76.

116. Ariadna Gromova, "V interesach istiny" [In the interest of truth], *Literaturnaya gazeta*, 9 August 1966. The "real person" involved was Moissey G. Kogan, who was captured by the Germans in 1941, who repeatedly escaped from captivity and was then recaptured, and who, between November 1942 and January 1943, worked in Stalingrad under a false identity (Armenian or Ukrainian) as an interpreter for the German command. Arrested by Soviet security services in February 1943, he was sentenced to ten years of forced labor for collaboration (art. 58, para. 1a), but the penalty did not include an accusation of denunciation. In 1957 he filed a petition to review the trial. For his version of the story, see Pinkus, *The Soviet Government*, 130–33.

117. For a general framework of Khrushchev's story, see Mitrokhin, *Russkaja partiya*, 160–68. For Khrushchev's personal position on the "Jewish question," see Shimon Redlich, "Khrushchev and the Jews," *Jewish Social Studies* 34, no. 4 (1972): 343–53. For the pamphlet, see Trochym K. Kychko, *Iudayizm bez prykras* [Judaism without embellishment] (Vydavnyctvo Akademiï Nauk URSR, 1963). The pamphlet was printed in a run of twelve thousand copies at a very low price.

118. Trochym K. Kychko (1905–?) was expelled from the Communist Party in 1948 for alleged collaboration during the war. Reinstated in 1954, he was active from 1957 as

an author of articles and volumes criticizing Judaism and later Zionism. See *Iudejs'ka religiya, ïï pochodzhennja i sut'* [The Jewish religion, its origin and essence] (Tovarystvo dlja poshirennja politychnych ta naukovych znan' Ukraïns'koï RSR, 1957); *Pro iudejs'ku relihiyu* [On the Jewish religion] (Tovarystvo dlja poshirennja politychnych ta naukovych znan' Ukraïns'koï RSR, 1959); and *Iudaïzm i sionizm* [Judaism and Zionism] (Tovarystvo "Znannja" Ukraïns'koï RSR, 1968).

119. See the thorough analyses of the text by Moshe Decter, "'Judaism Without Embellishment': Recent Documentation of Soviet Anti-Semitism," *New Politics* 3, no. 1 (1964): 102–18; Decter, "'Judaism Without Embellishment': Recent Documentation of Soviet Anti-Semitism," in *The Unredeemed: Anti-Semitism in the Soviet Union*, ed. Ronald I. Rubin (Quadrangle Books, 1968), 135–45. For the context, see Kostyrchenko, *Tajnaja politika Chrushchëva*, 222–25.

120. Kychko, *Iudayizm bez prykras*, 161.

121. See the special dossier "'Judaism Without Embellishment': An Examination of Anti-Semitism in Soviet Propaganda Against Religion," *Jews in Eastern Europe* 2, no. 5 (1964): 4–51, particularly the extensive review of the international press, "World Reaction—Soviet Confusion: Western Communists Join in Protests," *Jews in Eastern Europe* 2, no. 5 (1964): 24–35. For example, the *New York Times*, 27 February and 14 March 1964, wrote that in Ukraine a volume had been published with "Nazi-style" caricatures.

122. See a series of interventions in *Ukrainians and Jews: A Symposium* (Ukrainian Congress Committee of America, 1966), 97–106, 157–58, 163–68, 177–89, and for Communist policies, see 190.

123. For example, *L'Humanité*, 24 March 1964; *Paese Sera*, 25 March 1964; *L'Unità*, 30 March 1964. Among the reactions, see also "Soviet Anti-Semitism: The Kichko Book," *Political Affairs* 63, no. 6 (1964): 1–12; "Soviet Anti-Semitism: The Status of Soviet Jews," *Political Affairs* 63, no. 7 (1964): 1–15; Bohdan Osadchuk, "Skandal u Kyjevi abo deshcho pro suchasnyj radjans'kyj antysemityzm" [Scandal in Kyiv or something about contemporary Soviet antisemitism], *Suchasnist'* (Munich), no. 6 (1964): 115–18. For a broader analysis, see Moshe Decter, *The Soviet Book That Shook the Communist World* (Midstream—The Theodor Herzl Foundation, 1964); Solomon M. Schwarz, *Evrei v Sovetskom Sojuze s nachala vtoroj mirovoj vojny (1939–1965)* [Jews in the Soviet Union since the beginning of World War II (1939–1965)] (Amerikanskij evrejskij rabochij komitet, 1966), 314–21.

124. The weekly *L'Express*, 20 March 1964, scrutinized T. Kychko's book, highlighting the contradictions of the Soviet government and noting that appeals against antisemitism, like the one made by Yevtushenko to Khrushchev, seemed to go unheeded. Less international attention was drawn to another antisemitic publication, the novel by Ivan M. Shevtsov, *Tlja (Roman-pamflet)* [The flea (pamphlet-novel)] (Sovetskaja Rossija, 1964), with a preface by academic Aleksandr I. Laktionov, who soon after, however, disavowed it; Ivan M. Shevtsov, *Tlja (Roman-pamflet)*, 2nd ed. (Sovetskaja Rossija, 2003). Drafted during the decline of the campaign against cosmopolitanism, the work had failed to obtain proper authorization for publication. It became relevant again in the changed conditions of the 1960s, following Khrushchev's speeches on art and literature, especially thanks to the main theme addressed (the struggle of "Russian realist" artists against "Jewish formalists"), sparking a wide critical debate at home. For

context, see Zubok, *Zhivago's Children*, 239–40; Kostyrchenko, *Tajnaja politika Stalina*, 412–14.

125. "V ideologicheskoj komissii CK KPSS" [In the ideological commission of the Central Committee of the CPSU], *Pravda*, 4 April 1964; Schwarz, *Evrei v Sovetskom Sojuze*, 319–20; Kostyrchenko, *Tajnaja politika Stalina*, 226–27.

126. See "Ob odnoj neponjatnoj shumiche" [On an incomprehensible uproar], *Izvestia*, 5 April 1964; "Antisemitskiy pamflet v Sovetskom Sojuze" [An antisemitic pamphlet in the Soviet Union], *Socialisticheskiy vestnik*, no. 3 (1965): 66–75 (the article is signed Obozrevatel' [an observer]); Schwarz, *Evrei v Sovetskom Sojuze*, 320–21; Kostyrchenko, *Tajnaja politika Stalina*, 227. The ambiguities of the Soviet leadership are confirmed by the simultaneous publication of Aleksandr A. Osipov, *Katechizis bez prikras* [Catechism without embellishment] (Gospolitizdat, 1963), an anti-Orthodox booklet that also resorted to explicitly antisemitic arguments that were even more violent than those used by T. K. Kychko. On the issue, see "Anti-Semitism in the USSR: Questions Raised by Kichko Book," *Jews in Eastern Europe* 2, no. 5 (1964): 7–8.

127. For the official Soviet position, see "World Reaction—Soviet Confusion," 35–42. A few years later, the Supreme Soviet of Ukraine awarded T. Kychko an honorary diploma "for his work in favor of atheism propaganda" (*Pravda Ukrainy*, 20 January 1968). See "The Kichko Affair: Additional Documents," *Soviet Jewish Affairs*, no. 1 (1971): 109–13.

128. Anatoly Kuznetsov, "Prodolzhenie legendy: Zapiski molodogo cheloveka" [The legend continues: Reflections of a young man], *Yunost*, no. 7 (1957): 6–59 (Goslitizdat, 1958); Italian translation, *La leggenda continua* (Editori Riuniti, 1961). On "confessional prose and self-fashioning," see Oleg Kharkhordin, *The Collective and the Individual in Russia: A Study of Practices* (University of California Press, 1999), 343–54.

129. Kuznetsov, *Babiy Jar*, 16–17; Italian translation, 23–24. See the attentive and reasoned reading of the novel by Giovanna Brogi Bercoff, "La tragedia di Babyn Jar," in *Rappresentare la Shoah*, ed. Alessandro Costazza, *Quaderni di Acme*, no. 75 (2005): 327–37. Concerning the use of reality as a cultural category in Kuznetsov's novel, see Sidra DeKoven Ezrahi, *By Words Alone: The Holocaust in Literature* (University of Chicago Press, 1980), 28–30.

130. Concerning the figure of the poet, writer, and translator Shlomo Even-Shoshan (1910–2004), his relations with the Russian literary world, and his special interest in Babi Yar, which he visited in 1963 guided by V. Nekrasov, see Grigory Kipnis, "V gostjach u Shlomo, druga Viktora Nekrasova" [At the home of Shlomo, friend of Viktor Nekrasov], *Pravda Ukrainy*, August 16, 1994, 3. The first edition of the correspondence is A. Anatoly [Anatoly Kuznetsov], *Pis'ma v Izrail' (1964–1971)* [Letters to Israel (1964–1971)], ed. Feliks Rakhlin, 22, no. 131 (2004): 151–87; I use the revised and integrated reedition in *Literaturno-chudozhestvennyj al'manach Trediakovskiy*, 5 October 2009, http://www.trediakovsky.ru/pisma-v-izrail-1964-1971.

131. Kuznetsov to Sh. Even-Shoshan from Tula, 16 August 1964, in Anatoly, *Pis'ma v Izrail'*. In the same letter, Kuznetsov recalled that, at the time he accompanied Yevtushenko to the massacre site and the poet composed his famous verses, "there was nothing left there except thick black layers of ash sticking out from under the sand."

132. Kuznetsov to Sh. Even-Shoshan from Tula, 28 October 1964, in Anatoly, *Pis'ma v Izrail'*.

133. For an analysis of the "documentary fiction" technique in Kuznetsov's novel, see James E. Young, *Writing and Rewriting the Holocaust: Narrative and the Consequences of Interpretation* (Indiana University Press, 1988), 53–59; Young, "Holocaust Documentary Fiction: The Novelist as Eyewitness," in *Writing and the Holocaust*, ed. Berel Lang (Holmes and Meier, 1988), 202–9, which also reconstructs the case of the "plagiarism" conducted by D. M. [Donald Michael] Thomas in *The White Hotel* (1981).

134. Kuznetsov, *Babiy Jar*, 119; Italian translation, 117. After the book's publication in the USSR, Dina Pronicheva wrote to Kuznetsov that she had been visited by another Babi Yar survivor who at the time of the massacre was a boy who had been hidden and then adopted by a Ukrainian family, from whom he took his name on his identity card. He had never told anyone his story: "Judging by the details he recalled, his story was true. But he just sat there reminiscing—and left without saying his name" (119; Italian translation, 117).

135. Kuznetsov, *Babiy Jar*, 300; Italian translation, 284. See also Davydov's testimonies about his arrest in *Istoricheskaja topografiya: Chronologiya sobytiy* [Historical topography: Chronology of events], ed. Tatiana Evstafeva and Vitaly Nachmanovich (Vneshtorgizdat Ukrainy, 2004), doc. 71, p. 338, doc. 87, p. 366.

136. Kuznetsov to Sh. Even-Shoshan from Tula, 17 May 1965, in Anatoly, *Pis'ma v Izrail'*.

137. Kuznetsov to Sh. Even-Shoshan from Tula, 2 June 1965, in Anatoly, *Pis'ma v Izrail'*.

138. Kuznetsov, *Babiy Jar*, 484; Italian translation, 454.

139. Anatoly Kuznetsov, *Babiy Jar: Roman-dokument*, published in *Yunost*, no. 8–10 (1966). At that time the magazine's circulation was two million copies.

140. Anatoly Kuznetsov, *Babiy Jar: Roman-dokument* (Molodaya Gvardiya, 1967), print run of 150,000 copies. It was on this version that the first Italian translation was based: Anatoly Kuznetsov, *Babiy Jar: Romanzo documentario* (Paravia, 1970); here, however, I will continue to refer to the unabridged Posev edition of 1970 and the Adelphi Italian translation of 2019. The author was also offered a film adaptation (see a letter to Sh. Even-Shoshan, Tula, 17 July 1968, in Anatoly, *Pis'ma v Izrail'*), but the project, sponsored by Lenfilm, was not completed. Concerning the general issue of the treatment of the Babi Yar massacre in cinematic form, see Karel Berkhoff, "Babyn Yar in Cinema," in *Babyn Yar: History and Memory*, ed. Vladyslav Hrynevych and Paul R. Magocsi (Duch i Litera, 2016), 239–57. More specifically, on Mark S. Donskoy's film *Nepokorënnye* [The indomitable] (1945), based on the story of the same name by Boris L. Gorbatov (Gosudarstvennoe izdatel'stvo chudozhestvennoj literatury, 1943); Italian translation, *Gli indomabili* (La Nuova Biblioteca, 1945), which presented as a key scene a mass execution shot at Babi Yar, see Jeremy Hicks, "Confronting the Holocaust: Mark Donskoi's 'The Unvanquished,'" *Studies in Russian Soviet Cinema* 3, no. 1 (2009): 33–51; Mark Donskoi, *First Films of the Holocaust: Soviet Cinema and the Genocide of the Jews, 1938–1946* (University of Pittsburgh Press, 2012), 134–56; Olga Gershenson, *The Phantom Holocaust: Soviet Cinema and Jewish Catastrophe* (Rutgers University Press, 2013), 40–57; Donskoi, "Between the Permitted and the Forbidden: The Politics of Holocaust Representation in *The Unvanquished* (1945)," in *Soviet Jews in World War II: Fighting, Witnessing, Remembering*, ed. Harriet Murav and Gennady Estraikh (Academic Studies Press, 2014), 168–86.

141. Dokia K. Humenna, *Chreshchatyj Jar (Kyïv 1941–43): Roman-chronika* [Chresh-chatyj Jar (Kyiv 1941–43): Novel-chronicle] (Slovo, 1956). For an analysis of Dokia K. Humenna's work compared with the diary kept by the writer in the first two years of the war, see Myroslav Shkandrij, *Jews in Ukrainian Literature: Representation and Identity* (Yale University Press, 2009), 201–4; Shkandrij, *Ukrainian Nationalism: Politics, Ideology, and Literature, 1929–1956* (Yale University Press, 2015), 253–67; Shkandrij, "Dokia Humenna's Representation of the Second World War in Her Novel and Diary," in *Zhnyva: Essays Presented in Honor of George G. Grabowicz on His Seventieth Birthday*, ed. Roman Koropeckyj, Taras Koznarsky, and Maxim Tarnawsky (Harvard Ukrainian Studies, 2015), 665–78; Shkandrij, "Dokia Humenna's Depiction of the Second World War and the OUN in Khreshchatyi iar: How Readers Responded," *Journal of Ukrainian Studies* 3, no. 1 (2016): 89–109.

142. Kuznetsov, *Babiy Jar*, 18–19; Italian translation, 25.

143. Kuznetsov, *Babiy Jar*, 20; Italian translation, 26.

144. Kuznetsov to Sh. Even-Shoshan from Tula, 16 August 1964, in Anatoly, *Pis'ma v Izrail'*.

145. Kuznetsov to Sh. Even-Shoshan from Tula, 17 May 1965, in Anatoly, *Pis'ma v Izrail'*.

146. This is what Kuznetsov stated in April 1967 in an intervention in *Sputnik*; see William Korey, "No Monument over Babi Yar," in *The Soviet Cage: Anti-Semitism in Russia* (Viking Press, 1973), 116–17.

147. Kuznetsov to Sh. Even-Shoshan from Tula, 29 December 1966, in Anatoly, *Pis'ma v Izrail'*.

148. Kuznetsov, *Babiy Jar*, 5; Italian translation, 13–14. Kuznetsov specified in this regard: "I did not at all set my book [against his poem]; simply the scale of the novel allowed for much more to be told about Babi Yar, and in all its aspects. In some foreign editions, my novel is even introduced by Yevtushenko's poem as a kind of preface, which is eloquent in itself" (6; Italian translation, 14).

149. Kuznetsov, *Babiy Jar*.

150. Kuznetsov, *Babiy Jar*, 8–9; Italian translation, 16.

151. Kuznetsov, *Babiy Jar*, 9–10; Italian translation, 16, 18.

152. Kuznetsov to Sh. Even-Shoshan from Tula, 29 December 1966, in Anatoly, *Pis'ma v Izrail'*, which also includes a list of errata sent to the correspondent. See a series of other clarifications for the text translation in a letter from Tula dated 1 November 1967, in Anatoly, *Pis'ma v Izrail'*.

153. Kuznetsov to Sh. Even-Shoshan from Tula, 20 January 1967, in Anatoly, *Pis'ma v Izrail'*.

154. Kuznetsov, *Babiy Jar*, 11–12; Italian translation, 18–19.

155. Semen Gluzman, "Babiy Jar," *Fokus*, 29 September 2006, http://www.kby.kiev.ua/komitet/ru/polemics/art00021.html.

156. Kuznetsov to Sh. Even-Shoshan from Tula, 20 January 1967, in Anatoly, *Pis'ma v Izrail'*.

157. Among the most positive reviews, see Aleksandr Borshchagovskiy, "Proshloe ne umiraet" [The past does not die], *Literaturnaya gazeta*, 26 November 1966, 4; Ariadna Gromova, "Pravda, tol'ko pravda . . ." [The truth and nothing but the truth . . .], *Novyj mir*, no. 2 (1967): 247–50. A letter from Dina M. Pronicheva published in

Literaturnaya gazeta, 22 February 1967, emphasized the specific Jewish nature of the massacre and detailed how she and her husband (of Russian nationality) managed to save their son, who was a little over two years old, from being shot. For the novel's reception, see Korey, "No Monument," 118–19, 122–23. George St. George's book *The Road to Babyi-Yar* (Spearman, 1967) is largely based on Kuznetsov's text.

158. Kuznetsov, *Babiy Jar*, 12–13; Italian translation, 20.

159. For the methods of the "escape," see the recollections of Leonid Vladimirov [Leonid V. Finkel'shtejn], "Zhizn' nomer dva" [Life number two], *Vremja i my*, no. 144 (1999): 253–56.

160. I rely upon "Obrashchenie k ljudjam" [Appeal to the people], in Vladimir Batshev, "Delo Anatoliya Kuznecova" [The Anatoly Kuznetsov affair], *Vremja i my*, no. 148 (2000): 227–28. The reference is to Anatoly V. Kuznetsov, "Ogon" [Fire], *Yunost*, no. 3–4 (1969).

161. "Obrashchenie k ljudjam," 229.

162. "Obrashchenie k ljudjam," 230–31. See also the autobiographical note sent attached to the cited letter to Sh. Even-Shoshan, 9 November 1970, in Anatoly, *Pis'ma v Izrail'*, and some clarifications on the new name (and not pseudonym) in a letter to Sh. Even-Shoshan, 1971, London.

163. Kuznetsov himself discussed this in an interview with journalist David Floyd, "The Russian Writer and the KGB," *Sunday Telegraph*, 10 August 1969. See Batshev, "Delo Anatoliya Kuznecova," 243–45. See also Yuri Shapoval, "Nevozvrashchenie Anatoliya Kuznecova" [The defection of Anatoly Kuznetsov], *Den'*, 24 December 2004, http://www.day.kiev.ua/ru/article/istoriya-i-ya/nevozvrashchenie-anatoliya-kuznecova. The collaboration is confirmed in a report by KGB chairman Yuri V. Andropov to the Central Committee of the CPSU, 4 August 1969, in *Sovetskiy archiv* [Soviet archive], comp. Vladimir Bukovsky, http://www.bukovsky-archives.net/pdfs/dis60/kgb69-2.pdf.

164. The incident provoked the critical reaction of dissident Andrei A. Amalrik. See the open letter he addressed to Kuznetsov on 1 November 1969 in Andrei Amalrik, *Stat'i i pis'ma, 1967–1970* [Articles and letters, 1967–1970] (Fond imeni Gercena, 1971), 12–27. More sympathetic is the reaction of dissident writer Anatoly T. Gladilin, *Ulica generalov: Popytka memuarov* [The street of generals: An attempt at memoirs] (Vagrius, 2008), 118–33.

165. Autobiographical information attached to a letter to Sh. Even-Shoshan, 9 November 1970, in Anatoly, *Pis'ma v Izrail'*.

166. Kuznetsov, *Babiy Jar*, 12; Italian translation, 19–20. A meticulous analysis of Kuznetsov's novel in the broader context of Soviet censorship of the time is Herman Ermolaev, *Censorship in Soviet Literature, 1917–1991* (Rowman and Littlefield, 1997), 181–221.

167. "K chitateljam v Izraile" [To readers in Israel], *Literaturno-chudozhestvennyj al'manach Trediakovskiy*, 5 October 2009, http://www.trediakovsky.ru/kchitatelyam-v-izraile.

168. Vladimirov, "Zhizn' nomer dva," 256.

169. "K chitateljam v Izraile."

170. Kuznetsov, *Babiy Jar*, 94; Italian translation, 95–96. The censored text is in italics.

171. Kuznetsov, *Babiy Jar*, 102–3; Italian translation, 103–4. The added text is in square brackets.

172. Kuznetsov, *Babiy Jar*, 88; Italian translation, 90. The added text is in square brackets.

173. Kuznetsov, *Babiy Jar*, 204–5; Italian translation, 197–98. The censored text is in italics; ellipsis added. For a comparison between the first edition and the uncensored one, see Edith W. Clowes, "Entwürfe zur Erinnerung an den Holocaust: Evtushenkos und Kuznecovs 'Babiy Jar,'" in *Zerstörer des Schweigens: Formen künstlerischer Erinnerung an die nationalsozialistische Rassen- und Vernichtungspolitik in Osteuropa*, ed. Frank Grüner, Urs Heftrich, and Heinz-Dietrich Löwe (Böhlau, 2006), 115–27.

Chapter 5. Profane, Erase, Redeem

1. A. Anatoly [Anatoly Kuznetsov], *Babiy Jar: Roman-dokument* [Babi Yar: Documentary novel] (Posev, 1970), 476–85; Italian translation, *Babiy Jar: Romanzo-documento* (Adelphi, 2019), 447–54.

2. Kuznetsov, *Babiy Jar*, 481–82; Italian translation, 452. A letter dated 7 October 1964 addressed to the first secretary of the Central Committee of the Communist Party of Ukraine reported the discovery of the remains of other prisoners from the Syrets camp. The remains were buried in common graves in the Lukyanivka military cemetery. An investigative commission was also appointed to identify any other burial sites of prisoners and to shed light on the activities of the Communist resistance within the camp. See Tatiana Evstafeva and Vitaly Nachmanovich, eds., *Istoricheskaja topografiya: Chronologiya sobytiy* [Historical topography: Chronology of events] (Vneshtorgizdat Ukrainy, 2004), doc. 159, p. 538, doc. 160, p. 540. For other cases of discovery, see Tatiana Evstafeva, "Babiy Jar vo vtoroj polovine XX v." [Babi Yar in the second half of the twentieth century], in Evstafeva and Nachmanovich, *Istoricheskaja topografiya*, 193; Evstafeva, "Babiy Jar: Poslevoennaja istoriya mestnosti" [Babi Yar: Postwar history of the site], in *Babyn Jar: Masove ubyvstvo i pam'jat' pro n'oho; Materialy mizhnarodnoï naukovoï konferenciï 24–25 zhovtnja 2011 r., m. Kyïv* [Babi Yar: Mass murder and memory of it; Proceedings of the International Scientific Conference, Kyiv, 24–25 October 2011], ed. Mykhailo Tyahlyi and Vitaly Nachmanovych (Ukraïns'kyj centr vyvchennja istorii Holokostu, Hromads'kyj komitet dlja vshanuvannja pam'jati zhertv Babynoho Jaru, 2012), 24–25. Even in recent times, human bones have been found during excavation work, for example, in the fall of 2000 on Melnykova Street. See Mikhail Milman, "Babiy Jar: Zapiski ekskursovoda" [Babi Yar: Notes of a guide], *Evrejskiy obozrevatel'*, 26 October 2001, http://www.jewukr.org /observer/jo12_15/po21_r.html.

3. Concerning the issue of the "reassignment" of cemeteries, see Mordechai Altshuler, *Religion and Jewish Identity in the Soviet Union, 1941–1964* (Brandeis University Press, 2012), 213–15. The modernization and reconstruction of the road network caused significant disturbances, as is well documented in the verses of Sava O. Holovanivsky, "Vulytsya Melnykova" [Melnykova Street] (1968), in *Babiy Jar: Spasiteli i spasënnye* [Babi Yar: Rescuers and rescued], ed. Ilya M. Levitas (Stal, 2005), 406–7, which recall the victims' walk toward Babi Yar. As of 7 November 2018, the history of that walk was erased by renaming it Yuriy Illjenko Street.

4. Mikhail Kalnicky and Boris Chandros, "Evrejskiy nekropol' Kieva do 1917 goda" [The Jewish necropolis of Kyiv before 1917], *Evrejskiy obozrevatel'*, 20 September 2004, http://www.jewukr.org/observer/eo2003/page_show_ru.php?id=762; Mikhail Kalnicky, *Evrejskie adresa Kieva: Putevoditel' po kul'turno-istoricheskim mestam* [Jewish addresses of Kyiv: Guide to cultural-historical places] (Duch i Litera, 2012), 336–39.

5. Report by P. Vilkhovy, 13 March 1953, in Mikhail Mitsel, *Obshchiny iudejskogo veroispovedaniya v Ukraine (Kyiv, L'vov: 1945–1981 gg.)* [Jewish religious communities in Ukraine (Lviv: 1945–1981)] (Institut Iudaiki, 1998), 75–76; Vladimir Khanin, ed., *Documents on Ukrainian Jewish Identity and Emigration, 1944–1990* (Frank Cass, 2003), doc. 19, pp. 95–96. The climate of the time is outlined in Mikhail Mitsel, "Zima 1953 goda v Kieve i na Ukraine: 's gnevom i vozmushcheniem'" [The winter of 1953 in Kyiv and Ukraine: "with anger and indignation"], in *Ksenofobiya: Istoriya, ideologiya, politika* [Xenophobia: History, ideology, politics], ed. Konstantin Yu. Burmistrov, Rashid M. Kaplanov, and Viktoriya V. Mochalova (Centr nauchnych rabotnikov i prepodavatelej iudaiki v VUZach "Sefer," 2003), 131–59.

6. Resolution no. 988 of the executive committee of the City of Kyiv, 26 June 1962, on the liquidation of the Kopylovo cemetery and the old Karaite Jewish cemetery, in Evstafeva and Nachmanovich, *Istoricheskaja topografiya*, doc. 149, pp. 525–26. The resolution also ordered the final dismantling of the small Christian cemetery of Kopylovo (1.5 hectares), closed to burials in 1927 and already devastated due to the Kurenivka disaster in 1961. See Mikhail Kalnicky and Boris Chandros, "Evrejskiy nekropol' Kieva v sovetskoe vremja" [The Jewish necropolis of Kyiv in Soviet times], *Evrejskiy obozrevatel'*, 29 September 2004, http://www.jewukr.org/observer/eo2003/page_show_ru.php?id=778; Kalnicky, *Evrejskie adresa Kieva*, 339–40.

7. A. Sharandak to the secretary of the provincial committee of the Communist Party of Ukraine, V. A. Boichenko, and the president of the executive committee of the City Council of Workers' Deputies, O. J. Davydov, 1 December 1962, in Mitsel, *Obshchiny iudejskogo veroispovedaniya*, doc. 29, pp. 113–14. The remains of Ber Borochov were transferred to Israel in 1963 and buried in the Kvutzat Kinneret cemetery near the Sea of Galilee next to those of other socialist figures from the Zionist movement. The remains of Max E. Mandelstamm were instead reburied in the Berkovetske cemetery in Kyiv.

8. K. F. Polonik, 10 January 1963, in Mitsel, *Obshchiny iudejskogo veroispovedaniya*, doc. 30, pp. 117–18.

9. Resolution no. 1603 of the executive committee of the City of Kyiv, 15 October 1963, on the planning of a park of culture and leisure on the territory of the suppressed Jewish and Karaite cemeteries, in Evstafeva and Nachmanovich, *Istoricheskaja topografiya*, doc. 151, pp. 528–29; Resolution no. 1017 of the executive committee of the City of Kyiv, 28 July 1964, on the allocation of a plot of land for the construction of the Avangard sports complex, in Evstafeva and Nachmanovich, *Istoricheskaja topografiya*, doc. 155, pp. 533–34.

10. Letter from the director of the Kievgorstroy no. 1 trust, A. Bardash, to the president of the DSO Avangard of the provincial council of Kyiv with observations on the assignment of the project for the construction of a sports complex, 7 September 1965, in Evstafeva and Nachmanovich, *Istoricheskaja topografiya*, doc. 161, p. 541.

11. Kuznetsov, *Babiy Jar*, 482; Italian translation, 452.

12. Viktor Nekrasov, "Kamen' v Bab'em Jaru" [A stone at Babi Yar], in *Izhoj: Viktor Nekrasov u spohadach suchasnykiv* [Rebel: Viktor Nekrasov in the memories of contemporaries] (Duch i Litera, 2014), 201, and in Nekrasov, *Arestovannye stranicy: Rasskazy, interv'ju, pis'ma iz archiva KGB* [Seized pages: Stories, interviews, letters from the KGB archive], ed. Lyubov' Chazan (Laurus, 2014), 191, ellipsis added. The text was written in 1973, but the manuscript—seized by the security services—remained unpublished for a long time.

13. Nekrasov, "Kamen' v Bab'em Jaru," 201–2; Nekrasov, *Arestovannye stranicy*, 191–92.

14. Nekrasov, "Kamen' v Bab'em Jaru," 203; Nekrasov, *Arestovannye stranicy*, 192–93. The writer used similar words to describe the destruction of the Jewish cemetery ("they desecrated and shattered the sepulchral monuments") in Viktor Nekrasov, "Babiy Jar—45 let" [Babi Yar—45 years], *Novoe russkoe slovo*, 29 August 1986.

15. Viktor Nekrasov, "Zapiski zevaki" [Reflections of a wanderer], *Kontinent*, no. 4 (1975): 81–83. Concerning the writer's interest in necropolises, see Nekrasov, "Po obe storony Steny: Chast' vtoraja" [On both sides of the wall: Part two], *Kontinent*, no. 19 (1979): 119–20.

16. The goal was to complete within a year one structure to commemorate the people murdered at the bottom of the ravine and another one dedicated to the prisoners of war who died in the Darnytsia concentration camp. The project was undertaken by resolution of the Central Committee of the Communist Party of Ukraine on 30 May 1965. See Evstafeva, "Babiy Jar," 25–26. The announcement made no reference to the Jewish victims, but that aspect was emphasized in the information publicized at the international level: "City of Kyiv to Memorialize Jewish Victims of Babi Yar Massacre," *JTA Daily News Bulletin*, 27 August 1965.

17. K. Grigoriev, "Pamiatnik na meste Bab'ego Jara i v Darnice" [Monument at the site of Babi Yar and in Darnytsia], *Literaturnaya gazeta*, 30 November 1965, 1; "Proyektn far a denkmol in Babiy Jar" [Projects for a monument in Babi Yar], *Sovietish haimland*, no. 3 (1966): 158. See Yevgeny Zhovnerovskij [Zhovnirovskij], "Konkurs na pamjatnik" [The competition for the monument], in *Babiy Jar*, ed. Efrem Baukh (Izdanie Sojuza zemljachestv-vychodcev iz SSSR, 1981), 105–7; Aleksandr Naiman, "Babiy Jar: Tragediya i pamjat'" [Babi Yar: Tragedy and memory], *Evrejskij obozrevatel'*, 3 April 2002, http://www.jewukr.org/observer/joo7_26/po104_r.html; and the testimony of one of the participants in the competition: Aleksandr Shteinberg, "Dokumenty zabytoj pamjati" [Documents of a forgotten memory], *Evrejskiy obozrevatel'*, 24 July 2002, http://www.jewukr.org/observer/jo14_33/po101_r.html.

18. Viktor Nekrasov, "Novye pamjatniki" [New monuments], *Dekorativnoe iskusstvo SSSR*, no. 12 (1966): 23.

19. Shteinberg, "Dokumenty zabytoj pamjati." With few exceptions, the plans and drawings presented to the selection committee did not refer to the extermination of the Jews. This was emphasized by the statement "Soviet Designs for Babi Yar Memorial Do Not Identify Victims as Jews," *JTA Daily News Bulletin*, 9 March 1966.

20. See Sergei V. Babushkin, Dmitri Brazhnik, Irma I. Karakis, and Andrei Puchkov, eds., *Architektor Iosif Karakis: Sud'ba i tvorchestvo (Al'bom-katalog k stoletiyu so dnja rozhdeniya)* [Architect Iosif Karakis: Fate and work (album-catalog for the centenary of his birth)] (Informacionno-izdatel'skij centr "Simvol-T," 2002); Boris L.

Erofalov-Pilipchak, *Architektura sovetskogo Kieva* [The architecture of Soviet Kyiv] (Izdatel'skij dom A+S, 2010), 441–63; Andrei Puchkov, "Kievskiy arkhitektor Iosif Karakis: K voprosu o kovke mastera v tigljach sovetskoj epochi" [The Kyiv architect Josyp Karakis: On the work of a master in the forges of the Soviet era], *MIST: Mystectvo, istoriya, suchasnist', teoriya*, no. 9 (2013): 176–209; Oleg Yunakov, *Arkhitektor Iosif Karakis: Zhizn', tvorchestvo i sud'ba* [The architect Josyp Karakis: Life, work and fate] (Almaz, 2016), and the site dedicated to his work: http://karakys.narod.ru/.

21. Recollection of Tamara V. Ustenko on the occasion of an exhibition for the ninetieth anniversary of the birth of Yu. J. Karakis, reported by Puchkov, "Kievskiy arkhitektor Iosif Karakis," 186; Yunakov, *Arkhitektor Iosif Karakis*, 274–75. Among those pushing for the petition was the student Mikhail P. Budilovsky, also of Jewish origin, who later participated in the 1965 competition with a project together with A. Miletsky, V. Rybachuk, and V. Melnychenko. The reaction of part of the student body confirms the division produced in academic circles by the campaign against "cosmopolitanism." See Benjamin Tromly, *Making the Soviet Intelligentsia: Universities and Intellectual Life Under Stalin and Khrushchev* (Cambridge University Press, 2014), 80.

22. I use the summary of the three project variants in http://karakys.narod.ru/Virtual/60/ListVirtual60.html.

23. Zhovnerovskij, "Konkurs na pamjatnik," 105–6.

24. Tatiana Evstafeva, "K istorii ustanovleniya pamjatnika v Bab'em Jaru" [On the history of the installation of a monument at Babi Yar], *Evrejskij obozrevatel'*, 5 June 2002, http://www.jewukr.org/observer/jo11_30/p0102_r.html. See also Avraam Miletsky, "Skorbota, tysha i pam'jat'" [Grief, silence, and memory], *Arkhitektura Ukraïny*, no. 1 (1993): 42; Miletsky, *Naplyvy pamjati* [Memory dissolves] (Filobiblon, 1998).

25. See Ada F. Rybachuk and Volodymyr V. Melnychenko, *"Kogda rushitsja mir . . .": Kniga-rekviem, kniga- pamjatnik* ["When the world collapses . . .": Requiem book, memorial book] (Jurinform, 1991), 11; Karl Kantor, "Der steinerne Kranz der Qualen: Ein Denkmal für Babi Yar," *Via Regia—Kulturstrasse des Europarates*, no. 15 (1994), http://www.via-regia.org/bibliothek/pdf/heft15/kantor_babijjar.pdf.

26. Shteinberg, "Dokumenty zabytoj pamjati."

27. Interview with Anatoly F. Ignashchenko (former student of Joseph Yu. Karakis) conducted by Vladimir Platonov, "Babiy Jar: Tragediya o tragedii" [Babi Yar: A tragedy about the tragedy], *Zerkalo nedeli*, 27 September 1997.

28. Document signed by the president of the jury and vice chairman of the Council of Ministers of the USSR, Sergey N. Andrianov, 17 February 1966, in Shteinberg, "Dokumenty zabytoj pamjati." It appears that there were three projects that explicitly referred to the extermination of the Jews (Naiman, "Babiy Jar").

29. The jury chose a project representing a figure with a flag, the work of architects Aleksandr Ya. Shteinberg and Yuri A. Paskevych and sculptors Inna A. Kolomiyets and Georgy Ya. Khusid, but the work was not realized (Shteinberg, "Dokumenty zabytoj pamjati").

30. Ion Degen, "Viktor Platonovich Nekrasov: Gl. iz kn. 'Portrety uchitelej'" [Viktor Platonovich Nekrasov: Chapter from the book *Portraits of teachers*], *Raduga*, no. 5–6 (2005): 110. See also Degen, *Portrety uchitelej* [Portraits of teachers] (Tip. Rama-Press, 1992), 194–213. Nekrasov's reference was to the monumental sculptor Yevgeny V.

Vuchetich, author at that time (1959–67) of the allegorical statue *The Motherland Calls!* for the memorial dedicated to the heroes of the Battle of Stalingrad.

31. Lazar Lazarev, "Iz ognja . . . : O Viktore Nekrasove" [From the fire . . . : About Viktor Nekrasov], in *Shestoj etazh, ili perebiraja nashi daty* [The sixth floor, or reexamining our anniversaries] (Knizhnyj Sad, 1999), 187; Lazarev, *Zapiski pozhilogo cheloveka: Kniga vospominaniy* [Reflections of an elderly man: Book of memories] (Vremja, 2005), 45.

32. Letter to Aleksandr M. Grossman, 28 May 1966, in *"Byli by vokrug tebja gorod i ljudi . . ."*: *Pis'ma Viktora Nekrasova* ["If only there were a city and people around you . . .": Letters of Viktor Nekrasov], ed. Tatiana A. Rogozovskaya, *Egupec*, no. 20 (2011): 297.

33. Viktor Nekrasov, "Slova 'velikie' i prostye" [Words "great" and simple], *Iskusstvo kino*, no. 5 (1959): 55–61; Nekrasov, *Sochineniya* [Works] (Knizhnaja Palata, 2002), 1121–26. It was a reflection on the recent films *Poema o more* [Poem of the sea] (1958) by Aleksandr Dovzhenko (actually made by his wife, Yuliya I. Solntseva, based on a screenplay by the recently deceased director) and *Dva fёdora* [The two fedoras] (1958) by Marlen M. Khutsiev. Nekrasov explicitly criticized the former for its lack of verisimilitude in response to the support of Dovzhenko's monumentalistic principle as expressed by Yakov L. Varshavsky, "Dusha geroja" [The hero's soul], *Iskusstvo kino*, no. 11 (1958): 23–24. For the broader ensuing debate, see Les Tanyuk, "Viktor Nekrasov i Ukraïna" [Viktor Nekrasov and Ukraine], in *Izhoj*, 151–54, 156–57.

34. I use Viktor Nekrasov, "Slova 'velikie' i prostye," 1121–22. Stanislavski's influence is also emphasized in Yakov L. Varshavsky's reply, "Nado razobrat'sja" [We need to understand], *Iskusstvo kino*, no. 5 (1959): 61–65, centered on the accusation of "microrealism." See also a portrait of K. S. Stanislavsky in Viktor Nekrasov, "V zhizni i v pis'mach: Vospominaniya" [In life and letters: Memories], *Novyj mir*, no. 9 (1969): 110–17; and Nekrasov, *V zhizni i v pis'mach: Memuarnye ocherki* [In life and letters: Memoirs] (Sovetskij Pisatel', 1971), 126–38.

35. Viktor Nekrasov, *Front-Line Stalingrad*, trans. David Floyd (Harvill, 1962).

36. Tanyuk, "Viktor Nekrasov i Ukraïna," 149–50.

37. Konstantin S. Stanislavsky, "Rabota aktёra nad soboj" [The actor's work on himself], in Stanislavsky, *Sobranie sochineniy v devjati tomach* [Collected works in nine volumes] (Iskusstvo, 1989), 2/1:236–37, 266; Italian translation, *Il lavoro dell'attore su se stesso* [The actor's work on himself] (Laterza, 1996), 142–43, 163, ellipsis added.

38. Viktor Nekrasov, *V okopach Stalingrada* [In the trenches of Stalingrad] (Sovetskij Pisatel', 1947); Italian translation, *Nelle trincee di Stalingrado* [In the trenches of Stalingrad] (Mondadori, 1964), 106.

39. Nekrasov, "Slova 'velikie' i prostye," 1122–23.

40. Nekrasov, "Slova 'velikie' i prostye," 1126. To the readers of the article, published in the most respected Soviet film magazine of the time, Nekrasov's reference to the now proverbial maxim of Dovzhenko was clear: "Eliminate all the copper truths. Preserve only the pure gold of truth." See Aleksandr Dovzhenko, "Slovo v scenarii chudozhestvennogo fil'ma" [The word in the art film script], in *Voprosy kinodramaturgii* [Questions of cinematic dramaturgy] (Iskusstvo, 1954), 1:5–25; Dovzhenko, *Izbrannoe* [Selected works] (Iskusstvo, 1957), 586–605.

41. After a number of modifications, the film obtained censorship approval but with limited distribution. See *Apparat CK KPSS i kul'tura, 1953–1957: Dokumenty* [The apparatus of the Central Committee of the CPSU and culture, 1953–1957: Documents] (Rosspen, 2001), doc. 147, pp. 548–49, doc. 152, pp. 562–63, doc. 161, p. 600.

42. Suffice it to consider the general ostracism of the theme of disability (anatomical and physiological, but especially psychological). See Vera Dunham, "Images of the Disabled, Especially the War Wounded," in *The Disabled in the Soviet Union: Past and Present, Theory and Practice*, ed. William O. McCagg and Lewis H. Siegelbaum (University of Pittsburgh Press, 1989), 151–64; Beate Fieseler, "The Bitter Legacy of the 'Great Patriotic War': Red Army Disabled Soldiers Under Late Stalinism," in *Late Stalinist Russia: Society Between Reconstruction and Reinvention*, ed. Juliane Fürst (Routledge, 2006), 46–61; Fieseler, "Soviet-Style Welfare: The Disabled Soldiers of the 'Great Patriotic War,'" in *Disability in Eastern Europe and the Former Soviet Union: History, Policy and Everyday Life*, ed. Michael Rasell and Elena R. Iarskaia-Smirnova (Routledge, 2014), 18–41; Elena Iarskaia-Smirnova and Pavel Romanov, "Heroes and Spongers: The Iconography of Disability in Soviet Poster and Film," in Rasell and Iarskaia-Smirnova, *Disability in Eastern Europe*, 67–96.

43. Viktor Nekrasov, "Listki iz bloknota: Zametki" [Notebook leaves: Notes], *Yunost*, no. 6 (1961): 62–63.

44. Nekrasov, "Listki iz bloknota," 64–65.

45. Viktor Nekrasov, "O proshlom, nastojashchem i chut'-chut' o budushchem: Zametki ob architecture" [On the past, the present, and a little about the future: Notes on architecture], *Literaturnaya gazeta*, 20 February 1960, 1–2. Nekrasov's reference is, quite clearly, to Le Corbusier, *Vers une architecture* [Toward an architecture] (Crès, 1923), 16; Italian translation, *Verso un'architettura* [Toward an architecture] (Longanesi, 1984).

46. Viktor Nekrasov, *Pervoe znakomstvo: Iz zarubezhnych vpechatleniy* [First acquaintance: Impressions from abroad] (Sovetskij Pisatel', 1960), 104 (with a brief profile of Le Corbusier); Italian translation: *Sovietico in Italia* (Vallecchi, 1960), 76. The writer has returned on several occasions to the influence of and correspondence and meeting with Le Corbusier, "idol" of his youth. See Viktor Nekrasov, "Mesjac vo Francii" [A month in France], *Novyj mir*, no. 4 (1965): 102–63; Nekrasov, "Le Korbjuz'e" [Le Corbusier], in *V zhizni i v pis'mach: Memuarnye ocherki*, 139–48.

47. Nekrasov, "O proshlom," 2.

48. Nekrasov, "Novye pamjatniki," 23–27. A significant part of the article is reproduced, with slight modifications and some cuts, in Nekrasov, "Zapiski zevaki," 78–81.

49. Nekrasov, "Novye pamjatniki," 23, 25.

50. Stanislavski, "Rabota aktëra nad soboj," 2/1:239–41; Italian translation, 144–45.

51. Nekrasov, "Novye pamjatniki," 25.

52. Nekrasov, "Novye pamjatniki," 25–26. For the development of Nekrasov's reflection on the notion of "tragedy," his notes on the meeting with Pier Paolo Pasolini during his trip to Italy in March 1962 are very important. See Viktor Nekrasov, "Po obe storony okeana" [On both sides of the ocean], *Novyj mir*, no. 11 (1962): 127–29; Italian translation, *Di qua e di là dall'oceano* [On both sides of the ocean] (Mondadori, 1965), 50–54. On relations with the Italian cultural world, see Marco Sabbatini, *Viktor Nekrasov e l'Italia: Uno scrittore sovietico nel dibattito culturale degli anni Cinquanta*

[Viktor Nekrasov and Italy: A Soviet writer in the cultural debate of the 1950s] (Universitas Studiorum, 2018).

53. Nekrasov, "Novye pamjatniki," 26.

54. Nekrasov, "Novye pamjatniki," 26.

55. Nekrasov, "Novye pamjatniki," 26–27.

56. Stanislavski, "Rabota aktëra nad soboj," 2/1:242; Italian translation, 146–47.

57. Nekrasov, "Novye pamjatniki," 27, ellipsis added.

58. Stanislavski, "Rabota aktëra nad soboj," 2/1:266; Italian translation, 163.

Chapter 6. Claiming the Place

1. "Podrazhaniye 11 Psalmu" [Imitation of Psalm 11] (15 February 1859), *Osnova*, no. 10 (1861): 1.

2. "Znyshchennja vitrazhu T. Shevchenka v Kyïvs'komu Universyteti" [The destruction of the T. Shevchenko stained glass at Kyiv University], *Suchasnist'* (Munich) 6, no. 54 (1965): 104–7.

3. See Lyudmila M. Alexeyeva, *Istoriya inakomysliya v SSSR: Novejshiy period* [The history of dissent in the USSR: The modern period] (Vest', 1992), 12–21; Georgiy V. Kasianov, *Nezhodni: Ukraïns'ka intelihenciya v rusi oporu 1960–80-ch rokiv* [Dissenters: The Ukrainian intelligentsia in the resistance movement of the 1960s–1980s] (Lybid', 1995), 12–31; Serhy Yekelchyk, *Ukraine: Birth of a Modern Nation* (Oxford University Press, 2007), 163–69; Yekelchyk, "The Early 1960s as a Cultural Space: A Microhistory of Ukraine's Generation of Cultural Rebels," *Nationalities Papers* 43, no. 2 (2015): 45–62; Benjamin Tromly, "An Unlikely National Revival: Soviet Higher Learning and the Ukrainian 'Sixtiers,'" *Russian Review* 68, no. 4 (2009): 607–22; Simone A. Bellezza, "The 'Shistdesiatnytstvo' as a Group of Friends: The 'Kompaniia' of the Club of the Creative Youth of Kyiv (1960–1965)," *Snodi: Pubblici e privati nella storia contemporanea*, no. 5 (2010): 64–82; Bellezza, *The Shore of Expectations: A Cultural Study of the Shistdesiatnyky* (University of Alberta Press, 2021).

4. Kasianov, *Nezhodni*, 20. Starting on 29 July 1958, spontaneous and unauthorized gatherings of young people had begun in Moscow near the monument to Vladimir V. Mayakovsky, on Majakovka, to read verses or conduct informal debates. See Lyudmila V. Polikovskaya, *"My—predchustvie . . . predtecha . . .": Ploshchad' Majakovskogo 1958–1965* ["We—premonition . . . prelude . . .": Mayakovsky Square, 1958–1965] (Zven'ja, 1997).

5. For example, on 22 May 1964 the gathering aimed to protest the ban on celebrating the anniversary of the poet's funeral.

6. Israel Kleiner, "The Jewish Question and Ukrainian-Jewish Relations in Ukrainian 'Samizdat,'" in *Ukrainian-Jewish Relations in Historical Perspective*, ed. Peter J. Potichnyj and Howard Aster (Canadian Institute of Ukrainian Studies Press, 1990), 421–36; Yohanan Petrovsky-Shtern, *Reconceptualizing the Alien: Jews in Modern Ukrainian Thought*, Ab imperio 4 (2003): 556–76.

7. In 1941 Yom Kippur fell on 1 October.

8. Emmanuel (Amik) Diamant, "Babiy Jar, ili Pamjat' o tom, kak v narod prevrashchalos' stroptivoe plemja" [Babi Yar, or memory of how a stubborn generation turned into a people], *My zdes'*, 15–21 September 2011, http://www.kby.kiev.ua/komitet/ru/history/art00065.html. The role of Amik Diamant in organizing the gathering was

recalled by V. Nekrasov on the occasion of the thirty-fifth anniversary of the massacre, which he celebrated in Israel together with Diamant: Viktor Nekrasov, "Vzgljad i nechto: Chast' vtoraja (okonchanie)" [A look and something: Part two (end)], *Kontinent*, no. 13 (1977): 58; and emphasized by Rafaïl Nachmanovych in "Babiy Jar—1966: Kak eto bylo" [Babi Yar—1966: How it was], *Obozrevatel'*, 29 September 2009, http://kiyany.obozrevatel.com/news/2006/9/28/22982.htm (interview conducted by Konstantin Gedz).

9. Ivan M. Dziuba (1931–2022), writer and literary critic, had previously been threatened with expulsion from the Union of Ukrainian Writers in 1962 for his "wrong political views." *Internacionalizm chy rusyfikaciya* was initially published in a very limited print run and distributed only among party organization staff. As soon as it was withdrawn from circulation, it entered the realm of samizdat. The first edition printed abroad, in Munich (Suchasnist', 1968; extracts also in *Suchasnist'* [Munich] 2, no. 86 [1968]: 61–87, and 4, no. 88 [1968]: 63–77) was followed by numerous translations (Italian translation, *L'oppressione delle nazionalità in URSS* [The oppression of nationalities in the USSR] [La nuova sinistra, 1971]).

10. Leonid Pljušč, *Na karnavale istorii* [At the carnival of history] (Overseas Publications Interchange, 1979), 195–96; Italian translation, *Nel carnevale della storia: Memorie* [In the carnival of history: Memoirs] (Mondadori, 1978), 190–91. Leonid Ivanovich Pliusch (1938–2015), mathematician, writer, and member of the Initiative Group for the Defense of Human Rights in the USSR, was arrested in January 1972 on charges of anti-Soviet activities and in January 1973 was sentenced to confinement in a psychiatric hospital for the "social danger" of his actions. He was released in December 1975 following international mobilization and emigrated with his family.

11. The "doctors' plot" was a conspiracy theory that predominantly Jewish medical professionals planned to murder leading communist party and govementment officials.

12. Ivan Dziuba, "To, chto vzyvaet k sovesti" [What appeals to conscience], *Evrejskij obozrevatel'*, 24 October 2006, 6–7, http://www.jewukr.org/observer/eo2003/page_show_ru.php?id=1756.

13. Svyatoslav Josypovych Karavansky (1920–2016), poet and translator, was sentenced to twenty-five years at forced labor in 1944. Amnestied after seventeen years spent in camps in the Arctic region, he returned to Odessa, his hometown, but in 1965 he was again arrested and sent without trial to a camp in Mordovia to serve the remainder of his first sentence. The petition written in prison circulated in clandestine form before being published in the West: Svyatoslav Y. Karavansky, "To the Council of Nationalities of the USSR," *New Leader*, 15 January 1968, 12–15; repr., *Ukrainian Quarterly* 24, no. 2 (1968): 108–16.

14. Karavansky, "To the Council," *Ukrainian Quarterly*, 109.

15. Ivan Dziuba, "Ne sdavshiysja lzhi" [Not yielding to lies], in *O Viktore Nekrasove: Vospominaniya (Chelovek, voin, pisatel')* [Recollections of Viktor Nekrasov (man, warrior, writer)] (Ukraïns'kyj Pys'mennyk, 1992), 92–93; first published in *Raduga*, no. 2 (1990): 106–16.

16. Vladimir N. Voinovich, *Avtoportret: Roman moej zhizni* [Self-portrait: Novel of my life] (Eksmo, 2010), 600–601.

17. Testimony of Gely Snegiryov, *Roman-donos* [Denunciation novel] (Duch i Litera, 2000), 119.

18. Viktor Nekrasov, "Gorodskie progulki" [City walks], *Yunost*, no. 7 (1988): 22. On several occasions, the writer recalled having opened his speech with words from Anatoly V. Lunacharsky, *Ob antisemitizme* [On antisemitism] (Gosudarstvennoe Izdatel'stvo, 1929), a volume that had been given to him many years earlier by the author himself. See, for example, Viktor Nekrasov, "Lunacharskiy," in *V zhizni i v pis'mach: Memuarnye ocherki* [In life and letters: Memoirs] (Sovetskij Pisatel', 1971), 96; Nekrasov, "Vzgljad i nechto," 63; Nekrasov, "On opjat' podnimaet golovu (Ob anti-semitizme)" [Again raises his head (on antisemitism)], *Novoe russkoe slovo*, 18 January 1985.

19. Ion Degen, "Viktor Platonovich Nekrasov: Gl. iz kn. 'Portrety uchitelej'" [Viktor Platonovich Nekrasov: Chapter from the book *Portraits of teachers*], *Raduga*, no. 5–6 (2005): 110. Aleksandr Parnis also recalled "an astonishing quiet, the painful silence of a huge crowd" ("Viktor Nekrasov i Babiy Jar" [Viktor Nekrasov and Babi Yar], *Alef*, 24 July 2007, http://www.alefmagazine.com/pub448.html). See also Parnis, *Viktor Nekrasov: Do i posle . . .* [Viktor Nekrasov: Before and after . . .], in *Viktor Nekrasov: Vozvrashchenie v Dom Turbinych* [Viktor Nekrasov: Return to the house of the Turbins], ed. Tatiana A. Rogozovskaya (Feniks, 2004), 9.

20. Pljušč, *Na karnavale istorii*, 196, 197–98; Italian translation, 191–92.

21. Zachariy Belotserkovskiy, "Dissident Lënja" [The dissident Lënja], *Boruch: Elektronnyj al'manach*, 15 October 2015, http://boruh.info/tvorchestvo/proza/115-dissident-ljonya (the text erroneously refers to the date of 29 September 1971).

22. See Snegiryov, *Roman-donos*, 119; Anatoly [Anatoly Kuznetsov], *Babiy Jar: Roman-dokument* [Babi Yar: Documentary novel] (Posev, 1970), 482; Italian translation, *Babiy Jar: Romanzo-documento* (Adelphi, 2019), 452.

23. I use Ivan Dziuba, "U 25-ti rokovyny rozstriliv u Babynomu Jaru" [On the twenty-fifth anniversary of the executions in Babi Yar], *Suchasnist'* (Munich) 11, no. 83 (1967): 32–35, reproduced from *Ukraïns'ke slovo*, 8 October 1967, then *Egupec*, no. 1 (1995): 4–8, and in Dziuba, "To, chto vzyvaet k sovesti." See Ivan Dzyuba, "On the Twenty-Fifth Anniversary of the Murders in Baby Yar," *Polin: Studies in Polish Jewry* 26 (2014): 381–89.

24. Yuri I. Shapoval, "Sprava Ivana Dziuba" [The case of Ivan Dziuba], *Z archiviv VUChK-GPU-NKVD-KGB* 1, no. 36 (2011): 259–60.

25. Viktor Nekrasov, "Kamen' v Bab'em Jaru" [A stone at Babi Yar], in *Izhoj: Viktor Nekrasov u spohadach suchasnykiv* [Rebel: Viktor Nekrasov in the memories of contemporaries] (Duch i Litera, 2014), 198; Nekrasov, *Arestovannye stranicy: Rasskazy, interv'ju, pis'ma iz archiva KGB* [Seized pages: Stories, interviews, letters from the KGB archive], ed. Lyubov' Chazan (Laurus, 2014), 187. Large fragments of Dziuba's speech are reported in Nekrasov, "Zapiski zevaki" [Reflections of a wanderer], *Kontinent*, no. 4 (1975): 77–78.

26. Viktor Nekrasov, "Ivan Dziuba, kakim ja ego znaju" [Ivan Dziuba as I know him] (1974), in *Sochineniya* [Works] (Knizhnaja Palata, 2002), 1131.

27. Dziuba, "U 25-ti rokovyny rozstriliv," 32.

28. Dziuba, "U 25-ti rokovyny rozstriliv," 33. In the version of the speech published in 1967, which we use, there was at this point a reference that would be removed in later versions: "It seems that Lenin's directives on the fight against antisemitism have

been forgotten, just as those on the national development of Ukraine have been forgotten."

29. Dziuba, "U 25-ti rokovyny rozstriliv," 33–34.

30. Dziuba, "U 25-ti rokovyny rozstriliv," 34–35. In the 1967 published version, Dziuba also referred, naively and with the scantiest understanding of political reality, to the example of coexistence that had been achieved in neighboring socialist Poland between Poles and Jews.

31. Dziuba, "U 25-ti rokovyny rozstriliv," 35.

32. Circulation in the West was facilitated by its inclusion as a supplement in *Lycho z rozumu (portrety dvadcjaty "zlochynciv"): Zbirnyk materialiv* [What a misfortune to have sense! (portraits of twenty "criminals"): Collection of materials], comp. Vyacheslav Chornovil (First Ukrainian Print Shop in France, 1967), 307–12; Vyacheslav Chornovil, ed., *The Chornovil Papers* (McGraw-Hill, 1968), 222–26; then in Abraham Brumberg, ed., *Quest of Justice: Protest and Dissent in the Soviet Union Today* (Praeger, 1970), 200–204. Concerning the phenomenon of samizdat in Ukraine and, more specifically, on the circulation of Dziuba's essay, see Oleh Bazhan, "'Samvydav' jak zasib poshireniya ob'jektyvnoj informaciï v 60–80 rokach" [The *samvydav* as a means of spreading objective information in the 1960s–1980s], *Z archiviv VUChK-GPU-NKVD-KGB* 1–2, no. 6–7 (1998): 357–64; Oles Obertas, *Ukraïns'kyj samvydav: Literaturna krytyka ta publicystyka (1960-i-pochatok 1970-ch rokiv)* [Ukrainian *samvydav*: Literary criticism and journalism (1960s–early 1970s)] (Smoloskyp, 2010), 111–17 (particularly on "oral *samvydav*").

33. Nekrasov, "Kamen' v Bab'em Jaru," 197; Nekrasov, *Arestovannye stranicy*, 186. See also Nekrasov, "Ivan Dziuba, kakim ja ego znaju," 1131.

34. Published in *Egupec*, no. 1 (1995): 9–10, and reprinted in Dziuba, "To, chto vzyvaet k sovesti," emphasis added. The document should be considered within the context of the final phase of the repressions of Dziuba's activities: on 2 March 1972 he was unanimously expelled from the Union of Ukrainian Writers for violating its statutes and contributing to the preparation and dissemination of material with a high nationalistic content; on 18 April of that same year, he was arrested. Tried between 11 and 16 March 1973, he was sentenced to five years of forced labor and five years of exile under article 62 of the penal code of the Ukrainian Soviet Socialist Republic ("anti-Soviet agitation and propaganda"). He was released after a public letter renouncing his "previous erroneous opinions" (Ivan Dziuba, "Do redakciï gazety 'Literaturna Ukraïna': Zajava" [To the editorial office of the newspaper *Literaturna Ukraïna*: Statement], *Literaturna Ukraïna*, 9 November 1973, 4). The retraction provoked negative reactions in dissident circles. V. P. Nekrasov, however, defended Dziuba and continued to support his loyalty. See Nekrasov, "Ivan Dziuba, kakim ja ego znaju," 1126–31; and Nekrasov, *Arestovannye stranicy*, 194–206. The text was written in 1974 but remained unpublished until the early 1990s because it had been confiscated by the security services. It later appeared in *Voprosy literatury*, no. 2 (1993): 301–11, accompanied by Ivan Dziuba, "Vmesto poslesloviya: Znal takim, kakim chotel videt'" [Instead of an afterword: I knew what I wanted to see], 312–14. See Alexeyeva, *Istoriya inakomysliya v SSSR*, 14–15, 17, 20, 25; Kasianov, *Nezhodni*, 23–27, 96–104, 129–32; Shapoval, "Sprava Ivana Dziuba," 259–94.

35. See the recollections of Rafaïl A. Nachmanovych in "Babiy Jar—1966." Eduard L. Timlin managed to preserve some frames showing Nekrasov that were later used in the documentary film by R. Nachmanovych, *Viktor Nekrasov na svobodi i doma* [Viktor Nekrasov at liberty and at home] (1991) and other works. Director and documentary filmmaker Rafaïl A. Nachmanovych (1927–2009) joined Ukrkinochronika in Kyiv in 1954 and worked there until 1997. He shot over sixty documentaries, some of which were destroyed or banned from public viewing. On several occasions, he was suspended from authorization to film. He had met Nekrasov in 1946 in the context of the activities of the magazine *Radjans'ke mystectvo*. He made three documentary films based on screenplays by the writer: *Neizvestnomu soldatu* [To the unknown soldier] (1961), *Syn soldata* [The soldier's son] (1962), and *Zhil chelovek . . .* [There was a man . . .] (1964). He is also the author of *Evrejskoe kladbishche* [The Jewish cemetery] (1989), the first documentary film on Jewish culture, religion, and identity in the USSR.

36. Concerning the fate of this material, see Diamant, "Babiy Jar, ili Pamjat' o tom."

37. Recollections of Nachmanovych in "Babiy Jar—1966"; Parnis, "Viktor Nekrasov i Babiy Jar."

38. Vladimir Khanin, ed., *Documents on Ukrainian Jewish Identity and Emigration, 1944–1990* (Frank Cass, 2003), doc. 39, p. 145. O. P. Botvyn's report was prepared based on some reports received the previous day that were published in Mikhail Mitsel, *Obshchiny iudejskogo veroispovedaniya v Ukraine (Kyiv, L'vov: 1945–1981 gg.)* [Jewish religious communities in Ukraine (Kyiv, L'vov: 1945–1981)] (Institut Iudaiki, 1998), 120–23.

39. Khanin, *Documents on Ukrainian Jewish Identity*, doc. 39, p. 146.

40. Protocol no. 31 of the meeting of the Kyiv City Committee of the Communist Party of Ukraine, 12 October 1966, in Lev Drobyazko, *Materialy o Viktore Nekrasove* [Materials on Viktor Nekrasov], http://aej.org.ua/History/634.html; *Izhoj*, 179–80, ellipses added.

41. Rafaïl Nachmanovych, *Vozvrashchenie v sistemu koordinat, ili Martirolog meteka* [Return to the coordinate system, or the Martyrology of the metic] (Feniks, 2013), 49–50; Gely Snegiryov, *Avtoportret-66* [Self-portrait-66] (Duch i Litera, 2001), 83–88.

42. The speech is reported in full in Snegiryov, *Roman-donos*, 114–21. *Roman-donos* is an original novel verité, published posthumously, in which the author describes events and protagonists of the Kyiv dissent movement, interspersing the narrative with documents of various kinds (letters, stenograms and minutes of party meetings, drawings, etc.). Seized by the KGB, it came to light only in the 1990s. Gely Ivanovych Snegiryov (1927–78), director and set designer at Ukrkinochronika, became known as a writer with the publication of the story "Rodi mne tri syna" [Give me three sons], *Novyj mir*, no. 6 (1967): 122–30. Later, after learning that his mother had once been close to Ukrainian nationalist youth organizations, he conducted an investigation into the events that led to the 1930 show trial of the so-called Spilka Vyzvolennja Ukraïny (Union for the Liberation of Ukraine): "Mama moja, mama . . . Liriko-publicisticheskoe issledovanie" [My mother, my mother . . . A lyrical-journalistic investigation], *Kontinent*, no. 11 (1977): 11–53; no. 12 (1977): 163–209; no. 13 (1977): 173–203; no. 14 (1977): 152–92; no. 15 (1978): 90–122. He published in the dissident press and abroad until his

arrest on 22 September 1977. This was followed by a public retraction, weighed down by the writer's serious health conditions, including blindness and partial paralysis. See Gely Snegiryov, "Soromljus' i zasudzhuju" [I am ashamed and condemn], *Radjans'ka Ukraïna*, 1 April 1978; Snegiryov, "Styzhus' i osuzhdaju . . ." [I am ashamed and condemn . . .], *Literaturnaya gazeta*, 12 April 1978, 9. He died in the hospital on 28 December 1978. His prison memoirs were published posthumously with a preface by V. P. Nekrasov and an editorial title: Gely Snegiryov, "Kak na duchu . . ." [Without hiding anything . . .], *Kontinent*, no. 21 (1979): 89–145. See also Viktor Nekrasov, "Po obe storony Steny: Chast' pervaja" [On both sides of the wall: Part one], *Kontinent*, no. 18 (1978): 108–13.

43. Snegiryov, *Roman-donos*, 117.

44. Nekrasov, "Kamen' v Bab'em Jaru," 199; Nekrasov, *Arestovannye stranicy*, 188. See also Nekrasov, "Zapiski zevaki," 78.

45. The declaration is reported in Snegiryov, *Roman-donos*, 119–20. Nekrasov also recalled that he had not prepared a speech for the occasion and that the words came out spontaneously "among those who were crying and sobbing" ("Zapiski zevaki," 76).

46. Efim Etkind, "Pravda Viktora Nekrasova" [The truth of Viktor Nekrasov], *Vremja i my*, no. 109 (1990): 218.

47. Nekrasov, "Zapiski zevaki," 78.

48. Nahum Korzhavin, "Psichologiya sovremennego entuziazma" [Psychology of contemporary enthusiasm], *Kontinent*, no. 9 (1976): 125.

49. Korzhavin, "Psichologiya," 140, ellipsis added. N. Korzhavin's reference was particularly to the antisemitic work of Ivan M. Shevtsov already mentioned.

50. Resolution no. 1537 of the Kyiv City Committee of the Communist Party of Ukraine and the Executive Committee of the City Soviet of Workers' Deputies, 20 October 1966, DAK, f. R-1, op. 8, spr. 535, ark. 80. See Tatiana Evstafeva, "Babiy Jar: Poslevoennaja istoriya mestnosti" [Babi Yar: Postwar history of the site], in *Babyn Jar: Masove ubyvstvo i pam'jat' pro n'oho: Materialy mizhnarodnoï naukovoï konferencii 24–25 zhovtnja 2011 r., m. Kyïv* [Babi Yar: Mass murder and memory of it: Proceedings of the International Scientific Conference, Kyiv, 24–25 October 2011], ed. Mykhailo Tyahlyi and Vitaly Nachmanovych (Ukraïns'kyj centr vyvchennja istorii Holokostu, Hromads'kyj komitet dlja vshanuvannja pam'jati zhertv Babynoho Jaru, 2012), 27.

51. Shmuel Spector and M. Kipnis, eds., *Babiy Jar: K pjatidesjatiletiyu tragedii 29–30 sentjabrja 1941 goda* [Babi Yar: On the fiftieth anniversary of the tragedy of 29–30 September 1941] (Biblioteka-Alija, 1991), 184; "Iz pisem," in *Babiy Jar*, ed. Efrem Baukh (Izdanie Sojuza zemljachestv-vychodcev iz SSSR, 1981), 64.

52. Ilya Ehrenburg to Solomon K. Rozenblat, 16 December 1966, in *"Na cokole istorii . . .": Pis'ma 1931–1967* ["At the base of history . . .": Letters 1931–1967], ed. Boris Ya. Frezinskiy (Agraf, 2004), 605–6.

53. Kuznetsov, *Babiy Jar*, 483; Italian translation, 453.

54. Vladimir Khanin, "Judaism and Organized Jewish Movements in the USSR/CIS After World War II: The Ukrainian Case," *Jewish Political Studies Review* 11, no. 1–2 (1999): 85. Concerning the Jewish nationalist movement in Ukraine, see Oleh H. Bazhan and Yuri Z. Danylyuk, *Opozyciya v Ukraïni (druha polovyna 50-ch-80-ti rr. XX st.)* [Opposition in Ukraine (second half of the 1950s–1980s of the twentieth century)] (Ridnyj Kraj, 2000), 353–85; Bazhan, "Represyvni zachody radjans'koï vlady shchodo

hromadjan jevrejs'koï nacional'nosti v URSR (1960-ti-1980-ti rr.)" [Repressive measures by the Soviet authorities against citizens of Jewish nationality in the USSR (1960s–1980s)], *Z archiviv VUChK-GPU-NKVD-KGB* 1–2, no. 22–23 (2004): 112–20; Nati Cantorovich and Irena Cantorovich, "The Impact of the Holocaust and the State of Israel on Soviet Jewish Identity," in *The Jewish Movement in the Soviet Union*, ed. Yaacov Ro'i (Woodrow Wilson Center Press and Johns Hopkins University Press, 2012), 119–36.

55. The speeches delivered at official ceremonies were exemplary and therefore took on a repetitive and ritualistic character over time, as noted by Nekrasov: "The secretary . . . delivers a speech, largely devoted to the successes of his district regarding housing construction and the fulfillment of the plan in various sectors. Then some shock workers speak, and among them, obligatory it seems, there is one of Jewish nationality . . . who talks about Zionist atrocities in Israel. Then the national anthem is played, and the meeting is declared closed. At this point, those who bring bouquets and wreaths of flowers appear" ("Zapiski zevaki," 75, ellipses added). Starting from 22 May 1968, an annual official ceremony was also organized in front of the monument dedicated to Taras Shevchenko, with a large deployment of artists, amateur speakers, Komsomol members, military personnel, and other volunteers. See the brief reports on the 1968–69 demonstrations in *Chronika tekushchich sobytij*, 31 December 1968 and 30 June 1969.

56. The case of Boris L. Kochubievsky was publicized by *Chronika tekushchich sobytij*, 28 February 1969 and 30 June 1969. It thus gained immediate international resonance with extensive dissemination of the trial materials against the dissident. See Moshe Decter, ed., *A Hero for Our Time: The Trial and Fate of Boris Kochubiyevsky* (Academic Committee on Soviet Jewry, 1970); *Jews in Eastern Europe* 4, no. 3 (1970): 11–29; Peter Reddaway, ed., *Uncensored Russia: The Human Rights Movement in the Soviet Union* (Jonathan Cape, 1972), 301–6; Abram I. Rozhansky, ed., *Antievrejskie processy v Sovetskom Sojuze (1969–1971 gg.): Dokumenty i juridiceskiy kommentariy* [The trials against Jews in the Soviet Union (1969–1971): Documents and legal commentary] (Hebrew University of Jerusalem—Center for Research and Documentation of East European Jewry, 1979), 1:1–22.

57. Decter, *A Hero for Our Time*, 33–35; Rozhansky, *Antievrejskie processy*, 1–3. The text was found during a search and used as evidence in the subsequent trial against Kochubievsky.

58. *Chronika tekushchikh sobytiy*, 28 February 1969; Decter, *A Hero for Our Time*, 14–15; Rozhansky, *Antievrejskie processy*, 7–9.

59. Abraham J. Heschel, foreword to Decter, *A Hero for Our Time*, 3.

60. The letter is published in English and Russian in Decter, *A Hero for Our Time*, 13, 37. See also *Jews in Eastern Europe* 4, no. 2 (1969): 57–58; Rozhansky, *Antievrejskie processy*, 4–5.

61. Decter, *A Hero for Our Time*, 13, 37, ellipsis added.

62. Kochubievsky rejected all accusations and denied the falsity of his statements, asserting that even if some were found to be inaccurate, it was not due to deliberate falsehood, as he spoke convinced of the truth of his words. See *Chronika tekushchikh sobytiy*, 30 June 1969; Decter, *A Hero for Our Time*, 16; Rozhansky, *Antievrejskie processy*, 12.

63. Decter, *A Hero for Our Time*, 16, 19; Rozhansky, *Antievrejskie processy*, 10–11, 17–18; Pljušč, *Na karnavale istorii*, 261, 287–88; Italian translation, 256–57, 277–79.

64. Decter, *A Hero for Our Time*, 19–20; Rozhansky, *Antievrejskie processy*, 11–12; Mikhail Mitsel, "Zapret na uvekovechenie pamjati kak sposob zamalchivaniya Cholokosta: Praktika KPU v otnoshenii Bab'ego Jara" [The ban on perpetuating memory as a method of silencing the Holocaust: The practice of the Communist Party of Ukraine regarding Babui Yar], *Holokost i Suchasnist'* 1, no. 2 (2007): 14.

65. Decter, *A Hero for Our Time*, 21; Rozhansky, *Antievrejskie processy*, 16–17.

66. Decter, *A Hero for Our Time*, 22; Rozhansky, *Antievrejskie processy*, 19.

67. Alexeyeva, *Istoriya inakomysliya v SSSR*, 115–33. See also Yaacov Ro'i, *The Struggle for Soviet Jewish Emigration, 1948–1967* (Cambridge University Press, 1991); Pauline Peretz, *Combat pour les Juifs soviétiques: Washington-Moscow-Jerusalem, 1953–1989* (Armand Colin, 2006); Stuart Altshuler, *From Exodus to Freedom: A History of the Soviet Jewry Movement* (Rowman & Littlefield, 2005).

68. "Ob emigracii iz SSSR" [On emigration from the USSR], in *Dokumenty Moskovskoj Chel'sinkskoj gruppy, 1976–1982* [Documents of the Moscow Helsinki Group, 1976–1982], ed. Dmitri I. Zubarev and Gennady V. Kuzovkin (Moskovskaja Chel'sinkskaja Gruppa, 2006), doc. 91, p. 374. The document is dated 4 June 1979 and is signed by Elena G. Bonner, Sofia V. Kallistratova (Sofiya Kalistratova), Malva N. Landa, Viktor A. Nekipelov, Tatiana S. Osipova, and Yuri N. Yarym-Agaev.

69. Viktor Nekrasov, "Personal'noe delo kommunista Jufy" [The personal case of the Communist Jufa], *Vremja i my*, no. 5 (1976): 6. The *personal'noe delo* is, in the Soviet era, a hearing conducted by a party organization to take measures regarding the conduct of a member who has violated internal discipline or the criminal code.

70. Nekrasov, "Personal'noe delo kommunista Jufy," 8.

71. Nekrasov, "Personal'noe delo kommunista Jufy," 26–27, first ellipsis added.

72. Bazhan, "Represyvni zachody radjans'koï vlady," 114–15.

73. In the West, starting in the 1960s, the works of Solomon M. Schwarz, *Evrei v Sovetskom Sojuze s nachala vtoroj mirovoj vojny (1939–1965)* [Jews in the Soviet Union since the beginning of World War II (1939–1965)] (Amerikanskij evrejskij rabochij komitet, 1966), 359–71; William Korey, "The Forgotten Martyrs of Babi Yar," in *The Unredeemed: Anti-Semitism in the Soviet Union*, ed. Ronald I. Rubin (Quadrangle Books, 1968), 127–34; Korey, "Babi Yar Remembered," *Midstream* 15, no. 3 (1969): 24–39; Korey, "No Monument over Babi Yar," in *The Soviet Cage: Anti-Semitism in Russia* (Viking Press, 1973), 98–124; Korey, "Forty Years Ago at Babi Yar: Reliving the Crime," *Present Tense: The Magazine of World Jewish Affairs* 9, no. 1 (1981): 27–31; Korey, "A Monument over Babi Yar?," in *The Holocaust in the Soviet Union: Studies and Sources on the Destruction of the Jews in the Nazi-Occupied Territories of the USSR, 1941–1945*, ed. Lucjan Dobroszycki and Jeffrey S. Gurock (M. E. Sharpe, 1993), 61–74; Benjamin Pinkus, *The Soviet Government and the Jews, 1948–1967: A Documented Study* (Cambridge University Press, 1984), 96–99, 114–26, 435–38; and Nora Levin, *The Jews in the Soviet Union Since 1917: Paradox of Survival* (Tauris, 1990), 2:611–14, contributed to keeping the focus on Babi Yar.

74. Lucy Dawidowicz, "Babi Yar's Legacy," *New York Times Magazine*, 27 September 1981.

75. Baukh, *Babi Yar*, 113–14.

76. *Chronika tekushchikh sobytiy*, 31 October 1970; Alexeyeva, *Istoriya inakomysliya v SSSR*, 120.

77. *Chronika tekushchikh sobytiy*, 31 October 1970.

78. "Chto mozhno sdelat' iz dvukh treugol'nikov" [What can be done with two triangles], in Baukh, *Babi Yar*, 130. The fragment is taken from Izrail' Klejner, *Anekdoticheskaja tragediya* [An anecdotal tragedy] (Krug, 1978).

79. Pljušč, *Na karnavale istorii*, 343–44; Italian translation, 321–22 (which I modified). The dissident Plyushch, in reporting the dialogue, was well aware of the difference between the five-pointed star and the six-pointed star.

80. Pljušč, *Na karnavale istorii*, 344; Italian translation, 322. Some time later, Plyushch planned to publish a miscellany with Ivan Dziuba titled *Babiy Jar* on the contemporary antisemitism of the Communist Party, also drawing on materials on prerevolutionary anti-Judaism, but the project was not completed (Pljušč, *Na karnavale istorii*, 390; Italian translation, 360).

81. See the report of the first secretary of the Kiev City Committee, O. P. Botvyn, to the Central Committee of the Communist Party of Ukraine, 17 November 1969, in Khanin, *Documents on Ukrainian Jewish Identity*, doc. 47, pp. 176–78. See another report by O. P. Botvyn to the Central Committee, 16 September 1969, in Khanin, *Documents on Ukrainian Jewish Identity*, doc. 46, p. 176, which also announced "counterpropaganda" actions.

82. See the report of the first secretary of the Communist Party of Ukraine, P. Yu. Shelest, to the Central Committee of the CPSU, 11–12 March 1971, in Khanin, *Documents on Ukrainian Jewish Identity*, doc. 50, pp. 184–86.

83. Nekrasov, "Kamen' v Bab'em Jaru," 200; Nekrasov, *Arestovannye stranicy*, 189. The long quote is from Nekrasov, "Zapiski zevaki," 75.

84. Themes elaborated in all their facets by Vladimir V. Bol'shakov, *Sionizm na sluzhbe antikommunizma* [Zionism in the service of anti-Communism] (Politizdat, 1972), 23–45.

85. *Pravda*, 12 March 1970; Bol'shakov, *Sionizm na sluzhbe antikommunizma*, 39.

86. Letter to the *Daily Telegraph*, in "Kuznetsov Says Letter by Soviet Jews Implicating Zionism in Babi Yar Beyond Belief," *JTA Daily News Bulletin*, 27 March 1970.

87. Nekrasov, "Kamen' v Bab'em Jaru," 199–200; Nekrasov, *Arestovannye stranicy*, 189.

88. Concerning the preparations for the ceremony, see the report of the secretary of the Kiev Regional Committee, F. Rudych, to the Central Committee of the Communist Party of Ukraine, 23 August 1971, in Khanin, *Documents on Ukrainian Jewish Identity*, doc. 57, pp. 200–201.

89. Baukh, *Babi Yar*, 140; *Chronika tekushchikh sobytiy*, 10 November 1971; Alexeyeva, *Istoriya inakomysliya v SSSR*, 120. See also the personal testimony of the dissident Iosif Begun, "Zapret na pamjat' o Cholokoste" [The ban on remembering the Holocaust], in *Ten' Cholokosta: Materialy II mezhdunarodnogo simpoziuma "Uroki Cholokosta i sovremennaja Rossiya," Moskva 4–7 maja 1997 g.* [The shadow of the Holocaust: Proceedings of the Second International Symposium "The lessons of the Holocaust and contemporary Russia," Moscow, 4–7 May 1997], ed. Ilya A. Altman (Cholokost, 1998), 111.

90. Anatoly Feldman, "Evrejskoe nacional'noe dvizhenie v Kieve (mart–sentjabr' 1971 g.)" [The Jewish national movement in Kiev (March–September 1971)], *Egupec*, no. 16 (2006): 358–59. Feldman wrote his brief memoir in Vienna on 22 September 1971 while in transit to Israel.

91. Feldman, "Evrejskoe nacional'noe dvizhenie v Kieve," 360–61; *Chronika tekush-chikh sobytiy*, 11 September 1971; Yakov Ingerman, ed., *Evrei i evrejskiy narod: Peticii, pis'ma i obrasheniya evreev SSSR* [The Jews and the Jewish people: Petitions, letters, and appeals of Soviet Jews] (Hebrew University of Jerusalem—Center for Research and Documentation of East-European Jewry, 1974), 4:75–76. See also a report on "the plans of these Zionist elements" sent by Yuri V. Andropov to the Central Committee of the CPSU, 10 August 1971, in Boris Morozov, *Documents on Soviet Jewish Emigration* (Frank Cass, 1999), doc. 29, p. 119. Concerning the intensification of countermeasures by the security organs, the Ministry of Internal Affairs, and the prosecutor general in Ukraine, see Bazhan, "Represyvni zachody radjans'koï vlady," 115–16.

92. See the report of the secretary of the Kiev Regional Committee of the Communist Party, E. Litvinov, to the Central Committee of the Communist Party of Ukraine, 8 September 1972, in Khanin, *Documents on Ukrainian Jewish Identity*, doc. 71, p. 256.

93. *Chronika tekushchikh sobytiy*, 15 October 1972. On 11 April 1972 there was another unauthorized demonstration at Babi Yar that attracted the authorities' attention to commemorate the Warsaw Ghetto uprising. See the report by O. P. Botvyn to P. Yu. Shelest, 12 April 1972, and the related communication of the first secretary to the Central Committee of the CPSU, in Khanin, *Documents on Ukrainian Jewish Identity*, doc. 61, pp. 214–17.

94. Report by V. V. Shcherbytsky to the Central Committee of the Communist Party, October 1973, HDA SBU (Haluzevyi derzhavnyi arkhiv Sluzhby bezpeky Ukrainy, Sectoral State Archive of the Security Services of Ukraine), f. 16, spr. 1027, ark. 258–60.

95. Snegiryov, *Roman-donos*, 454 (diary note dated 21 May 1974). The allusion was to the vans used by the political police, often disguised as food transport trucks.

96. Report by O. P. Botvyn to the Central Committee of the Communist Party of Ukraine, 18 September 1974, in Khanin, *Documents on Ukrainian Jewish Identity*, doc. 77, p. 266.

97. Ingerman, *Evrei i evrejskiy narod*, 8:265.

98. See the aforementioned report by O. P. Botvyn to the Central Committee of the Communist Party of Ukraine, 18 September 1974, in Khanin, *Documents on Ukrainian Jewish Identity*, doc. 77, p. 266. On 26–27 September some initiatives (a television interview and the planned newspaper article) were indeed undertaken that mentioned the monument project (report by O. P. Botvyn himself, 30 September 1974, in Khanin, *Documents on Ukrainian Jewish Identity*, doc. 78, p. 267). The term *otkazniki* was already in use, albeit unofficially, to refer to those who had formally requested an emigration visa but had received a refusal (*otkaz*) from the authorities.

99. Report by V. V. Fedorchuk to V. V. Shcherbytsky, 21 September 1974, HDA SBU, f. 16, spr. 1037, ark. 77–80.

100. Viktor Nekrasov, "Komu eto nuzhno?" [Who needs this?], *Znamya*, no. 5 (1990): 17. This is an autobiographical text dated "Moscow, 5 March 1974." It circulated among Nekrasov's friends and was reported in Snegiryov, *Roman-donos*, 246–49.

It was first published by the emigration newspaper *Russkaja mysl'*, 11 April 1974, and broadcast by Radio Svoboda, gaining immediate resonance in dissent circles (*Chronika tekushchikh sobytiy*, 17 July 1974).

101. In Aleksandr Parnis, "Tragediya Bab'ego Jara: Ob odnoj nezakonchennoj knige Viktora Nekrasova" [The tragedy of Babi Yar: An unfinished book by Viktor Nekrasov], *Den'*, 28 September 2006, http://www.day.kiev.ua/ru/article/kultura/tragediya -babego-yara. Regarding those photographs, during an interview on 26 January Nekrasov explained: "The photographs, evidence of the state of the Jewish cemetery, were sent along with a cover letter from me . . . to the Central Committee of the Communist Party with an invitation to review them and take the necessary measures to restore order" (Nekrasov, *Arestovannye stranicy*, 139, ellipsis added).

102. Anna Berzer, "O Viktore Nekrasove" [About Viktor Nekrasov], *Druzhba narodov*, no. 5 (1989): 150.

103. Lazar Lazarev, "Vernost' pravde: Tvorcheskiy put' Viktora Nekrasova" [Loyalty to the truth: The creative path of Viktor Nekrasov], *Literatura*, no. 18 (2002): 5–9.

104. Nekrasov, "Zapiski zevaki," 104, ellipsis added. Concerning the effects these events had on Nekrasov's personality, see the recollections of Ananij Rochlin, "Pisatel' i vremja" [The writer and time], in Viktor Nekrasov, *V samych adskich kotlach pobyval . . . Sbornik povestej i rasskazov, vospominaniy i pisem* [I have been in the most hellish cauldrons . . . Collection of stories and tales, memories and letters] (Molodaya Gvardiya, 1991), 386–89.

105. Nekrasov, "Komu eto nuzhno?," 18–19. That photo album on Babi Yar and the ravaged Jewish cemetery, "now stored in the KGB archives," is still remembered in Nekrasov, "Vzgljad i nechto: Chast' vtoraja" [A look and a certain something: Part two], *Kontinent*, no. 12 (1977): 90.

106. The letter is published in Rogozovskaya, *Viktor Nekrasov*, 72–73; Les Tanyuk, "Viktor Nekrasov i Ukraïna" [Viktor Nekrasov and Ukraine], in *Izhoj*, 181–82; and reported in Snegiryov, *Roman-donos*, 456–57. The theme of voluntary exile is clearly present in Nekrasov, "Komu eto nuzhno?," 16.

107. In the essay "10 let vo Francii" [Ten years in France], *Novoe russkoe slovo*, 9– 16 December 1984, Nekrasov writes that he never received an official communication about the measure and only learned of it when he was already abroad. On 3 January 1975 the presidium of the board of the Union of Writers of Ukraine approved Nekrasov's expulsion for his "antisocial behavior, which conflicts with the Statute of the Union of Writers of the USSR" (the decision did not need ratification by the Union of Writers of the USSR and was therefore final). See the extract of resolution no. 1, 3 January 1975, CGAMLI Ukrainy, f. 590, op. 5, od. zb. 351, l. 18, http://www.nekrassov -viktor.com/Documents/Vipiska-isklychenie-iz-soyuza-pisateley.aspx. See also Grigory I. Kipnis, "I tol'ko pravdu . . ." [Only the truth . . .], in *O Viktore Nekrasove*, 139– 40. All of Nekrasov's books, whatever the language of their publication, were officially banned by decree no. 31, 13 August 1976, of the Glavlit (General Directorate for Literature and Publishing Affairs) and therefore withdrawn from libraries. The writer's Soviet citizenship was revoked in 1979.

108. Information by V. V. Shcherbytsky, 15 July 1974, in Mikhail Mitsel, "Neproduktivnyy pisatel Sovetskoy Ukrainy" [An unproductive writer of Soviet Ukraine], *Vestnik*, 20 July 1999, http://www.vestnik.com/issues/1999/0720/koi/mitsel.htm.

109. A broad picture of Nekrasov in exile can be drawn thanks to Viktor Kondyrev, "Vsë na svete, krome shila i gvozdya: Vospominaniya o Viktore Platonoviche Nekrasove (Kiev–Paris, 1972–87 gg.)" [Everything except an awl and a nail: Recollections of Viktor Platonovich Nekrasov (Kyiv–Paris, 1972–1987)] (AST-Astrel', 2011).

110. Among the fragments brought to light is the essay written in 1973, here used repeatedly, Nekrasov, "Kamen' v Bab'em Yaru," 194–203; see also Nekrasov, *Arestovannye stranicy*, 183–93.

111. Nekrasov, "Komu eto nuzhno?," 17.

112. Etkind, "Pravda Viktora Nekrasova," 221–22. "Travel notes" (*putevye zapiski*) are one of Viktor Nekrasov's favorite genres. See in particular the impressions on the trip to Italy and France in April 1957: "Pervoe znakomstvo: Iz zarubezhnykh vpechatleniy" [First acquaintance: Impressions from abroad], *Novyj mir*, no. 7 (1958): 142–81, and no. 8 (1958): 123–59 (illustrated by drawings and photographs by the author himself); *Pervoe znakomstvo: Iz zarubezhnykh vpechatleniy* (Sovetsky Pisatel', 1960); Italian translation, *Sovietico in Italia* (Vallecchi, 1960); and those on the trip to Italy and the United States in March 1962: "Po obe storony okeana," *Novyj mir*, no. 11 (1962): 112–48, and no. 12 (1962): 110–52; Italian translation, *Di qua e di là dall'oceano* [On both sides of the ocean] (Arnaldo Mondadori, 1965).

113. Lazar Lazarev, "Iz ognja . . . : O Viktore Nekrasove" [From the fire . . . : About Viktor Nekrasov], in *Shestoj etazh, ili perebiraja nashi daty* [The sixth floor, or reexamining our anniversaries] (Knizhnyj Sad, 1999), 187; Lazarev, *Zapiski pozhilogo cheloveka: Kniga vospominaniy* [Reflections of an elderly man: Book of memories] (Vremja, 2005), 46.

114. Nekrasov, "Zapiski zevaki," 30–31. The censorship of Nekrasov's essay was preceded by the dismantling of the liberal editorial board of *Novyj mir* and the removal of the editor in chief, Aleksandr T. Tvardovsky.

115. Nekrasov, "Zapiski zevaki," 35. See Nekrasov, "Kak ya pechatalsya v posledniy raz" [My last publication] (1975), *Znamya*, no. 5 (1990): 19–21.

116. The first edition, which I've always utilized, is the previously cited: Viktor Nekrasov, "Zapiski zevaki," *Kontinent*, no. 4 (1975): 13–172; then Nekrasov, *Zapiski zevaki* (Posev, 1976). The original version, titled "Gorodskie progulki," was published in the Soviet Union only after the author's death in *Yunost*, no. 7 (1988): 8–31, formerly *Novyj mir* (editor Anna S. Berzer).

117. Nekrasov, "Gorodskie progulki," 21; Nekrasov, "Zapiski zevaki," 72–73 (with minimal variations).

118. Nekrasov, "Gorodskie progulki," 21; Nekrasov, "Zapiski zevaki," 73–74 (with minimal variations).

119. Nekrasov, "Gorodskie progulki," 22, ellipsis added.

120. Viktor Nekrasov, "Posle 'Holocaust'a'" [After "Holocaust"], *Egupec*, no. 18 (2009): 222–23, second ellipsis added.

121. *Pravda*, 23 June 1976.

122. The architect A. F. Ignashchenko later testified that during the work to lay the foundations, a thick layer of human ash was found. According to his research, gravestones from the Jewish cemetery had been piled up at that place to "sift" the ashes of the already incinerated bodies over them to isolate and remove gold teeth, rings, and other valuable objects. See Tymur Litovchenko, "Pro novitni plany zvedennya chogos'

hrandioznogo u Babynomu Jaru chutky khodyly shche torik" [Rumors about immi-nent plans to build something grandiose in Babyn Yar circulated already last year], *PIK (Polityka i kul'tura)*, 21–28 May 2002, 43, in Evstafeva, "Babiy Jar," 28.

123. Mikhail M. Shulkevich and Talida D. Dmitrenko, *Kiev: Arkhitekturno-istoricheskiy ocherk* [Kyiv: Architectural-historical essay], 5th ed. (Budivel'nyk, 1978), 364.

124. Recollections of Oleksandr P. Vitryk collected by Yulia Melnichuk, "Kogda prishla nastoyashchaya nishcheta, odin iz avtorov pamyatnika v Bab'em Yaru Viktor Suchenko dobrovol'no ushel iz zhizni" [When real poverty came, one of the authors of the monument in Babyn Yar, Viktor Suchenko, voluntarily left life], *Fakty*, 2 July 2003, 5, http://fakty.ua/79175-kogda-prishla-nastoyacshaya-nicsheta-odin-iz-avtorov-pamyatnika-v-babem-yaru-viktor-suhenko-dobrovolno-ushel-iz-zhizni.

125. Aleksandr Naiman, "Babiy Jar: Tragediya i pamjat'" [Babi Yar: Tragedy and memory], *Evrejskij obozrevatel'*, 3 April 2002, http://www.jewukr.org/observer/joo7_26/po104_r.html.

126. See the resolutions no. 1595 (4 October 1971), DAK, f. R-1, op. 8, spr. 1004, ark. 115–16; no. 166 (17 February 1975), DAK, f. R-1, op. 8, spr. 1379, ark. 293–96; no. 492 (19 May 1975), DAK, f. R-1, op. 8, spr. 1394, ark. 103; no. 972 (30 September 1975), DAK, f. R-1, op. 8, spr. 1411, ark. 75–76; no. 508 (17 May 1976), DAK, f. R-1, op. 8, spr. 1565, ark. 88–89, again a reference to the "construction of a monument to Soviet citi-zens and soldiers and officers prisoners of war who died at the hands of Nazi occupiers in the Syrets district of Kyiv."

127. Evstafeva, "Babiy Jar," 28. The official press in Yiddish provided an account of the monument's creation by the poet Arn Vergelis, "Der denkmol in babi yar vet shteyn ledoyres" [A monument in Babi Yar for future generations], *Sovetish heymland*, no. 6 (1975): 158–64.

128. Quoted from the family archive in Lyudmila Lysenko, "Dve monumental'nye istorii" [Two monumental stories], based on materials presented in the communica-tion "Two Memorials: To the Victims of BabijYar and to the Great Patriotic War (1941–45)," international conference, "La mémoire sculptée de l'Europe," Strasbourg, 3–4 December 2001, http://kulupa.livejournal.com/328747.html.

129. This is reported by Victoria Khiterer, "Memorialization of the Holocaust in Minsk and Kiev," in *Holocaust Resistance in Europe and America: New Aspects and Dilemmas*, ed. Victoria Khiterer and Abigail S. Gruber (Cambridge Scholars Publish-ing, 2017), 120.

130. Recollections of O. P. Vitryk in Melnichuk, "Kogda prishla nastoyashchaya nishcheta."

131. Recollections of Anatoly F. Ignashchenko collected by Vladimir Platonov, "Babiy Jar: Tragediya o tragedii" [Babi Yar: A tragedy about the tragedy], *Zerkalo nedeli*, 27 September 1997; and of Aleksandr Shteinberg, "Dokumenty zabytoj pam-jati" [Documents of a forgotten memory], *Evrejskij obozrevatel'*, 24 July 2002, http://www.jewukr.org/observer/jo14_33/po101_r.html; Lysenko, "Dve monumental'nye istorii."

132. Shulkevich and Dmitrenko, *Kiev*, 393. The project was entrusted to the archi-tects Vadym I. Hopkalo, Vadym M. Grechina, and Volodymyr Ye. Kolomiyets.

133. Shulkevich and Dmitrenko, *Kiev*, 344.

134. *Chronika tekushchikh sobytiy*, 8 October 1976; Natan Shcharansky (Natan Sharansky), *Ne uboyus' zla* [I am not afraid of evil] (Vek-Olimp, 1991), 21. See also the testimony of the dissident Begun, "Zapret na pamyat' o Cholokoste," 112, who was part of a group of people detained by the police while they were about to reach Babi Yar and held until late at night to prevent them from attending the gathering.

135. *Chronika tekushchikh sobytiy*, 30 November 1977.

136. Korzhavin, "Psichologiya," 140.

137. Naum Meiman, "Monument u Bab'ego Yara" [The monument at Babi Yar], *Kontinent*, no. 15 (1978): 179–80 (the article is dated 15 September 1977).

138. Meiman, "Monument u Bab'ego Yara," 181.

139. Meiman, "Monument u Bab'ego Yara," 184.

140. Meiman, "Monument u Bab'ego Yara," 181–82.

141. Meiman, "Monument u Bab'ego Yara," 182–83.

142. Elie Wiesel, *Paroles d'étranger: Textes, contes et dialogues* [Words from a stranger: Texts, tales, and dialogues] (Seuil, 1982), 84–85; Italian translation, *Parole di straniero* [Words of a foreigner] (Spirali, 1986), 82–83. See also Wiesel, *. . . e il mare non si riempie mai: Memorie 2* [. . . and the sea never fills: Memoirs 2] (Bompiani, 2003), 279, original edition, *Mémoires 2: . . . et la mer n'est pas remplie* [Memoirs 2: . . . and the sea is not full] (Seuil, 1996).

143. Wiesel, *Paroles d'étranger*, 85–86; Italian translation, 84.

144. Wiesel, *. . . e il mare non si riempie mai*, 279–80.

145. Wiesel, *. . . e il mare non si riempie mai*, 280. See also Wiesel, *Paroles d'étranger*, 87; Italian translation, 85. On Wiesel's visit and the American delegation, see the report of the head of the department for foreign tourism in Mitsel, "Zapret na uvekovechenie pamyati," 23–24.

146. To follow the development of the strategies of struggle, see Marina A. Morozova, *Anatomiya otkaza* [Anatomy of refusal] (RGGU, 2011), 95–139.

147. *Chronika tekushchikh sobytiy*, 3 August 1980; Alexeyeva, *Istoriya inakomysliya v SSSR*, 130.

148. "Repressii protiv evreev-otkaznikov v Kieve" [Repressions against Jewish refuseniks in Kyiv], in Zubarev and Kuzovkin, *Dokumenty Moskovskoj Chel'sinkskoj gruppy*, doc. 149, pp. 482–83 (document of 25 November 1980, signed by Elena G. Bonner, Sofiya V. Kalistratova, Naum N. Meiman, Ivan S. Kovalev, and Feliks A. Serebrov).

149. *Presledovaniya evreev-otkaznikov prodolzhayutsya* [Persecutions of Jewish refuseniks continue], in Zubarev and Kuzovkin, *Dokumenty Moskovskoj Chel'sinkskoj gruppy*, doc. 173, p. 523 (document of 8 July 1981, signed by Elena G. Bonner, Sofiya V. Kalistratova, Ivan S. Kovalev, and Naum N. Meiman).

150. Mark Ya. Azbel, *Refusenik: Trapped in the Soviet Union* (Houghton Mifflin, 1981), 372. Mark Yakovlevich Azbel (1932) applied to immigrate to Israel in 1972. He was allowed to leave the Soviet Union in 1977.

151. *Chronika tekushchikh sobytiy*, 31 December 1981. A previous collective denunciation by Kyiv's refuseniks, signed by ninety-seven people, was delivered to the Central Committee of the CPSU and the Ministry of Internal Affairs of the USSR on 7 February 1980 (*Chronika tekushchikh sobytiy*, 3 August 1980). Regarding the cases of persecution reported: V. Pilnikov was sentenced to five years for "deliberate hooliganism

[*zlostnoe chuliganstvo*]" (article 206/2 of the penal code of the Ukrainian SSR); K. Fridman to one year for "deliberate refusal of labor activity [*zlostnoe uklonenie ot trudovoy deyatel'nosti*]" (article 214/1 of the penal code); V. Kislik to three years for "deliberate hooliganism" (article 206/2 of the penal code); S. Zubko to four years for illegal possession of a firearm (article 222/1 of the penal code) and illegal possession of narcotics (article 229.6/1 of the penal code). See Zubarev and Kuzovkin, *Dokumenty Moskovskoj Chel'sinkskoj gruppy*, 483, 521–23, 533–34.

152. *Chronika tekushchikh sobytiy*, 31 December 1981, ellipsis added.

153. "40-ya godovshchina massovykh rasstrelov evreev v Bab'em Yare" [The fortieth anniversary of the mass shootings of Jews in Babyn Yar], Zubarev and Kuzovkin, *Dokumenty Moskovskoj Chel'sinkskoj gruppy*, doc. 184, pp. 541–42. The document is dated 23 October 1981.

154. Azbel, *Refusenik*, 373. For further information on the significance of Babi Yar as a place of memory during the 1970s and 1980s, see Vladyslav Hrynevych, "Babyn Yar After Babyn Yar," in *Babyn Yar: History and Memory*, ed. Vladyslav Hrynevych and Paul R. Magocsi (Duch i Litera, 2016), 135–43.

155. Nekrasov, "Posle 'Holocaust'a,'" 223. See also Viktor Nekrasov, "Babiy Jar—45 let" [Babi Yar—45 years], *Novoe russkoe slovo*, 29 August 1986.

156. Nekrasov, "Posle 'Holocaust'a,'" 224–25.

157. Nekrasov, "Zapiski zevaki," 81.

158. Nekrasov, "Kamen' v Bab'em Yaru," 195; Nekrasov, *Arestovannye stranicy*, 184.

159. Nekrasov, "Po obe storony Steny," 141.

160. A survey in *Babyn Yar: Masove ubyvstvo i pam'jat'*, 221–250. See also Vitaliy Nakhmanovych, "Babyn Yar: A Place of Memory in Search of a Future," in Hrynevych and Magocsi, *Babyn Yar: History and Memory*, 291–314.

161. See http://babynyar.org/en for the guidelines. Karel Berkhoff, ed., *Basic Historical Narrative of the Babi Yar Holocaust Memorial Center* (Babi Yar Holocaust Memorial Center, 2018), can also be found at http://api.babiyar.org/uploads/files/fund/ff5be4721f4ef9d0cee21b34e17e8c05.pdf.

Epilogue

1. Nahum Korzhavin, "Poema sushchestvovaniya" [Poem of existence], *Vremya i my*, no. 1 (1975): 115–26; Korzhavin, *Vremena: Izbrannoe* [Times: Selected works] (Frankfurt am Main: Posev, 1976), 311–37. For this work, I have been guided by the reflections of Martha C. Nussbaum, *Giustizia poetica: Immaginazione letteraria e vita civile* (Mimesis, 2012), original edition, *Poetic Justice: Literary Imagination and Public Life* (Beacon Press, 1995); Nussbaum, *L'intelligenza delle emozioni* (Il Mulino, 2009), original edition, *Upheavals of Thought: The Intelligence of Emotions* (Cambridge University Press, 2001); Nussbaum, *Emozioni politiche: Perché l'amore conta per la giustizia* (Il Mulino, 2014), original edition, *Political Emotions: Why Love Matters for Justice* (Belknap Press of Harvard University Press, 2013).

Index

Akhmatova, Anna, 76

Aksyonov, Vasily P., 136

Alabyan, Karo S., 90

Aleichem, Sholem, 159

Aleksandrov, Georgy Fedorovich, 36–37, 56

Aliger, Margarita, 76

Alperin, V., 26

Anatoly, A. *See* Kuznetsov, Anatoly Vasilyevich

Anstei, Olga Nikolaevna, 40–41, 220–21n8

antisemitism: censorship and, 137–38; communism and, 126–29; cosmopolitanism and, 78–79; within Kyiv, 58–63; and remembering Babi Yar, 162–64; Shostakovich and, 117–19, 124; Ukrainians and, 159–61, 164–67, 248–49n23; Yevtushenko and, 102, 105–7, 109–12; Zionism and, 171–73. *See also* nationalism; Zionism

Antokolsky, Pavel G., 51–53, 79, 224–25n49, 224n47, 225n50

Antonenko-Davydovych, Borys D., 162

Arab-Israeli War, 170

At Babi Yar (Prorokov), 89

Auschwitz, 190

Avraam (Holovanivsky), 80

Azbel, Mark Ya., 194

"Babi Jar" (Ozerov), 200–201

Babi Yar: abandonment of site of, 69–72; accounts of the events at, 13–21; coming back to/early commemorations of, 65–69; dam collapse at, 96–100, 245n70; demonstrations at, 158, 161–69, 175–82; erasure of, 190–91, 196–98; executions at, 3, 5–6; liberation and, 33–38; march in remembrance of, 72–75; measures to prevent gatherings at, 194–96; monument at, 84, 89–91, 93–94, 133, 145–49, 153–56, 158, 169–70, 187–91, 196–99, 243n41, 265n16, 266nn28–29, 282n134; Nekrasov on, 186–87, 265n14; news reports of, 27–30; official reports about, 35–38; operation to erase traces of executions at, 30–32; pilgrimages to, 94–96, 100–101; poetry about, 39–41, 64, 72, 85–89, 102–17; redevelopment of, 94–96, 139, 141–42, 264nn9–10; survivors of, 24–27; as a symbolic space, 170–73, 275n55. *See also Babi Yar* (Kuznetsov); "Babi Yar" (Yevtushenko); Ehrenburg, Ilya; Kyiv; Lukyanivka Jewish cemetery; memorials (for Jewish victims)

"Babi Yar" (Ehrenburg), 50

Babi Yar (Kuznetsov), 129–38, 260n140, 261n148, 262n164. *See also* censorship

285

George L. Mosse Series in the History of
European Culture, Sexuality, and Ideas

STEVEN E. ASCHHEIM, ANNETTE BECKER, SKYE DONEY, AND DAVID J. SORKIN
Series Editors

Of God and Gods: Egypt, Israel, and the Rise of Monotheism
JAN ASSMANN

*Messengers of Disaster: Raphael Lemkin, Jan Karski, and
Twentieth-Century Genocides*
ANNETTE BECKER; TRANSLATED BY KÄTHE ROTH

*Respectability and Violence: Military Values, Masculine Honor, and
Italy's Road to Mass Death*
LORENZO BENADUSI; TRANSLATED BY ZAKIYA HANAFI

The Enemy of the New Man: Homosexuality in Fascist Italy
LORENZO BENADUSI; TRANSLATED BY SUZANNE DINGEE AND
JENNIFER PUDNEY

*The Holocaust and the West German Historians: Historical Interpretation
and Autobiographical Memory*
NICOLAS BERG; TRANSLATED AND EDITED BY JOEL GOLB

Surreal Geographies: A New History of Holocaust Consciousness
KATHRYN L. BRACKNEY

Collected Memories: Holocaust History and Postwar Testimony
CHRISTOPHER R. BROWNING

Contemporary Europe in the Historical Imagination
EDITED BY DARCY BUERKLE AND SKYE DONEY

Cataclysms: A History of the Twentieth Century from Europe's Edge
DAN DINER; TRANSLATED BY WILLIAM TEMPLER WITH JOEL GOLB

*Fascination with the Persecutor: George L. Mosse and
the Catastrophe of Modern Man*
EMILIO GENTILE; TRANSLATED BY JOHN AND ANNE C. TEDESCHI

La Grande Italia: The Myth of the Nation in the Twentieth Century
EMILIO GENTILE; TRANSLATED BY SUZANNE DINGEE AND JENNIFER PUDNEY

The Invisible Jewish Budapest: Metropolitan Culture at the Fin de Siècle
MARY GLUCK

*Carl Schmitt and the Jews: The "Jewish Question," the Holocaust,
and German Legal Theory*
RAPHAEL GROSS; TRANSLATED BY JOEL GOLB

*Unlearning Eugenics: Sexuality, Reproduction, and Disability
in Post-Nazi Europe*
DAGMAR HERZOG

Reason After Its Eclipse: On Late Critical Theory
MARTIN JAY

Rescue and Remembrance: Imagining the German Collective After Nazism
KOBI KABALEK

*Some Measure of Justice: The Holocaust Era Restitution
Campaign of the 1990s*
MICHAEL R. MARRUS

*The Best Weapon for Peace: Maria Montessori, Education,
and Children's Rights*
ERICA MORETTI

Confronting History: A Memoir
GEORGE L. MOSSE

Nazi Culture: Intellectual, Cultural, and Social Life in the Third Reich
GEORGE L. MOSSE

Last Days of Theresienstadt
EVA NOACK-MOSSE; TRANSLATED BY SKYE DONEY AND
BIRUTĖ CIPLIJAUSKAITĖ